Handbook for SAP PP in S/4HANA

Production Planning and Execution in SAP S/4HANA

Himanshu Goel

Handbook for SAP PP in S/4HANA: Production Planning and Execution in SAP S/4HANA

Himanshu Goel
Germany, Germany

ISBN-13 (pbk): 978-1-4842-8565-7
https://doi.org/10.1007/978-1-4842-8566-4

ISBN-13 (electronic): 978-1-4842-8566-4

Managing Director, Apress Media LLC: Welmoed Spahr
Acquisitions Editor: Divya Modi
Development Editor:Laura Berendson
Coordinating Editor: Divya Modi
Copyeditor: Kezia Endsley

Cover designed by eStudioCalamar

Cover image designed by Freepik (www.freepik.com)

Distributed to the book trade worldwide by Springer Science+Business Media New York, 1 New York Plaza, New York, NY 10004. Phone 1-800-SPRINGER, fax (201) 348-4505, e-mail orders-ny@springer-sbm.com, or visit www.springeronline.com. Apress Media, LLC is a California LLC and the sole member (owner) is Springer Science + Business Media Finance Inc (SSBM Finance Inc). SSBM Finance Inc is a **Delaware** corporation.

For information on translations, please e-mail booktranslations@springernature.com; for reprint, paperback, or audio rights, please e-mail bookpermissions@springernature.com.

Apress titles may be purchased in bulk for academic, corporate, or promotional use. eBook versions and licenses are also available for most titles. For more information, reference our Print and eBook Bulk Sales web page at http://www.apress.com/bulk-sales.

Any source code or other supplementary material referenced by the author in this book is available to readers on GitHub (Github.com/apress). For more detailed information, please visit http://www.apress.com/source-code.

Printed on acid-free paper

To my beloved mother, I LOVE YOU! I will always cherish the time that I got to spend with you. Hope to see you again someday.

To my wife, you are awesome! I LOVE YOU!

To my dearest son, You're rare, special in every which way possible! You have the most beautiful smile and you're the most amazing son in the whole world! Daddy and Mommy love you the most!

Table of Contents

About the Author

Himanshu Goel is an SAP certified solution architect. He has more than 15 years of experience in designing and deploying SAP solutions, primarily in production planning and execution, quality management, and plant maintenance. He's a supply chain professional focused on solving business problems and delivering customer-centric solutions. He has worked on several large-scale, end-to-end SAP implementation and rollout projects. He has authored the e-bite *Introducing the Material Master in SAP S/4HANA*, published by SAP Press, and has also contributed several entries on `blogs.sap.com`. He is passionate SAP professional and loves all things SAP.

About the Technical Reviewer

 **Diwakar Sharma** is an ERP and business transformation professional with more than 18 years of experience in SAP implementations. Currently, he is working with Accenture as Senior Manager. His specific focus is on the supply chain, production planning, manufacturing, quality management, logistics, and integration with non-ERP applications. Diwakar has worked internationally, managing project teams located in different countries and both on-site and offshore resources.

Acknowledgments

First of all, I would like to thank my beloved wife Akanksha for all her support and encouragement, which kept me going through the writing process.

I would like to thank my dear friend Diwakar Sharma for his guidance and thorough review of the book.

This book wouldn't be possible without Jawad Akhtar. He connected with me one fine day after reading one of my SAP blogs and planted the idea of writing a book on SAP in my head.

I would like to give a big thank you to the entire team at Apress!

I would like to thank Divya Modi, coordinating editor at Apress, for her great support during the process and her patience with my hectic schedule. Furthermore, many thanks to Laura Berendson, development editor at Apress, who provided her valuable suggestions during the review process.

CHAPTER 1

Introduction

Welcome to the exciting world of SAP! In this chapter, you will learn about:

- SAP, the company and its flagship products

- The evolution of ERP (Enterprise Resource Planning)

- The history of SAP and its major milestones

- SAP production planning

What Is SAP?

First things first, SAP is pronounced S-A-P. You say the individual letters S-A-P (ess-ay-pee). This is due to the fact that SAP is an initialism and not an acronym. If you have been pronouncing it as "SAP," now you know it's wrong.

Which of the following do you think SAP is?

- Technology

- Programming language

- Application/tool

What if I told you that SAP is none of these? As a matter of fact, SAP is a German company that was founded in 1972 by five ex-IBM engineers. SAP stands for "Systeme, Anwendungen und Produkte in der Datenverarbeitung" in German, which translates to "Systems, Applications, and Products in Data Processing" in English.

SAP AG develops software products used by companies to manage their business operations, best known for its ERP (Enterprise Resource Planning). But it also develops many other products and solutions such as Ariba, Concur, IBP, several cloud-base products, and more. SAP S/4HANA is SAP's latest product and it's the successor to SAP ERP. It's built for the SAP HANA in-memory database.

© Himanshu Goel 2022
H. Goel, *Handbook for SAP PP in S/4HANA*, https://doi.org/10.1007/978-1-4842-8566-4_1

SAP S/4HANA is an abbreviation of "SAP Business Suite 4 SAP HANA," which is an enterprise resource planning (ERP) software package. SAP S/4HANA is the successor to SAP ECC (SAP ERP Central Component). Generation 4 is the first SAP business suite to run only on the proprietary SAP HANA (High-Speed Analytical Appliance) database platform.

The SAP S/4HANA business suite is used by companies across the globe to manage their operations, including sales, procurement, planning (advanced), production, inventory management, warehouse management, transport management, finance, human resources, and more. The biggest strength of SAP lies in the unified integration of all business functions, which help businesses run their operations in real time. Companies all over the globe use SAP S/4HANA as a single source of truth for informed decision-making. SAP S/4HANA combines analytical and transactional capabilities.

Now that you know what SAP stands for and how it is correctly pronounced, I want to share some funny acronyms for SAP that you may come across in your SAP career. SAP has been known to be called Slow and Painful, Slow and Problematic, Seriously Annoying Program, and Submit and Pray, to name a few.

Introduction to ERP

ERP stands for Enterprise Resource Planning. Companies need software systems to run their day-to-day business operations, including sales, manufacturing, procurement, finance, human resources, and so on. ERP aids organizations in running their business functions, like logistics, supply chains, finance, human resources, and so on. The strength of ERP lies in the fact that it integrates all business functions into a single platform.

Figure 1-1 shows the evolution of ERP. During the 1960s, companies relied on standalone software tools to manage their sales, finances, inventories, and so on. MRP (Material Requirements Planning) systems were used to manage the inventory and keep the stock level in control.

Figure 1-1. *History of ERP*

In the 1980s, a new concept evolved that integrated MRP with sales, purchasing, finance, and production. It was called MRP II. The new system, MRP II, proved extremely beneficial to companies. It provided extended functionalities to handle capacity planning and scheduling and direct integration with production processes and various business functions.

MRP II laid the foundation for a new concept, called ERP, which changed the way companies operated their business. ERP was introduced in the 1990s and it took MRP II to the next level. ERP integrated business functions like human resources, project systems, and customer relationship management (CRM) to MRP II. It also provided real-time reporting, thus helping businesses make informed decisions.

With the introduction of high-speed Internet and cloud computing in the 2010s, ERP was again revolutionized. ERP suites are now available on the cloud, which means companies can run ERP on browser-based platforms that allow users to access and run ERP tools from anywhere in the world.

The History of SAP

SAP was started by five ex-IBM employees in 1972. In 1973, they launched their first product, which was an accounting system called RF. This eventually led to the development of SAP R/1, where R stands for real time.

In 1979, SAP R/2 was launched. It was much more powerful than SAP R/1. The capabilities of the software were extended to support other business functions, like material management and production planning, logistics, and human resources. R/2 operated on mainframe computers.

SAP's flagship product—SAP R/3—was launched in 1992. It operated on a client-server architecture. The 3 refers to a three-tier architecture. The three layers of SAP

R/3 were database, application server, and presentation server. SAP R/3 could operate on OSes like Microsoft Windows and UNIX. SAP R/3 laid the founding for the next generation of ERP so much so that it still remains the basis of the current ERP systems.

SAP revamped the architecture completely and introduced mySAP ERP in 2004. The old SAP R/3 was replaced with SAP ERP Central Component (SAP ECC). Several new products—including SRM (Supplier Relationship Management), CRM, PLM (Product Lifecycle Management), and SCM (Supply Chain Management)—were introduced in mySAP ERP. The new SAP ECC enabled users to run SAP Business Warehouse and SAP Strategic Enterprise Management and Internet Transaction Server in SAP ECC.

In 2015, SAP launched their latest ERP, called SAP S/4HANA. Also called Suite for HANA. The new ERP runs on SAP's in-memory database, HANA. SAP S/4HANA not only integrates several business functions and industry solutions, but it also integrates parts of SAP Business Suite products, such as SAP SRM, SAP CRM, and SAP SCM. SAP S/4HANA can be implemented to run in the cloud, on-premises, and in hybrid mode. The major milestones of SAP are shown in Figure 1-2.

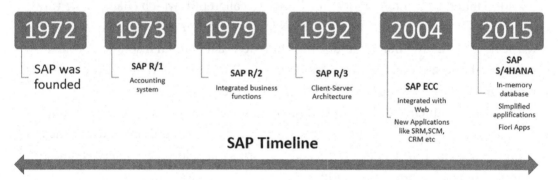

Figure 1-2. *The SAP timeline*

Introduction to SAP Production Planning

SAP ERP provides solutions to cover end-to-end business processes and functions in an organization, including sales and distribution, production planning, materials management, finance and control, plant maintenance, supply chain management, human resources, and more. Refer to Figure 1-3.

Figure 1-3. *Business functions in SAP S/4HANA*

Production planning and execution is the mainstay of a manufacturing organization. It is of utmost importance for a manufacturing organization to plan and forecast their production. They must be able to set up streamlined production processes to maximize efficiency and effectiveness and meet or exceed customer expectations. The SAP PP module helps organizations effectively plan and produce their products.

This book discusses production planning tools like sales and operations planning (S&OP), demand management, master production scheduling (MPS), materials requirements planning (MRP), and capacity requirements planning (CRP). You'll also learn about manufacturing execution processes, ranging from discrete manufacturing to repetitive manufacturing to the process industry process.

Manufacturing processes are broadly divided into two segments:

- Manufacturing planning
- Manufacturing execution

Manufacturing planning determines the quantities of materials to be produced to meet customer demands. It considers the available capacity in the plant. Production planning aids procurement of raw materials and other equipment needed for production as well as planning of labor and other staff.

Manufacturing planning helps the organizations optimize their production process and thus minimize production costs.

In SAP PP, various tools are available to support production planning, as shown in Figure 1-4. These tools help companies plan their production in the most effective way:

- Sales and Operations Planning

- Demand Management

- Master Production Scheduling (MPS)

- Material Requirement Planning (MRP)

- Capacity Requirement Planning (CRP)

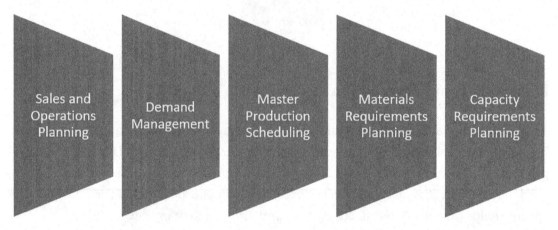

Figure 1-4. *Tools for production planning*

Manufacturing execution determines how the raw materials are transformed into finished goods. SAP has provided three production execution methodologies, as shown in Figure 1-5.

- Production order-based manufacturing

- Repetitive manufacturing

- Process order-based manufacturing

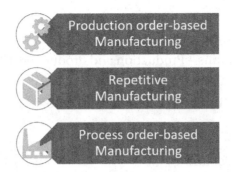

Figure 1-5. *Manufacturing execution methodologies*

Manufacturing Industry Types

The manufacturing industries are broadly divided into two industry types—discrete manufacturing and process manufacturing.

Discrete Manufacturing

Discrete manufacturing is a production methodology used to produce materials or assemblies that can be disassembled, completely or partially, into the original state of the components used. The methodology uses complex, multi-level BOMs and products change frequently from order to order. Lots of different products can be produced on the same production line with a little variation of machine parameters/settings. The products are manufactured using process like assembly, welding, machining, punching, stamping, and so on. Industries such as automotive, electronics, medical devices, and heavy machinery use discrete manufacturing to produce products like bicycles, cars, computers, mobile phones, forklifts, heavy earth movers, and so on.

Process Manufacturing

Process manufacturing is a production methodology where the production involves a special process that transforms the ingredients into a totally new product. The production process is quite intricate as it involves formulas or recipes. The production involves highly composite processes like casting, grinding, blending, boiling, and so on. Chemicals and food products go through a chemical process. Industries like chemical, pharma, FMCG (fast-moving consumer goods), and food and beverage use process manufacturing to manufacture products such as chemicals, medicines, food products, and so on.

Unlike discrete manufacturing, the finished goods in process manufacturing cannot be disassembled into their original raw materials.

SAP designed two solutions—Production and Production-Process—that cater to these two industries types: discrete and process.

SAP provides three production execution methodologies:

- Production order-based manufacturing

- Repetitive manufacturing

- Process order-based manufacturing

Production order-based manufacturing is a methodology where production is executed based on orders. The materials are produced in lots or batches as the products change quite frequently. The Production order is a detailed document and contains tons of information. This is in addition to the ones available in planned orders, such as operation details, system status, user status, planned cost, actual cost, component's overview, operations overview, and many more. There are also lots of functions available, like release, cost, availability check, capacity planning, read PP master data, technically closure of production order, and so on. You can also display goods movement, cost analysis, confirmation details, and so on.

The strength of discrete manufacturing lies in the fact that every aspect of production can be traced back with respect to the production order. To support traceability in discrete manufacturing, you use the batch management functionality.

The cost of production is settled at order level. The settlement receiver is usually a material for make-to-stock production and sales order for make-to-order production.

Repetitive manufacturing is a period-based production. The same product is manufactured over a period of time, and products do not change frequently. The planned order is a simple document containing only essential details, such as material, quantity, production dates, production version, and components. The planned order disappears forever once the backflush is posted.

The strength of repetitive manufacturing lies in the simplicity and effortlessness. Thus, it requires less effort from the business for the backflush process.

The cost of production is settled on a product cost collector, which acts as a bucket for storing the cost of production. A product cost collector is created for plant/material/production version. The settlement is carried out periodically. (Usually monthly.)

Process order-based manufacturing is similar to production order-based manufacturing but is used in discrete manufacturing. Process order-based manufacturing is used in process industries.

In PP-PI, production is executed based on process orders, which are similar to production orders. However, there are some differences between production order-based manufacturing and process order-based manufacturing.

In PP-PI, you use resources instead of work centers, master recipes instead of routing, and process orders instead of production orders.

One of the more unique features of PP-PI are the PI sheets. In a PI sheet, you can describe the entire production cycle of a product or part of a production process. If the PI sheet represents part of the production process, you usually need several PI sheets to manufacture a product. You can define the control and picking information for the individual production steps in the PI sheets. The PI sheet is used to inform the process operator about the individual production steps that need to be performed. They can interactively maintain the SAP PI sheet according to the phase sequence.

Table 1-1 shows the differences between the different master data objects used in each of the production execution methodologies—discrete manufacturing, process industry, and repetitive manufacturing.

Table 1-1. *Master Data Objects in SAP PP*

Discrete Manufacturing	Process Industry	Repetitive Manufacturing
Material Master	Material Master	Material Master
Bill of Materials (BOM)	Bill of Materials (BOM)	Bill of Materials (BOM)
Work Center	Resources	Production Line
Routing	Master Recipe	Rate Routing
Production Version	Production Version	Production Version
Production Resources and Tools	N/A	Production Resources and Tools
N/A	PI Sheets/ X-Steps	N/A
N/A	N/A	Product Cost Collector

Table 1-2 shows the differences between the production execution methodologies based on the functions available for each.

Table 1-2. *Production Execution Methodologies*

	Discrete Manufacturing	Process Manufacturing	Repetitive Manufacturing
Production Resources and Tools	Yes	No	Yes
Order Splitting	Yes	No	No
PI Sheets/X-Steps	No	Yes	No
Trigger Point	Yes	No	No
User Status	Yes	Yes	No
Digital Signature	No	Yes	No
Active Ingredient	No	Yes	No
Setup Matrix	Yes	Yes	No
Campaign Production	No	Yes	No

SAP manufacturing consultants often think that the industry should steer them to which type of manufacturing to use: PP or PP-PI. The decision about whether you want to implement PP or PP-PI should be based on the functionality that you want to use.

Similarly, the decision to use order-based production (discrete and process) or orderless production (repetitive) depends on your business requirements. Consider requirements such as manufacturing processes on the shop floor, production reporting and data capturing, traceability, collect/report costs per order or per time period, and so on.

Note   Production order-based manufacturing is referred to as *discrete manufacturing* in SAP, which is misleading due to the fact that order-based manufacturing and repetitive manufacturing are both execution methodologies used in discrete manufacturing. In this book, we refer to order-based production as simply discrete manufacturing, since that's how it is referred to in SAP.

Business Case

Assume that SuperGears AG is a manufacturer and supplier of gear box assemblies to major automobile OEMs (Original Equipment Manufacturers). SuperGears is rolling out a big project to implement SAP S/4HANA to streamline their business processes. The project scope is to cover end-to-end business process such as order-to-cash, procure-to-pay, plan-to-produce, and record-to-report. The SAP project team must implement core SAP modules like SD (Sales and Distribution), MM (Material Management), PP (Production Planning and Execution), FICO (Finance and Controlling) , and so on. In this book, we place emphasis on the production planning and execution modules.

Consider this discussion between the production manager at SuperGears and the SAP S/4HANA production planning and execution functional consultant.

1. *What do you produce?*

   We're a leading manufacturer and supplier of gear boxes to automotive OEMs. Our parts are built with the latest cutting-edge technology to achieve a greater degree of efficiency. Constant Mesh Gear box is our flagship product, which constitutes 70% of our total sales.

2. *What components are used for manufacturing a gear box assembly?*

   The major components that we use for production are a counter shaft, clutch shaft, dog clutch, main shaft, and reverse gear (see Figure 1-6).

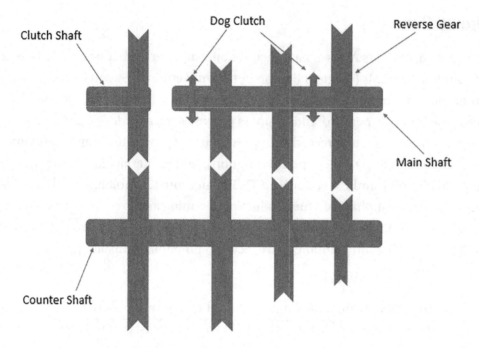

Figure 1-6. *Constant mesh gear box*

3. *Can you explain your manufacturing process?*

The shaft and gears are fabricated with high-quality steel, which is procured from vendors. In our machine line, gears go through a series of operations like machining, drilling, and boring on high-precision CNC machines. Turning is performed on shafts on lathe machines. Finally, the gears and shafts are assembled into the gear box assembly on our assembly line.

Now that you know the business process for SuperGears AG, the next step is to transform the business process into SAP. First you have to create master data objects like material master, bill of material, work center, and so on.

Summary

In this chapter, you learned about ERP, including the history of ERP and the importance of SAP production planning. You also learned about the different manufacturing execution methodologies, including production order-based manufacturing, repetitive manufacturing, and process order-based manufacturing. You'll learn more about these in the coming chapters.

The next chapter covers master data objects for SAP production planning and execution. It explores all the relevant master data objects for SAP PP and discusses how each master data object is created in SAP.

CHAPTER 2

Master Data in SAP PP

This chapter explains the master data objects required for the manufacturing process in SAP: material master, bill of materials, work center, routing, and production version.

Master Data

In SAP, two types of data are created—master data and transaction data.

Master data is static data that is used to drive key processes in the organization. Once the master data is created, it is seldom changed. Master data acts as a prerequisite to run business processes.

Transaction data is dynamic data used to capture day-to-day business transactions. Master data is used during the creation of transactional data.

Business scenario: The purchasing department at SuperGears AG wants to run their purchasing process using the SAP S/4HANA. The first thing they need to do is create their master data, including the material master, the vendor master, the purchase info records, the source list, and so on. One master data object can be used in another master data object. For example, material master and vendor master are used in the purchase info record. All these master data objects are eventually used in purchase requisitions or purchase orders, which are transaction data. When there is a raw material shortage, MRP will generate a purchase requisition to procure the material from the vendor. The purchase requisition is converted to a purchase order. The master data objects are created once and can be referred to in hundreds or thousands of transactions. However, each transaction is unique and is identified by a unique document number. For example, the purchasing department can issue hundreds of purchase orders to the vendor. All the purchase orders will have unique order numbers, while the master data remains the same.

© Himanshu Goel 2022
H. Goel, *Handbook for SAP PP in S/4HANA*, https://doi.org/10.1007/978-1-4842-8566-4_2

Now that you have learned about master data and its importance, this section covers the master data objects relevant for SAP PP:

Material master: The material master is essentially the most important master data for any company. In the manufacturing industry, a company produces a product and eventually needs semifinished assemblies and raw materials for the production process. All the information related to the materials a company produces, procures, stores, or sells is captured in the material master. SAP users often confuse material with raw material, but the two are separate and distinct. In SAP, materials can be finished or semifinished products, raw components, trade goods, or services and packaging.

Bill of materials (BOM): A bill of materials is a comprehensive list of the components that make up a product or assembly. The list includes the material number of each component, together with the quantity and unit of measure. You can create single-level and/or multilevel BOMs. For instance, you would create a BOM for a semifinished assembly and then create a BOM for a finished assembly that's made up of the semifinished assembly and additional components.

Work center: This refers to a place or a workstation where an activity or an operation is performed during the production process. A work center can be a machine or a labor (a manual operation such as quality inspection). Work centers are used in routing and subsequently in production orders.

Task list: This is a list of the production steps. It contains the following important information:

- *Operations* that should be performed during the production of a finished/semifinished assembly.

- The *work center* on which the operation should be performed.

- The *time* needed to set up machines during change over, including operation or machine time for each process, labor time, and so on.

Task lists have different nomenclature in different manufacturing execution methodologies:

- A task list with task list type N is called a *routing* and is used in discrete manufacturing.

- A task list with task list type R is called a *rate routing* and is used in repetitive manufacturing.

- A task list with task list type 2 is called a *master recipe* and is used in the process industry.

- Task lists with task list type S and M are referred to as reference operation set and reference rate routing, respectively. These task lists can be used as template routings.

Production Version: This defines a unique production technique for producing a material. For example, the gearbox might use `Counter_Shaft01` or `Counter_Shaft02`. Either of the two counter shafts can be used to assemble the gearbox. This scenario can be handled using an alternate BOM in SAP (see Figure 2-1). You can create two alternative BOMs for gearbox, each using a different counter shaft.

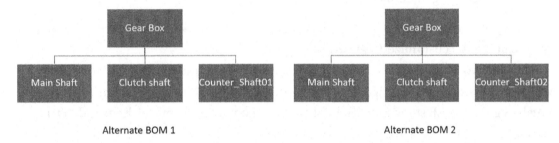

Figure 2-1. *Alternate BOMs*

Similarly, you can produce a finished/semifinished assembly on two different production lines. For example, the gearbox can be assembled on `Assembly_Line_01` or `Assembly_Line_02`. This scenario is handled using a group counter in routing. You must create two routings that can assemble the gearbox on different assembly lines.

Based on the BOM and routing, you can create four production versions for each permutation and combination of BOM and routing for this assembly. You can also create multiple production versions based on the production lot size or validity dates.

As you might have guessed, discrete manufacturing is the manufacturing industry type that's relevant to SuperGears AG. In the next section, you see how to create master data for the gearbox assembly in a discrete manufacturing environment.

Material Master

A material master record is a central library for storing all relevant information from various departments—for instance, the production department maintains data in the Material Requirements Planning (MRP) and Work Scheduling views, while the sales and marketing teams store sales-related data in the Sales views of a material master. Likewise, every logistics department, including purchasing, production, sales, quality, and warehouses, store relevant data in the material master. The application of the material master is not limited to logistics functions; rather, finance and controlling departments also use the material master to store the data that is relevant for them.

It is quite common to define several types of materials, including:

- Finished assembly (FERT)

- Semifinished assembly (HALB)

- Raw material (ROH)

- Packaging material (VERP)

There are many more material types available in standard SAP. Moreover, material types can also be customized as needed.

Are you wondering what FERT and HALB mean? They are abbreviated from German words. FERT stands for "Fertigteil" or "Fertigerzeugnis" in German, which means a finished good. HALB stands for "Halbfabrikat," which means semifinished, and ROH stands for "Rohteil," which means a raw material.

Each material master record is uniquely identified by a material number that can be up to 40 characters long in SAP S/4HANA. In SAP ERP ECC, the material number can be up to 18 characters long. The material number can be internal or external. A material master number is generated automatically when creating a material master record using an internal number range. Users can also choose a specific number for the material master number within an external number range. External numbers can be used when a company is using multiple systems (for instance, a Product Lifecycle Management system) and prefers to have synchronous material numbers.

Different views of the material master data are maintained at different organization levels. For instance, sales views are maintained at the sales area level, MRP and work scheduling tabs are maintained at the plant level, and accounting information is maintained at the valuation area level. The valuation area is an organization level at which materials are valuated; it can use a plant or company code.

For starters, to create a material master record, you need to define the following:

- Material number

- Industry sector

- Material type

- Material description

Material Number

The material number is a unique number that identifies a material. Any material that is procured, produced, or stored in a plant must have a material master record created for it, and this is represented with a unique material number. A material number can be created uniquely using an internal number range or an external number range.

This is one of the improvements in SAP S/4HANA. In SAP ERP, material numbers can be created with up to a maximum of 18 characters. However, SAP S/4HANA permits you to create a material number of up to 40 characters. This is an optional feature. It is also worth noting that the impact of this extension on custom code, interfaces, and other SAP applications must be evaluated before using the 40-character extension by switching it on.

Industry Sector

The industry sector determines the industry segment for which the material is created—for example, mechanical engineering, the chemical industry, pharma, and so forth. It also determines the views and fields that can be used to maintain the material master record. For instance, the industry sector could be configured to determine which views and in what sequence users can display the material master. Also, it can be configured so that a field is required, optional, display only, or hidden.

Material Types

The material type determines if the material is

- Finished assembly

- Semifinished assembly

- Raw material

- Packaging material

Material type plays a very vital role, as it determines the business process for the material—for instance, a finished assembly (Material Type FERT) does not have purchasing views, while raw materials do not have sales views.

It is important to choose the material type correctly, especially in complex organizations like multinational corporations. The same material can be a product in one part of the organization, a trade material in another, and a raw material in yet another. So, choosing the right material type can be tricky, as material type is independent of organizational level.

When creating a material master record, the material type determines the following (see Figure 2-2):

- Which departments can maintain the material master record

- Whether the material number is assigned internally or externally

- Which number range interval the material number comes from

- Which screens appear and in which sequence

- Which department-specific data you must enter

- Which special material types are allowed; for example, configurable material

- Which procurement type is allowed—internal production or external procurement

- Whether quantity changes in the material master record are updated

- Whether value changes to financial accounting stock accounts are updated

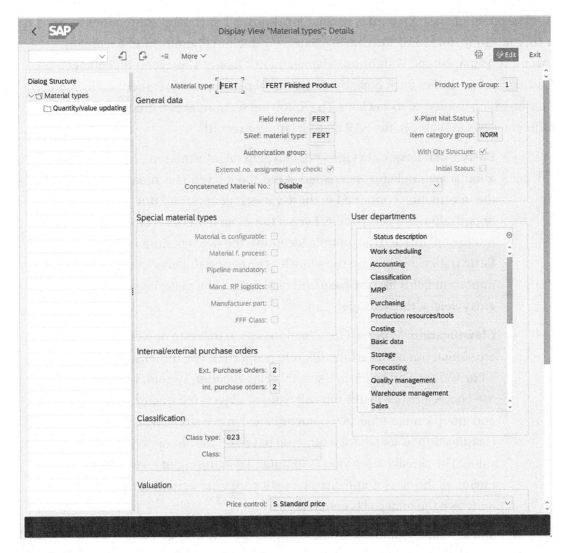

Figure 2-2. Material types

Material Description

A material description is a detailed description of the material. For instance, you can describe the product name using configuration details of the finished assembly. The material description is initially maintained in the login language. You can also maintain material description translations in multiple languages.

The material master record is created for almost all the business functions in an organization, including Purchasing, Sales, Production Planning and Execution, Inventory Management, Warehouse Management, Quality Management, Finance, Costing, and so on. For each business function there is separate segment in the material master, which is referred to as *views*. The following section takes a quick look of the different views available in the SAP material master record.

- **Basic Data:** Basic data views contain general information about a material and are created at the client level. This means the information contained in these views is generic and not organizational-level specific. Even if the same material is created for multiple plants across multiple locations, the fields maintained in Basic Data views remain the same for the material. This view contains important fields like the base unit of measure, the material group, the gross weight, the net weight, and so on.

- **Classification:** Material classification is used to group objects that are similar but have certain different properties, like dimension, color, weight, and so forth. Using this classification system, you can use characteristics to describe all types of objects (characteristics) and group similar objects (characteristics) in classes. You can use classification to search for a material based on the characteristics value. The classification view is maintained at the client level, which means all the classes and characteristics are valid across all the plants for which the material is created.

- **Sales:** Data maintained in Sales views is used by the Sales and Distribution module of SAP for any activities pertaining to selling and distributing the material to reach the customers. There are five views for sales—Sales: Sales Organization 1, Sales: Sales Organization 2, Sales: General/Plant, International Trade: Export, and Sales Text.

- **Purchasing:** Purchasing is a component of SAP S/4HANA Sourcing and Procurement that is responsible for procuring material from the vendor. Data maintained in the purchasing view of the material master is used in any activities pertaining to buying and procuring the material from the vendor. There are three views for purchasing—Purchasing, International Trade: Import, and Purchase Order Text.

- **Production Planning and Execution Views:** The production planning and executions tabs are spread over eight views: MRP1, MRP2, MRP3, MRP4, Forecasting, Advanced Planning, Extended SPP, and Work Scheduling. The fields in these views play a significant role in the material planning and production process.

- **General Plant Data/Storage:** The Plant Data/Storage views (i.e., General Plant Data/Storage 1 and General Plant Data/Storage 2) contain fields and data that determine how the shelf-life of a material is determined, how the physical inventory process should be carried out, and so on.

- **Quality Management:** In the Quality Management view of the material master, you can define the parameters that control the process for quality inspections throughout the logistics supply chain. You can also define various inspection parameters based on the inspection type—for example:

  - How the quality inspections are triggered

  - If the inspection should be done with or without a task list

  - If the inspection should be done with or without a material specification

  - Whether result recordings should be done for inspection characteristics

- **Accounting:** The Accounting views (i.e., Accounting 1 and Accounting 2) of the material master hold specific data about how the material is valuated, along with other accounting data.

- **Costing:** The Costing view is used to determine the product cost. It can involve various inputs, but for production, the most important is the costing lot size—an optimal lot size used for product cost estimates.

- Now let's create a new material master for the gear assembly, which is a finished material. I'm only creating a finished good. Similarly, you must create a material master record for all the components, semifinished assemblies, packaging materials, and so on.

- Choose Logistics ➤ Production ➤ Master Data ➤ Material Master
  ➤ Material ➤ Create (General) ➤ Immediately. You can also use
  Transaction Code (T-Code) MM01 to create a material master record.
  Figure 2-3 shows the initial screen of a material master, where you
  can enter the material number (if an external number range is
  permitted), industry segment, and material type. Then you can select
  the views that you want to create for the material.

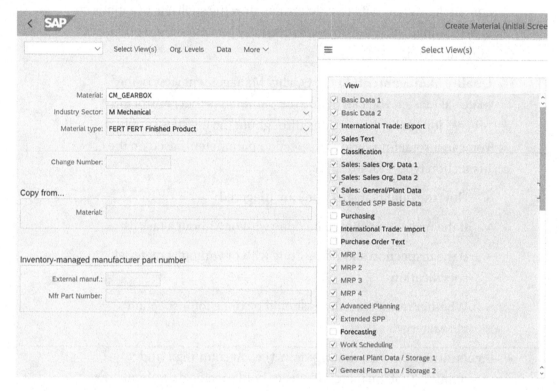

Figure 2-3. *Create material master*

The screen shown in Figure 2-4 appears, where you can maintain the organization data relevant to the material. For example, you can enter the plant, storage location, sales organization, distribution channel, warehouse number, and storage type.

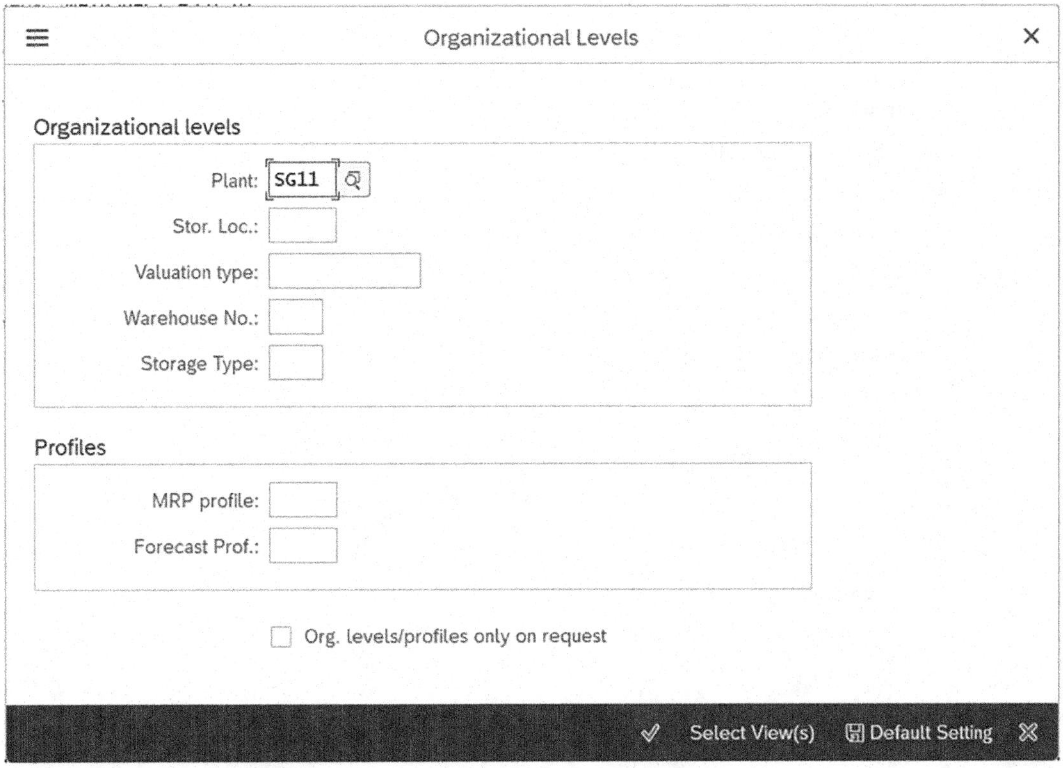

Figure 2-4. *Create material master: organizational levels*

In the Basic Data 1 view, you can maintain a material description, a base unit of measure, the material group, and other important fields like gross weight, net weight, and so on, as shown in Figure 2-5.

Figure 2-5. *Material master: basic data 1*

The next section discusses some of the most important fields in the MRP views of the material master.

MRP1 View

This section discusses some of the most important fields in the MRP1 view of the material master. The MRP1 view contains three sections—General Data, MRP Procedure, and Lot Size Data. Figure 2-6 displays the MRP1 view of the material master.

< ⚙ MRP 1   ⚙ MRP 2   ⚙ MRP 3   ⚙ MRP 4   ⚙ Advanced Planning   ⚙ Extended SPP   ⚙ Work scheduling

Material:	CM_GEARBOX
*Descr.:	Constant Mesh Gear Box
Plant:	SG11 SuperGears AG

General Data

*Base Unit of Measure:	EA	MRP Group:	
Purchasing Group:		ABC Indicator:	
Plant-Sp.Matl Status:		Valid From:	

MRP procedure

*MRP Type:	PD Forecast Consumption, No Planning Time Fence		
Reorder Point:		Planning time fence:	
Planning cycle:		MRP Controller:	SG1

Lot size data

Lot Sizing Procedure:	EX Lot-for-lot order quantity		
Minimum Lot Size:		Maximum Lot Size:	
Fixed lot size:		Maximum Stock Level:	
LS-Independent Costs:		Storage Costs Code:	
Assembly scrap (%):		Takt time:	
Rounding Profile:		Rounding value:	

Figure 2-6. *Material master: MRP1*

Base Unit of Measure (UoM): Each material master record must have a base unit of measure. This UoM is used for inventory management. It means the stock is maintained in a base unit of measure. Each business function can maintain its own UoM, such as a purchasing unit of measure or production unit of measure or sales unit of measure. All additional units of measure other than the base unit of measure are called *alternative units of measure.* SAP ERP comes supplied with the ISO (International Organization for Standardization) unit of measure tables, meaning that SAP ERP already has the conversions from kilograms to pounds. For nonstandard units, you must define the conversion factor of the alternative unit of measure to the base unit of measure for each alternate UoM; for example, converting pieces to pallets or cartons.

MRP Group: This is an important field, as several MRP parameters can be defined in it. The MRP group contains a lot of parameters, including the planning strategy group, consumption mode, order types to be used while converting a planned order to a production/process order, planning time fence, and so forth. Instead of using the MRP plant parameters, you can use MRP groups and then assign them to materials that share the same parameters.

Purchasing Group: This key identifies a person or a group of people who are responsible for activities related to the purchase of the materials. This field is only relevant to materials that are procured externally.

ABC Indicator: This key identifies the ABC classification of a material. The ABC classification is based on material consumption:

- A: High consumption part, thus considered the most important

- B: Medium consumption part, thus relatively less important

- C: Low consumption part, quite unimportant

You can define your own percentage for classifying according to the ABC analysis— for example, materials with 60% of consumption value can be classified as A, materials with 25% consumption value can be classified as B, and the remaining 15% can be classified as C.

In some organizations, materials classified as A get special attention and thus are planned through MPS (master production scheduling) instead of MRP (Material Requirements Planning).

Plant-Specific Material Status: This field indicates if a material is restricted for use in a particular business function. Table 2-1 shows the statuses and the areas for which materials are allowed. The system will throw a restriction message (i.e., a warning or an error message) if the material is used in a restricted way in the plant.

Table 2-1. *Plant Specific Material Status*

	Purchasing	MRP	Production	Plant Maintenance	Inventory Management	Costing
Blocked for procurement		X	X	X	X	X
Under development						X
Blocked for costing	X	X	X	X	X	
Blocked for production	X	X		X	X	X
Blocked for maintenance	X	X	X		X	X
Obsolete						

MRP Type: MRP is one of the most important functions in SAP.

In SAP, there are three broad types of MRP procedures, as shown in Figure 2-7:

- Materials requirements planning

- Master production scheduling

- Consumption-based planning

  - Reorder-point planning

  - Time-phased planning

  - Forecast-based planning

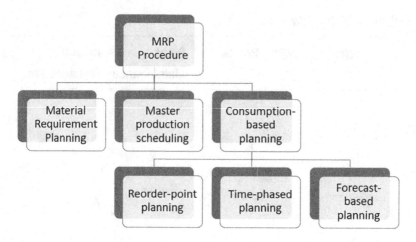

Figure 2-7. *The MRP procedure*

Material Requirements Planning (MRP): MRP is a planning engine used to calculate which materials (or components) should be produced (or procured), the quantities to be produced/procured, and the dates on which the material should be available. The function of MRP is to ensure material availability for production and thus on-time delivery to customers.

The standard SAP offers five MRP types:

- PD MRP

- P1 MRP, fixing type -1

- P2 MRP, fixing type -2

- P3 MRP, fixing type -3

- P4 MRP, fixing type -4

MRP types P1 to P4 are MRPs with a fixing type (or firming type). The firming type determines how order proposals are firmed and scheduled if you work with a planning time fence in the planning run.

Master Production Scheduling (MPS): MPS is exactly like MRP, except it is used to flag materials separately. Master production scheduling (MPS) is a form of MRP that concentrates the planning on the parts or products that have the greatest influence on the company's profitability or that dominate the entire production process by using critical resources. These items are marked as A parts in the ABC indicator field (MPS items) and are planned with extra attention. These items are selected for a separate MPS run that takes place before the MRP run. The MPS run is conducted without a BOM explosion so that the MRP controller can ensure that the master schedule items (MSI) are correctly planned before the detailed MRP run takes place.

MPS is run separately and can only be run at a single-level run. The materials planned with MPS are not included in the normal MRP run. This means a separate transaction is used in SAP for the MPS run.

The standard SAP offers five MPS types:

- M0 MPS, fixing type -0-

- M1 MPS, fixing type -1-

- M2 MPS, fixing type -2-

- M3 MPS, fixing type -3-

- M4 MPS, fixing type -4-

Consumption-Based Planning (CBP): As the name suggests, consumption-based planning procedures use past consumption data or historical data to calculate future requirements with the help of the material forecast or static planning procedures. The demand elements have no influence on CBP.

Consumption-based planning is further divided into three broad categories:

Reorder-point planning: The procurement is triggered when the sum of plant stock and firmed receipts falls below the reorder point. The following MRP types operate on the principles of reorder-point planning:

- V1 Manual reord.point w. ext.reqs

- V2 Autom. reord.point w. ext.reqs

- VB Manual reorder-point planning

Forecast-based planning: The future requirements are determined based on historical consumption data. The VV Forecast-based planning MRP type operates on the principles of forecast-based planning.

Time-phased planning: This planning type can be used when the materials are procured in a particular time interval. For example, say a vendor delivers the product every Monday. You can add the quantity for the entire week and send a cumulative requirement. The following MRP types operate on the principles of time-phased planning:

- R1 Time-phased planning

- R2 Time-phased w.auto.reord.point

- RR Tmphsd. repl. w. dyn.trgt.stck

- RS Time-phased replenishment plng

Reorder Point: If you are using reorder-point planning, you must maintain the reorder point. Whenever the stock falls below the reorder-point quantity, the system creates a procurement proposal during the next planning run. The MRP controller must maintain this value manually when using manual reorder-point planning. If you are using automatic reorder-point planning, the system updates this value automatically at defined intervals.

Lot Sizing Procedure: The lot size indicator helps determine the lot size (or the quantity to be procured/produced) during the net requirement calculation in the planning run. This means the MRP run will calculate the exact order quantity based on the lot size. The lot sizes are divided into three major types:

Static lot size: The procurement quantity is calculated based on the specified quantity in the material master.

- Fix order quantity

- Lot for lot order quantity

- Replenishment to a maximum stock level

Period lot size: You can add the requirement for a specified time interval. For example, you can group the demand for a time bucket (days, weeks, or months) and the system will create orders accordingly.

- Daily lot size

- Weekly lot size

- Monthly lot size

Optimum lot size: As the name suggests, this lot-sizing procedure aims to create optimal lots by minimizing costs like lot-size-independent costs (setup or order costs) and storage costs.

- Part period balancing

- Dynamic lot size

- Groff reorder procedure

Based on the selected lot size procedure, the following fields appear dynamically in the lot size data section of the MRP1 view.

Minimum Lot Size: The minimum quantity allowed for a procurement element. For example, say the minimum lot size for a material is 50 pcs. There is a requirement of 40 pcs, and the stock availability is 15 pcs. Based on the net requirement calculation, the procurement element should be 25 pcs. Due to the minimum lot size, the system creates a procurement element of 50 pcs.

Maximum Lot Size: The maximum quantity allowed for a procurement element. For example, say the maximum lot size for a material is 50 pcs. There is a requirement of 125 pcs, and the stock available is 5 pcs. Based on the net requirement calculation, the procurement element should be 120 pcs. Due to the maximum lot size of 50 pcs, the system creates two procurement elements of 50 each and a third procurement element for 20 pcs to cover the requirements.

Maximum Stock Level: The maximum allowed quantity for the material in the plant. This is used when you are using the HB - Replenish to Maximum Stock Level lot-sizing procedure.

Assembly Scrap: Usually, there is scrap during the production of assembly materials. You can maintain the scrap percentage so that scrap is considered during lot size calculation. For example, if you maintain an assembly scrap at 10% and there is a requirement of 100 pcs, the system will create an order proposal for 110 pcs to account for 10% scrap. Using assembly scrap also helps you plan components in a better way.

MRP2 View

This section discusses some of the important fields in the MRP2 view of the material master. The MRP2 view contains three sections—Procurement, Scheduling, and Net Requirements Calculation. Figure 2-8 displays the MRP2 view of the material master.

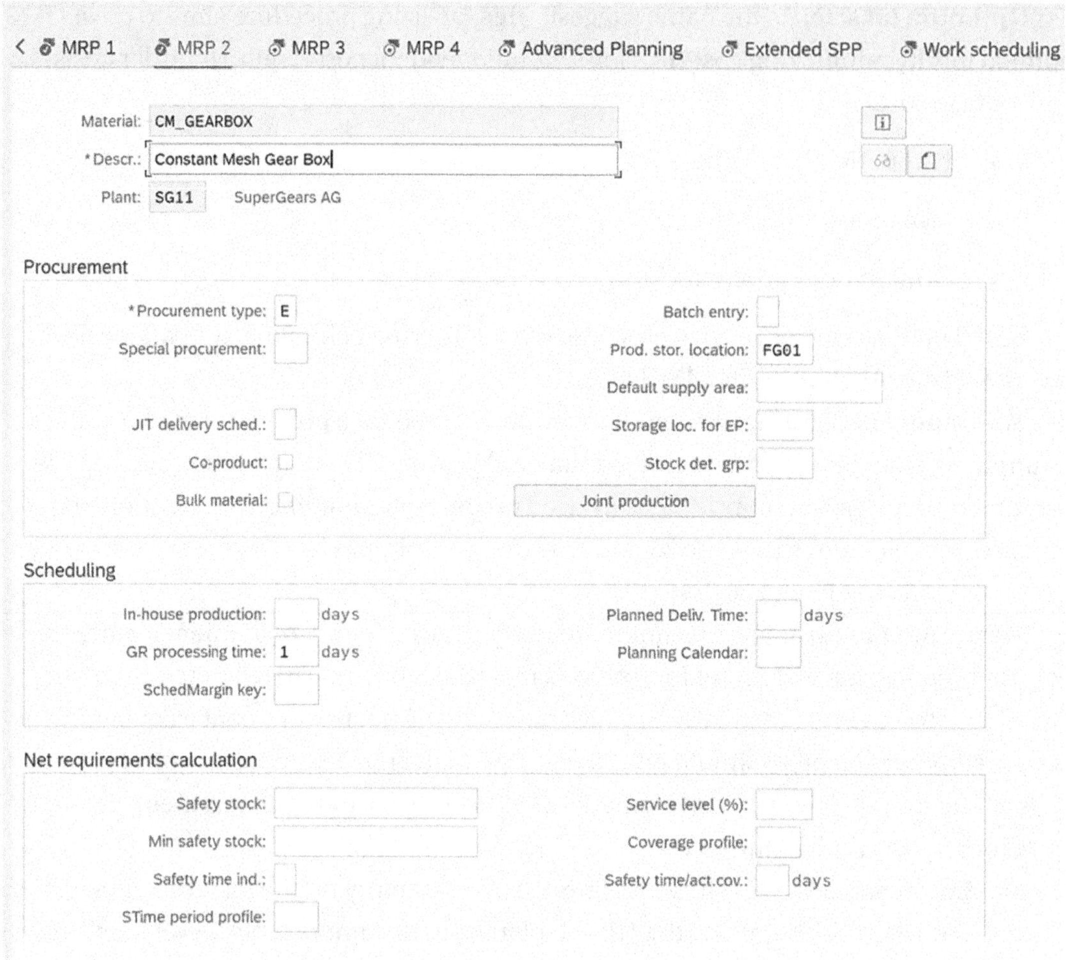

Figure 2-8. *Material master: MRP2*

Procurement Type: Using this key, you can decide how a material is procured (i.e., if the material is produced in-house or procured externally from a vendor). If the material is procured externally, the planning run creates a purchase requisition. If the material is produced in-house, the system creates a planned order. There could be some special materials that are mostly produced in-house; however, due to capacity constraints, the materials are sourced from vendors. For such materials, you can set the procurement type to Both Procurement and the system will generate a planned order during the planning run. The MRP controller can decide if the planned order should be converted to a production order for in-house production. If there are capacity constraints, then the planned order is converted to a purchase requisition, which is further converted to a purchase order.

Special Procurements: Some materials are procured in specific ways and thus are identified by a special procurement key.

Some of the special procurement types for in-house production are

- Phantom assembly

- Production in another plant

- Direct production/collective order

Some of the special procurement types for external procurement are

- Consignment

- Subcontracting

- Stock transfer

Backflush: Backflush refers to auto goods issue to the production order. You can skip the manual goods issue process using backflush. The backflush indicator can be activated in multiple master data objects. The highest priority is checked based on the following hierarchy:

- **Routing:** You can activate backflush for a component in component assignment.

- **Material Master:** You can activate backflush in the material master or let the work center decide.

- **Work Center:** If you opted for the work center to decide in the material master, you can activate backflush in the work center. This provides an advantage if you want to backflush all the components that are consumed in this work center and thus do not need to activate backflush for each material in the material master.

Batch Entry: This field is used to specify how the batches of the components are determined in a production/process order. You have the following options:

- The batches can be assigned manually in the order before the order is released.

- The batches can be determined automatically when the order is released.

- The batches are determined when the goods issue is posted.

- The batches must be entered in the order before the goods issue is posted, but not necessarily before the order is released.

Production Storage Location: This is the storage location that is populated automatically in an order (planned order, production order, or run schedule quantity in REM—repetitive manufacturing). For a material that is produced, the production storage location is where the finished goods are posted during goods receipt. For a component, this is the issuing storage location to which the backflush is posted.

In-House Production Time in Days: This field is used to maintain the lead time to produce a material. (Normally, the manufacturing lead time is the sum of the in-house production time and the GR processing time.) This is maintained on workdays and used to calculate the basic date for a planned order in a planning run. The time maintained in in-house production time is lot-size independent, which means the planned dates remain the same, irrespective of how many parts are produced.

Planned Delivery Time in Days: This field is used to maintain the lead time for procuring material externally from the vendor. (Normally, the purchasing lead time is a sum of the planned delivery time and the GR processing time.) This is maintained in workdays and specifies the time from when it is ordered until it is received in the warehouse. Like in-house production time, it helps the material controller plan the components effectively, as planned delivery time is calculated in the purchase requisition.

GR Processing Time (in Days): This is the time needed for inspection and placing the materials in the stock once the stock is received. Goods receipt processing time is also considered in total replenishment lead time.

Schedule Margin Key: This key is used to determine floats or buffer time that should be considered during lead time scheduling. The floats are generally used for administrative activities or to compensate for interruptions during production. Float before production or after production can be used as a buffer for unforeseen interruptions. Float before production is used to compensate for any delays in material staging of components, or delays caused by capacity constraints. The float after production can be used to compensate for unexpected interruptions during the production.

Safety Stock: This is the quantity of the material that should always be in stock to mitigate the risk of running out of stocks during uncertain times. Safety stock acts as a buffer to meet unexpected high demands from the customer or to continue production even if there is an interruption in delivery from the vendor. It can be maintained manually using manual reorder-point planning. The safety stock is determined automatically when using automatic reorder-point planning or forecast-based planning.

Minimum Safety Stock: This is used during the automatic calculation of the safety stock to ensure it doesn't fall below the minimum in case the system determines the safety stock to be too low.

MRP3 View

This section discusses some of the important fields in the MRP3 view of the material master. The MRP3 view contains four sections—Forecast Requirements, Planning, Availability Check, and Plant-Specific Configuration. Figure 2-9 displays the MRP3 view of the material master.

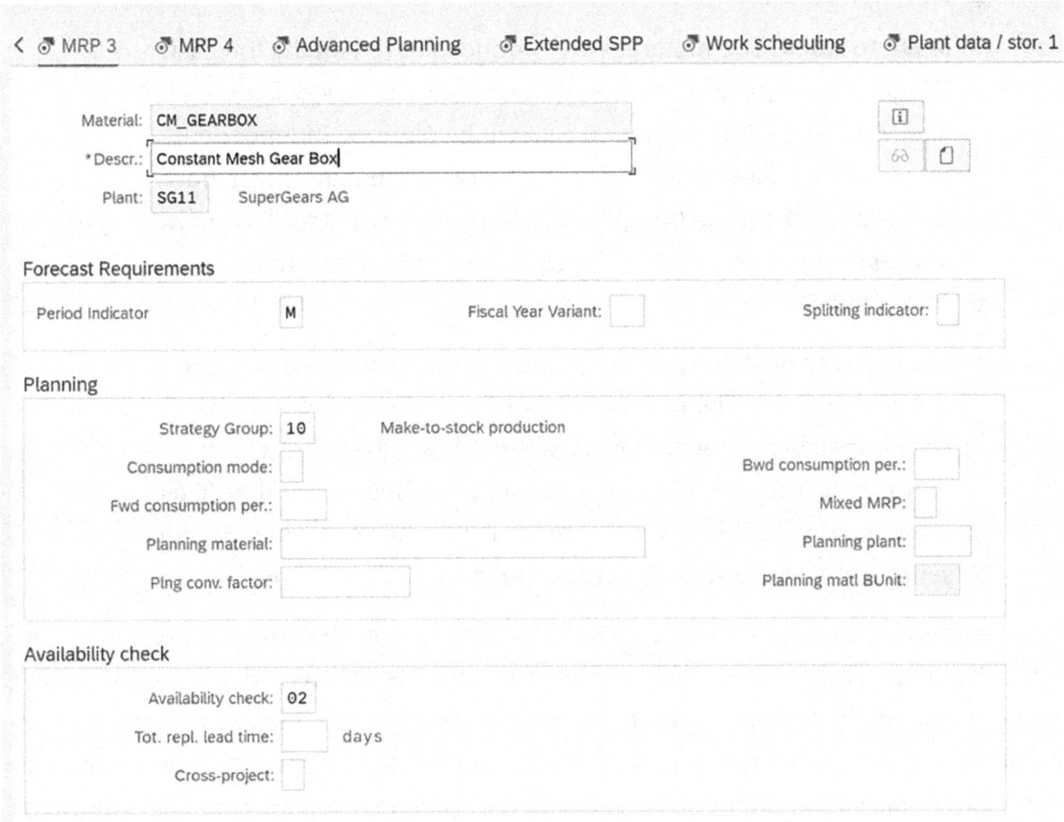

Figure 2-9. *Material master: MRP3*

Strategy Group: A strategy group is used to group all the planning strategies that can be used for a material. However, in most cases, only one planning strategy is used for a material.

A planning strategy is used to determine the planning procedure for a material. You can choose to produce a material in one of the following production environments:

- **Make to order:** The materials are produced for a specific sales order only. The material is not planned with a planned independent requirement, and the planning run (MRP) does not consider planned independent requirements, if any. There is a clear relation between production and sales, and each production order has an assignment and is created with reference to a sales order. The cost of production is settled on the sales order. The most common make-to-order planning strategies are 20, 50, and 60.

- **Make to stock:** The materials are produced based on the forecast. Demand management plays a vital role in make-to-stock production, and MRP plans the production against the planned independent requirements. Sales orders are not considered in planning in pure make-to-stock production. The cost of production is settled on the material. The most common make-to-stock planning strategies are 10, 11, and 40.

- **Assemble to order:** A product is assembled only when the sales order is received. The assemble-to-order environment is used in industries where a lot of finished assemblies are produced and they use the same components and semifinished assemblies. This gives you the flexibility to procure the key components and produce semifinished assemblies in a make-to-stock environment.

Consumption mode: This key is used to determine how the forecasts are consumed by the demands. The planned independent requirements are created as forecasts, which can be consumed by customer requirements or other demands. (Sales order, dependent requirements, or material reservations.) You can use backward consumption to consume forecasts that fall earlier than the requirement date of demands or forward consumption to consume forecasts that fall after the requirement date of demands.

Figure 2-10 shows how the planned independent requirements are consumed by customer requirements in backward and forward consumption mode.

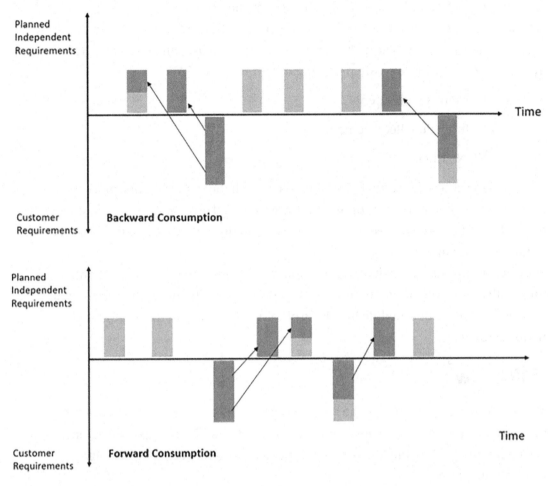

Figure 2-10. *Consumption mode*

Backward Consumption Period: If you are using backward consumption, you can specify the period for which planned independent requirements are consumed by sales orders, dependent requirements, or material reservations. The backward period is calculated from the current date.

Forward Consumption Period: If you are using forward consumption, you can specify the period for which planned independent requirements are consumed by sales orders, dependent requirements, or material reservations. The forward period is calculated from the current date.

Availability Check: This field is rather important, as it helps determine if products can be delivered on time to the customers while creating a sales order, during planned order or production order creation. During the availability check, the system considers several parameters, including MRP elements (production order, sales order, purchase order, and so on), stock, planned independent requirements, and so forth. The following availability checking groups are preconfigured in standard SAP:

- 01 Daily Requirements

- 02 Individual Requirements

- KP No Check

Checking group 01 means the system adds up all the requirements for a day and MRP creates a procurement proposal for the cumulated quantities. This also means that only one line is displayed in the MD04 Stock Requirement List with cumulated requirement quantities.

Checking group 02 means all requirements are considered individually and thus MRP creates procurement proposals for each requirement. Each requirement, such as sales order or schedule line, is displayed individually in the MD04 Stock Requirement List.

MRP4 View

This section discusses some of the most important fields in the MRP4 view of the material master. The MRP4 view contains three sections—BOM Explosion/Dependent Requirements, Discontinued Parts, and Repetitive Manufacturing/Assembly/Deployment Strategy.

Figure 2-11 shows the MRP4 view of the material master.

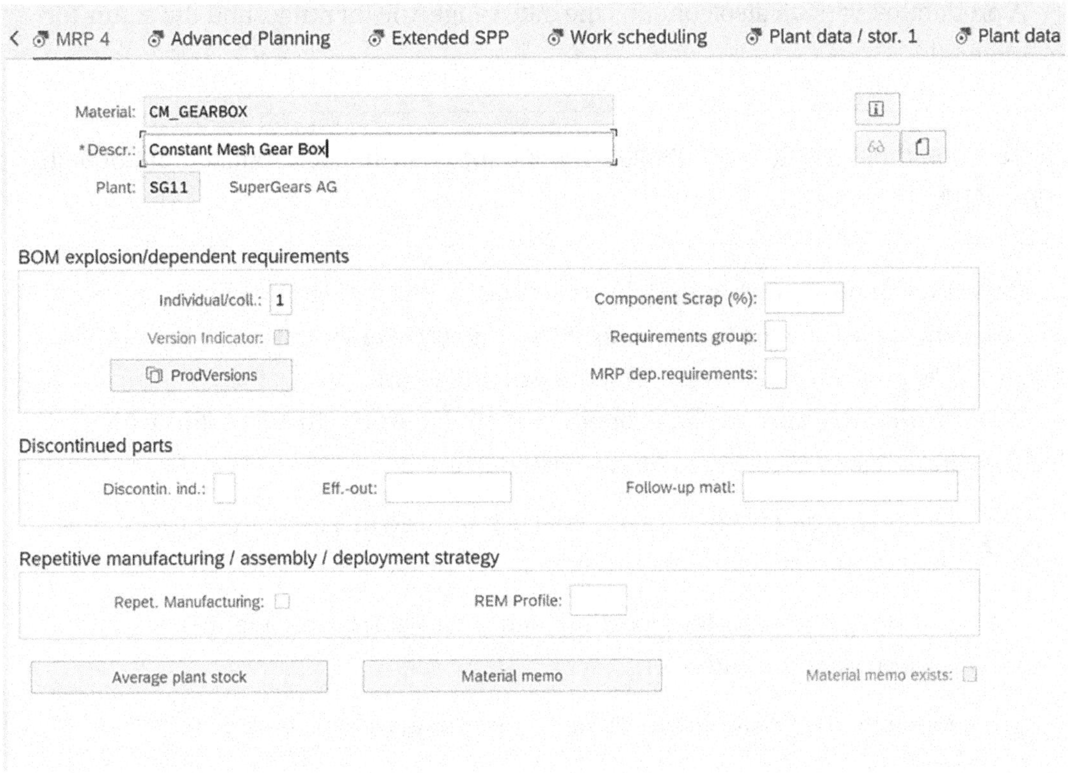

Figure 2-11. Material master: MRP4

Individual/Collective: This indicator is used to determine if the dependent requirements of a material are planned separately or grouped together. You can choose if you want to group material components individually for each sales order or if you want to group the dependent requirement into one order.

Production Version: This specifies a unique production method for the material. For example, material A001 can be manufactured using components B001 and C001 or components B001 and D001. You must create two alternate BOMs, specifying which components should be used to produce material A001. Similarly, the material can be produced on two production lines with different production processes. Routing must be created with two group counters, each describing the appropriate production process.

The Production Version button can be used to create production versions in a new popup screen. With reference to the previous example, you can create four production versions for a unique combination of alternate BOMs and routing groups.

A production version also contains the date range, the lot range, and the status for the material.

Note   You must create a production version for an in-house produced material in S/4 HANA.

Repetitive Manufacturing Indicator: Setting up this indicator means you are activating the material to be manufactured in a repetitive environment. You must also assign a REM profile if you're using repetitive manufacturing.

REM Profile: You must assign a repetitive manufacturing (REM) profile, which decides certain parameters based on the customization:

- Order type determines if a material is produced in a make-to-stock or make-to-order environment.

- Control parameters for reporting point, error correction, planned order reduction, and so on.

- Movement types for goods receipt, goods issue, scrap, and so on.

Work Scheduling View

This view contains production-relevant information and is mandatory to maintain if you are operating in the discrete/process industry. Otherwise, the system will not allow you to create a production/process order. Figure 2-12 shows the work scheduling view of the material master.

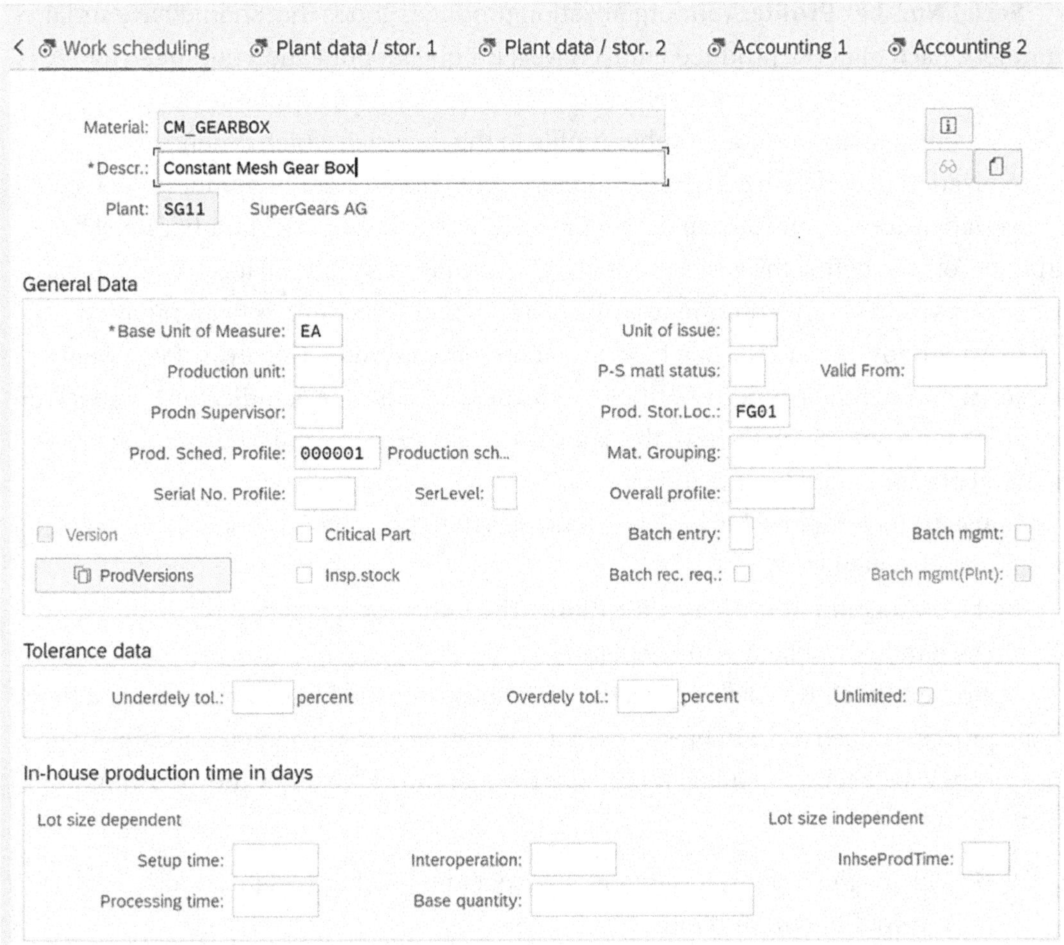

Figure 2-12. *Material master: work scheduling*

Production Supervisor: This key is used to identify a person or a group of people responsible for the production of the material. A production scheduling profile can be assigned to a production scheduler and thus it can be used to determine scheduling parameters, as described in the next field.

Production Scheduling Profile: This is used to determine how certain functions are triggered in the production or process order. You can release an order automatically or print shop floor papers. You can trigger automatic goods receipt during order confirmation. You can assign the order type to be used when converting a planned order to a production Order. You can specify an overall profile for capacity leveling.

Serial Number Profile: Your organization produces goods that should have serial numbers. Each material produced must have a unique identification number—for example, a chassis number for a vehicle or IMEI number for a cellphone device. Then you must assign a serial number profile to the material, which is defined in customization to establish certain parameters about how the serial numbers are created.

Serialization Level: You can define the level at which the serial number must be unique. You can define the serial number to be unique at a material level, which means the system checks for the uniqueness of a material and serial number combination. This means another material can have the same serial number. However, if you want the serial number to be unique at the client level, you must check indicator 1, and it will ensure that no two materials have the same serial number. You must ensure that every material master record has the indicator 1.

Batch Management: This indicator specifies that the material should be handled in batches at the client level.

Batch Management Indicator for Plant: The indicator specifies if the material should be handled in batches in the plant.

Approved Batch Record Required: This indicator is used only if you are operating in the process industry. If you have checked this indicator in the material master, then the system will check if the batch record has been approved to allow the following postings:

- Making the usage decision for an inspection lot of the origin goods receipt from production

- Changing the batch status from restricted to unrestricted

Batch Entry: This field specifies how the batches of components are determined in a production/process order. You have the following options:

- The batches can be assigned manually in the order before the order is released.

- The batches can be determined automatically when the order is released.

- The batches can be determined when the goods issue is posted.

- The batches must be entered in the order before the goods issue is posted, but not necessarily before the order is released.

Underdelivery Tolerance: You can specify a permissible lower tolerance limit for the quantity that can be accepted against the order quantity. Say you have an order quantity of 100 with an underdelivery tolerance limit of 5%. In that case, the system will not allow Goods receipt below 95.

Overdelivery Tolerance: You can specify a permissible upper tolerance limit for the quantity that can be accepted against the order quantity. Say you have an order quantity of 100 with an overdelivery tolerance limit of 5%. In that case, the system will not allow goods receipt over 105.

Unlimited Overdelivery Tolerance: You can use this indicator to specify that there is no limit for overdelivery and underdelivery. The system will allow you to post any amount of goods receipt.

Now that you have created material master records for finished goods, semifinished goods, and components, you can create a BOM (bill of materials) for the gearbox assembly.

Bill of Materials

A bill of materials (BOM) is a comprehensive list of the components that make up a product or assembly. The list includes the material number of each component, together with the quantity and unit of measure, among other details. SuperGears AG needs components like a counter shaft, a clutch shaft, a dog clutch, a main shaft, and a reverse gear to produce their gear assembly, for example.

You can create a bill of materials using Transaction Code CS01 or by choosing Logistics ➤ Production ➤ Master Data ➤ Bill of Materials ➤ Bill of Materials ➤ Material BOM ➤ Create.

Figure 2-13 shows the initial screen called Create Material BOM. Enter the material number of the final assembly for which you want to create the BOM, the plant number of the production plant, and BOM usage.

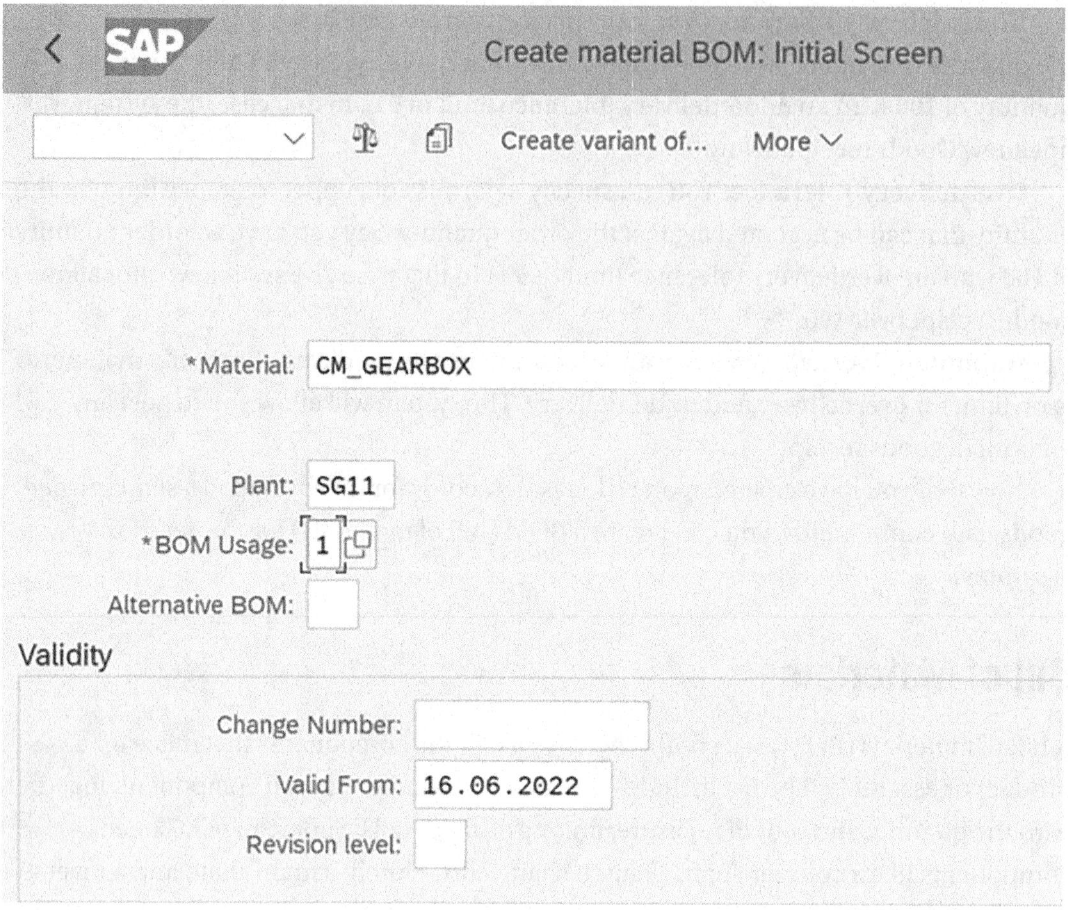

Figure 2-13. *Create a bill of materials*

BOM Usage: This is used to state the application area where the BOM can be used. For example, the Engineering team at SuperGears creates a BOM for Engineering/ Design to list all the components needed for gear assembly during the design phase. The BOM created with usage Engineering/Design is not exploded during the MRP run or cannot be used in a production order. Once the Engineering team approves the design of the gear assembly for production, a BOM with usage Production is created, which can be used for the MRP run and the production orders.

Similarly, you can create a BOM for Sales & Distribution, Plant Maintenance, Costing, and so on. If you create a BOM with usage Universal, it can be used for all business functions. Figure 2-14 shows the BOM uses available in SAP.

BOM Usage (1)   16 Entries found

Restrictions

Usage	Prod.	Eng/des.	PM	Spare	CostRel	Sales	Usage text
1	+	.	-	.	.	.	Production
2	.	+	-	.	.	-	Engineering/Design
3	.	.	-	.	.	.	Universal
4	-	-	+	.	.	-	Plant Maintenance
5	.	.	-	.	.	+	Sales and Distribution
6	.	.	-	.	+	.	Costing
7	.	-	-	-	.	.	Empties
8	-	.	-	-	-	-	Stability Study
B	.	.	-	.	.	+	Sales Bundles (IS-HT-SW)
C	-	-	+	.	.	-	Configuration Control
L	+	.	-	.	.	.	Production Charminar Casting
M	.	.	.	.	.	.	External Munitions Display
S	-	-	.	-	-	-	Customer Management
U	.	-	.	-	-	-	IUID Embedded Items

Figure 2-14. BOM usage

Alternative BOM: If a finished/semifinished assembly can be produced in multiple ways using different components, you can use an alternative BOM to record different ways for producing that material. SuperGears AG uses counter shafts, clutch shafts, dog clutches, main shafts, and reverse gears to manufacture the constant mesh gearbox. While creating the BOM, the system will generate the BOM with Alternative BOM 1 by default. A gearbox can use Counter_Shaft01 or Counter_Shaft02. Either of the two counter shafts can be used to assemble the gearbox. This scenario can be handled using an alternate BOM in SAP. You can create two alternative BOMs for the gearbox, each using different counter shafts.

Thus, the primary BOM is created using Counter_Shaft01 with Alternative BOM 1. You also need to create another BOM using Counter_Shaft02 and the system will set the alternative BOM 2. The system allows you to create up to 99 alternative BOMs.

Figure 2-15 shows the header screen of the BOM.

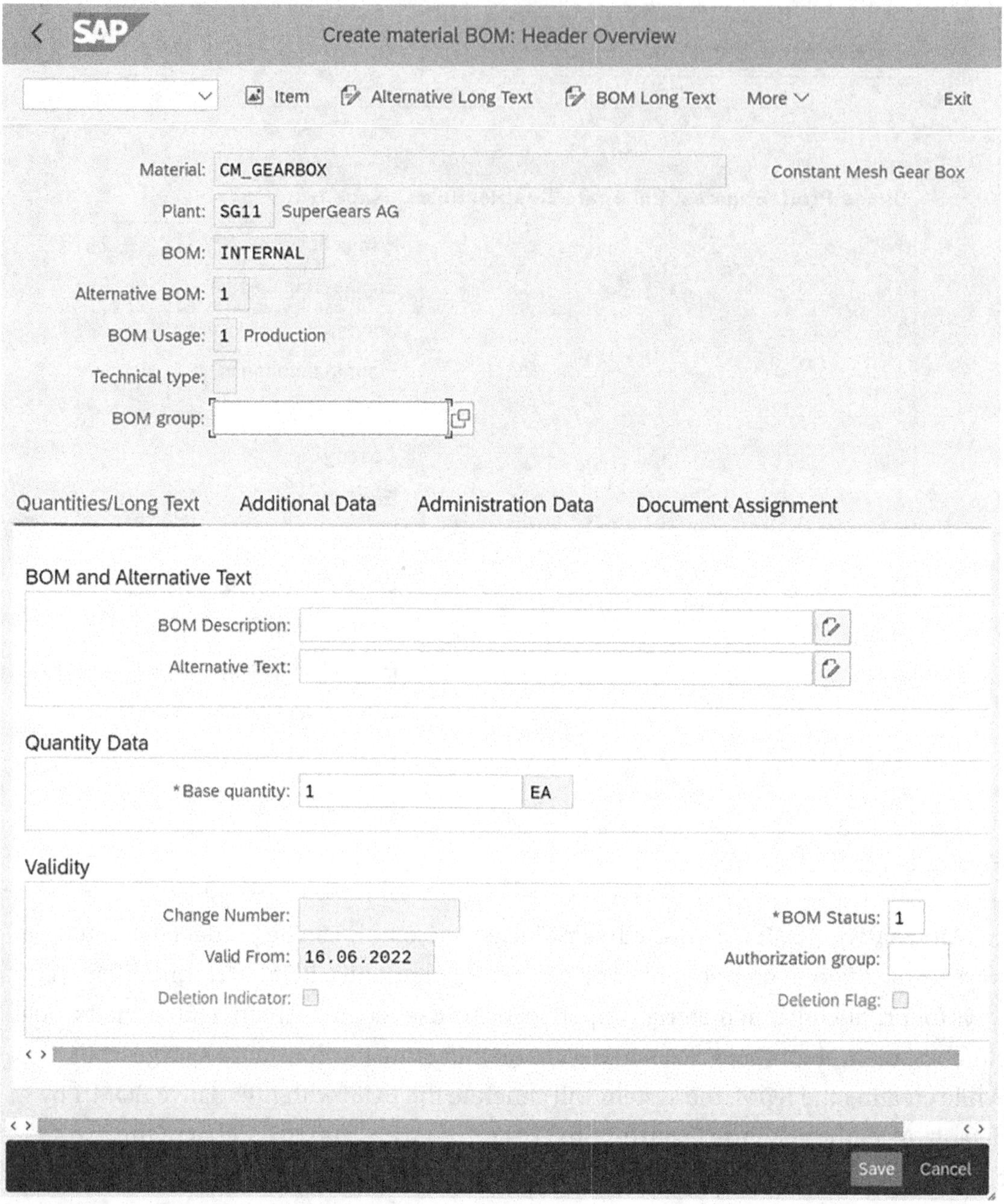

Figure 2-15. *Create material BOM header*

BOM: A BOM number is generated automatically by the system to each material and BOM category. All the alternative BOMs created for a material are grouped in the same BOM number. Similarly, all the variants in a variant BOM are also grouped in the same BOM number.

Base Quantity: Base quantity is the quantity to which all component quantities in a BOM relate. For example, the base quantity for gear assembly would be 1 and you would assign a quantity of each component required to produce one gear assembly. However, if you're producing cheese, you might need approximately 80 kgs of milk to produce 10 kgs of cheese. In this case, the base quantity for cheese would be 10 kgs and you'd allocate quantities for components with reference to the base quantity of the parent material.

BOM Status: This identifies if the BOM is active or inactive, as shown in Figure 2-16. New status keys can be customized by specifying an application area like MRP explosion, planned order, costing, and so on.

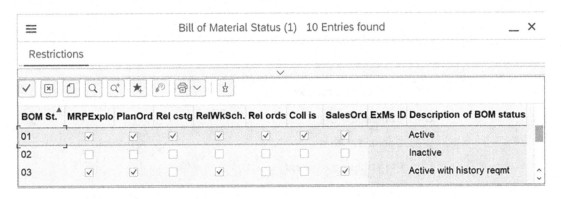

BOM St.	MRPExplo	PlanOrd	Rel cstg	RelWkSch.	Rel ords	Coll is	SalesOrd	ExMs ID	Description of BOM status
01	✓	✓	✓	✓	✓	✓	✓		Active
02	☐	☐	☐	☐	☐	☐	☐		Inactive
03	✓	✓	☐	✓	☐	☐	✓		Active with history reqmt

Figure 2-16. *Bill of materials status*

Valid From: This specifies the date from which the BOM is valid. The system defaults the current date on which BOM is created as valid from date.

Let's look at some of the important data in item overview by clicking the Item Overview button.

Item Number: This number refers to the sequence of BOM components. Usually, the item increment is 10, starting with 0010 for the first component.

Item Category: The item category identifies the type of material and influences how the material can be used in the BOM. Common item categories are stock item, non-stock item, variable-size item, text item, document item, and intra material, as shown in Figure 2-17.

Stock Item: Most of the components are kept in stock and must have a material master record so that the inventory situation can be analyzed and procurement can be triggered based on stock consumption.

Non-Stock Item: These are components in BOM that are rarely used and thus you don't need to maintain the stock of this component. It is not mandatory to create a material master record; you can just enter a material description for this component.

Text Item: The system stores your text in a text file using the long text processing function.

Document Item: You can use document item to attach documents like design drawing, catalogue, user manual, and so on.

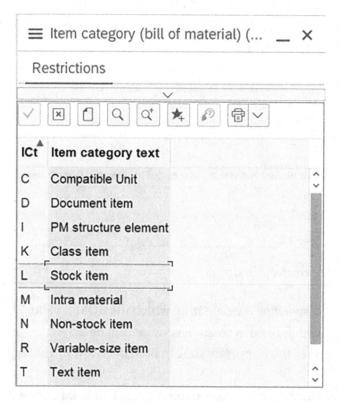

Figure 2-17. *Item category*

Component: You must assign the material number from the material master record of the component, as shown in Figure 2-18.

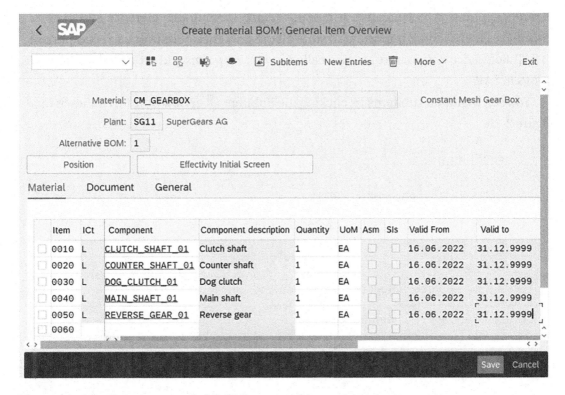

Figure 2-18. *Create material BOM: general item overview*

Component Description: Component description is populated automatically from the material master record. If you're using a non-stock item, you can just enter the component description along with other details, like quantity, price, purchasing group, material group, and so on.

Quantity: Assign the quantity of the component with reference to the base quantity of the finished assembly.

Unit of Measure: The unit of measure for component is populated from the material master record automatically.

Assembly Indicator: If the component is a semifinished assembly and has its own BOM, the Assembly indicator is assigned automatically by the system.

Subitems Indicator: If you have maintained subitems, this flag is set by the system automatically.

Business Case: This scenario involves the Electrical and Electronics industry, where it is important to store reference designators in SAP and eventually send this information to the MES system. This marks the exact place where a component (for example, a capacitor or a relay) should be placed on the PCB. The same components could be used at multiple points, which means a component can have multiple reference designators. This makes it even more important to store all the reference points for each component in SAP. Reference designators are also called *mounting points* and are called *installation points* in SAP.

You can maintain subitems by clicking the Subitem Overview button, as shown in Figure 2-19.

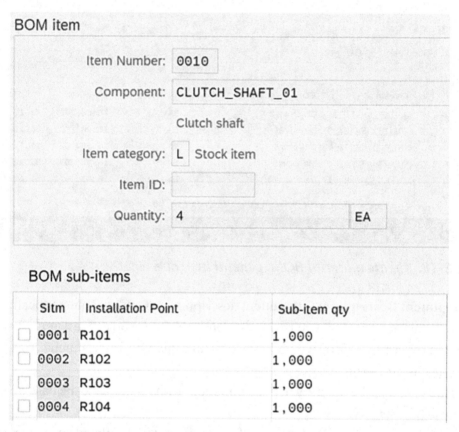

Figure 2-19. *Create material BOM: subitems*

Note: The subitems have been assigned just to show the functionality. However, the installation points are not relevant in the example of the gearbox assembly.

Valid From: Specifies the date from which the component is valid. The system defaults the current date on which BOM is created as the Valid From date. When a new component is assigned to an existing BOM, the current date is assigned as the Valid From date for the component. If you're using a change number, the Valid From date is populated from the change number.

Valid To: Specify the date until which the component is valid. The system defaults the valid to date as 31.12.9999. If a component is replaced by another component, the Valid To date is changed accordingly.

Change number: You can use the change number to create or change master data objects, like the material master, BOM, routing, and so on. When using change master in BOM, you can control certain parameters:

- Valid From date of BOM header or components

- Track the changes/history of the BOM

Phantom: If the component is assigned phantom in the material master record, the system sets this indicator automatically.

SAP phantom assembly is a virtual assembly that's neither produced nor purchased. You don't keep inventory of the phantom assembly either. The purpose of the phantom assembly is to create a BOM so that all the components can be grouped, but you don't want to create a separate production order. You can also say that phantom assemblies are assembled "on the go" and immediately consumed by some other assembly in the production process.

For example, the reverse gear and dog clutch are mounted on the main shaft forming a phantom assembly. But you don't have to create a separate production order and keep the phantom assembly in stock, as it is immediately assembled with a counter shaft and a clutch shaft.

Work Center

This refers to a place or a workstation where an activity or an operation is performed during the production process. A work center can be a machine/group of machines or a labor process (manual operation like quality inspection)/group of machines or even a combination of machine and labor. Work centers are used in routing and subsequently in production orders.

You can create a work center using Transaction Code CR01 or by choosing Logistics ➤ Production ➤ Master Data ➤ Work Centers ➤ Work Centers ➤ Create.

Plant: Enter the plant, the name of the work center, and the work center category, as shown in Figure 2-20.

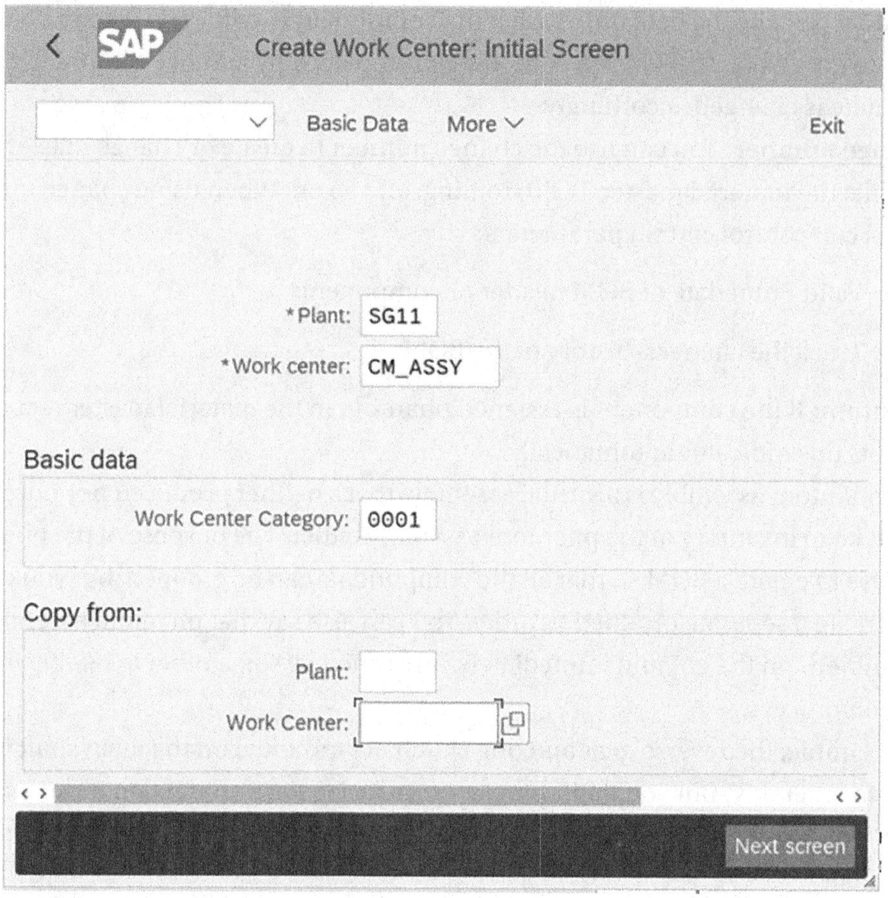

Figure 2-20. *Create work center*

Work Center: You can define an eight-digit alphanumeric unique name for the work center.

Business Case: At SuperGears AG, the gears that are procured from external vendors go through a series of operations like machining, drilling, and boring on the machine line. Similarly, turning is performed on shafts on lathe machines. And finally, the gears and shafts are assembled into gearbox assembly on the assembly line. To map this process, you must create work centers for the machine line, the lathe machine, and the assembly line.

Let's consider an example of an assembly line only to keep the process simple. Let's create a work center called CM_ASSY, which will be used to assemble the gearbox.

Work Center Category: Work center category determines the data that can be maintained in the work center, as shown in Figure 2-21.

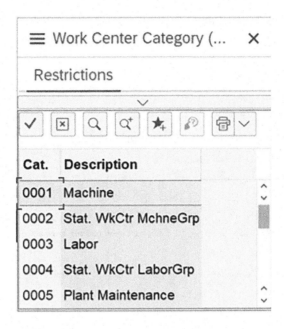

Figure 2-21. *Work center category*

It also identifies the application areas where the work center can be used, as shown in Figure 2-22. For example, the work center created with the Machine category can be used for maintenance, production, or quality inspection, as shown in Figure 2-22.

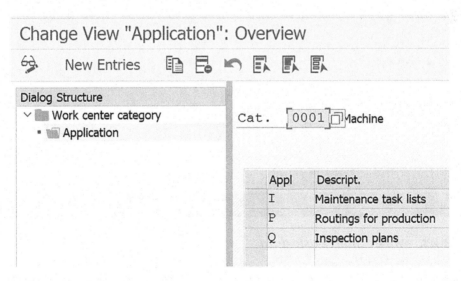

Figure 2-22. *Work center category application*

The work center master contains five tabs—Basic Data, Default Values, Capacities, Scheduling, and Costing. The next sections discuss some of the important fields in each of these tabs.

Basic Data View

Figure 2-23 shows the basic data view of the work center.

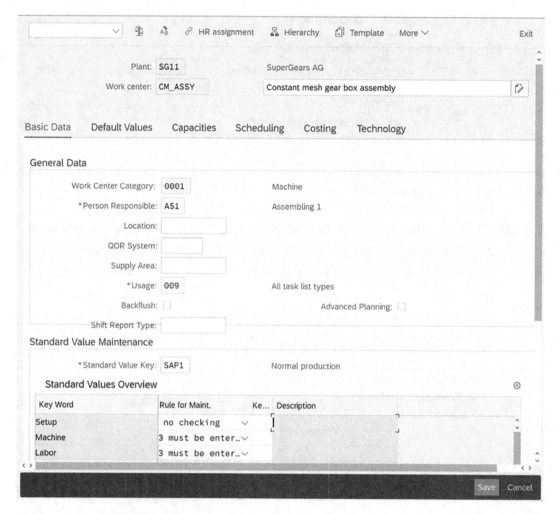

Figure 2-23. *Work center: basic data*

Description: In the Work Center header, you can see that the plant and work center name are populated from the initial screen. You must enter the Work Center description and provide more specific details of the work center for CM_ASSY. Then you must specify the description of the work center as Constant Mesh Gearbox Assembly.

Production Supply Area: The production supply area serves as interim storage on the shop floor. Components are received from the warehouse and stored temporarily in production supply area, also called the PSA. The components are then used for production directly from PSA, thus reducing the wait time. The PSA is used in Kanban and JIT outbound processing and in extended warehouse management.

Task List Usage: This key can be used to determine the task lists in which a work center or production resource/tool may be used. Task list usage shouldn't be confused with the work center category. The Work Center category determines the application areas like production, maintenance, and so on. The task list usage determines the task list type where the work center can be used. For example, the work center category called 0001 Machine specifies the application as P Routings for Production. With Task List Usage, you can restrict the use of work center for only routings or rate routings or master recipes.

Backflush: This refers to automatic goods issue to production orders. You can skip the manual goods issue process using backflush. The backflush indicator can be activated in multiple master data objects. The highest priority is checked based on the following hierarchy:

- **Routing:** You can activate backflush for a component in component assignment.

- **Material Master:** You can activate backflush in the material master or let the work center decide.

- **Work Center:** If you opted for the work center to decide in the material master, then you can activate backflush in the work center. This provides an advantage if you want to backflush all the components that are consumed in this work center and thus do not need to activate backflush for each material in the material master.

Standard Value Key: When doing an operation on a work center, certain activities are performed. For example, when starting production, you need to set up the machine settings (for example, change the cutting tools or adjust the operating parameters on a CNC machine). This activity is referred to as setup. Similarly, you can have other activities like machine or labor time, which are used to calculate cycle time and costs for each operation, and so on. Other activities can be power, depreciation, overhead, and so on.

All these activities are also referred to as parameters. A standard reference key can contain up to a maximum of six parameters for activities, as shown in Figure 2-24. The activities are then populated in routing and are used to calculate capacity, scheduling, costing, and so on. The SAP1 standard value key, as shown in Figure 2-24, contains three activities—Setup, Machine, and Labor.

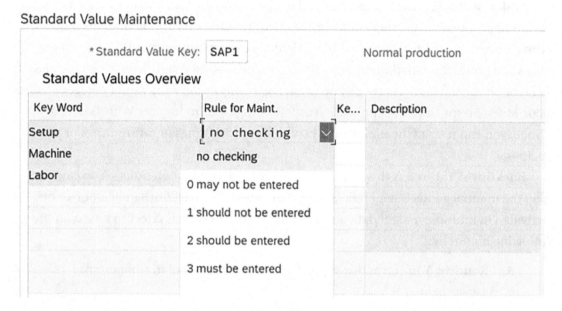

Figure 2-24. *Work center: standard value key*

You can also create new standard value keys, which can include a maximum of six activities. For example, setup, machine, labor, power, depreciation, and overhead.

Rule for Maintenance: This determines whether it is optional or mandatory to maintain a value for an activity in an operation of a routing.

Default Values View

Figure 2-25 shows the Default Values view of the work center.

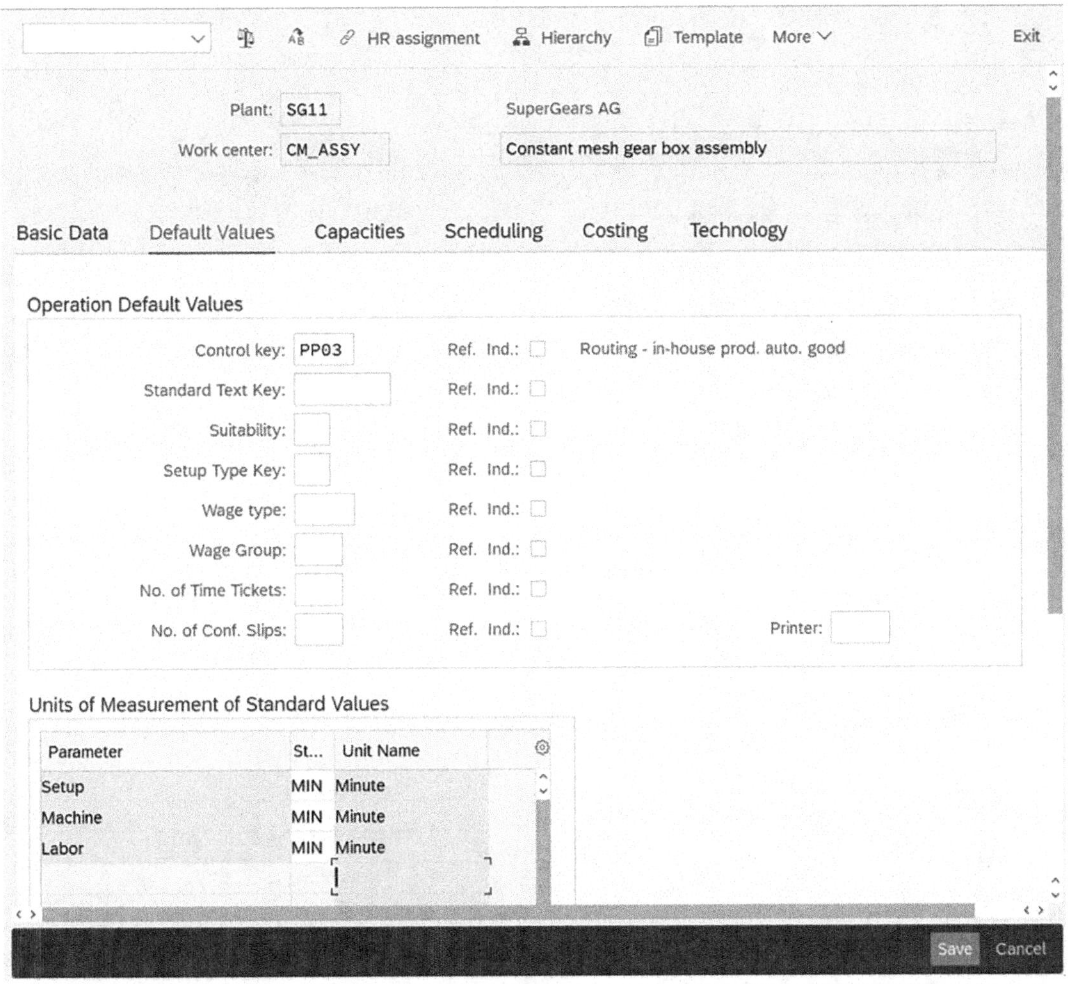

Figure 2-25. *Work center: default values*

Control Key: This is used to determine how an operation is processed. It controls a lot of parameters, including scheduling, capacity requirements, costing, external processing, confirmation, and so on. Figure 2-26 shows all the parameters for control key PP01.

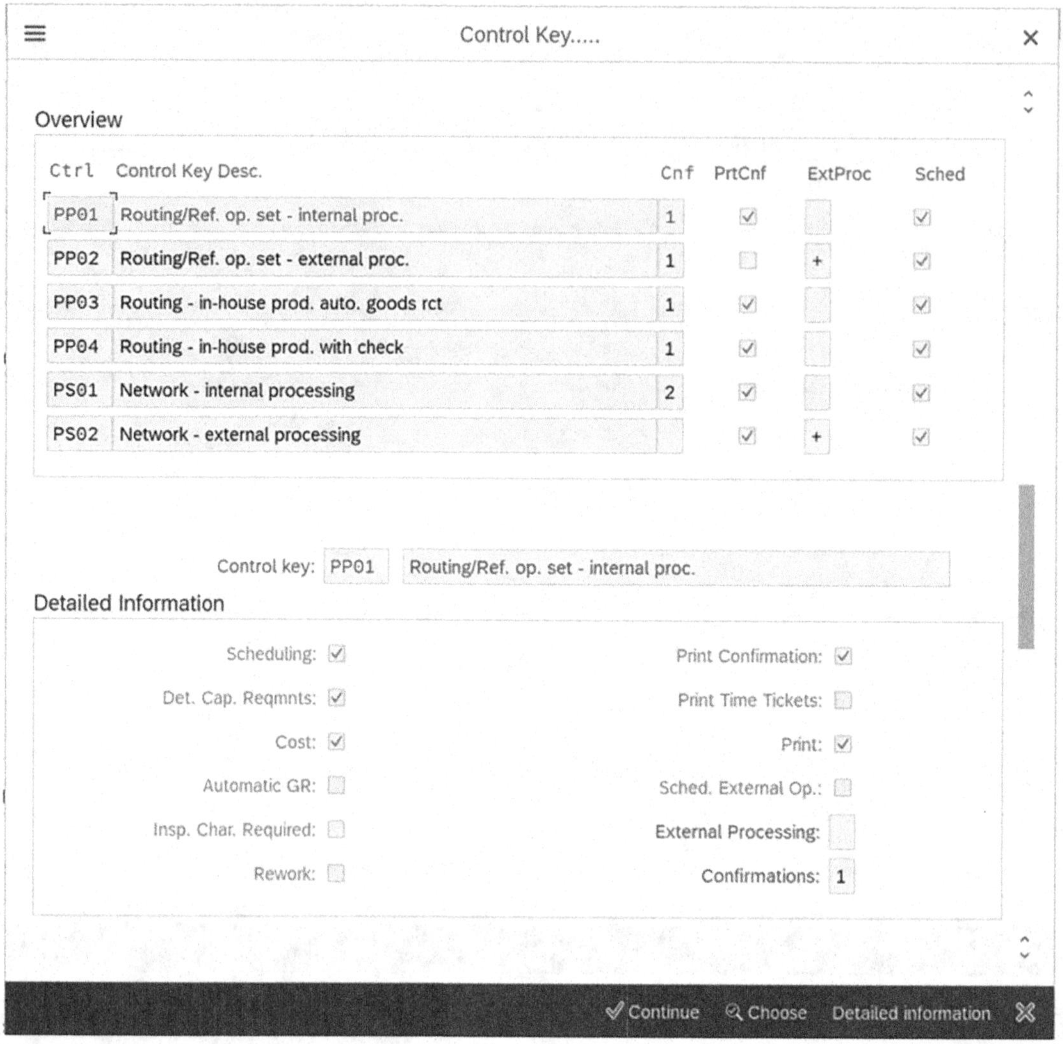

Figure 2-26. *Control key*

- The Scheduling check box determines if scheduling is performed on this work center.

- Determine Capacity Requirements controls whether capacity requirement records are generated for an operation on this work center.

- Cost Indicator determines if the activities performed on this work center should be costed.

- Automatic Goods Receipt specifies that a goods receipt for an order is posted automatically for the confirmation. This means if a control key with Automatic Goods Receipt is assigned to an operation and a confirmation is posted, the system also posts goods receipts automatically.

- Externally Processing specifies that the operation is processed by an external vendor, which is also referred to as operation subcontracting.

- Confirmation Parameters specifies whether an object is to be confirmed if it has the control key you selected. You can also specify if milestone confirmations can be posted for this operation (see Figure 2-27).

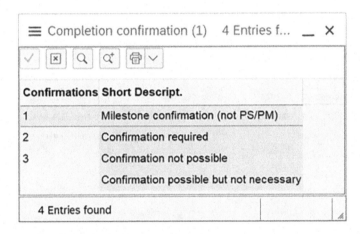

Figure 2-27. Confirmation parameters

Standard Text Key: A standard text is assigned to an operation by entering the standard text key in the operation. By changing this text within the operation long text, you can create an individual operation description.

Capacities

In the Capacities tab, you maintain available capacities, breaks, capacity utilization, and so on. You also maintain the formulas for setup, processing, teardown, and so on. The production order determines the time for an operation from the routing and, based on the formulas in the Capacities view of the work center, then generates its capacity requirement. Figure 2-28 shows the Capacities view of the work center.

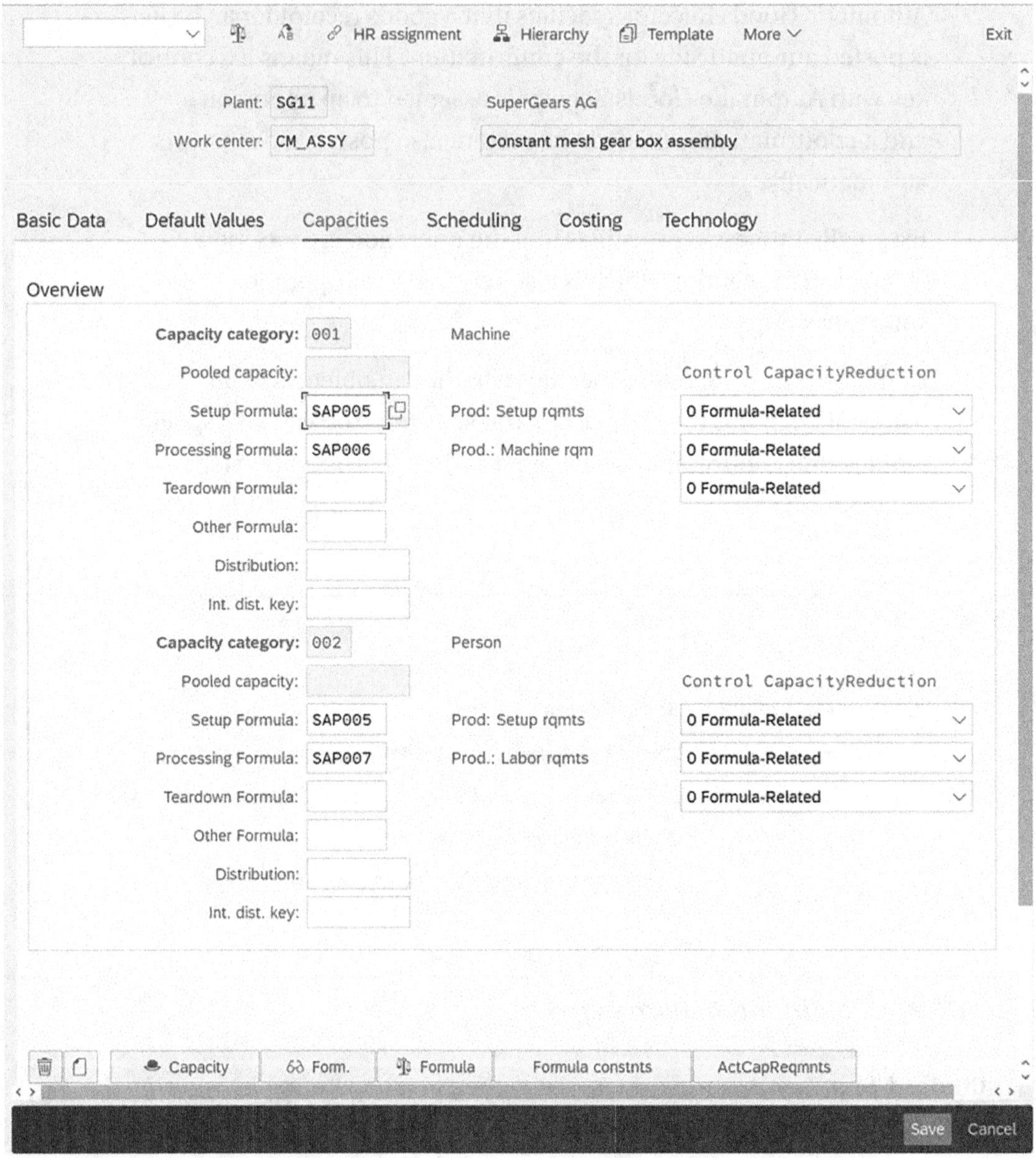

Figure 2-28. *Work center: capacities*

SAP comes preconfigured with capacity formulas that can be readily used, as shown in Table 2-2.

Table 2-2. *Formulas for Capacity*

Formula	Description
SAP001	Prod.: Setup time
SAP002	Prod.: Machine time
SAP003	Prod.: Labor time
SAP004	Proj:Netw/Maint.Time
SAP005	Prod: Setup rqmts
SAP006	Prod.: Machine rqmts
SAP007	Prod.: Labor rqmts

Click the Capacity Header at the bottom-left of the screen to navigate to the Work Center Capacity: Header. From this screen, you can maintain the parameters that are important to determine the capacity of the work center, like factory calendar, start time, end time, length of breaks, capacity utilization, and so on, as shown in Figure 2-29.

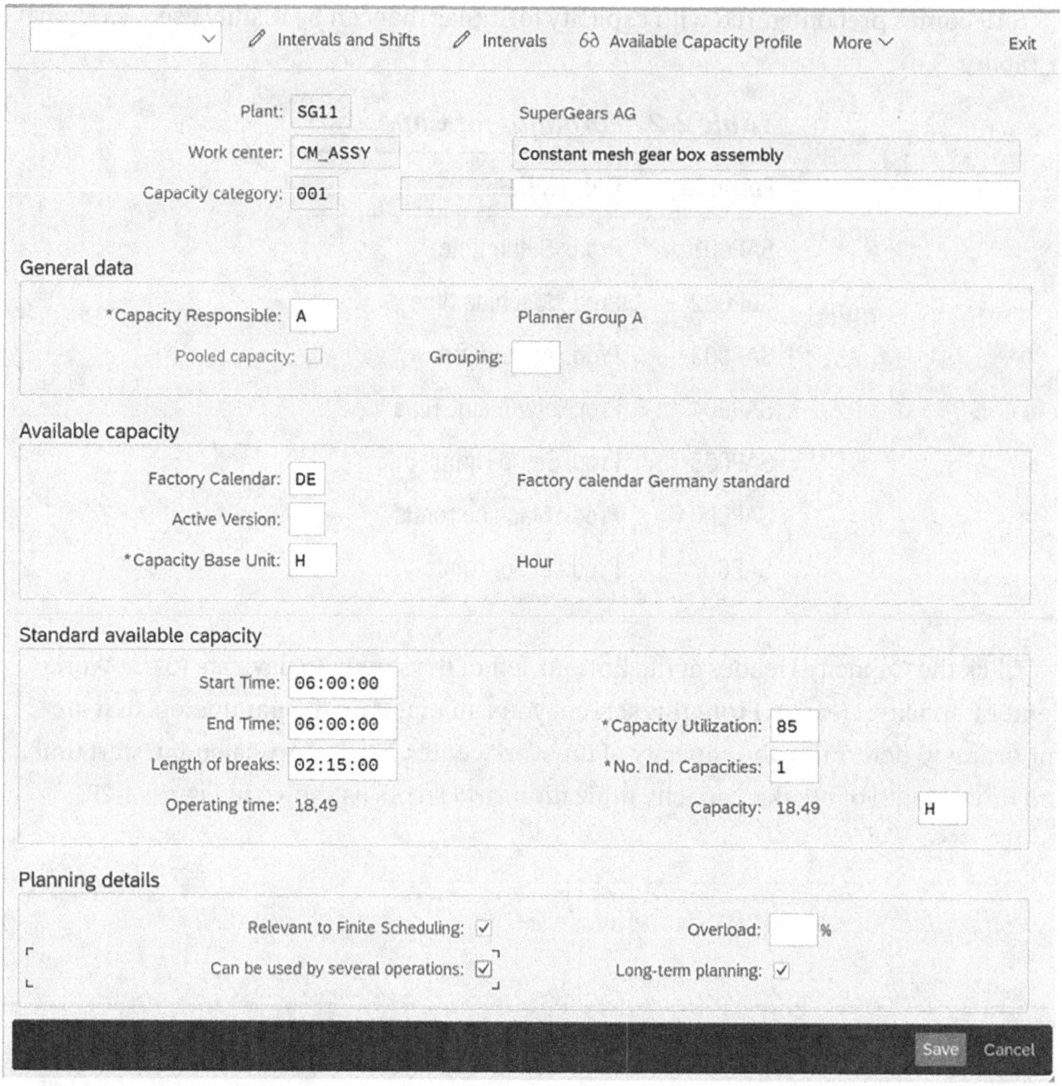

Figure 2-29. Work center: capacity header

Factory Calendar: This is a country-specific calendar that specifies the working day for the plant as well as a list of public holidays (maintained via the holiday calendar). Each plant is assigned a factory calendar. You can assign a factory calendar in the work center or the system can use the factory calendar maintained at the plant level. Here, the factory calendar helps schedule the production order (i.e., scheduling is not performed on a holiday).

Capacity Base Unit: The unit in which available capacity is maintained; for example, hours or minutes.

Start Time: This is the start time of the shift for the work center. For example, at SuperGears the first shift starts at 06:00 AM.

End Time: This is the end time of the shift of the work center. For example, SuperGears runs three shifts a day and the third shift ends at 06:00 AM the next day.

Length of Breaks: This is the duration of the total breaks during all shifts in a day. For example, SuperGears has break time of 45 mins during each shift, so the total break is 02:15 hours.

Capacity Utilization: Capacity utilization rate measures actual output realized against the potential output. Say the capacity for a work center is 500 pieces per day. On calculating the total production for a year, the average production turns out to be 450 pieces per day. Thus, the capacity utilization is 90%.

*Capacity Utilization: Actual Output / Potential Output * 100*

It is unlikely for a company to operate at a 100% capacity rate ,as there are always hurdles in the production process (such as the malfunction of equipment or unequal distribution of resources, and so on). Usually, a capacity utilization rate of 80-85% is considered good.

Based on the start time, end time, breaks, and capacity utilization, the operating time is calculated as 18,49 hours, as shown in the Standard Available Capacity section in Figure 2-30.

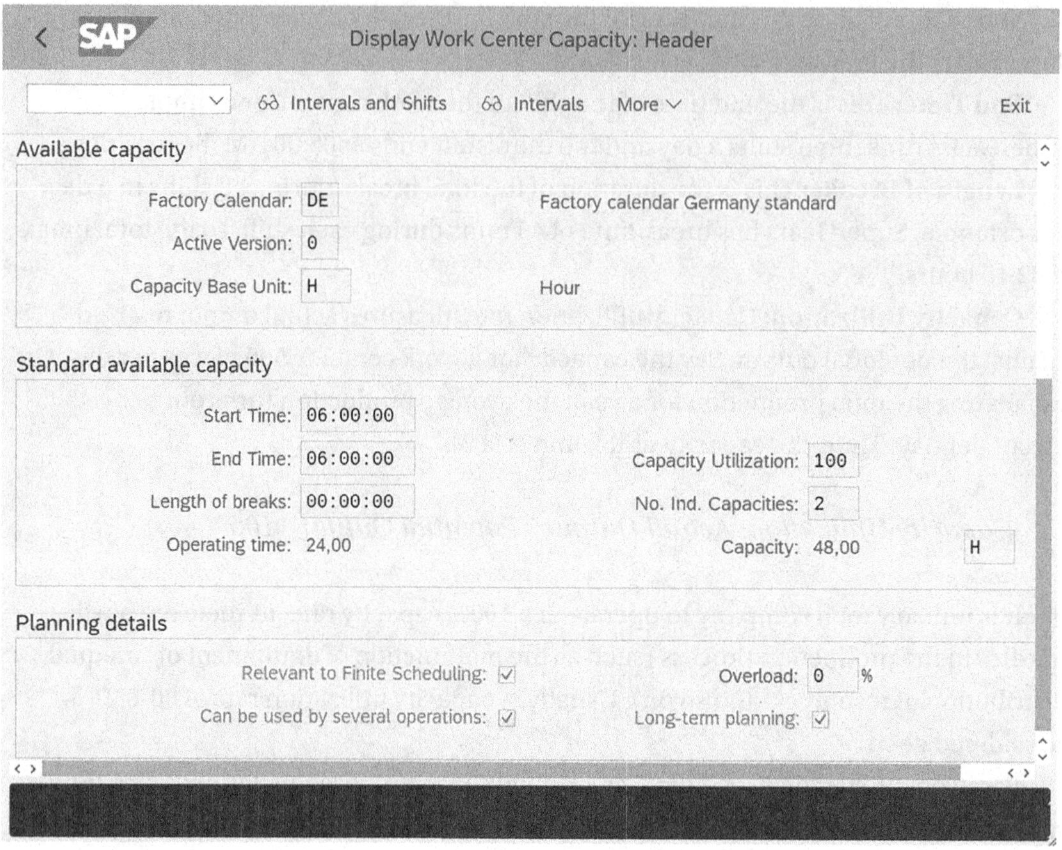

Figure 2-30. *Work center: standard available capacity*

Number of Individual Capacities: Say you have five machines that are used for the same kind of operation or activity, such as lathe machines. You can group the capacities of these five lathe machines as one work center "lathe" and assign the number of individual capacities as 5. Figure 2-31 shows that the operating time for the work center is 18,49 while the total capacity is 92,44 hours due to the fact that capacity is five times the operating time due to a number of individual capacities.

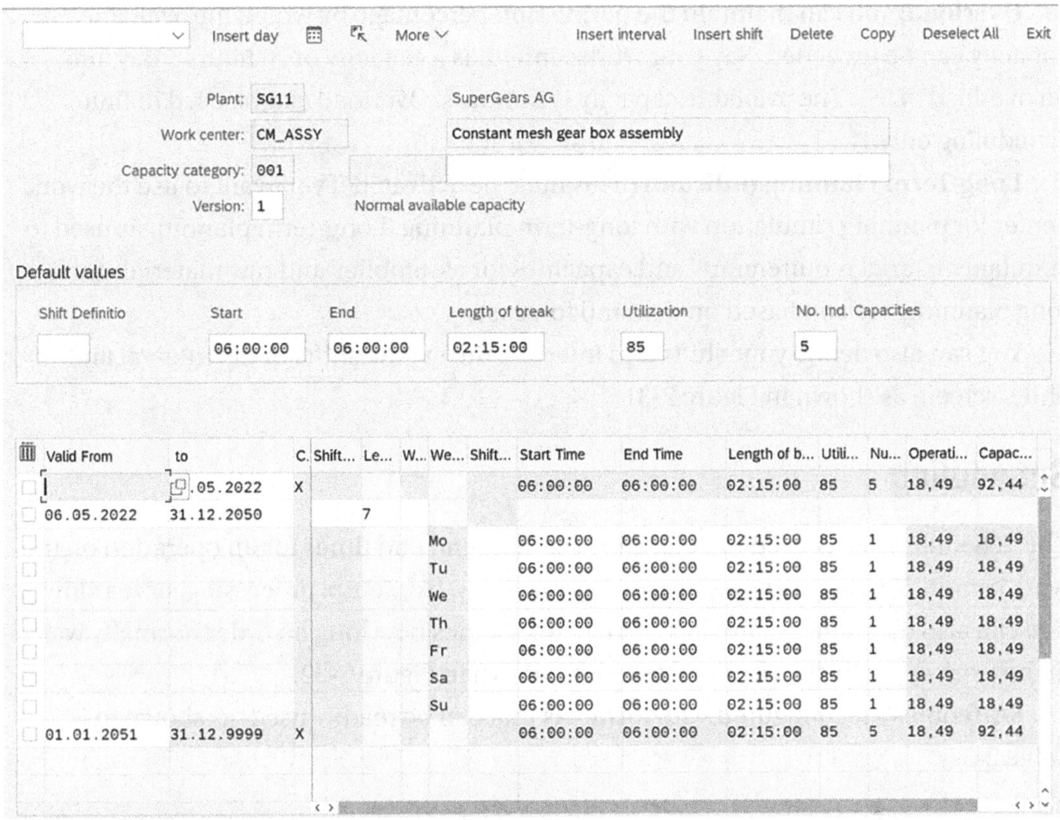

Figure 2-31. *Intervals of available capacity*

Let's learn about some of the important indicators in the Planning Details section, as shown in Figure 2-30.

Relevant to Finite Scheduling Indicator: This indicator is important as it determines if the capacity of the work center should be considered during finite scheduling.

Can Be Used by Several Operations: You can use this indicator to specify that the work center can be used by several operations or the same work center can be used by more than one production order simultaneously.

Business Case: Each gear produced by SuperGears should go through a Heat Treatment process. Say you created a work center for heat treatment that has a capacity to treat 500 gears at the same time. Gears from several different production orders can be treated in the heat treatment process simultaneously given its high capacity. You use the Can Be Used By Several Operations indicator to allow this.

Overload: You can maintain the permission percentage by which the available capacity can be exceeded. Say your work center has a capacity of 20 hours a day and an overload of 5%. The available capacity is 21 hours. Overload can be used in finite scheduling only.

Long-Term Planning Indicator: This must be activated if you want to use the work center for planning simulation with long-term planning. Long-term planning is used to simulate material requirements and capacities for assemblies and raw materials for a long planning horizon based on demand forecasts.

You can also define your shifts and intervals during the shifts in the Interval and Shifts screen, as shown in Figure 2-31.

Scheduling

The Scheduling tab is used to determine the start and end times for an operation on the work center. You can maintain processing formulas, like setup, processing, or teardown. You can also maintain queue time, which determines how long an order normally waits at the work center before it is processed, as shown in Figure 2-32.

SAP comes preconfigured with formulas that can be readily used, as shown in Table 2-3.

Table 2-3. *Formulas for Scheduling*

Formula	Description
SAP001	Prod.: Setup time
SAP002	Prod.: Machine time
SAP003	Prod.: Labor time
SAP004	Proj:Netw/Maint.Time
SAP005	Prod: Setup rqmts
SAP006	Prod.: Machine rqmts
SAP007	Prod.: Labor rqmts

Capacity view is used to identify the capacities needed on a work center, machine and labor that could work in parallel. The Scheduling view is used to determine the start and end times of an operation. Let's say there is a manual operation for testing gearboxes. Typically, 100 gearboxes can be tested in two hours. But if you assign two people for testing, the operation can be finished in one hour. Here the scheduling time is reduced, but the capacity remains the same, as two people are employed.

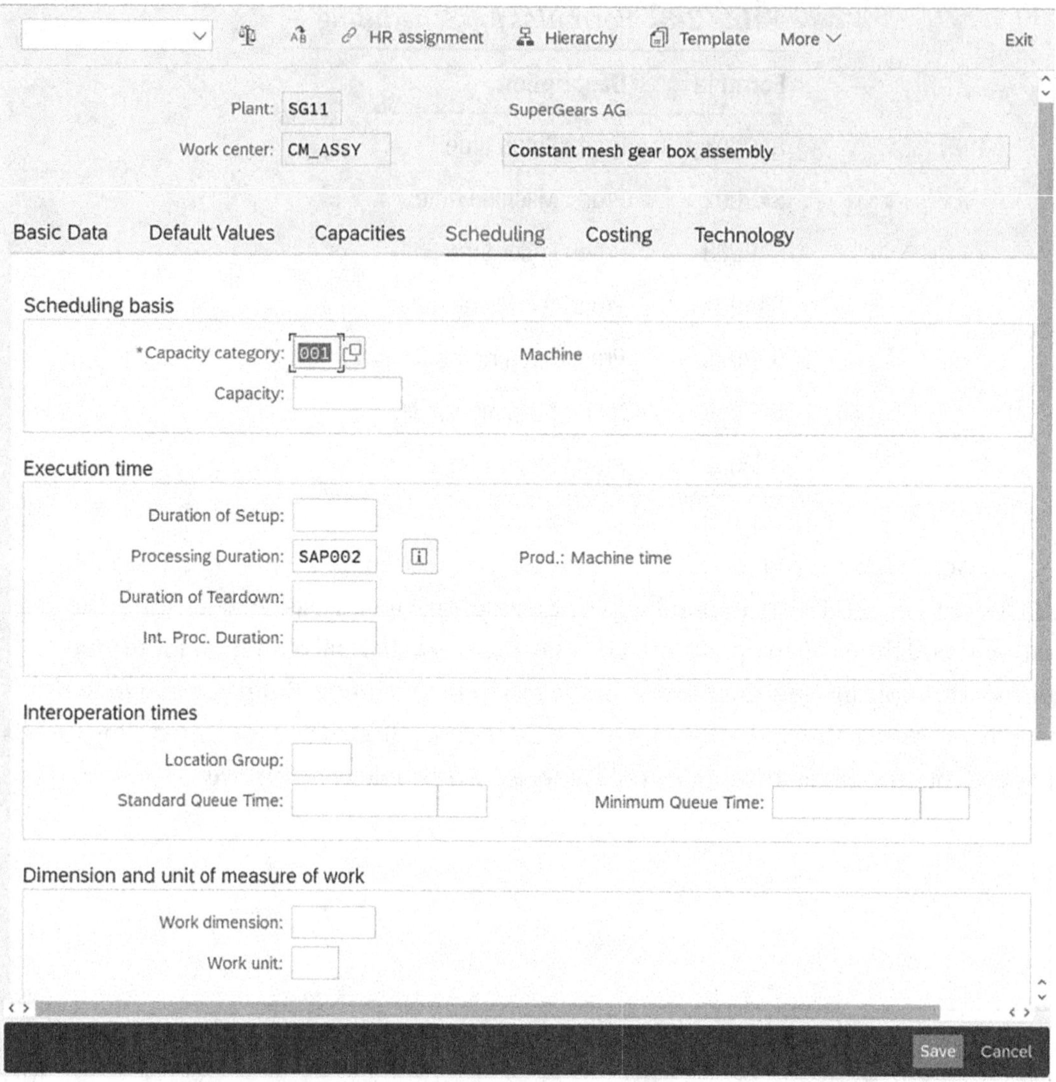

Figure 2-32. *Work center: scheduling*

Costing

The Costing tab is quite important, as it serves as an integration point between PP and CO. For each work center, you must assign a cost center to which all the costs of production on the work center are allocated. A cost center can have multiple work centers assigned to it; however, you can have only one cost center assigned in a work center.

Figure 2-33 shows the Costing view of the work center. Let's learn about important fields in the Costing view of the work center in the following section.

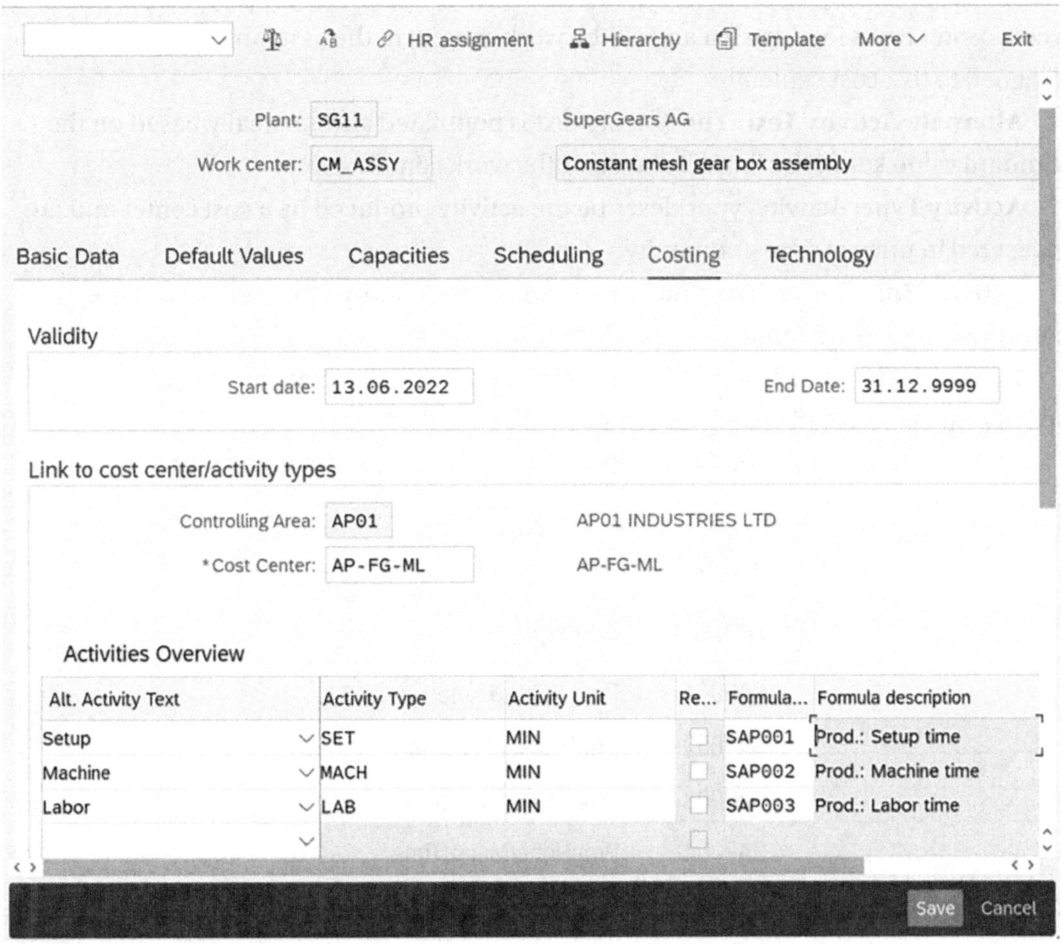

Figure 2-33. *Work center: costing*

Controlling Area: The controlling area is an organizational unit in accounting used to subdivide the business organization from a cost accounting standpoint. It is populated automatically based on plant assignment to company code and company code assignment to controlling area in the enterprise structure, which is defined in the customization.

Cost Center: A cost center is an organizational unit within a controlling area to which costs can be accumulated. You must assign a cost center where the system will accumulate the cost of production on a given work center. For example, you can have a cost center for assembly area and all the work centers in the assembly line can be assigned to this cost center.

Alternate Activity Text: The Activity text is populated automatically based on the standard value key in the Basic Data tab or the work center.

Activity Type: Activity types describe the activity produced by a cost center and are measured in units of time or quantity.

Activity Unit: The activity unit is the time or the quantity unit used to post the consumed activity quantities.

Formula: This specifies the key for formula that's used to calculate the costs of activity type performed on a work center.

SAP comes preconfigured with costing formulas that can be readily used, as shown in Table 2-4.

Table 2-4. *Formulas for Costing*

Formula	Description
SAP001	Prod.: Setup time
SAP002	Prod.: Machine time
SAP003	Prod.: Labor time
SAP004	Proj:Netw/Maint.Time
SAP005	Prod: Setup rqmts
SAP006	Prod.: Machine rqmts
SAP007	Prod.: Labor rqmts

Reference Indicator: If the reference indicator is set, you cannot change the values defined on the work center when creating a routing. If there are frequent changes to the costing activities, you must use this indicator, so that you can make changes in the work center and the objects will be updated in all the routings where the work center is used.

Routing

Routing is simply a production process or a series of processes that transform raw materials to finished products. It details important information such as:

- Operations that should be performed in the production of a finished/semifinished assembly

- The work center on which operation should be performed

- The time needed to set up machines during changeover, operation time for each process, and so on

- Materials needed for each operation

- Production resource and tools needed for production

You can create a routing process using Transaction Code CA01 or by choosing Logistics ➤ Production ➤ Master Data ➤ Routings ➤ Routings ➤ Standard Routings ➤ Create.

Figure 2-34 shows the initial screen called Create Routing. Enter the material number of the gearbox assembly to create the routing and enter the plant number of the production plant.

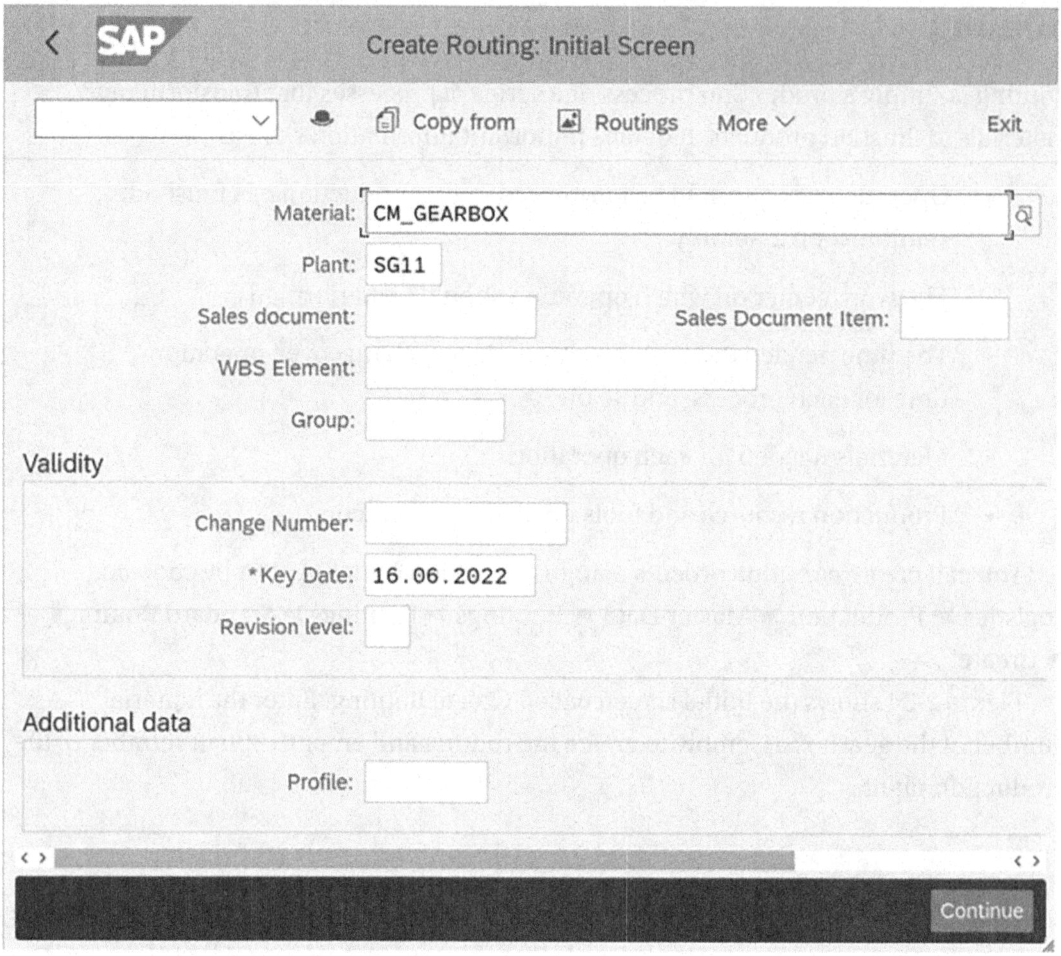

Figure 2-34. *Create routing: initial screens*

Change Number: You can use the change number to create or change master data objects like Material Master, BOM, Routing, and so on. When using the change master in routing, you can control the following parameters:

- Valid from date of routing

- Track the changes/history of the routing process

Key Date: Specifies the date from which the routing is valid. The system defaults to the current date on which the routing is created as the key date. For instance, if the key date for routing is 16.06.2022 and you are creating a Production version or production order for 15.05.2022, the system will give you an error message No Task List Exists, which means the routing is not created for the usage date.

Figure 2-35 shows the header screen of the routing process.

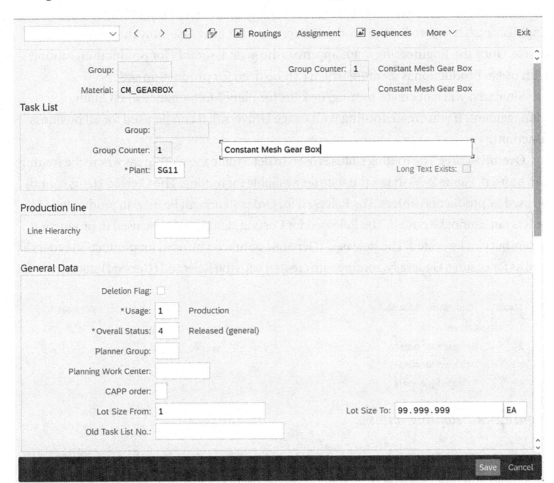

Figure 2-35. *Routing: header details*

Group: A unique key used to group routings.

You can create a routing with or without reference to a material. Routings without material numbers can be used by many materials that use the same production process, production line, or manufacturing steps.

Group Counter: A group counter together with group is used to identify a unique routing. For instance, when you create a routing for a material, a group (number) is generated automatically by the system with group counter 1 as the default. However, the group counter can be changed manually if need be. A new routing can be created for the same material with group counter 2 or so on. Thus, you can create multiple routings for the same material within the same (routing) group.

Usage: Task List usage is used to state the application area where routing can be used. For example, the Engineering team at SuperGears creates a routing for Engineering/Design to list the production process for gear assembly during the design phase. Once the Engineering team approves the gear assembly for production, routing with usage Production is created, which can be used for production orders.

Similarly, you can create routing/task list for Plant Maintenance and Quality Management. If you create routing with usage Universal, it can be used for all business functions.

Overall Status: The routing status is used to determine the work areas where the routing can be used. Figure 2-36 shows the statuses available for routing. The Created status cannot be used by production orders. The Released for Order status can be used in production orders but cannot be costed. The Released for Costing status cannot be used in production orders but can be costed. The Released (General) status can be used for production orders as well as for costing. Generally, routings are created with the Released (General) status.

Status	Description of the Status	RelInd	Cstng	Cons.chk.
1	Created	☐	☐	☐
2	Released for order	✓	☐	✓
3	Released for costing	☐	✓	✓
4	Released (general)	✓	✓	✓

Figure 2-36. *Routing statuses*

Lot Size From/To: The lot size defines the minimum and maximum quantities for the production order for which the routing can be used. For instance, SuperGears has two furnaces that they use for heat treatments. The small one has a capacity of up to 500 pieces, while the big one is used for bigger lot sizes from 500-1000 pieces. So, two routings should be created because both the furnaces have different operating timings, as shown in Table 2-5.

Table 2-5. *Routings per Lot Sizes*

Material	Product 1	Product 1
Group	50000001	50000001
Group Counter	1	2
Lot Size from	1	500
Lot size to	500	1000

Therefore, you need to assign different work centers and other details in the next screen, as explained in next section.

Click the Operation Overview button to navigate to the screen in Figure 2-37 in order to maintain the production process.

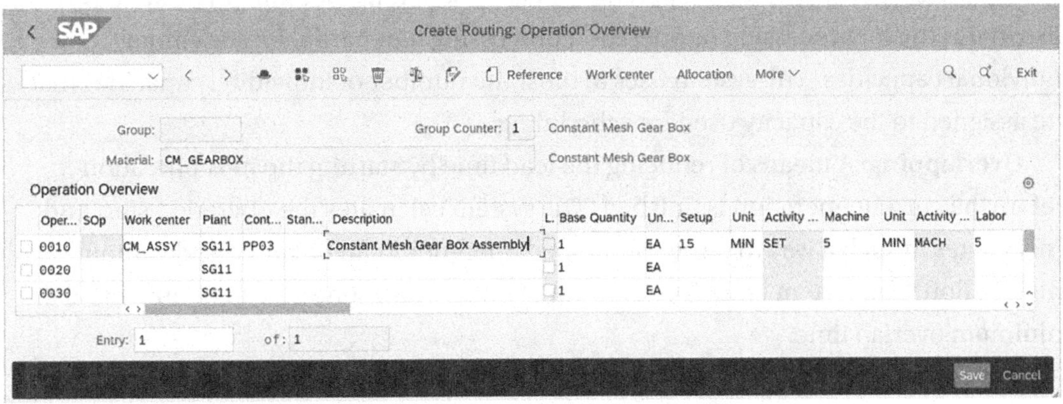

Figure 2-37. *Routing operation overview*

Operation: This number refers to the sequence of operations in the routing. Usually, the operation increment is 10, starting with 0010 for the first operation.

Sub-operation: This is subordinate to an operation and is used for more detailed planning of the process step described in the operation.

Work Center: You must maintain the work center that was created earlier as a separate master data object. Enter the CM_ASSY work center, which is the assembly line for the constant mesh gearbox assembly.

Note: The parameters assigned in Standard Value Key and Activity Type from the work center are reflected in the operation. You must assign a relevant activity time for each of these parameters—setup, machine, and labor.

Setup Time: When starting the production, you need to set up the machine settings (for example, changing the cutting tools or adjusting the operating parameters on one of the machines on the assembly line). This activity is referred to as setup.

Machine Time/Labor Time: Machine or labor time is used to calculate cycle time and costs for each operation. It's used for scheduling the operation, capacity requirement calculations on the work center, and calculating the costs of the operation.

Some of the other parameters that can be used for scheduling are Queue Time, Move Time, and so on.

Queue Time: This is the time an order normally waits at the work center before it is processed.

Move Time: This is the time normally needed between the current operation and the next one for the move from one work center (location group) to another.

Splitting: Specifies that the operation must be split for scheduling. The system distributes the lot processing or operation processing into partial lots or among individual capacities. The system uses at most the number of individual capacities that are assigned to the capacity used for scheduling.

Overlapping: A means of reducing the lead time by starting the next operation before the current operation is finished. The system calculates the operation start and finish dates in such a way that the overlapped operations can be processed without interruption. The system takes into account the minimum send-ahead quantity and the minimum overlap time.

The cost of each activity is calculated based on the time specified in routing. The Activity Type acts as an integration object between PP and CO. The price per unit of an activity is maintained in Transaction Code KP26.

Control Key: Used to determine how an operation is processed. It controls a lot of parameters like scheduling, capacity requirements, costing, external processing, confirmation, and so on. Figure 2-38 shows all the parameters for control key PP01.

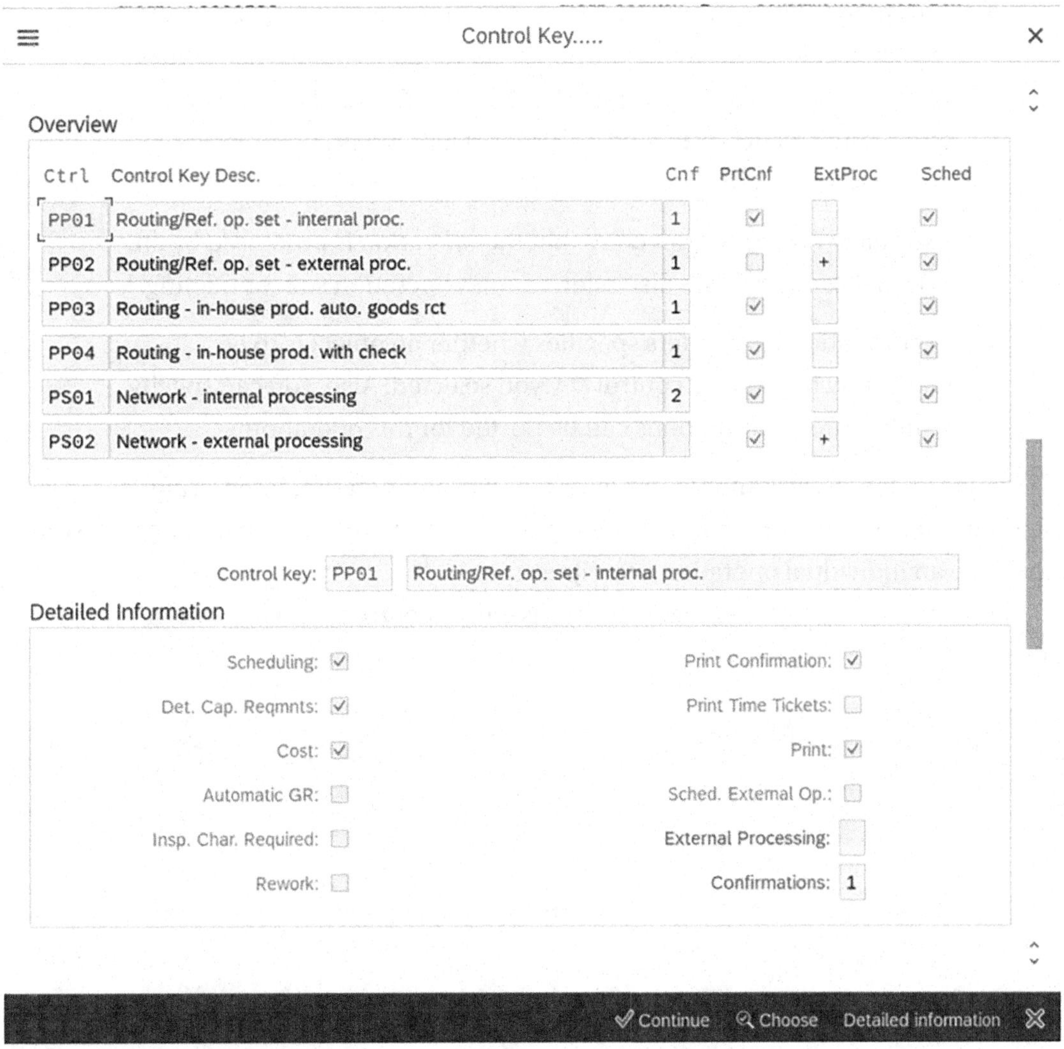

Figure 2-38. *Control key*

- The Scheduling parameter determines if scheduling is performed on this work center.

- Determine Capacity Requirements controls whether capacity requirement records are generated for an operation on this work center.

- Cost Indicator determines if the activities performed on this work center should be costed.

- Automatic Goods Receipt specifies that a goods receipt for an order is posted automatically for the confirmation. This means if a control key with Automatic Goods Receipt is assigned to an operation and a confirmation is posted, the system also posts goods receipts automatically.

- Externally Processing specifies that the operation is processed by an external vendor; this is also referred to as operation subcontracting.

- Confirmation Parameters specifies whether an object is to be confirmed if it has the control key you selected. Also, you can specify if milestone confirmations can be posted for this operation.

Standard Text Key: Standard text is assigned to an operation by entering the standard text key in the operation. By changing this text in the operation long text, you can create an individual operation description.

Standard text keys are created using Transaction Code CA10, as shown in Figure 2-39.

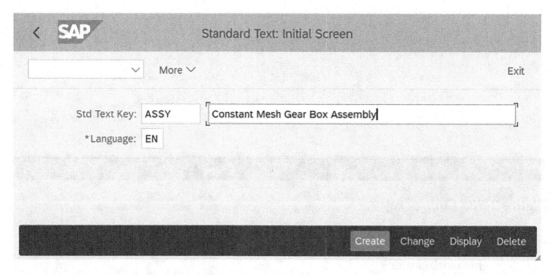

Figure 2-39. *Standard text: initial screen*

Click Create and enter the description of the standard text key, as shown in Figure 2-40.

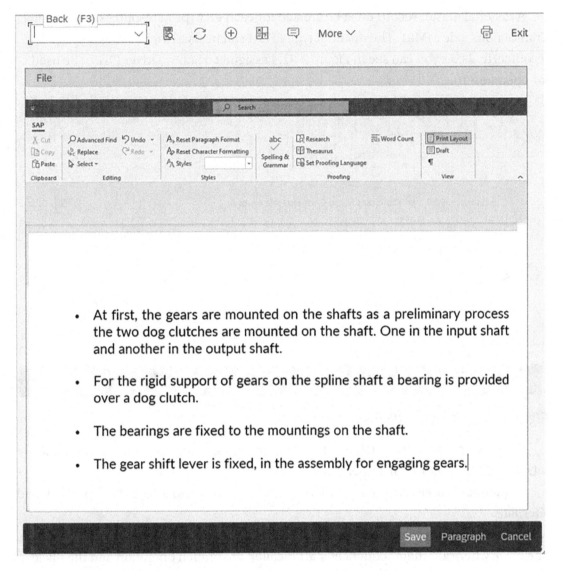

Figure 2-40. *Standard text*

The standard text key then can be assigned to work center or routing.

Description: You can maintain short text for operations describing the details of which activity needs to be performed on the work center.

Long Text Exists: This indicator specifies if a long text exists for the operation.

PRT (Indicator: Production Resource/Tools): You can assign production resource/tools like fixtures, molds, cutting tools, and so on, that should be used to perform the operation on the work center by clicking the Prod Resources/Tools button on the Operations screen.

A material master record must be created for each PRT (prod resources/tools) using Transaction Code MM01. The material type FHMI can be used for creating production resource/tools. As you can see in Figure 2-41, I assigned a Screw Driver PRT to be used for operation 10.

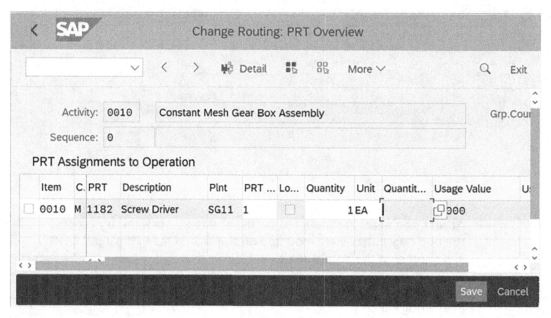

Figure 2-41. *Routing: PRT overview*

If you assigned Production Resource/Tools to an operation, the system automatically sets the PRT indicator for the operation.

Sequences: Three types of sequence are available in routing—standard, parallel, and alternate.

Alternate sequences are linked to the standard sequence, which is the main sequence. The place where alternate sequences start is called the branch operation and the place where it joins the standard sequence is called the return operation.

Parallel sequences are a set of operations that run parallel to the standard sequence. For example, in the chemical industry, this can be analytical processes that occur parallel to the main production process.

Alternate sequences consist of sets of operations other than the standard sequence so that either of the sequences can be run for a production process. Generally, branch operations in the standard sequence are ignored in this process.

Component Allocation: All the components for the finished/semifinished assembly as defined in the BOM are automatically populated in the routing. You can allocate each component on individual operations where the component will be used so that you have better overview of where the components will be consumed. While performing Operation confirmation, only the components allocated on the said operation will be consumed while posting goods issue to a production order.

The system allocates the components from the BOM to the first operation by default, which means all the components will be consumed while posting confirmation for the first operation.

You have now created a routing procedure that defines the production process for the gear assembly. However, you may have many finished gear assemblies that follow the same production process. Is it possible to create new routings using this routing as a template?

Actually, there is a better solution!

You can click the Assignment button on the Routing Header screen to assign materials in the routing. You can assign all the products (finished/semifinished assemblies) that will use the same routing. This way, you can create just one routing and assign multiple materials to it. This not only saves time and effort, but also eliminates redundant data leading to less load on the database and thus better performance.

As you can see in Figure 2-42, I assigned the CM_GEARBOX and CM_GEARBOX_01 materials to the same routing with group number 70000158 due to the fact that both gearboxes are assembled on the same assembly line using the same process.

≡		Material Assignment					×
	Group: 70000158	Key Date: 16.06.2022		Change No.:			
Material TL Assignments							
GrC	Description	Material	Plnt	Sales Doc.	Item	WBS Element	
1	Constant Mesh Gear Box	CM_GEARBOX	SG11		0		
1	Constant Mesh Gear Box	CM_GEARBOX_01	SG11		0		

Figure 2-42. *Routing: material assignment*

Production Version

The production version defines a unique production technique for producing a material.

The production version can be created using Transaction Code C223 - Production Version: Mass Processing. You can also create a production version in the MRP4 view of the material master.

Let's create a production version in change Material Master – MM02, as shown in Figure 2-43.

Version: You must specify an alphanumeric key, up to four characters long, which is a unique production version of the plant and material, combined.

Production Version Text: You must specify a description of the production version that can be up to 40 characters long and provided some information about the production version.

Valid From: You must specify the date from which the production version is valid.

Valid To: You must specify the date until which the production version is valid.

REM Allowed: This indictor specifies if the production version can be used for repetitive manufacturing.

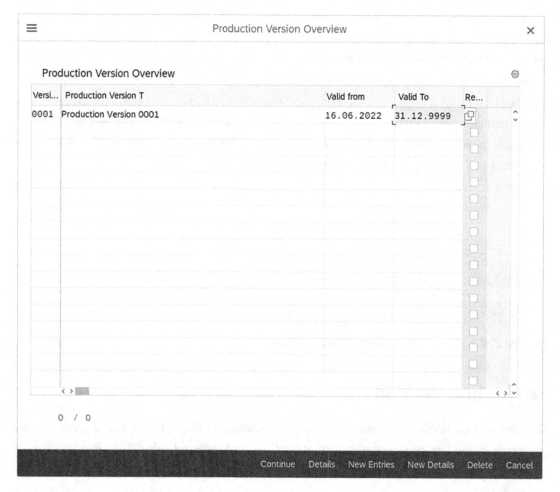

Figure 2-43. *Production version overview*

Double-click Production Version or click Details to navigate to the next screen to assign BOM and routing to the production version.

Minimum/Maximum Lot Size: The lot size defines the minimum and maximum quantities for which the production version can be used. For instance, SuperGears has two furnaces that they use for heat treatments. The small one has a capacity of up to 500 pieces, while the big one is used for bigger lot sizes from 500-1000 pieces. So, two routings must be created and two production versions should be created for different lot sizes.

Valid From: Specifies the date from which the production version is valid. The system defaults the current date on which production version is created as the Valid From date. You must ensure that BOM and routing exist for this date.

Valid To: Specifies the date until which the production version is valid. The system defaults the Valid To date as 31.12.9999. You must ensure that BOM and routing exist for this date.

In the Planning Data section, you must specify the routing data as follows:

Task List Type: You must select the task list type with which routing is created.

A task list specifies a series of operations that must be performed for different object types:

- In discrete manufacturing, you must create a routing as a task list.

- In repetitive manufacturing, you must create a rate routing.

- In process industries, you must create a master recipe.

Similarly, you can have an inspection plan or a maintenance task List for quality management and plant maintenance, respectively.

In this case, select N Routing for the Task List Type.

Group: You must enter the group number that was generated while creating the routing for the material.

Group Counter: You must enter the group counter that was generated while creating the routing for the material. If you have more than one group counter, you must enter the correct group counter.

In the Bill of Materials section, you must specify BOM data as follows:

Alternative BOM: You must enter the Alternate BOM created for the material.

BOM Usage: You must enter the BOM usage with which the BOM is created.

REM Allowed: You must activate this indicator if the production version can be used for repetitive manufacturing.

Production Line: The production line describes the capacities of repetitive manufacturing and can be represented in the system by an individual work center or by a line hierarchy. You can enter the production line in the production version. Figure 2-44 shows the production version details, including the lot size, routing, alternate BOM, and production line.

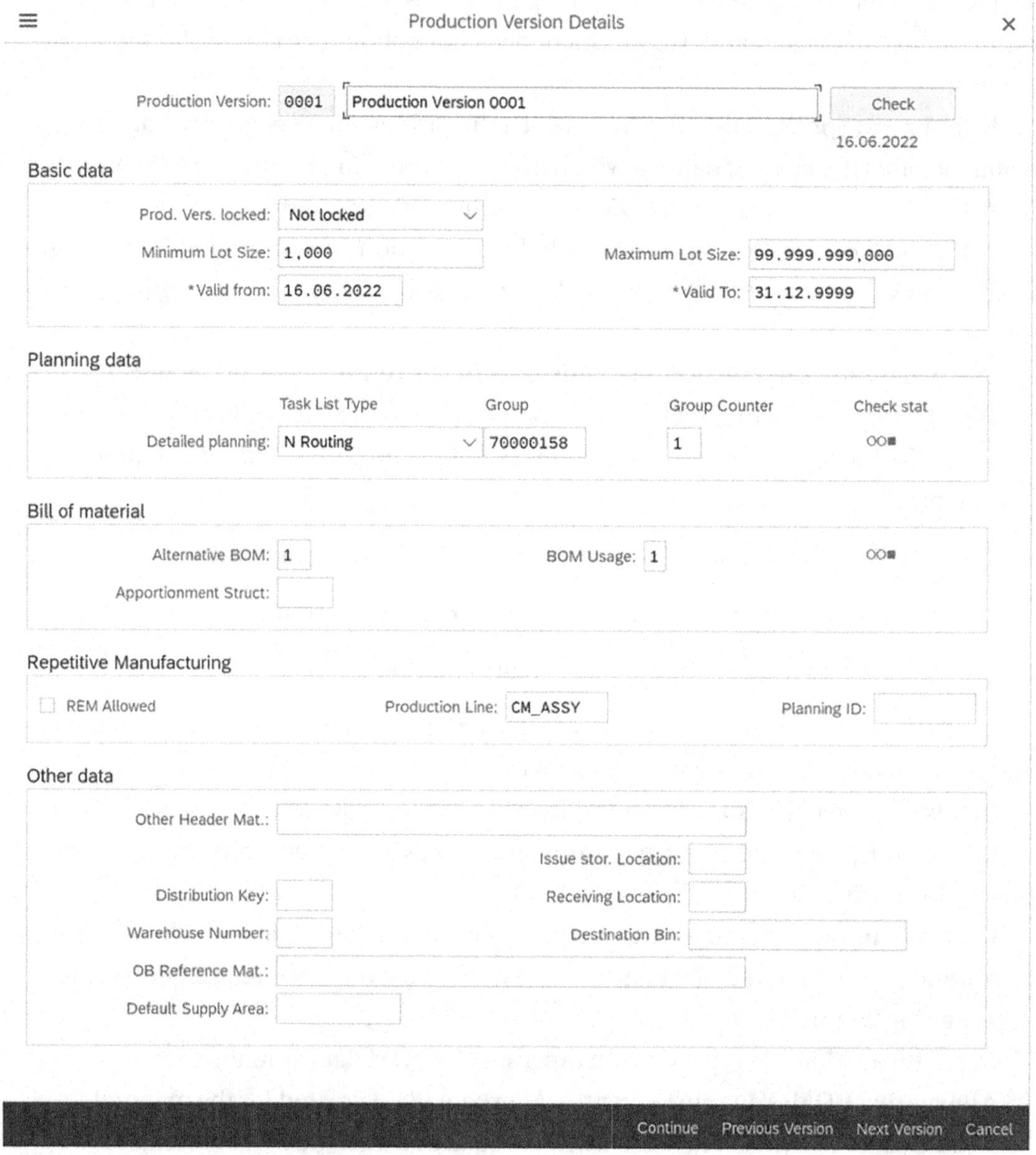

Figure 2-44. *Production version details*

The next section covers improvements made to S/4HANA.

Production Version Migration for BOM

SAP has a new tool for creating production versions. You can go to Transaction Code
SE38 and enter program name CS_BOM_PRODVER_MIGRATION. Click Execute to run the
program. Enter the material and plant number and then select one of the options for
migration execution—Run in Simulation Mode or Run in Actual Mode. Then press F8 or
click the clock icon to execute. Figure 2-45 shows the selection screen of the Production
Version Migration for BOM report.

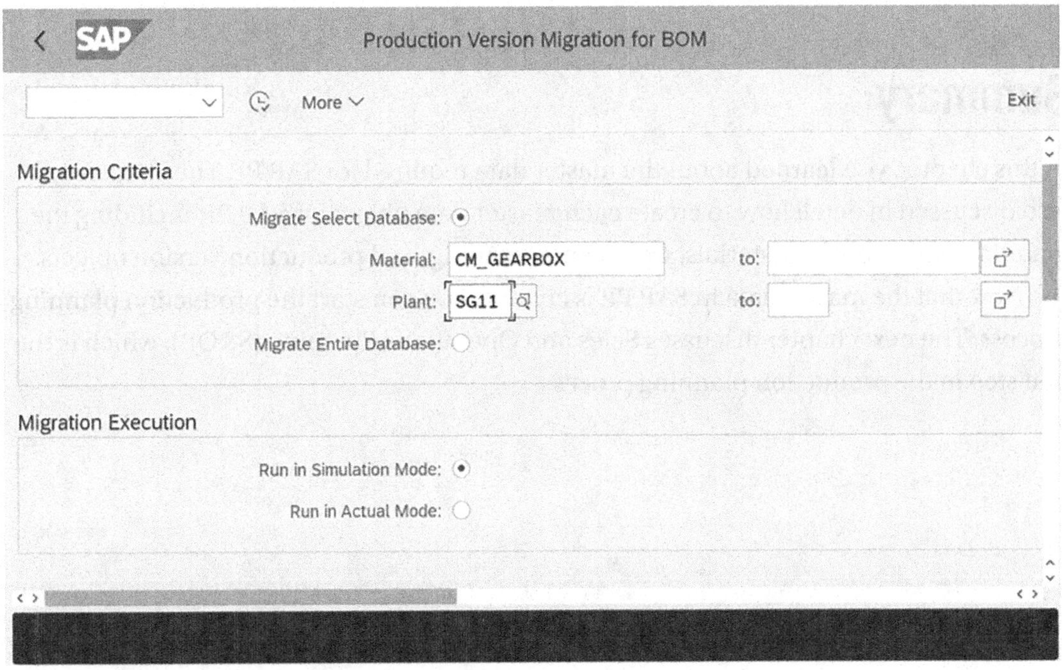

Figure 2-45. *Production version migration for BOM*

I'm executing the program in simulation mode. As you can see in Figure 2-46, the
system wants to create a production version 0002 with BOM Usage 1 and alternate BOM
1. If there are multiple BOMs created for the material (i.e., there is a BOM with multiple
alternate BOMs), the report will generate multiple production versions.

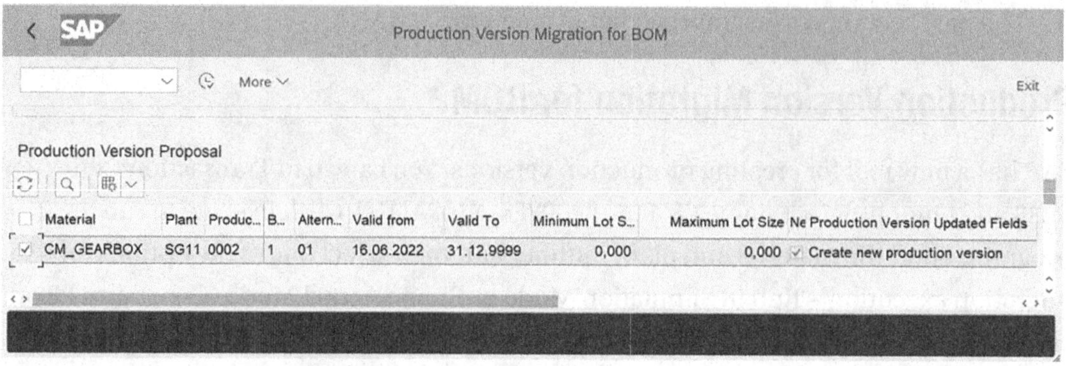

Figure 2-46. *Production version migration for BOM: proposal*

Summary

In this chapter, you learned about the master data required for SAP PP. The chapter also discussed in detail how to create each master data object for SAP PP, including the material master, bill of materials, work center, routing, and production version objects.

Now that the master data in SAP PP is created, you can start the production planning process. The next chapter discusses Sales and Operations Planning (S&OP), which is the first step in the production planning process.

CHAPTER 3

Sales and Operations Planning

APICS defines Sales and Operations Planning (S&OP) as the "Function of setting the overall level of manufacturing output (production plan) and other activities to best satisfy the current planned levels of sales (sales plan and/or forecasts), while meeting general business objectives of profitability, productivity, competitive customer lead times, etc., as expressed in the overall business plan." In this chapter, you learn how S&OP can be executed in SAP.

What Is Sales and Operations Planning (S&OP)?

S&OP is a flexible forecasting and planning tool with which sales, production, and other supply chain targets can be set based on historical, existing, and estimated future data to support the annual plan and the strategic direction. It is used to streamline and consolidate the company's sales and production operations. It is particularly suitable for long- and medium-term planning.

S&OP takes into account key supply chain drivers such as sales, marketing, demand management, and production and inventory management to get a holistic view of planning and thus help management make informed decisions.

Here are some of the key benefits of S&OP:

- It supports long-term and medium-term planning and thus strategic decision making.

- It helps organizations make informed decisions about a product's demand and supply.

- It helps organizations achieve higher customer service levels.

© Himanshu Goel 2022
H. Goel, *Handbook for SAP PP in S/4HANA*, https://doi.org/10.1007/978-1-4842-8566-4_3

- It helps organizations effectively manage demand change and develop flexibility.

- It helps manage inventory, lead-time, backlog, capacity, and demand.

- It helps create realistic production plans.

- It helps reduce/control costs through resource optimization.

The S&OP process links the objectives and strategies of formal business plans to actual production schedules. It also helps factory floor planning and execution support the annual plan and strategic direction.

S&OP consolidates inputs from the demand and supply sides as well as takes into consideration the econometric reviews. It also takes into account innovation and strategy, as shown in Figure 3-1.

Figure 3-1. *Elements of S&OP*

Standard SOP

Standard SOP can be used as a preconfigured solution with info structure S076. Standard SOP is used to plan production at the product group level and then disaggregate planning at the materials level, which is why its' called *level-by-level planning*.

Information structure (info structure) is a table that contains several fields that receive data from various business functions such as sales, purchasing, and so on. Information structures are used for analyses and evaluations.

An information structure consists of three parameters:

- **Period unit:** This is the time bucket during which planning is performed, such as a week, month, or year.

- **Characteristics:** Planning can be performed for various parameters/levels like sales organization, division, purchasing organization, plant, material, and so on.

- **Key figures:** Represent numerical values such as for sales history, production history, inventory level, and so on.

Figure 3-2 displays standard info structure S076, which is used for planning at the product group level.

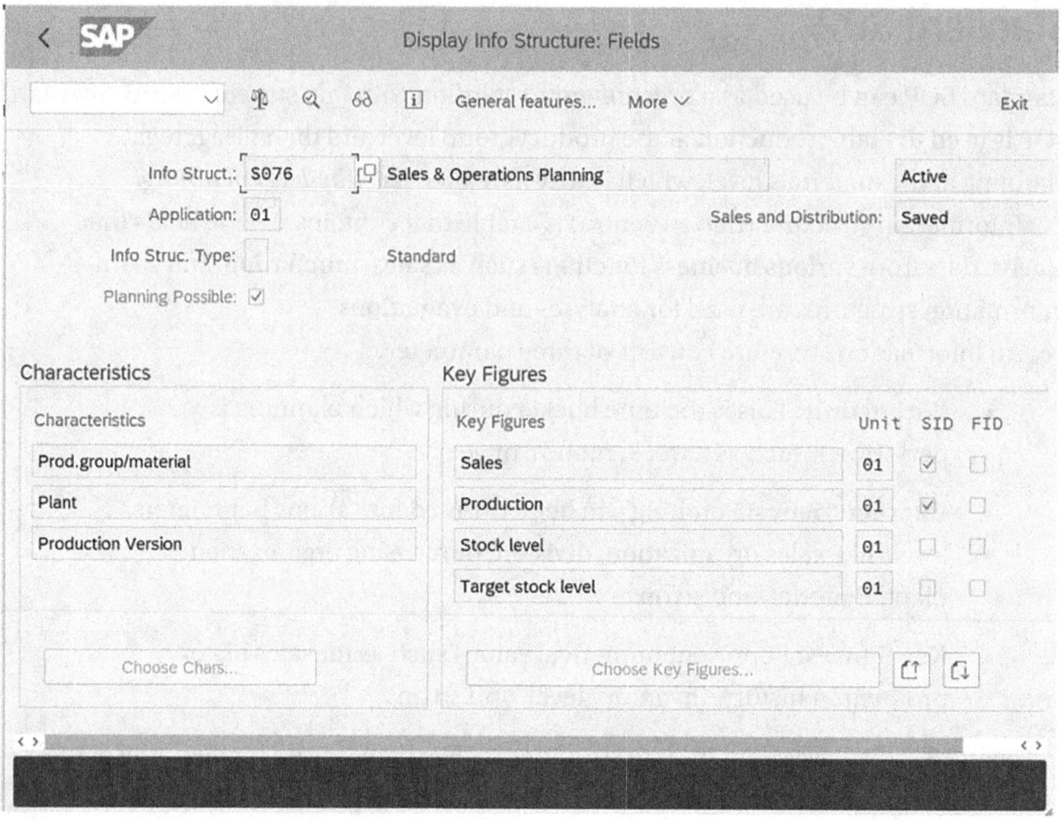

Figure 3-2. *Info structure S076*

Product Group

A product group is used to group similar materials or other product groups. If the product group contains materials as a member then it is called single level. Several product groups can also be grouped together to create multi-level product groups. In a multi-level product group hierarchy, the lowest level of the product group must contain materials as members.

A product group is used to plan the production for similar materials in a long-term planning period. For example, you can create a product group called the iPhone X. The product group may contain different variants of the iPhone X with different colors and other specifications. However, planning at the product group level will simplify the planning process, as the variants of the iPhone X will use similar components, capacities, and other resources. The iPhone X product group is a single level. You can also group various product groups for different iPhone models into the product range. In that way, iPhone is a multi-level product group.

SuperGears AG uses S&OP to plan and forecast their production, capacity, resources, financial budgeting, and so on.

Create a Product Group

Let's create a product group called Constant Mesh Gear Box, which is one of the main product families at our fictional SuperGears AG company.

Choose Logistics ➤ Production ➤ SOP ➤ Product Group ➤ Create. You can also use Transaction Code MC84 to create a product group. Figure 3-3 shows the initial screen of the product group, where you must enter the product group's name, description, plant, and base unit of measure. You must also specify whether the member elements will be materials or product groups.

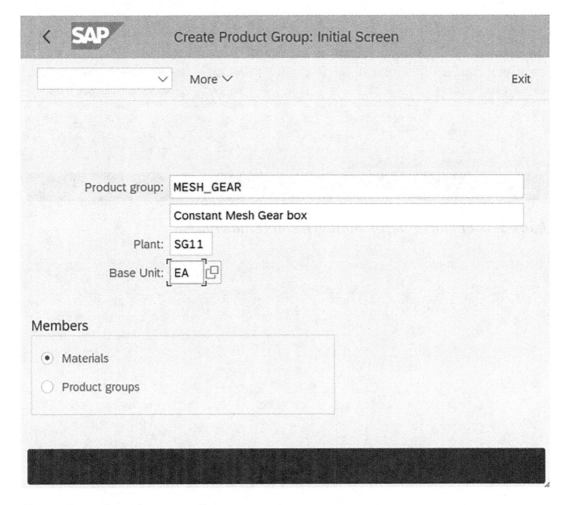

Figure 3-3. *Creating a product group*

When you press Enter, the screen in Figure 3-4 appears, where you must specify the materials and the percentage for each material proportional to the product group. I assigned two materials—CM_GEARBOX and CM_GEARBOX_01—each having a proportional factor of 50%.

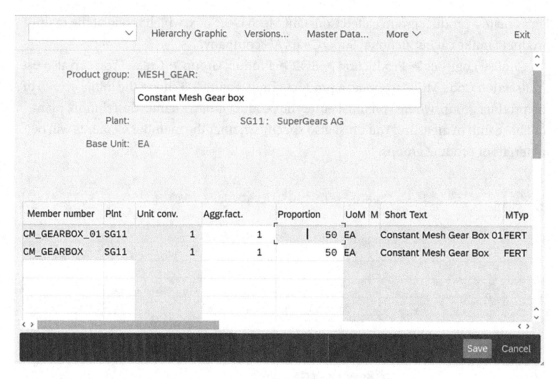

Figure 3-4. *Product group: maintain member materials*

You can click the Hierarchy Graphic button to display the product group and all its members graphically, as shown in Figure 3-5.

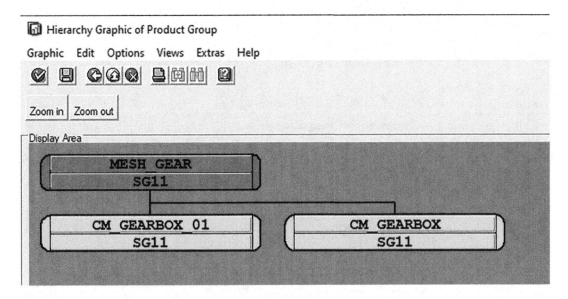

Figure 3-5. *Hierarchical graphic of the product group*

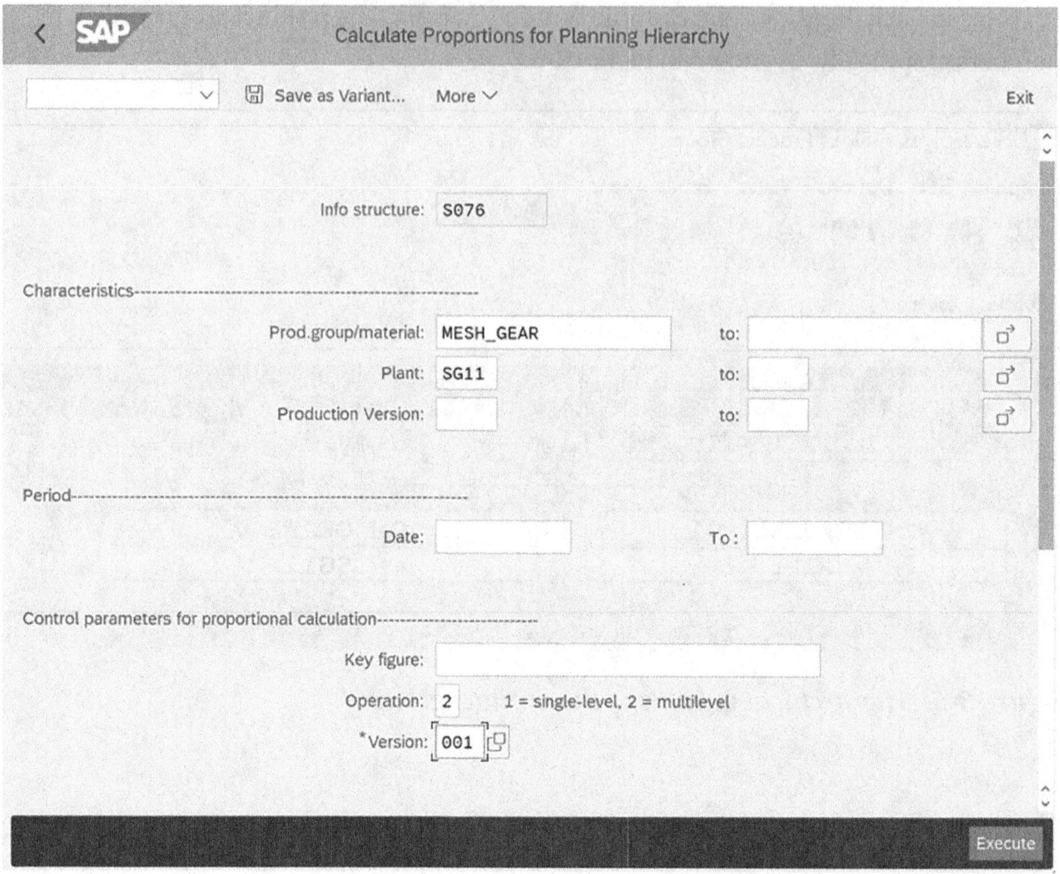

Figure 3-6. *Calculating proportions for the planning hierarchy*

The system can calculate the proportion factor automatically based on the historical data. Choose Logistics ➤ Production ➤ SOP ➤ Product Group ➤ Calculate Proportional Factors. You can also use the Transaction Code MC8L to generate the proportional factor automatically.

You can also distribute the proportional factors via More ➤ Edit ➤ Distribute Proportional Factors.

Create a Plan for the Product Group

Now that you have created a product group, the next step is to create a forecast (plan) at the product group level, which is also called a *rough-cut plan*. The rough-cut capacity planning (RCCP) is a capacity planning tool used for long-term planning for materials or product groups. It is used to determine the capacities needed to meet sales targets. Since this is a long-term plan, the forecast figures are created in monthly buckets.

Choose Logistics ➤ Production ➤ SOP ➤ Planning ➤ For Product Group ➤ Create. You can also use the Transaction Code MC81 to create a plan for the product group. Enter the product group and plant on the selection screen, as shown in Figure 3-7. When you press Enter, a popup window will appear to enter the version and description.

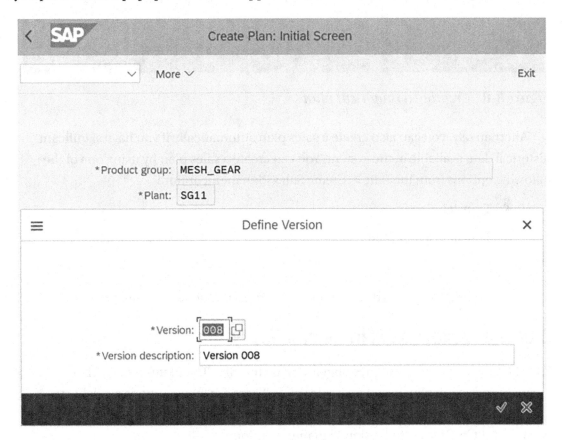

Figure 3-7. *Creating a plan: the initial screen*

Now enter the sales quantities as shown in Figure 3-8. I created a sales plan for June 2022 until December 2022.

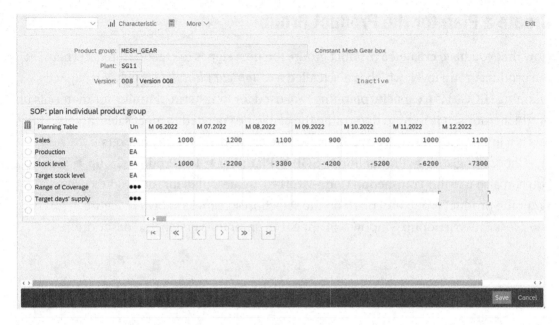

Figure 3-8. *Creating a rough-cut plan*

Alternatively, you can also create a sales plan automatically if you have significant historical data available in the system. You can create a sales plan by using one of the following options from the Edit ➤ Create Sales Plan menu option:

- Transfer plan from SIS

- Transfer CO-PA plan

- Forecast

- Transfer product group proportional from production or from sales

Create a Production Plan Automatically

You just saw how to create a sales plan for seven months. The planning table helps to create a production plan based on a sales plan. There are many options available to automatically create a production plan. You can choose one of the following options from the Edit ➤ Create Production Plan menu option:

- **Synchronous to sales:** The production plan is created to meet the sales requirement exactly, as you can see in Figure 3-9.

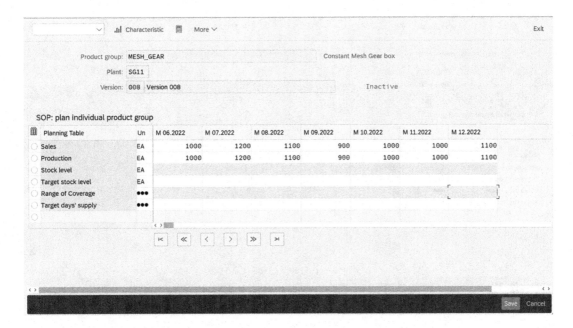

Figure 3-9. *Create a production plan synchronous to sales*

- **Target stock level:** You can maintain your target stock level and the system will generate production plan to reach the target stock level considering your sales plan.

As you can see in Figure 3-10, the target stock level has been maintained at 1000 for each month.

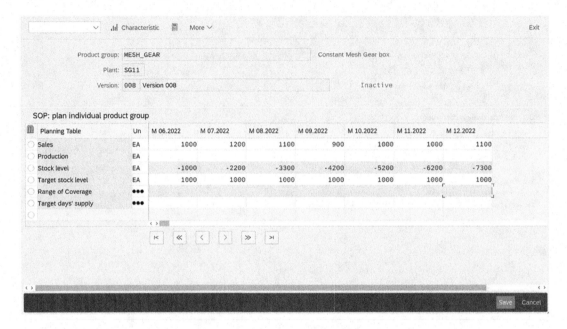

Figure 3-10. *Create a production plan from the target stock level*

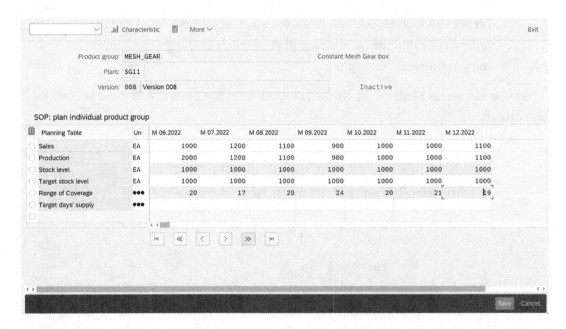

Figure 3-11. *Create a production plan based on the target stock level*

Choose Edit ➤ Create Production Plan ➤ Target Stock Level. The sales requirement for June 2022 is 1000 EA and the target stock level is 1000 EA. That's why the production plan is created for 2000 EA so that sales requirement for 1000 is fulfilled and there is a target stock of 1000 EA at month closing of June 2022. Similarly, the production plan is created for the rest of the months to reach the target stock level.

- **Target days' supply:** Similar to the target stock level option, you can also create a production plan to reach the target days' supply. The target days' supply is maintained at 5 for each month.

The days' supply for a period is calculated by the system based on the stock level divided by the average requirements. The average requirements are calculated as sales/number of workdays.

Choose Edit ➤ Create Production Plan ➤ Target Stock Level. The sales requirement for June 2022 is 1000 and the target days' supply is 5 days. The average requirements are calculated as sales/number of workdays.

Average Requirement = 1000/22 = 45.45

Target days' supply = 5

Stock level = average requirement * Target days' supply

Stock level = 45.45 * 5 = 227.27

Thus, the production is generated as 1250 EA to fulfill the sales requirement of 1000 EA and have a target days' supply of 5 days, as shown in Figure 3-13. The target range of supply is 5 and the production plan has been created so that the range of coverage is 5 days.

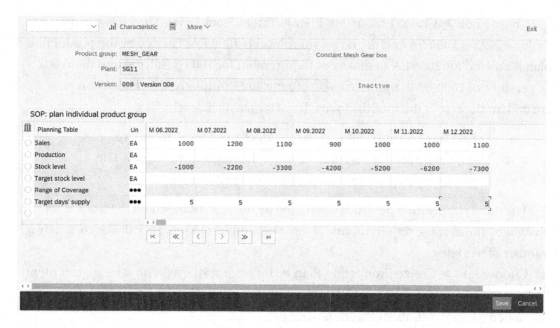

Figure 3-12. *Create a production plan based on the target days' supply*

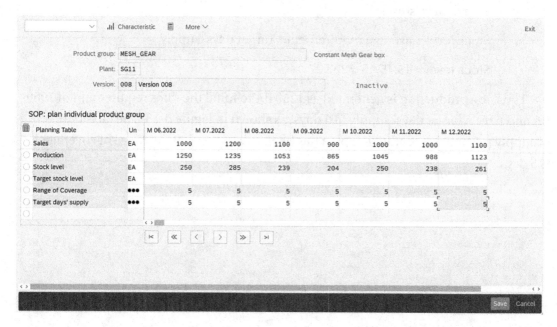

Figure 3-13. *Create a production plan based on the target days' supply*

- **Stock level = zero:** The production plan is calculated to achieve zero stock levels.

Choose Edit ➤ Create Production Plan ➤ Stock Level = 0. The production plan has been created to meet sales requirements and keep the stock at zero at the end of the planning bucket, as shown in Figure 3-14.

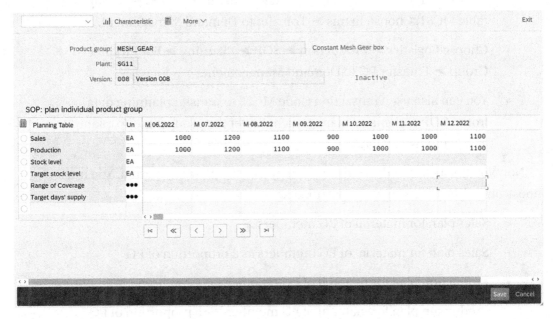

Figure 3-14. *Create a production plan based on zero stock level*

This production plan has no direct implication on actual production or operations. Several plans in the planning version can be created with inputs from various business functions, like sales, marketing, production, procurement, and so on. Once a common understanding is negotiated and agreed on, the final key figures are transferred to demand management as Planned Independent Requirements (PIRs).

The production plan is transferred from S&OP to demand management. The production plan is transferred as a PIR, which is the basis for the Material Requirement Planning (MRP).

Transfer to Demand Management

Planning figures can be transferred from S&OP to demand management in one of the following ways:

- Transfer from planning table MC81: The production planning figures can be transferred to demand management directly from planning table MC81. Choose Extras ➤ Transfer to Demand Management.

- Choose Logistics ➤ Production ➤ SOP ➤ Planning ➤ For Product Group ➤ Transfer PG to Demand Management.

- You can also use Transaction Code MC75 to transfer planning data from S&OP to demand management. Enter the product group, plant, and planning version.

Now you must choose the transfer strategy and the planning period. You must choose one of the following transfer strategies:

- Sales plan for material of PG members

- Sales plan for material of PG members as a proportion of PG

- Production plan for material of PG members

- Production plan for material of PG members as a proportion of PG

Sales Plan for Material of PG Members

The sales plan of the member materials of the product group is adopted when transferring the forecast figures to demand management.

Let's check the rough-cut plan for planning version 008. The sales plan is 1000 EA for each month, while the production plan is generated as 1000 EA. See Figure 3-15.

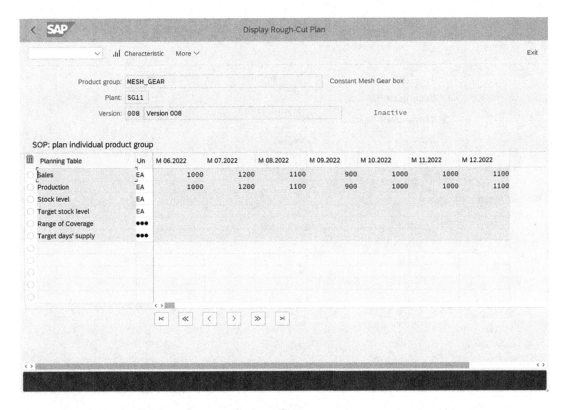

Figure 3-15. *Displaying the rough-cut plan*

Transfer the planning figures using the Sales Plan for Material of PG Members transfer strategy. The transfer period is June 2022 to December 2022.

You can also specify the requirement type and the version of PIR that should be considered when transferring the planning figures from S&OP to demand management. See Figure 3-16.

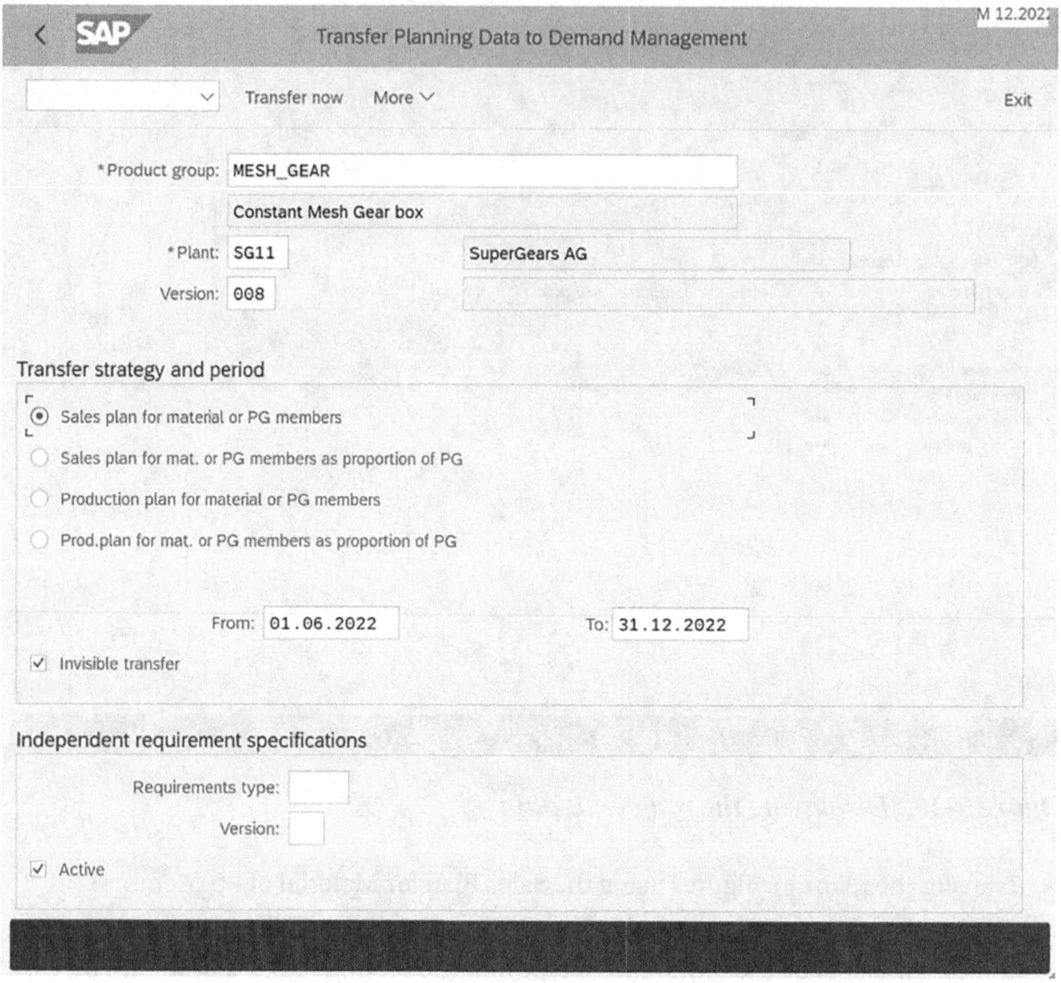

Figure 3-16. *Transfer the planning data to demand management*

Similarly, when using the Prod. Plan for Mat. or PG Members as a Proportion of PG transfer strategy, you can transfer the production plan from the planning version to demand management. When transferring the product group quantities to demand management, the production plan of the product group is disaggregated to the material level, according to the proportional factor defined earlier.

Planned Independent Requirements in Demand Management

You can verify the PIRs that have been transferred from S&OP using the SAP menu path Logistics ➤ Production ➤ Demand Management ➤ Planned Independent Requirements ➤ Display. Or use the Transaction Code MD63, as shown in Figure 3-17.

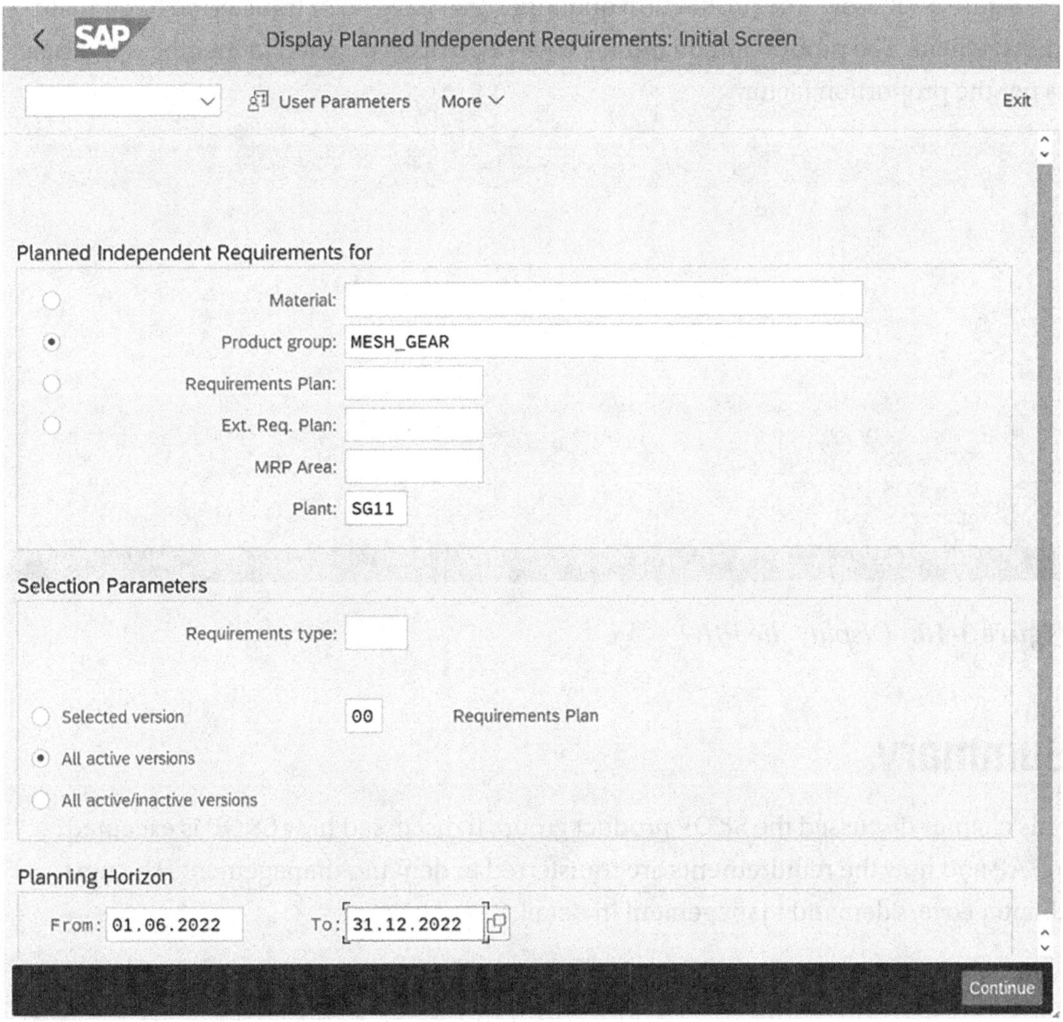

Figure 3-17. *Display a PIR: the initial screen*

You can display PIRs for individual materials or for product groups.

You can also create a requirement plan to create and identify one or more PIRs. For example, you can create a requirement plan to create PIRs for several materials so that you don't need to create separate PIRs for each material. Enter the product group for the mesh gear box.

Figure 3-18 shows the production quantities that have been transferred to demand management. The production quantities have been disaggregated to member materials as per the proportion factor.

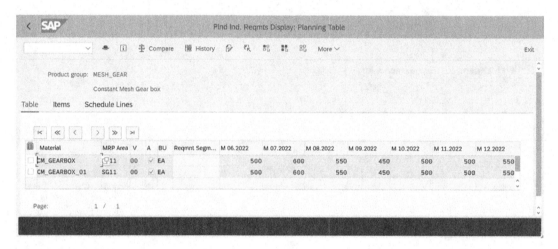

Figure 3-18. *Display the PIR*

Summary

This chapter discussed the S&OP product group. It discussed how S&OP is executed in SAP and how the requirements are transferred to demand management. The next chapter covers demand management in detail.

CHAPTER 4

Demand Management

Demand management is a planning tool that helps organizations forecast and manage the demands of their materials. In this chapter, you learn how demand management can be executed in SAP using the planned independent requirements (PIRs) and the customer independent requirements. You also learn how materials can be produced/procured in make-to-stock and make-to order environments.

What Is Demand Management?

Demand management is an important submodule of SAP manufacturing. It helps determine quantities and delivery dates for finished goods and/or assemblies. It is a link between sales and operations planning (S&OP) and material requirement planning. Demand management receives input from S&OP and provides inputs to MPS/MRP.

When requirements are entered, the demand program is updated. The demand program uses planned independent requirements or customer requirements.

In the previous chapter, which covered S&OP, you created a production plan for a product group. Then you disaggregated the plan as per the proportional factor to material level and transferred the forecast to demand management (planned independent requirements).

Demand management can use two elements—planned independent requirements and customer requirements. These are used to calculate net requirements during the MRP run.

Planned Independent Requirements

A planned independent requirement (PIR) is created for a material or a product group and contains at least one planned quantity and one date in a planning horizon. PIRs can be created in monthly or weekly buckets and can be split over time.

© Himanshu Goel 2022

H. Goel, *Handbook for SAP PP in S/4HANA*, https://doi.org/10.1007/978-1-4842-8566-4_4

PIRs can be created manually or transferred from S&OP, as shown in last chapter. See Figure 4-1.

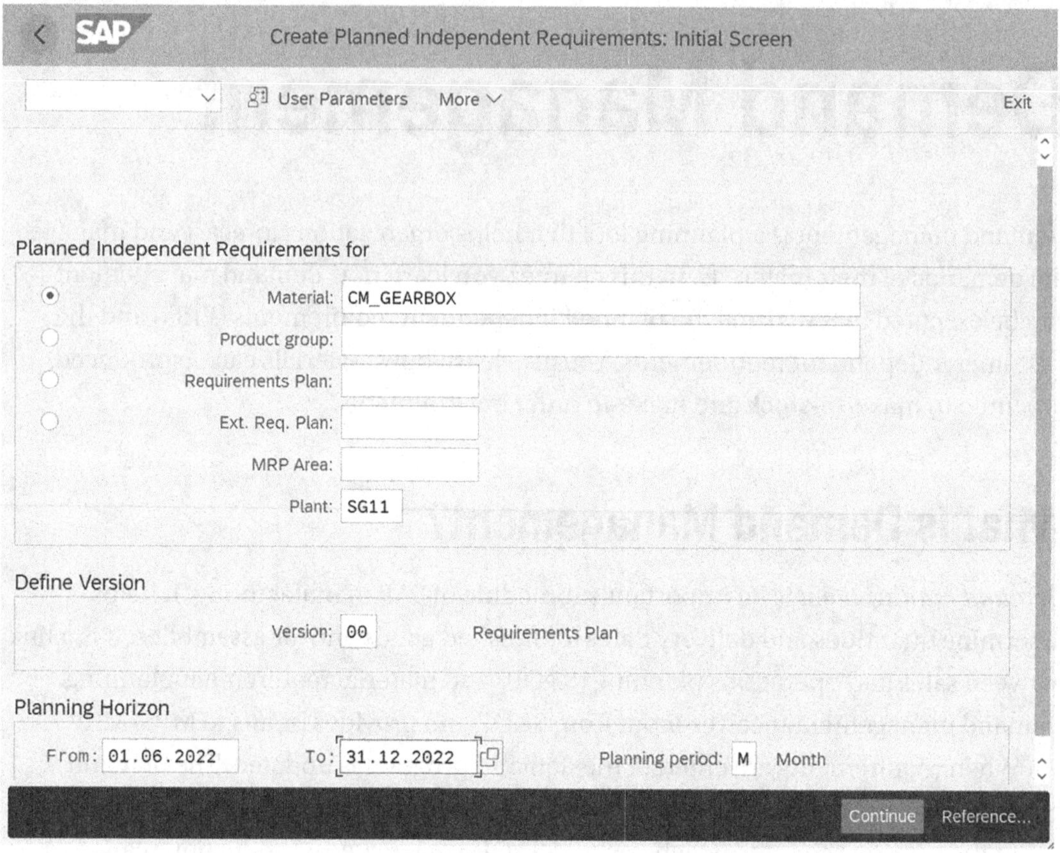

Figure 4-1. *Creating a planned independent requirement: initial screen*

Choose Logistics ➤ Production ➤ Production Planning ➤ Demand Management ➤ Planned Independent Requirements ➤ Create. You can also use Transaction Code MD61 to create PIRs. Enter the material or product group and plant on the selection screen.

PIRs can be created for a material or a product group. You need to enter the planning horizon and planning period. The planning period can be daily, weekly, or monthly.

The PIR consists of the following:

- Desired quantity

- Period indicator

- Requirement's date

- Planned quantity

Figure 4-2 shows the existing demands that were transferred from S&OP. However, the PIRs exist in monthly buckets. Click the Schedule Lines view to display the schedule of the PIRs, as shown in Figure 4-3.

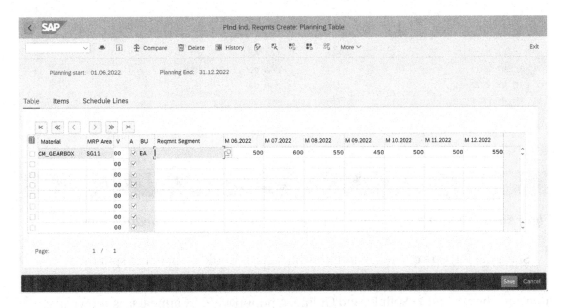

Figure 4-2. *Creating a planned independent requirement*

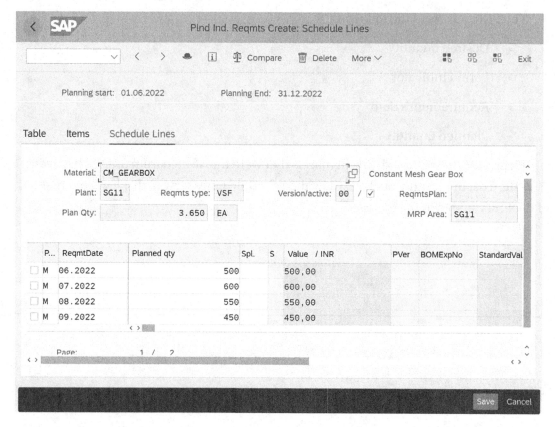

Figure 4-3. *Creating a planned independent requirement: schedule lines*

Since the PIRs are created in monthly buckets, it would be better to split them into weekly buckets to create a realistic demand. Select the demand for the month of June and choose Edit ➤ Split Period Online. A popup window appears, as shown in Figure 4-4, where you must specify the period you want to split. You can see that the planned quantity has been copied from the Schedule Line for the month of June. Change the Period Indicator from M – Month to W – Week.

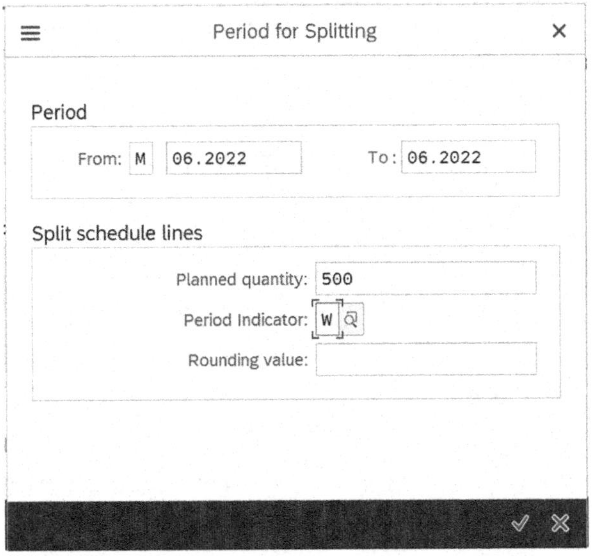

Figure 4-4. *Period for splitting*

As you can see in the Figure 4-5, the monthly schedule lines have been split into four weekly schedule lines. Similarly, you can split your schedule lines into daily buckets.

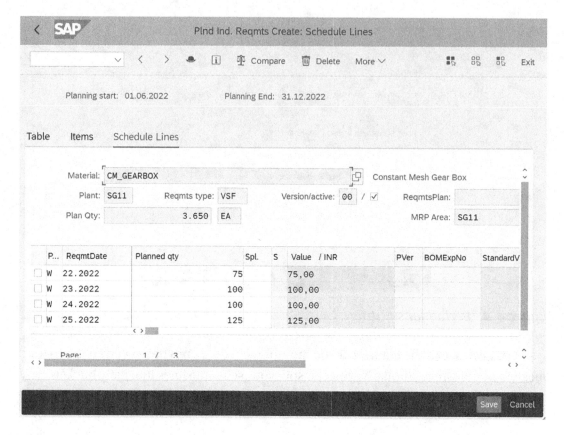

Figure 4-5. *Creating a planned independent requirement: schedule lines*

If you go back to the header screen of the PIR, you can see the requirements for the month of June are now displayed in weekly buckets, while the requirements for rest of the months are displayed in monthly buckets. See Figure 4-6.

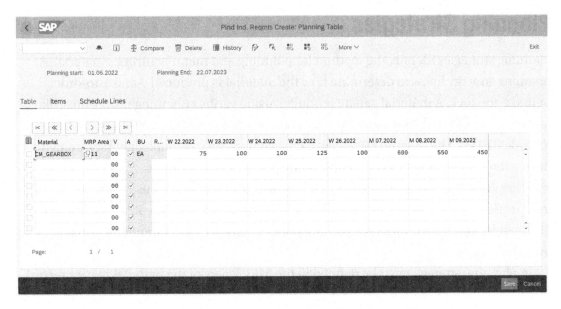

Figure 4-6. *Planned independent requirement: planning table*

Customer Requirements

Customer requirements represent the demands from the customers. Customer requirements can be received from customers as a sales order or as a scheduling agreement.

If you don't have a sales order, you can create customer independent requirements.

Choose Logistics ➤ Production ➤ Production Planning ➤ Demand Management ➤ Customer Requirements ➤ Create. You can also use Transaction Code MD81 to create customer independent requirements. Enter the requirements type and delivering plant on the selection screen and then enter the material, requirement type, and quantity to create customer independent requirements.

MD61 is a PIR that's used in a stock scenario, while MD81 is used to enter the customer requirement directly instead of using a sales order. The difference between the two lies in the requirement type, which decides the planning parameters—MTS (Make-to-Stock) or MTO (Make-to-Order). Customer independent requirement (MD81) is used for the make-to-order situation with requirement type set to KE and so on. The PIR is used for the make-to-stock situation with requirement type set to LSF, BSF, and so on.

Planning Strategies

Planning strategies identify the method for planning and manufacturing a material. A planning strategy helps to determine how the material is produced—make-to-order or make-to-stock. A material can be produced using various planning procedures, like Make-to-Stock (MTS), Make-to-Order (MTO), Assemble-to-Order (ATO), or Engineer-to-Order (ETO). The planning strategy plays a vital role in calculating net requirements during the MRP run and thus determines the production quantities.

The planning strategy also governs the consumption of warehouse stock and independent requirements. It is a key integration point between the PP module and the SD module, as it determines how the independent requirements should be consumed by the sales orders.

A planning strategy must be defined in the MRP3 view of the material master record.

Key Planning Strategies

Make-to-stock planning strategies support the make-to-stock environment. For example, you could plan a production based on forecast, then fulfil customer orders from the existing stock.

- Make-to-stock production (10)

- Planning with final assembly (40)

Make-to-order planning strategies support the make-to-order environment. For example, you wait for the customer order before you start production.

- Make-to-order (20)

- Planning w/o final assembly (50)

Assembly-to-order planning strategies support a combination of make-to-stock and make-to-order. For example, you could build sub-assemblies based on a forecast. Then, you wait for a customer order before assembling them into a finished product. This is also referred to as the assembly-to-order process.

- Assemble to order for finished product (81/82)

Make-to-Stock Strategies

Production is initiated based on forecasts, that is, PIRs; any customer requirements are not considered. Customer orders are fulfilled from stock. Once the materials are produced, they are placed into unrestricted stock and can be shipped to any customer.

Strategy 10, Make-to-Stock

Strategy 10 is particularly useful for pure make-to-stock scenarios, which means the production is done based on forecasts and the sales requirements have no effect on production. The production is based on production plans transferred via the demand program/manually entered PIRs. Warehouse stock is considered during net requirement calculations during the MRP run. Strategy 10 is also referred to as net requirements planning. A few important features of its strategy include:

- SOs (sales orders) are displayed for information only; they do not consume PIRs or change the demand plan. Sales orders have no influence on the production plan.

- Plant/warehouse stocks are taken into account and order quantities are adjusted accordingly.

- PIRs are not consumed by customer requirements (sales order/scheduling agreement) since customer requirements are not relevant for make-to-stock production.

- PIRs are consumed during PGIs (Post Goods Issue) for sales order delivery.

- It is often used in repetitive manufacturing.

The first step is to create finished goods with Strategy 10 in the MRP3 view of the material master, as shown in Figure 4-7.

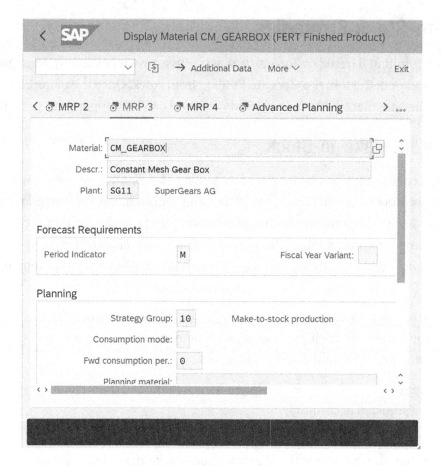

Figure 4-7. *Display material: planning strategy 10*

Since Strategy 10 is a make-to-stock strategy, you must create some PIRs. Once the PIRs are created, go to MD04 – Stock Requirement List to display the demands.

As you can see in Figure 4-8, there is an existing stock of 200 pcs and a few independent requirements were created to generate demand. Strategy 10 takes into account the existing stock and that's why the first two PIRs are fulfilled from the existing stock, while the third PIR is partially fulfilled.

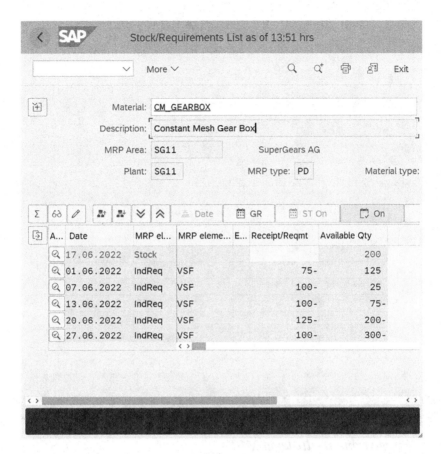

Figure 4-8. *Stock requirement list: planning strategy 10*

Now, let's run the MRP to generate receipt elements for the demand elements (the PIRs). Use Transaction Code MD02 to run the single item multi-level MRP with the parameters shown in Figure 4-9. Press Enter twice to run MRP.

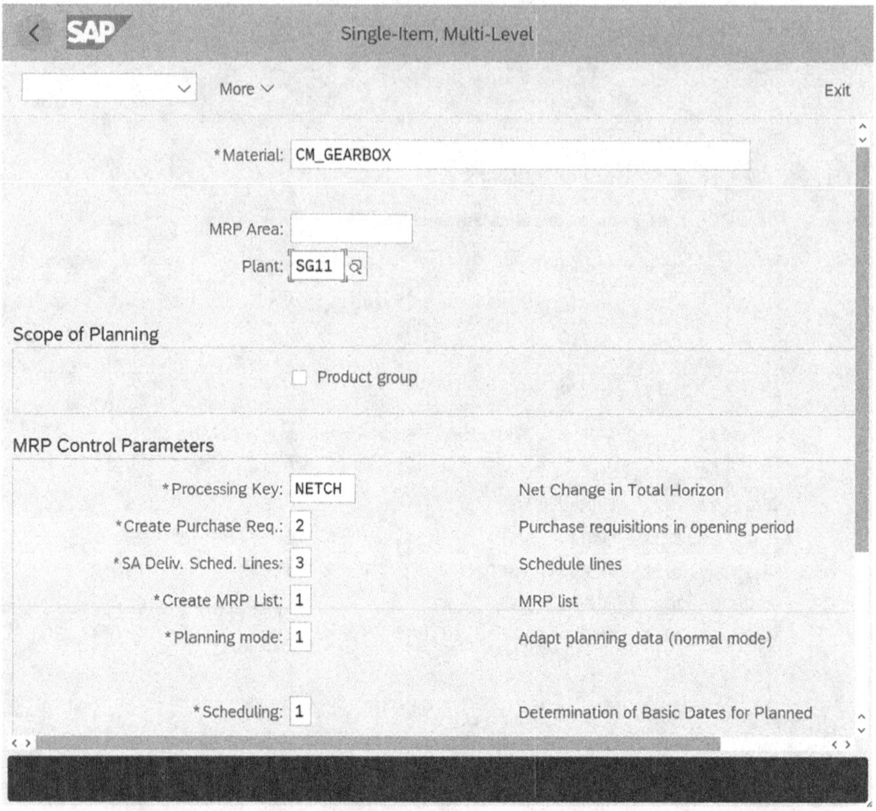

Figure 4-9. *Single item, multi-level MRP*

Go to MD04 again to see the planning situation, as shown in the Figure 4-10. Here, you can see that a few new planned orders have been generated to fulfil the requirements from the PIRs. The first three PIRs have a total requirement of 275 EA and there is an existing stock of 200 EA. That's why a planned order has been created for 75 EA to cover partial requirement of the third PIR. A few more planned orders have been generated to cover the requirements for the rest of the PIRs.

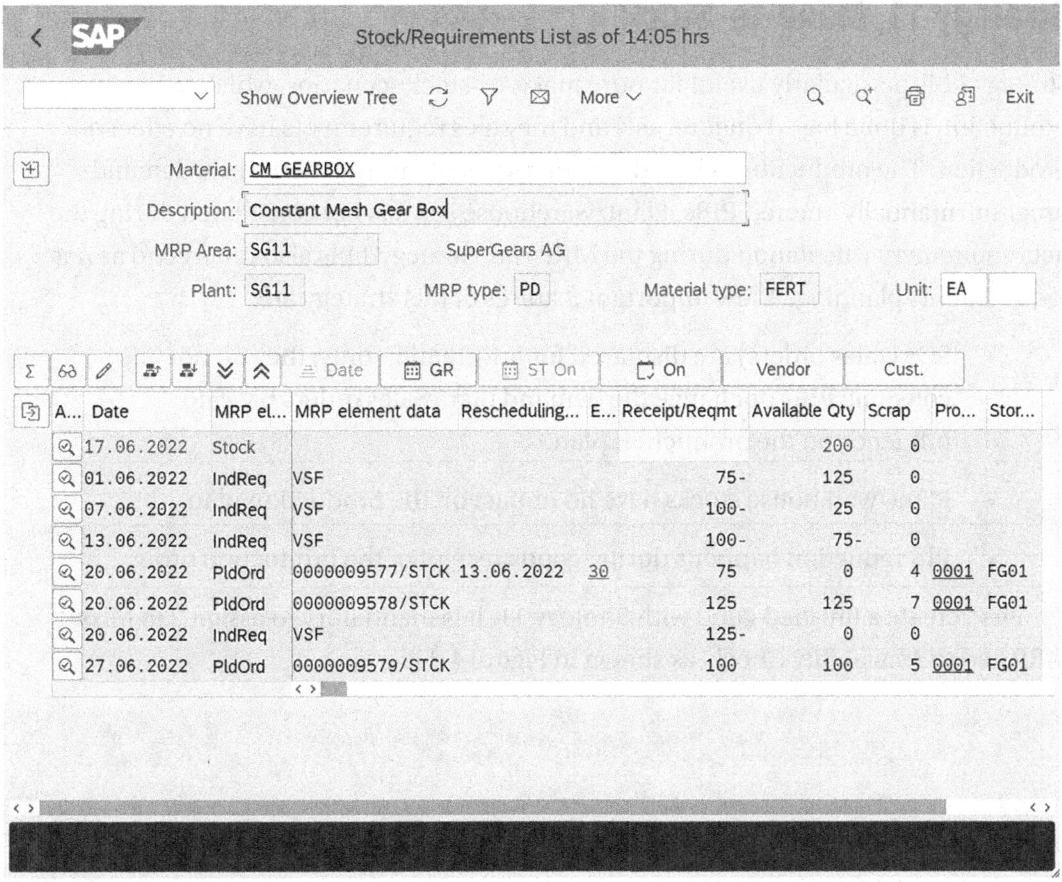

Figure 4-10. *Stock requirement list*

Let's look at the impact of the sales orders on the materials with Strategy 10. Let's create a sales order that's received from the customer. Use Transaction Code VA01 to create a sales order. Go back to MD04 and review the stock requirement list. You'll notice that the customer requirement (sales order) has no impact on the planning situation. Also, it can be noted that the PIR quantities have not been consumed. PIRs are not consumed by sales orders in Strategy 10, since the sales orders are not relevant for planning. When you create a delivery using Transaction Code VL01N and post the goods issue for delivery, the PIRs are reduced by the movement type 601 against the delivery.

Strategy 11, Make-to-Stock

Strategy 11 is particularly useful for pure make-to-stock scenarios, which means the production is done based on forecasts and the sales requirements have no effect on production. The production is based on production plans transferred via demand program/manually entered PIRs. Plant/warehouse stock is *not* considered during the net requirement calculation during the MRP run. Strategy 11 is also referred to as net requirements planning. A few important features of this strategy are:

- SOs (sales orders) are displayed for information only; they do not consume PIRs or change the demand plan. Sales orders have no influence on the production plan.

- Plant/warehouse stocks have no impact on the production plan.

- PIR reduction happens during goods receipt of the production order.

First, create a finished good with Strategy 11. It is mandatory to assign 2 to Mixed MRP and to Availability Check, as shown in Figure 4-11.

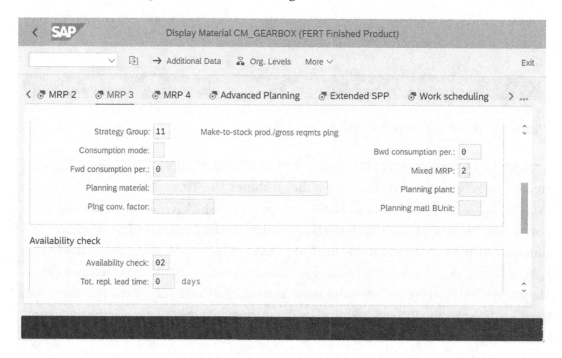

Figure 4-11. *Display material: planning strategy 11*

Since Strategy 11 is a make-to-stock strategy, create some PIRs using Transaction Code MD61 for the material CM_GEARBOX, which has Strategy 11.

Go to MD04 – Stock requirement List to display the forecasts created as PIRs. As you can see in Figure 4-12, there is an existing stock of 200 EA. Three independent requirements are displayed as demands with negative quantities. Since you're using Strategy 11, the stock is not taken into account. Despite the fact that there is existing stock of 200 EA, the system does not consider this stock for the independent requirements.

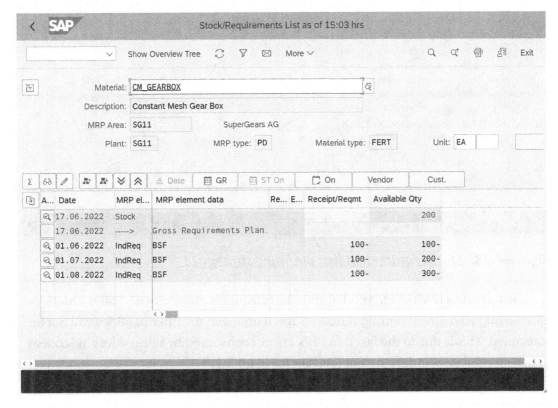

Figure 4-12. *Stock requirement list: planning strategy 11*

Now run the MRP to generate a planned order. Use Transaction Code MD02 to run single-item multi-level MRP with the parameters in Figure 4-13. Press Enter twice to run the MRP. Check the planning situation in the Stock Requirement List by using Transaction Code MD04. As you can see in Figure 4-13, three new planned orders have been generated to fulfil the PIRs. The existing stock is not considered and therefore three new planned orders are created for a total of 300 pcs to meet a total requirement of 300 pcs.

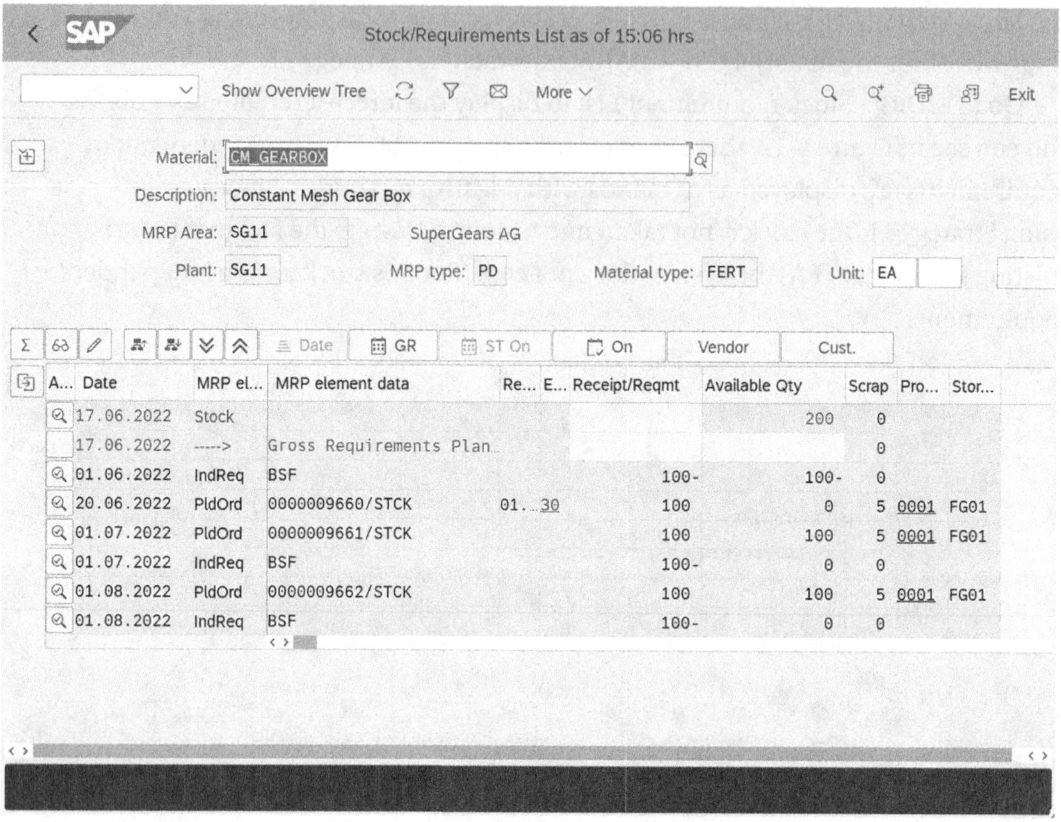

Figure 4-13. *Stock requirement list: planning strategy 11*

If you create a sales order, you'll notice that customer requirements (sales order) have no impact on the planning situation. You'll note that the PIR quantities will not be consumed. This is due to the fact that PIRs are not consumed by sales orders in Strategy 11 because the sales orders are not relevant for planning.

When using Strategy 11, the PIRs are reduced during goods receipt of the production order.

Did you notice the independent requirements for Strategy 10 were created with MRP element Type VSF (refer to Figure 4-8), while the independent requirements are created with MRP element Type BSF (refer to Figure 4-12)? This is because planning strategies contain requirement types for independent requirements and customer requirements. The requirements type contains important control parameters. The MRP element VSF and BSF are requirements types assigned to the strategies.

Strategy 40, Planning with Final Assembly

Strategy 40 is particularly useful for make-to-stock scenarios, which also consider Sales orders. The production is triggered based on forecast and the sales requirements consume the PIRs.

- Planning is done at the finished product level.

- Sales orders are taken into account, and they consume PIRs.

- If the sales order quantity exceeds the plan, the system will plan additional demand.

- If the sales order quantity is less than the demand, the stock is increased.

- Enables quick reactions to customer requirements.

Create a finished good with Strategy 40, as shown in Figure 4-14.

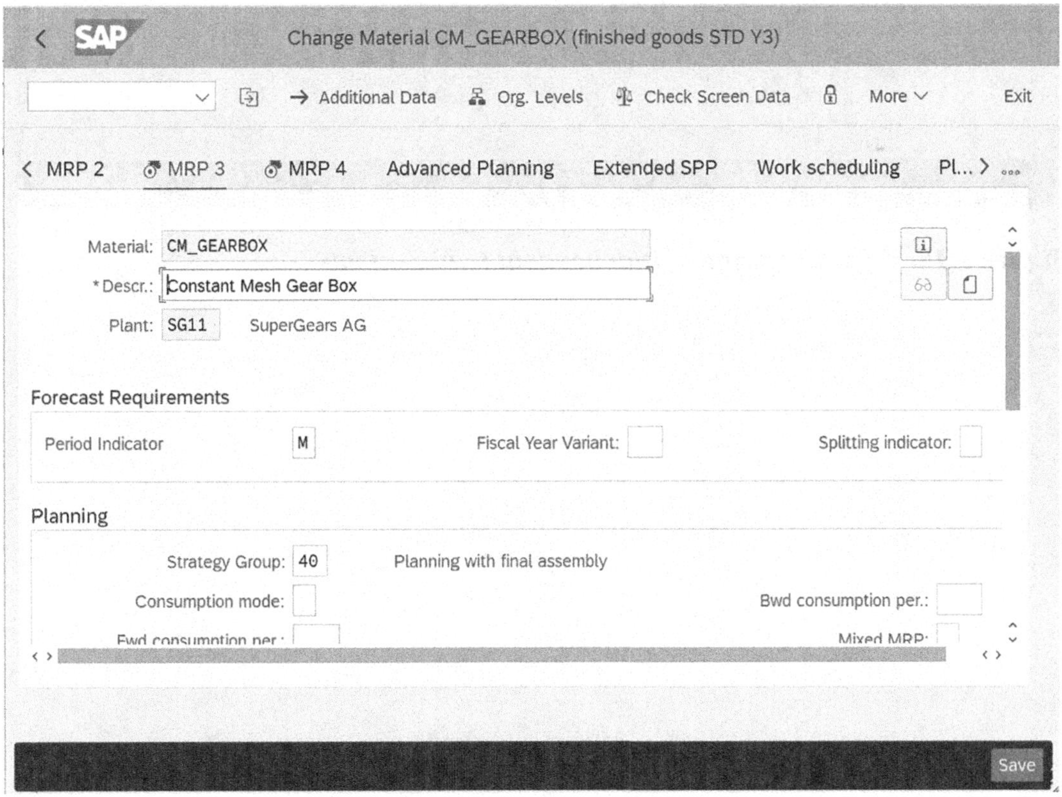

Figure 4-14. *Material master: MRP3 view*

Since Strategy 40 is a special make-to-stock strategy, let's create some PIRs. Use Transaction Code MD61 and enter the material, plant, planning period, and planning bucket information.

Enter the forecast as shown in the Figure 4-15. We created a forecast of 100 pcs each for weeks 26, 27, and 28.

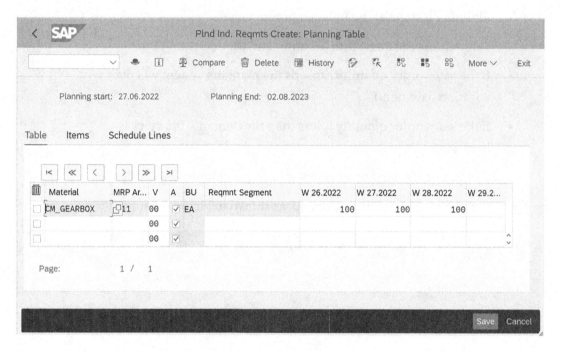

Figure 4-15. *Creating planned independent requirements*

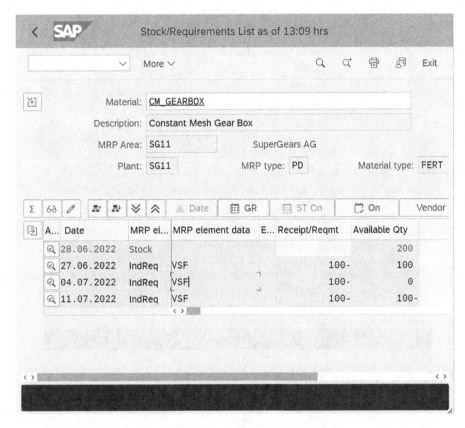

Figure 4-16. *Stock requirement list: planning strategy 40*

Save the PIRs. Now go to MD04 – Stock Requirement List to display the forecasts. As you can see, there is an existing stock of 120 pcs and three independent requirements of 100 pcs each. Since you're using Strategy 40, the stock is taken into account and that's why the total requirement for PIRs is reduced.

Now run the MRP to generate a planned order. Use Transaction Code MD02 to run single-item multi-level MRP. After running MRP, go to MD04 – Stock Requirement List again to check the current planning situation. You'll see that the system generated planned orders to cover the requirements from the PIRs.

The existing stock of 200 pcs is taken into account. There is a total requirement of 300 pcs and thus a new planned order is created for a 100 pcs since other demand from other PIRs can be fulfilled with existing stock.

Create a sales order for the finished assembly using Transaction Code VA01. The customer requirement (sales order) has consumed the PIRs since you're using Strategy 40, as shown in Figure 4-18.

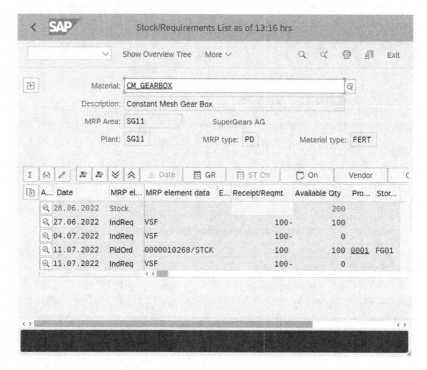

Figure 4-17. *Stock requirement list*

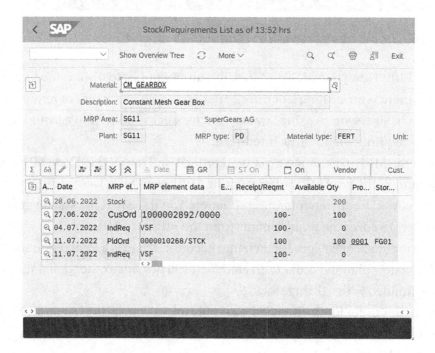

Figure 4-18. *Stock requirement list*

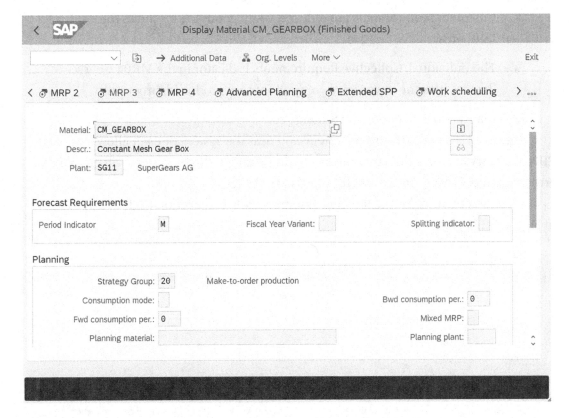

Figure 4-19. *Material master: MRP3 view*

Strategy 40 is one of the most widely used planning strategy across all industries.

Make-to-Order Strategies

Production is initiated based on customer requirements which can be received as sales order or scheduling agreements. Production is unique for each customer. The warehouse stock is built to satisfy the requirements of each sales order. The Production order is directly linked to the sales order and thus to the stock produced.

Strategy 20, Make-to-Order

Strategy 20 is particularly useful for make-to-order scenarios in which production is triggered based on sales orders.

- Each sales order item is displayed in an individual segment in the stock/requirement list and MRP list.

- Customer requirements are reduced when goods are issued to the sales order.

- The Individual/Collective Requirements Indicator in the MRP4 view decides how the lower-level components are produced/procured.

Let's create a finished good with Strategy 20.

Strategy 20 is a make-to-order strategy and thus the system doesn't allow it to create PIRs. If you try to create PIRs for materials using Strategy 20, the system will give you an error message: `Please Enter valid requirements type`.

Create a sales order for the finished assembly with Transaction Code VA01, as shown in Figure 4-20.

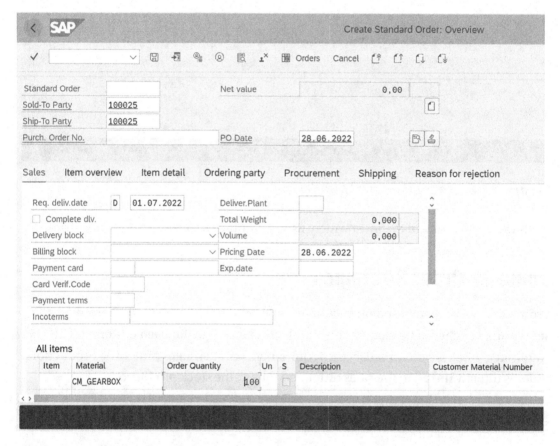

Figure 4-20. *Creating a sales order*

If you go to MD04 – Stock Requirement List, the sales order appears as a requirement.

Now run the MRP to fulfil demand. Use Transaction Code MD02 to run single-item multi-level MRP. You can also run the MRP for a specific sales order using Transaction Code MD50.

After the MRP run, use Transaction Code MD04 to check the planning situation. See Figure 4-21.

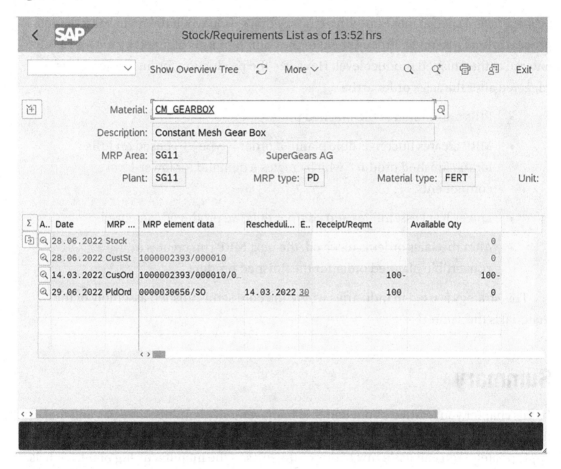

Figure 4-21. *Stock requirement list*

You can see that a new planned order has been generated to fulfil the customer requirements. In the MRP element data, you can see a planned order with /SO, which represents the sales order. This means the planned order has been generated for a material with Make-to-Order strategy. You can see the sales order in the Assignment View of the planned order.

Convert the planned order to production and then click the Green flag in the production order to release and save the order. Then, perform the manufacturing execution activities—goods issue to production order, order confirmation, and goods receipt against production order. Go to MD04 – Stock Requirement List; the stock is displayed as sales order stock and not as unrestricted stock.

Strategy 50, Planning without Final Assembly

Strategy 50 is a special make-to-order strategy that's used when the main value-added process is final assembly. Procurement of the components is planned by means of PIRs entered at the finished product level. However, the production for final assembly is triggered after the sales order arrives.

- PIRs are entered at the finished product level.

- MRP creates unconvertible planned orders (type VP) based on PIRs for the finished product, which creates a demand for lower-level components.

- Lower-level assemblies and components are produced/procured.

- After the sales order is received, the next MRP run creates a convertible planned order for the finished product.

This strategy is used in industries where the core semi-finished assembly of the material is the same.

Summary

In this chapter you learned about demand management planning strategies and make-to-stock and make-to-order strategies. These strategies will help you plan your materials appropriately. You can use a mix of these strategies in the manufacturing plant, such as using a Make-to-Order strategy for final assembly and a Make-to-Stock strategy for semi-finished assemblies.

The next chapter covers material requirement planning, which is the next step in the production planning process after demand management.

CHAPTER 5

Material Requirements Planning

Material requirements planning is probably the most powerful tool in logistics and supply chain management. This chapter cover material requirements planning and different MRP procedures. You also learn how to run MRP in SAP using classical MRP and MRP Live.

What Is Material Requirements Planning?

Material requirements planning (MRP) is the planning engine that ensures on-time material availability to meet demands which could be customer demands, planned independent requirements, or dependent requirements from high-level material.

The aim of MRP is to solve three basic questions:

- What (material) to produce/procure
- When (date) to produce/procure it
- How much of it (quantity of material)

MRP is the central component of ERP or in other words you can say that MRP is the heart of SAP. Any activity happening in the entire logistics/supply chain has a direct impact on MRP. Businesses can benefit greatly from MRP and solve a lot of problems, including non-optimal inventory levels (high inventory in most cases), delayed delivery to a customer, dead stock, capital lockup, and so forth.

MRP checks for requirements/demands and then checks if the material is in stock. If the material is not in stock, MRP creates procurement proposals (i.e., purchase requisitions) for materials procured from vendors and planned orders for materials produced in-house. (See Figure 5-1).

© Himanshu Goel 2022
H. Goel, *Handbook for SAP PP in S/4HANA*, https://doi.org/10.1007/978-1-4842-8566-4_5

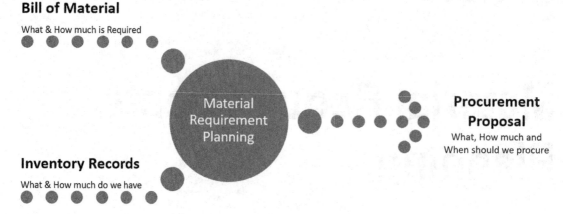

Figure 5-1. *Material requirements planning*

MRP takes input from demand elements, monitors stock situations, and generates supply elements as output.

Demand elements are MRP elements that generate the requirement for the material stock and thus credit (or reduce) the stock in the plant or warehouse. Demand elements are represented as -ve stock in the Stock Requirement list (Transaction Code MD04).

Some of the most common demand elements considered during MRP calculation are as follows:

- Concrete demands for finished goods from customers in terms of sales orders or schedule lines (make-to-order scenarios)

- Planned independent requirements for finished goods coming from S&OP/sales forecasts (make-to-stock scenarios)

- Material reservations

- Dependent requirements for semi-finished or raw materials

Supply elements are MRP elements that fulfill requirements and thus debit (or add) stock to the plant or warehouse. Supply elements are represented with +ve stock in the Stock Requirement list (Transaction Code MD04).

To ensure material availability for the demand, MRP checks the stock situation and if the stock is not available/enough, the system generates supply elements (i.e., purchase requisitions or planned orders), as shown in Figure 5-2:

- Purchase requisitions are for externally procured materials, which are then converted to purchase orders.

- Planned orders are for in-house produced materials, which are subsequently converted to production orders.

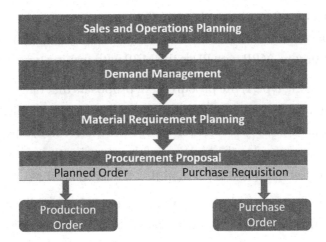

Figure 5-2. *Procurement proposal*

The master data maintained in the MRP1 – MRP4 views of the material master are extremely critical to MRP, as these parameters are considered during the MRP calculations. Thus, it is very important to maintain the master data correctly to ensure the MRP results are accurate. The fields of the MRP1 – MRP4 views in the material master are explained in Chapter 1.

You may assign one of the following MRPs to your material in the MRP1 view of the material master:

- PD   MRP

- P1   MRP, fixing type -1-

- P2   MRP, fixing type -2-

- P3   MRP, fixing type -3-

- P4   MRP, fixing type -4-

Planning Time Fence

You can use the planning time fence to protect automatic changes to the master plan during the planning run. Even if a new requirement arrives, the system will not create or change the procurement proposals within the planning time fence.

The MRP type for standard MRP is PD. MRP is also denoted with MRP Type P followed by firming type or fixing type. There are five firming types:

- 0: Firming type 0 means no firming. Therefore, procurement proposals are not firmed automatically even if they fall within the firming horizon. MRP type PD is the MRP with firming type 0.

- 1: With firming type 1, the procurement proposals that fall within the planning time fence are firmed automatically. If a new requirement arrives then the new procurement proposals are created, and the dates are moved to the end date of the planning time fence. Therefore, the new procurement proposals are not firmed.

- 2: With firming type 2, the procurement proposals that fall within the planning time fence are firmed automatically. If a new requirement arrives then new procurement proposals are not created (i.e., the shortage situation is not adjusted within the planning time fence).

- 3: With firming type 3, the procurement proposals that fall within the planning time fence are not firmed automatically. If a new requirement arrives then the new procurement proposals are created, and the dates are moved to the end date of the planning time fence.

- 4: With firming type 4, the procurement proposals that fall within the planning time fence are not firmed automatically. If a new requirement arrives, then new procurement proposals are not created (i.e., the shortage situation is not adjusted within the planning time fence).

Materials Requirements Planning
Steps in the MRP Run

Next, let's see how the MRP planning engine runs. There are six steps in the MRP run (see Figure 5-3):

1. Checking Planning File Entry

2. Net Requirement Calculation

3. Lot Size Calculation

4. Procurement Type

5. Scheduling

6. BOM Explosion

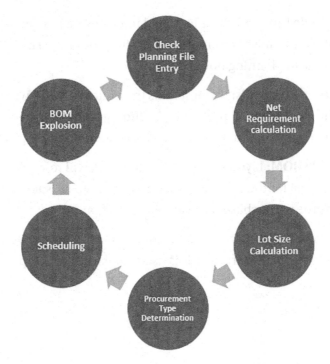

Figure 5-3. *MRP process*

Check Planning File Entry

Planning file entry is a list of all the relevant materials for the MRP run. New materials are created with MRP views, using a valid MRP type. If you have an MRP type called ND, the planning file entry will not be created, because ND means "No Planning". It is mandatory to have a valid MRP type assigned in the material master.

The planning file entry has several indicators or flags that determine how a material is treated during the MRP run. They can be generated manually or automatically.

You can manually create a planning file entry by choosing Logistics ➤ Production ➤ MRP ➤ Planning ➤ Planning File Entry ➤ Create. You can also use Transaction Code MD20 to create a planning file entry.

Enter the material and plant into the initial screen and select the indicators in the Planning File Entry section, as shown in Figure 5-4.

- **Net Change Planning:** This field indicates that the material is taken into account when running MRP with the processing key NETCH (Net Change in Total horizon).

- **Planning File Entry NETPL:** This field indicates that the material is taken into account when running MRP with processing key NETPL (Net Change in planning horizon).

- **Reset Order Proposals:** If you set this the indicator, MRP will delete all existing procurement proposals, including planned orders and purchase requisitions, and generate new procurement proposals.

- **Re-explode BOM:** If you set this indicator, MRP will re-explode the bill of material for the existing procurement proposal, such as the planned orders, purchase requisitions, and so on.

- **Planning Date:** This is the date on which the material should be considered for an MRP run. This is used primarily in time-phased planning.

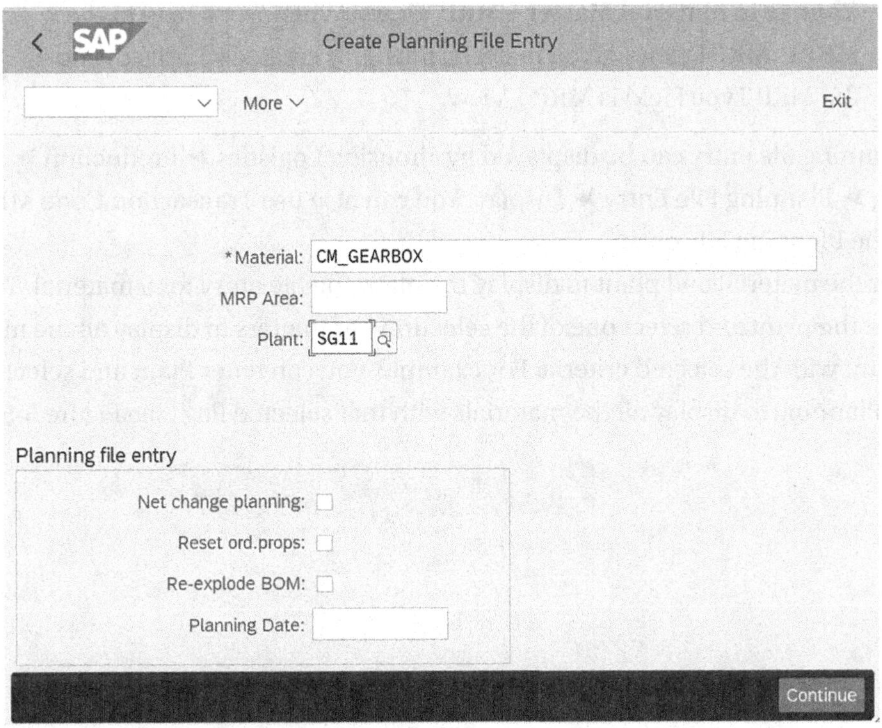

Figure 5-4. *Create Planning File entry*

Press Enter or click the Continue button. The system will give you a message that reads "The material CM_GEARBOX has been marked for the MRP run".

Automatically Creating a Planning File Entry

A planning file entry is created automatically for a material whenever any of the following activities happen:

- **Change in Inventory level:** Whenever the inventory level of the material changes due to a goods movement, such as a goods issue or goods receipt.

- **Change in Demand/Supply elements:** Whenever a new demand element is created (or changed) such as when a sales order arrives or a supply element is created (or changed), the quantity in the production order is changed.

- **Change in Material Master – MRP Views:** Whenever a field in the MRP1- MRP4 views of the material master is created/changed, and the MRP Type Field is MRP 1 View.

A planning file entry can be displayed by choosing Logistics ➤ Production ➤ MRP ➤ Planning ➤ Planning File Entry ➤ Display. You can also use Transaction Code MD21 to display the Planning File entry.

Enter the material and plant to display the planning file entry for a material. You can also enter the plant and select one of the selection parameters to display all the materials in the plant with the selected criteria. For example, you can enter Plant and select Net Change Planning to display all the materials with that selected flag (see Figure 5-5).

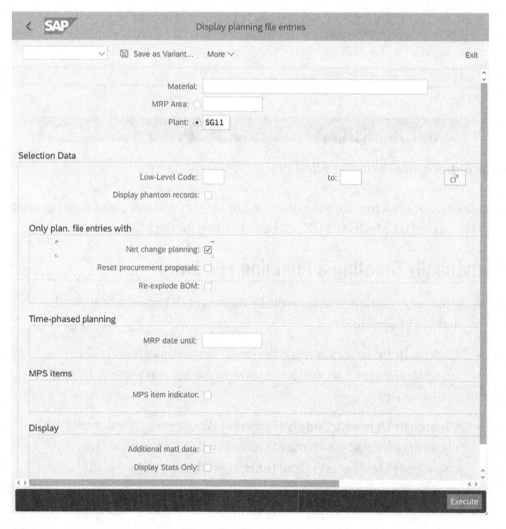

Figure 5-5. *Display Planning File entry: initial screen*

As shown in Figure 5-6, there are several indicators for the material.

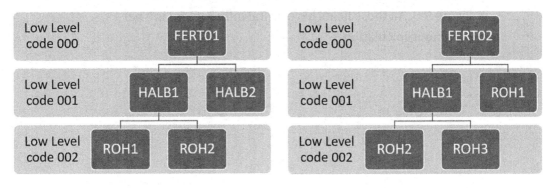

Figure 5-6. Display planning file entries

Record Type: This is used to determine if the material is an MRP material or a phantom assembly. This parameter is quite important, as the system doesn't generate a planned order if the material is a phantom assembly and is assigned as a BOM component.

Low-level code: This determines the lowest level at which a material is assigned in any BOM structure in an organization. A finished good has the low-level code 000 and then, based on the BOM structure, a semi-finished good will have low-level code 001, and so on. In the following example, ROH1 is placed at level 002 in the BOM structure for FERT01, whereas the ROH is placed at level 001 in the BOM structure for FERT02. Since the low-level code is calculated based on the lowest level at which the material is allocated in all the product structures in an organization, the low-level code for ROH1 is 002. If a material is not assigned in a BOM structure, the material will be assigned the low-level code 999. Figure 5-7 illustrates this.

Low Level code 000	FERT01		Low Level code 000	FERT02
Low Level code 001	HALB1 HALB2		Low Level code 001	HALB1 ROH1
Low Level code 002	ROH1 ROH2		Low Level code 002	ROH2 ROH3

Figure 5-7. Low-level code

Low-level code is determined by the system automatically and can be displayed in the material master by clicking the Information button.

MPS Indicator: This determines if the material should be included in the MPS (Master Production Scheduling) run.

The other indicators, like Net Change Planning, Planning File Entry, NETPL, and so on, are explained earlier.

Net Requirement Calculation

The MRP run calculates the net requirements based on the demands, the stock on hand, and the existing receipt elements. The first step is to identify the quantity to be produced/procured for the material based on the requirements. The system checks whether each requirement (demand element) can be covered by the existing warehouse stock. If the warehouse stock is not sufficient, then the requirements may be covered by one or more supply elements. If the requirements are not covered by stock on hand and the existing supply elements, a shortage quantity is calculated and the procurement proposals are created to cover the shortage.

During the net requirement calculation, several parameters are taken into account. Some of them are as follows:

- **Planning strategy:** This plays a vital role during net requirement calculation. For example, Strategy 10 takes into account the existing warehouse stock while Strategy 11 does not consider existing warehouse stocks.

- **Net requirement calculation section in MRP2 view of material master:** This section includes several important fields like Safety Stock, Coverage Profile, Safety Time, and so on, as shown in Figure 5-8. All these fields have a vital influence on the net requirement calculation.

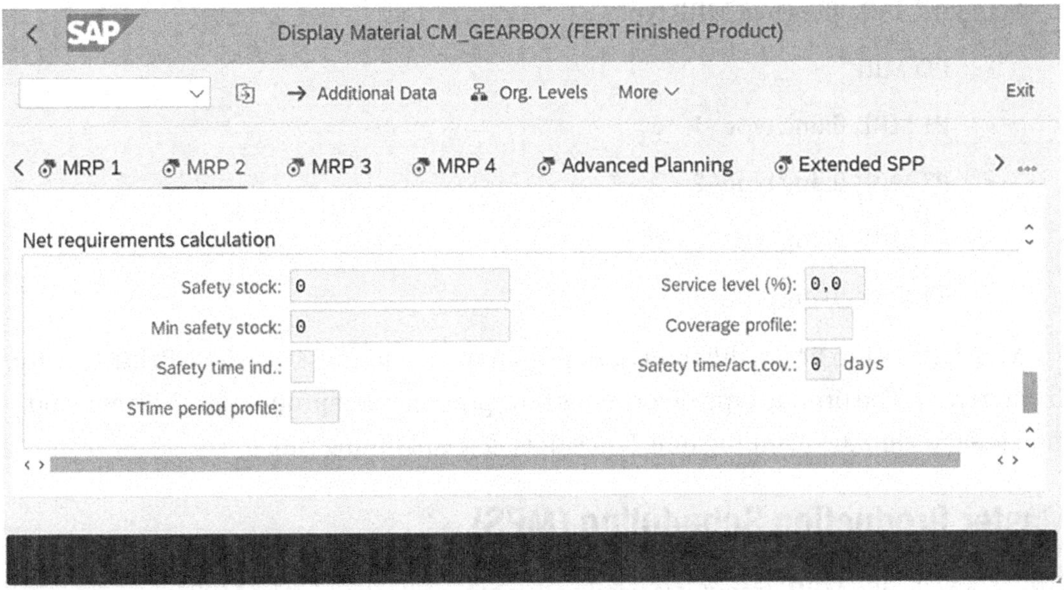

Figure 5-8. *Material master: net requirements calculation*

There are three broad types of material requirements planning, also called MRP procedures:

- Materials requirements planning

- Master production scheduling

- Consumption-based planning

    - Reorder-point planning

    - Time-phased planning

    - Forecast-based planning

Material Requirements Planning (MRP)

MRP is a planning engine that calculates which materials (or components) should be produced (or procured), the quantities to be produced/procured, and the dates on which the material should be available. The function of MRP is to ensure material availability for production and thus on-time delivery to the customers.

Standard SAP offers five MRP types:

- PD MRP

- P1 MRP, fixing type -1

- P2 MRP, fixing type -2

- P3 MRP, fixing type -3

- P4 MRP, fixing type -4

MRP types P1 to P4 are different options that run standard MRP with a fixing type (or firming type). The firming type determines how procurement proposals are firmed and scheduled within the planning time fence during the planning run.

Master Production Scheduling (MPS)

MPS is exactly like MRP, except it is used to flag materials separately. MPS is run for critical materials that have a huge impact on the company's profitability and require special attention.

MPS is run separately and can only be run at a single level. The materials planned using MPS are not included in the normal MRP run. This means a separate transaction is used in SAP for the MPS run. While doing an MPS run, you can run MRP flagged material together.

The standard SAP offers five MPS types:

- M0 MPS, fixing type -0-

- M1 MPS, fixing type -1-

- M2 MPS, fixing type -2-

- M3 MPS, fixing type -3-

- M4 MPS, fixing type -4-

Consumption-Based Planning

Consumption-based planning is a planning procedure that uses past consumption values (historical data) to calculate future requirements. The system calculates the requirement by applying the material forecasts or static planning procedures. The demand elements have no influence on CBP.

Consumption-based planning is further divided into three broad categories.

Reorder-Point Planning

The procurement proposals are created when the sum of plant stock and firmed receipts falls below the reorder point. The following MRP types operate on the principles of reorder-point planning:

- V1 Manual reord.point w. ext.reqs

- V2 Autom. reord.point w. ext.reqs

- VB Manual reorder-point planning

If you are using reorder-point planning, you must maintain the reorder point in the material master (MRP 1 View). Whenever the stock falls below the reorder-point quantity, the system creates a procurement proposal during the next planning run. The MRP controller must maintain this value manually when using manual reorder-point planning. If you are using automatic reorder-point planning, the system updates this value automatically at defined intervals.

Forecast-Based Planning

The future requirements are determined based on the historical consumption data. The MRP type called VV Forecast-Based Planning operates on the principles of forecast-based planning.

Time-Phased Planning

This planning can be used when the materials are procured in a particular time interval. For example, say a vendor delivers the product every Monday. You can add the quantity for the entire week and send a cumulative requirement. The following MRP types operate on the principles of time-phased planning:

- R1 Time-phased planning

- R2 Time-phased w.auto.reord.point

- RR Tmphsd. repl. w. dyn.trgt.stck

- RS Time-phased replenishment plng

Lot Size Calculation

The exact lot size of the procurement proposal is calculated based on the parameters defined in the Lot Size Data section of the MRP1 view of the material master. Based on parameters like Lot Sizing Procedure, Minimum Lot Size, Maximum Lot Size, Assembly Scrap, and so on, the system determines the lot size for the procurement element. See Figure 5-9.

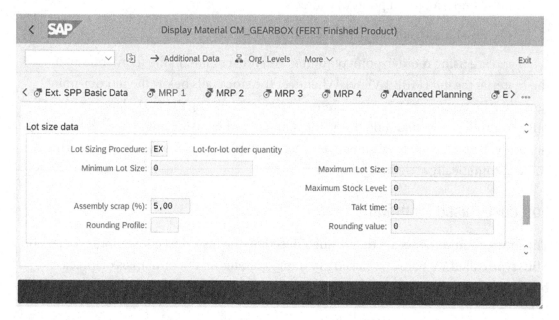

Figure 5-9. *Material master: lot size data*

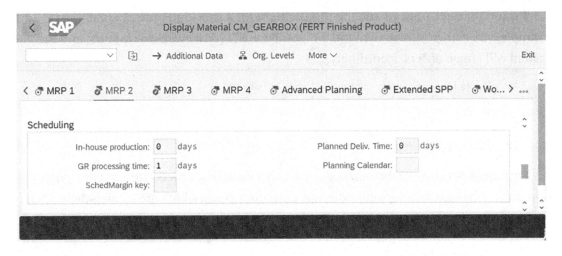

Figure 5-10. *Material master: scheduling*

The lot size indicator helps determine the lot size (or the quantity to be procured/produced) during the net requirement calculation in the planning run. This means the MRP run will calculate the exact order quantity based on the lot size. The lot sizes are divided into three major types:

- Static lot size

- Period lot size

- Optimum lot size

Static lot size: The procurement quantity is calculated based on the specified quantity in the material master.

- You can select the lot-size procedure FX: Fix Order Quantity and maintain the quantity in the Fix Lot Size field, and the system will create the order for the lot size as specified.

- Lot size indicator EX: Lot for Lot Order Quantity will create an order for the quantity that is an outcome of the net requirement calculation, which considers the demand/requirement and reduces the available stock.

Period lot size: You can add the requirement for a specified time interval. For example, you can group the demand for a time bucket (days, week, or month) and the system will create orders accordingly.

- Daily lot size

- Weekly lot size

- Monthly lot size

Optimum lot size: As the name suggests, this lot-sizing procedure aims to create optimal lots by minimizing setup, storage, and order costs, which are lot size-dependent.

- Part period balancing

- Dynamic lot size

- Groff reorder procedure

The system calculates the lot size of the procurement proposal based on the selected lot-sizing procedure and the values maintained in fields like Minimum Lot Size, Maximum Lot Size, Fix Lot Size, Rounding Value, and so on.

Procurement Type

Once the system has determined the lot size, the next step is to identify the procurement type for creating the procurement proposals. The Procurement section in the MRP2 view of the material master plays a vital role when creating a procurement proposal. The Procurement Type field determines if the material is produced internally or procured externally. Procurement Type is a mandatory field and one of the following procurement types must be selected, as shown in the Table 5-1.

Table 5-1. *Procurement Types*

E	In-house production
F	External procurement
Blank	No procurement
X	Both procurement types

For in-house produced materials with Procurement Type E, MRP generates planned orders, while for externally procured materials with Procurement Type F, MRP generates purchase requisitions or planned orders. In the case of planned orders generated for Procurement Type F, they need to be converted in the purchase requisition later.

Special Procurement Type: This is another important field. Some of the special procurement types for in-house production are:

Phantom assembly: This is a virtual assembly that's neither produced nor purchased and is not inventoried. Phantom assembly is used to group components together, but a separate production order is not created. You can also say that phantom assemblies are assembled "on the go" and immediately consumed by some other assembly in the production process.

Production in another plant: The materials are planned in the planning plant while they are produced in production plant.

Direct production/collective order: Direct production is used in special situations when sub-assemblies are produced and consumed directly by the higher-level production order, without the sub-assemblies being placed into stock. This means no goods receipt is posted for semi-finished assemblies. Likewise, there is no need for goods issue postings for these semi-finished assemblies, as they are consumed directly to the order of higher-level assembly. Such network of orders can also be referred to as collective orders.

Some of the special procurement types for external procurement are:

Consignment: In the consignment process, the goods are procured from the vendor. The vendor ships the materials and stores them at the buyer's premises. The material remains the property of the vendor even after delivery. The material is consumed from the consignment stock with special stock indicator K during goods issue.

Subcontracting: This refers to outsourcing a process to a vendor. The vendor is supplied with components from which goods are manufactured. A bill of material should be created for subcontracting materials to specify which material is sent to the vendor and which material is received. A purchase order with item category L is created for the vendor, which explodes the BOM to determine the components to be sent to the vendor.

Important: In S/4HANA, the production version is necessary for subcontracting the bill of materials.

Stock transfer: Materials are transferred from one plant to another within a company using a special purchase order called a stock transfer order. The receiving plant and issue plant are assigned during customization of this special procurement type.

Scheduling

The next step in the MRP run is to determine the dates of the procurement proposal. Scheduling determines the start and end dates for the planned orders or the delivery date for the purchase requisitions. The Scheduling section in the MRP2 view of the material master plays a vital role in determining the order dates.

In-House Production Time: Used to determine the dates for planned orders during the planning run. The in-house production time is independent of the order quantity.

Planned Delivery Time: The time (in workdays) needed by the vendor to deliver the goods after the purchase order is placed. In other words, it is the time between the date on which the order was placed and the date on which goods receipt is posted.

Goods Receipt Processing Time: Once a goods receipt is posted for a material then some time is needed for material inspection and for placing the goods in the warehouse. This is referred to as Goods Receipt Processing Time and it's applicable to all the materials that are produced in-house and procured externally.

BOM Explosion

During the planning run, MRP creates the procurement proposals with a lot size and then schedules them. The last step in the planning run is to explode the bill of materials (BOM) to calculate the quantity needed for semi-finished assemblies or raw materials. Once the BOM is exploded, all the steps of the MRP run (i.e., determining the planning file entry, net requirement calculation, lot size calculation, procurement type determination, and scheduling) are performed for every material of the BOM. Such a BOM explosion is applicable only when running a single item multi-level MRP run.

When running MRP at the plant level, the planning is carried out on the concept of low-level codes.

Low-level codes determine the lowest level at which a material is assigned in any BOM structure in an organization. A finished good has the low-level code 000, a semi-finished good has a low-level code 001, and so on. The planning is carried out for all the materials with the highest low-level code and then subsequently moves on to next level until it reaches the lowest low-level code.

MRP Procedures

As discussed, there are three types of material requirements planning:

- Materials requirements planning

- Master production scheduling

- Consumption-based planning

  - Reorder-point planning

  - Time-phased planning

  - Forecast-based planning

So far this chapter has discussed standard MRP. This section discusses MPS (Master Production Scheduling).

Master Production Scheduling

An MPS run is executed on the same principles as an MRP run. The main objective of MPS is to plan critical materials separately. MPS is used for materials that greatly influence company profits, or that take up critical resources. It is essential to plan these materials separately using special tools.

MPS aims to reduce storage costs and increase planning stability, thus ensuring on-time material delivery to customers.

The master plan of the critical materials planned with MPS greatly influences the entire production process, as the planning of the dependent parts depends on the planning result of the finished products and main assemblies.

The objective of MPS is to pay special attention to the critical materials. Therefore, these materials are planned with a separate planning run. These materials are not planned in the normal MRP runs. Planning the MPS materials separately ensures that these materials can be planned independently from the other planning.

You may assign one of the following MPS types to your material in the MRP1 view of the material master:

- M0   MPS, fixing type -0-

- M1   MPS, fixing type -1-

- M2   MPS, fixing type -2-

- M3   MPS, fixing type -3-

- M4   MPS, fixing type -4-

Planning Time Fence

You can use the Planning Time Fence to protect automatic changes to the master plan during the planning run. Even if a new requirement arrives, the system will not create or change procurement proposals within the planning time fence.

The MPS is represented with MRP Type M followed by the firming type or fixing type. There are five firming types:

- 0: Firming type 0 means no firming. Procurement proposals are not firmed automatically even if they fall within the firming horizon.

- 1: With firming type 1, the procurement proposals that fall within the planning time fence are firmed automatically. If a new requirement arrives then the new procurement proposals are created, and the dates are moved to the end date of the planning time fence. Therefore, the new procurement proposals are not firmed.

- 2: With firming type 2, the procurement proposals that fall within the planning time fence are firmed automatically. If a new requirement arrives then new procurement proposals are *not* created (i.e., the shortage situation is not adjusted within the planning time fence).

- 3: With firming type 3, the procurement proposals that fall within the planning time fence are *not* firmed automatically. If a new requirement arrives then the new procurement proposals are created, and the dates are moved to the end date of the planning time fence.

- 4: With firming type 4, the procurement proposals that fall within the planning time fence are *not* firmed automatically. If a new requirement arrives then new procurement proposals are not created (i.e., the shortage situation is not adjusted within the planning time fence).

You can run MPS using one of the following Transaction Codes:

- MD40   Master Production Scheduling Planning run

- MD41   MPS Single item, multi-level

- MD42   MPS Single item, single level

- MD43   MPS Single item, interactive

Consumption-Based Planning

As the name suggests, consumption-based planning is based on past data. The consumption values from the past are used to forecast future requirements. The planning procedure in consumption-based planning is quite different as compared to MRP or MPS. The procurement proposals are triggered when stock levels fall below a predefined reorder point or the past consumption values are used to forecast future requirements. The net requirement calculation is not triggered by sales orders or PIRs or dependent requirements.

Consumption-based planning is used to plan materials with relative low consumption, like C-parts (as identified by ABC classification). Such planning procedures are mostly used for raw materials and operating supplies.

The consumption pattern should be constant or linear with minimal irregularities for better forecast requirements. You must also ensure inventory management is always up-to-date to have a realistic picture of the stock situation.

Reorder Point Planning

In reorder point planning, procurement proposals are created when the sum of plant stock and firmed receipts falls below the *reorder point*. The reorder point is predefined in the MRP 1 view of the material master. This planning type can be used for a component that's not procured according to the BOM usage (C-parts).

In reorder point planning, the net requirement calculation is not triggered by sales orders or PIRs or dependent requirements. Rather, replenishment is triggered once the stock levels fall below the reorder point.

When using reorder point planning, it is recommended to use lot size HB Replenishment to Maximum Stock level. You must maintain the maximum stock level for the material. The reorder point should be defined in such a way that the average material requirements are covered during the replenishment lead time.

It is also important to maintain the safety stock (MRP 2 View) while using reorder point planning. This ensures that there is always enough stock to cover any unprecedented demand (for example, due to delivery delays or excessive material consumption). The safety stock should be able to cover demand during such situations. Figure 5-11 shows the reorder point planning procedure.

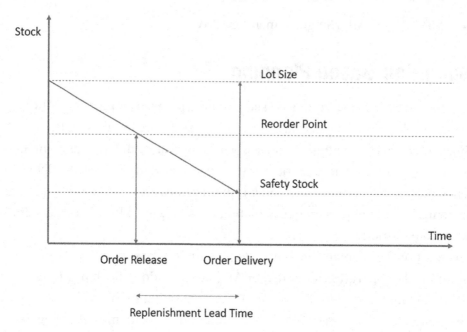

Figure 5-11. *Reorder point planning*

You can choose one of the following for reorder point planning:

Manual reorder point planning: You can use MRP Type VB Manual Reorder Point Planning or V1 Manual reord.point w. ext.reqs. Safety stock and reorder point are defined manually in the material master.

Automatic reorder point planning: You must assign MRP Type V2 Autom. reord.point w. ext.reqs. The system will determine the reorder point and safety stock automatically by the integrated forecasting program. The forecast program uses past consumption values to determine future requirements. These forecast requirements are then used to calculate the reorder point and safety stock considering the replenishment lead time and the expected service level (to be entered manually by the MRP controller in the material master).

Forecast-Based Planning

Like reorder point planning, forecast-based planning is based on historical material consumption. This planning method uses historical consumption values and forecast values to determine future requirements via the integrated forecasting program. The forecast values have a direct effect on MRP as automatically determined forecast requirements. Figure 5-12 shows the Forecasting view of the material master.

Figure 5-12. *Material master: Forecasting view*

The forecast is carried out on regular intervals based on the specified period (daily, weekly, monthly, or per accounting period) and the number of periods to be included in the forecast for each material. You can also specify the number of forecast periods to be considered during requirements planning.

The forecast requirements may or may not be adjusted based on consumption.

- If consumption is higher than the forecast requirements in the current month, the system also reduces future forecast requirements.

- If consumption is higher than the forecast requirements in the current month, the system does not reduce future forecast requirements.

- The reduction of the forecast requirements is based on average daily consumption. Actual consumption data is not relevant.

Important parameters to be defined in the material master for forecast-based planning are as follows:

- MRP Type VV Forecast-based planning should be assigned in the MRP1 view of the material master.

- Periodic lot size must be assigned.

- Period indicator must be specified in the MRP3 view of the material master.

- The Forecasting view of the material master must be maintained as per requirements.

- Maintain the correct Forecast Model view in the Forecasting view.

- Maintain the past consumption values in the additional data view called Consumption.

Once the master data is maintained, you can execute the forecasting run in the Forecasting view of the material master or you can execute the forecasting run using Transaction Code MP30.

Time-Phased Planning

You can use this to procure materials that are procured on a periodic basis. For example, a vendor delivers parts each Monday. You can plan these materials using time-phased planning and a planning calendar. The Planning Date file in the planning file entry is updated for the materials planned using time-phased planning. As the name suggests, the planning date is the date on which the material should be planned and is determined based on the planning cycle (the planning calendar). The date is set automatically when the material is created. After each planning (MRP) run, the planning date is redetermined.

Note: The Net Change Planning and Planning File Entry NETPL indicators in the planning file entry are irrelevant to materials planned using time-phased planning.

To plan materials using time-phased planning, you must maintain the following data in the material master:

MRP type for time-phased planning:

- R1   Time-phased planning

- R2   Time-phased w.auto.reord.point

- RE   Replenishment plnd externally

- RF   Replenish with dyn.TargetStock

- RP   Replenishment

- RR   Tmphsd. repl. w. dyn.trgt.stck

- RS   Time-phased replenishment plng

Planning cycle/planning calendar: The key that determines the day on which the material is planned. For example, if the material is delivered every Monday.

Planned delivery time in the MRP 2 view of the material master. This is quite important for determining the total replenishment lead time.

Lot size is maintained as Ex lot-for-lot order quantity in the MRP 1 view of the material master.

During the MRP run, the system checks the planning date in the planning file entry to determine if the material should be included in the next planning run. If the material should be included in the next planning run, the system calculates the requirements for the material.

The system determines a time interval using the following algorithm:

Time interval = MRP date + planning cycle + purchasing processing time + planned delivery time + goods receipt processing time.

The quantity to be ordered is calculated based on the forecast requirements in the time interval. The system also checks for stock on hand and firmed receipts (supply elements). Once the quantity to be ordered is determined, the procurement proposals are generated.

Although time-phased planning is conceptually designed under consumption-based planning, it can also be used with material requirements planning.

- **Time-phased planning using consumption-based planning:** In such a planning method, the requirements are generated using the material forecast. The forecast requirements are consumed based on the same parameters as in forecast-based planning.

- **Time-phased planning using material requirements planning:** In such a planning run, all the relevant requirements for MRP are considered in the net requirement calculation. Also, the forecast requirements are considered during the net requirement calculation. In such a planning method, it is mandatory to select an MRP type with the time-phased with requirements indicator.

How Do You Run MRP?

The MRP can be executed in one of the following ways:

- MD01   Material Requirements Planning run (MRP at Plant Level)

- MD02   MRP Single item, multi-level

- MD03   MRP Single item, single level

- MD01N   MRP Live

- MDBT   Total Planning: Background job

Total Planning Run

You can run MRP at the plant level or at the Scope of planning level using Transaction Codes MD01 and MD01N. The scope of planning is a key with which you can group together several plants or MRP areas, but it's not used in MD01N. Instead, you can directly input the materials. Therefore, you can run MRP (a total planning run) for a combination of several plants or several MRP areas. While running such an MRP, the system checks for all the materials flagged for the MRP run in the planning file entry. All the materials with the Net Change Planning flag and the planning file entry NETPL are planned in the planning run. The planning is carried out for all the materials with the highest low-level code and then moves to the next level until it reaches the lowest low-level code.

You can run total planning by choosing Logistics ➤ Production ➤ MRP ➤ Planning ➤ Total Planning ➤ Online or you can use Transaction Code MD01 (see Figure 5-13).

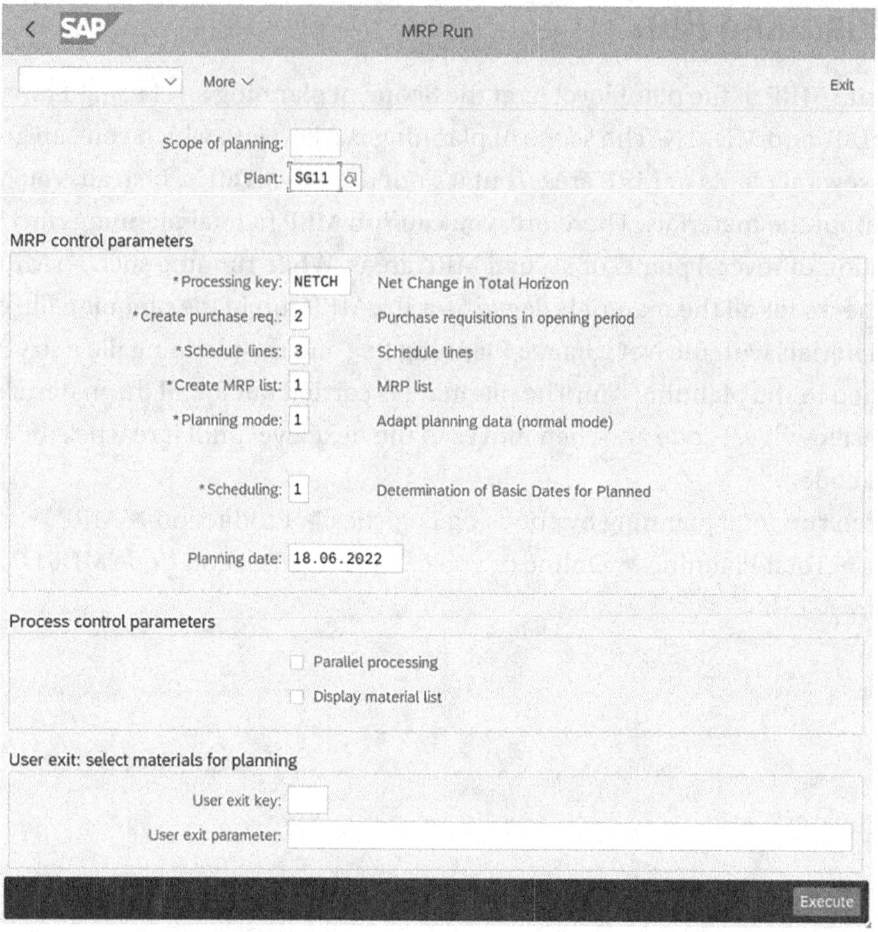

Figure 5-13. *Total planning: MRP run*

You can run total planning by choosing Logistics ➤ Production ➤ MRP ➤ Planning ➤ MD01N – MRP Live.

Background mode: You can also set up total planning to run in the background by choosing Logistics ➤ Production ➤ MRP ➤ Planning ➤ Total Planning ➤ As Background Job or you can set up the background job using Transaction Code MDBT.

Single Item, Multi-Level MRP Run

You can run MRP for a single material. The BOM is exploded and the planning run is executed for each material of the product structure. This planning run is usually executed for finished goods and the system will plan all the materials until the last level of the BOM structure. The planning file entry is *not* checked in such a planning run.

You can run single item, multi-level MRP by choosing Logistics ➤ Production ➤ MRP ➤ Planning ➤ Multilevel Single-Item Planning or you can use Transaction Code MD02 (see Figure 5-14).

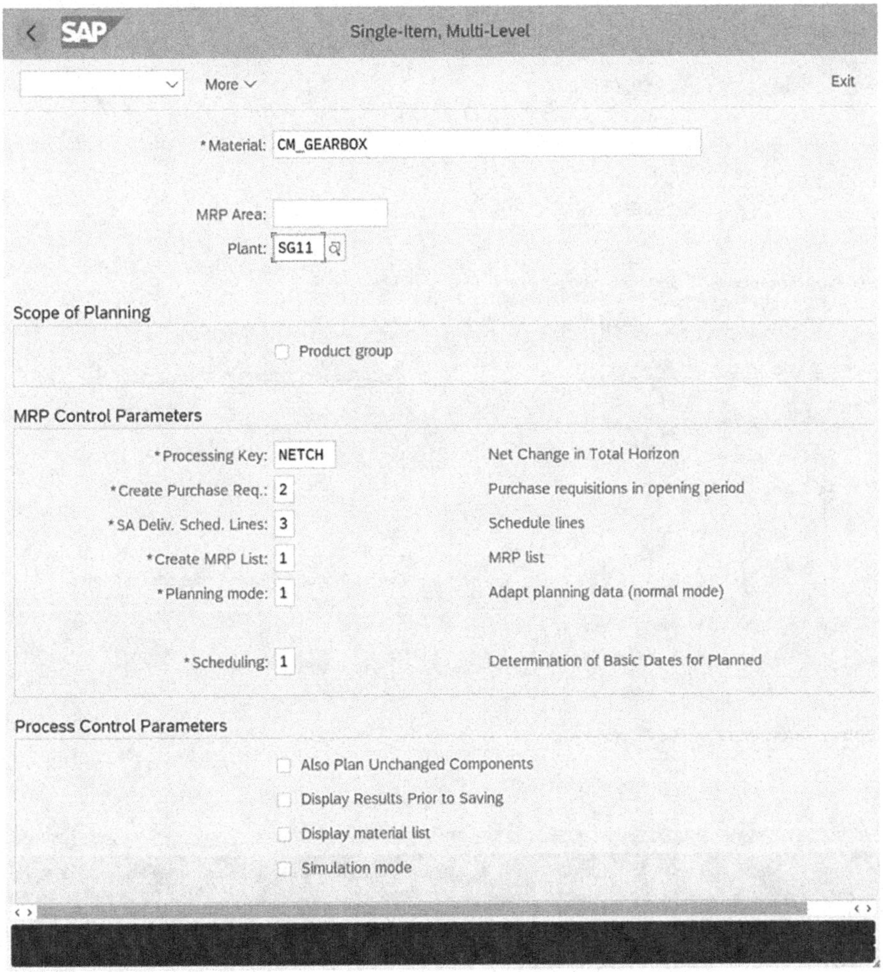

Figure 5-14. *Single item, multi-level*

Single Item, Single-Level MRP Run

You can run MRP for a single material only. In such a planning run, the BOM is not exploded, which means the components in the product structure are not planned.

You can run single item, single-level MRP by choosing Logistics ➤ Production ➤ MRP ➤ Planning ➤ Single-Level Single-Item Planning or you can use Transaction Code MD03 (see Figure 5-15).

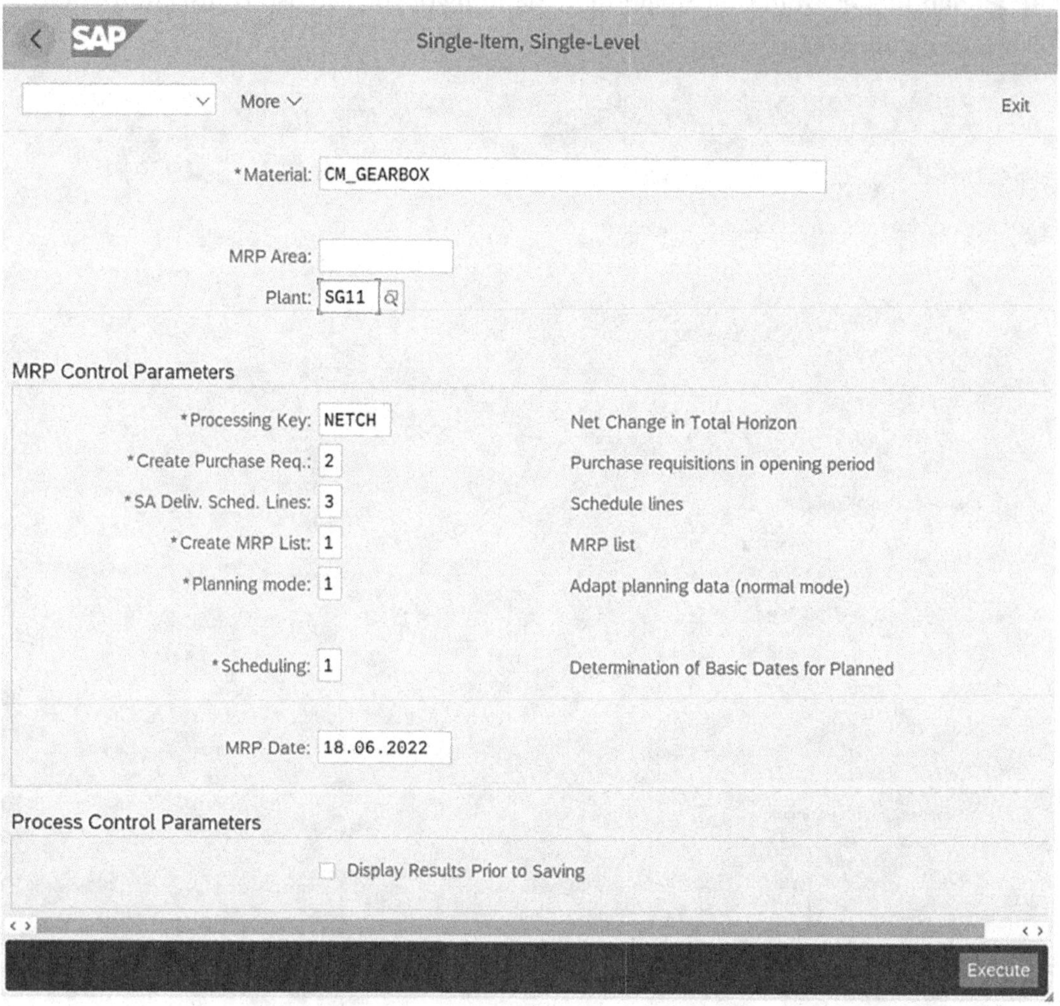

Figure 5-15. *Single-item, single-level*

MRP Control Parameters

While running MRP with any of the previous Transaction Codes, you must specify the control parameters.

Here is a list of MRP control parameters:

- Scope of planning

- Processing key

- Create purchase requisition

- Schedule lines

- Create MRP list

- Planning mode

- Scheduling

- Planning date

You can also choose Process Control Parameters to determine how the planning run is executed:

- Parallel processing

- Display material list

You can also activate the user exit to select which materials should be included in the planning run based on specific conditions:

- User exit key

- User exit parameter

Scope of Planning: This is a key with which you can group together several plants or MRP areas. Therefore, you can run MRP (a total planning run) for a combination of several plants or several MRP areas. Scope of planning can be customized with Transaction Code OMOE. As shown in Figure 5-16, a scope of planning SG00 is defined for SuperGears Group AG, which includes two plants (i.e., SG11- SuperGears AG & SG01 - SuperGears PL). Thus, the total planning run is executed for all the plants defined in the scope of planning. The planning run will happen in sequence—first for plant SG11 and then SG01. This field is only available in Transaction Code MD01.

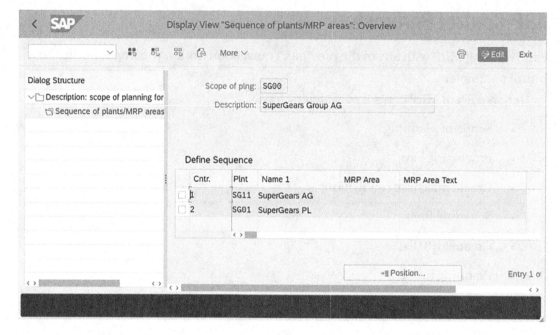

Figure 5-16. *Scope of planning: sequence of plants/MRP areas*

Processing Key

You can run MRP for all the materials or only for the materials for which the planning situation for the material has been changed. The following planning types are available in SAP:

Net Change Planning (NETCH): All the materials that have the Net Change in Planning flag in the planning file entry are planned during the MRP run. Whenever there is an MRP relevant change made to the material, the indicator is activated in the planning file entry. The planning run with NETCH is usually run daily (in background mode at night) to plan all the materials for which the planning situation has changed.

Net Change Planning in the Planning Horizon (NETPL): All the materials that have the Planning File Entry NETPL flag in the planning file entry are planned during the MRP run.

You can maintain the planning horizon at the plant level or the MRP group level. The planning horizon is the time in days that the requirements are considered during the planning run. For instance, if you maintain a planning horizon that's 100 days, the system will consider the materials that have an MRP relevant change for the next 100 days.

Regenerative Planning (NEUPL): All the materials for which a planning file entry exists are planned with regenerative planning. The system doesn't limit the planning run for materials using the NETCH or NETPL indictor in the planning file entry. It is recommended to run regenerative planning weekly or bi-weekly so that it will also plan those materials for which the planning situation is outdated. For example, there are some materials with old, planned orders. No MRP relevant changes were made to these planned orders, thus they were not rescheduled. Regenerative planning will replan such materials during the next planning run.

Create Purchase Requisition: The Create Purchase Requisition indicator determines if the system should create purchase requisitions or planned orders for the materials that are procured externally.

- **Purchase Requisitions:** Created for the total planning horizon.

- **Purchase Requisitions in Opening Period:** Created within the opening period. For all the requirements outside the opening period, planned orders are created.

- **Planned Orders:** Created for the entire planning horizon. These planned orders are later converted to purchase requisitions.

The Creation indicator for purchase requisitions can be maintained in customization at the MRP group level. If the Creation indicator is not maintained in customization at the MRP group level, the system checks the indicator selected on the initial screen of the planning run.

Purchase Requisition Creation in S/4HANA: The Create Purchase Requisition control parameter has been made obsolete in MRP Live. The planning run with MRP Live always creates purchase requisitions as procurement proposals for the materials that are procured externally. This is one of the simplifications in S/4HANA.

Schedule lines: The indicator controls if the system should generate schedule lines or not based on the following options:

- No schedule lines

- Schedule lines in the opening period

- Schedule lines

The creation indicator for schedule lines can be maintained in customization at the plant level or the MRP group level. If the creation indicator is not maintained in the customization at the plant level or MRP group level, the system checks the indicator selected on the initial screen of the planning run.

Create MRP list: This indicator controls if the system should generate an MRP list or not based on the following options:

- **MRP list:** MRP list is always generated for all the materials planned in the planning run.

- **Depending on the exception messages:** MRP list is generated only for a few materials that have specific exception messages.

- **No MRP list:** MRP list is not created for any of the planned materials.

Planning mode: The Planning Mode indicator determines how the existing procurement proposals are treated during the planning run. You can select one of the following planning modes:

- **Adapt planning data (Normal mode):** This is the recommended planning mode to be used for daily MRP runs. The unfirmed procurement proposals are adjusted based on the new planning situation. The planning mode takes into account the following changes:

  - **Change in requirement:** If there is a change in the requirement or demand element then the existing procurement proposals are adjusted accordingly.

  - **Changes in date and quantity:** If the date or quantity of the requirement or demand element is changed then the procurement proposals are adjusted accordingly.

  - **Changes in the MRP type or lot size in the material master:** If the MRP type or the lot sizing procedure is changed in the material master the existing procurement proposals are adopted based on the new parameters.

166

- **Re-explode BOM and Routing:** While using this planning mode, the system re-explodes the BOM and routing for all existing procurement proposals that are unfirmed. This planning mode is recommended to be used whenever there is a change in any of the following master data:

    - Material or sales BOM is changed

    - Phantom assembly BOM is changed

    - Material classification is changed

    - Production version is changed

Note   The Re-Explode BOM and Routing planning mode is not available in MD01N MRP Live.

Delete and recreate planning data: The system deletes all existing procurement proposals that are not firmed during planning run. It is not recommended to use this planning mode, as it slows down system performance since all existing procurement proposals are deleted and then recreated.

If you are using the Delete and Recreate Planning Data planning mode frequently, you need to keep eye on the planned order and purchase requisition number range. Using this planning mode will exhaust the number range soon.

Scheduling: Scheduling is a vital step during the planning run. It is used to determine the requirement dates for the procurement proposals. During scheduling, the system determines the start and end dates for the planned orders for the materials that are produced in-house. The requirement dates are determined in purchase requisition for the materials that are procured externally.

The Scheduling indicator determines whether the system should perform Basic Scheduling or Lead Time scheduling during the planning run.

Basic scheduling: During the planning run, the system determines the basic production dates for the planned orders. The basic start and end dates are calculated based on the in-house production time maintained in the MRP2 view of the material master. The in-house production time is independent of the lot size during the calculation of basic dates. Schedule margin key is not considered during the basic scheduling. The basic dates are accurate to the day.

Lead time scheduling: The system determines the production dates based on the time maintained in the routing. Various times can be maintained in the routing, such as setup time, processing time, queue time, interoperation time, and so on. All these times are maintained in the routing and are used to calculate the exact time required to produce a material based on the order lot quantity. During lead time scheduling, the system not only calculates the production date and time but also generates capacity requirements. The lead time scheduling calculates the exact production dates and the time to the accuracy of minutes and seconds. Figure 5-17 shows how the lead times are calculated considering float before production, operation times, and float after production.

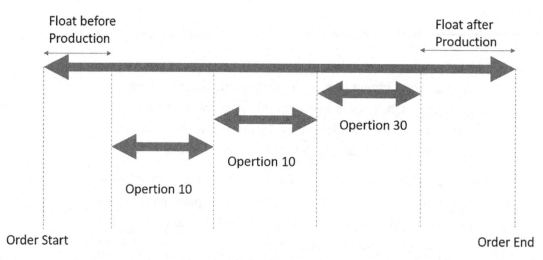

Figure 5-17. *Lead time scheduling*

Figure 5-18 shows the planned order with lead time scheduling. You can see basic and production dates, which are calculated based on exact time from routing. They also consider floats before/after production.

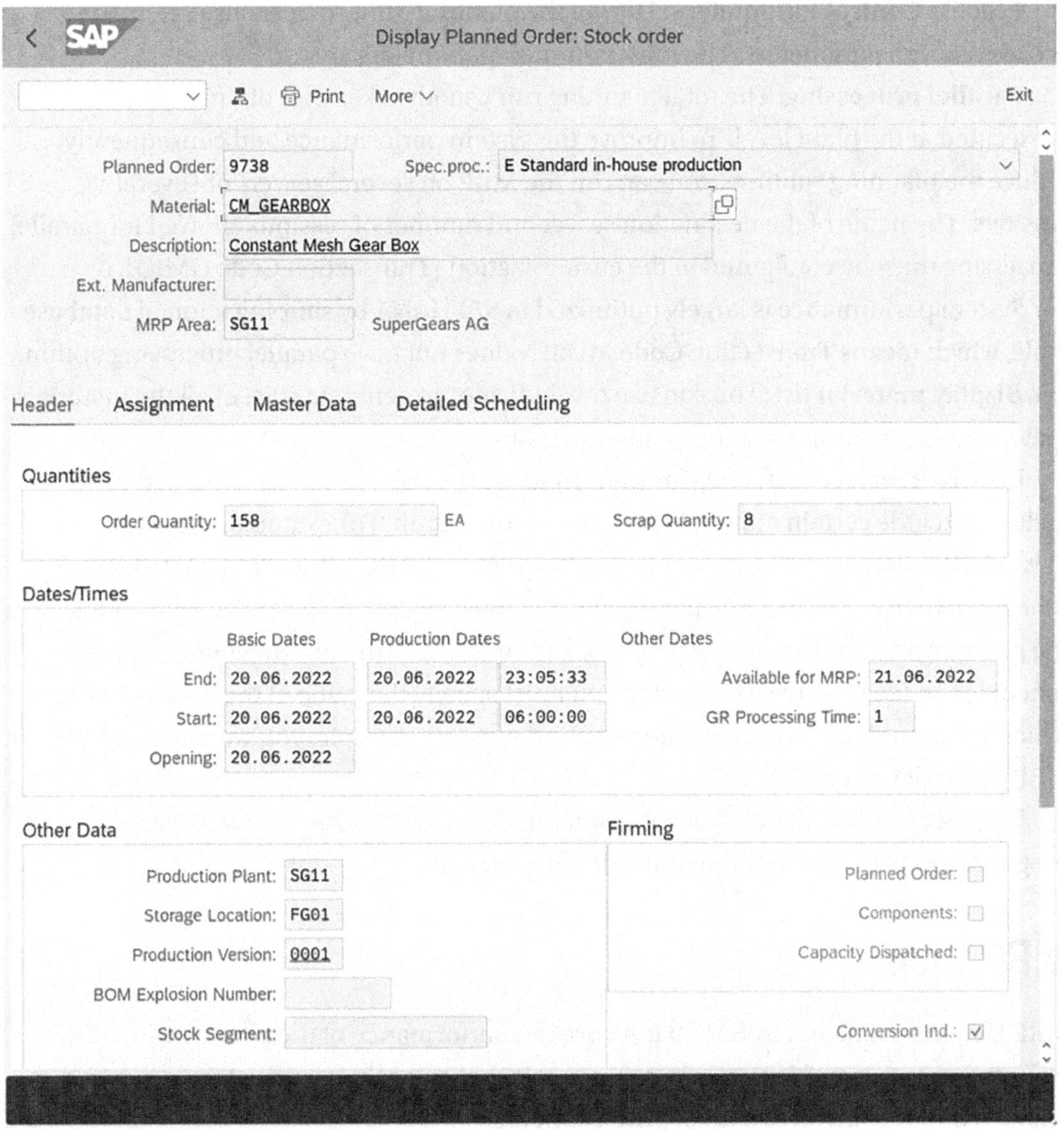

Figure 5-18. *Display planned order with lead time scheduling*

Planning Date: The planning date is only applicable to time-phased planning. Time-phased planning is used to plan the material on a periodic basis, such as every Tuesday or every Monday and Thursday. The system calculates the planning date for the next run and assigns the planning date in the planning file. The system checks the materials for which the planning date in the planning file is the same as the planning date in the initial screen of the planning run.

Process Control Parameters: During the planning run, you can also select the process control parameters. The most common parameters are:

Parallel processing: The total planning run usually takes a lot of time since the MRP is executed at the plant level. To improve the system performance and consequently reduce the planning runtime, you can run the MRP on several servers or several sessions. The name of the destination server and number of sessions allowed for parallel processing must be configured in the customization (Transaction Code OMIQ).

System performance is largely optimized in S/4 HANA by simplification of database table, which means Transaction Code MD01N does not have parallel processing option.

Display material list: You can use this indicator to generate a list of all the materials that have been planned during the planning run.

User Exit: Select materials for planning: A user exit can be implemented to include/exclude certain materials from the planning run. For example, you can choose to run MRP for materials that are assigned to a specific MRP controller or production scheduler. In the User Exit Key parameter, you must select the Control key for which the planning run should be executed. For example, the MRP controller or production scheduler. In the User Exit parameter, you must specify the value of the control key for which you would like to execute the planning run. For example, you want to run MRP for MRP controller 001 and 002.

The user exit M61X0001 must be implemented and the source code must be programmed to define how the user exit must execute.

MRP Live

MRP Live was launched by SAP to improve the performance of the planning run. The planning run is a complex process and can take hours, as thousands of materials are planned and that involves a lot of MRP elements.

With the launch of the SAP HANA database, which is an in-memory and column-oriented database, SAP realized that the performance of MRP could be improved by capitalizing on the capabilities of the HANA database. Hence SAP redesigned the entire logic around MRP to run it on the HANA database and thus improve the performance of the planning run.

The PPH_MRP_START program was copied from the RMMRP000 program (the technical program name for Classical MRP). The new program was reengineered keeping in mind the performance optimization by executing the planning run on an in-memory HANA database.

You can run total planning by choosing Logistics ➤ Production ➤ MRP ➤ Planning ➤ MD01N – MRP Live (see Figure 5-19).

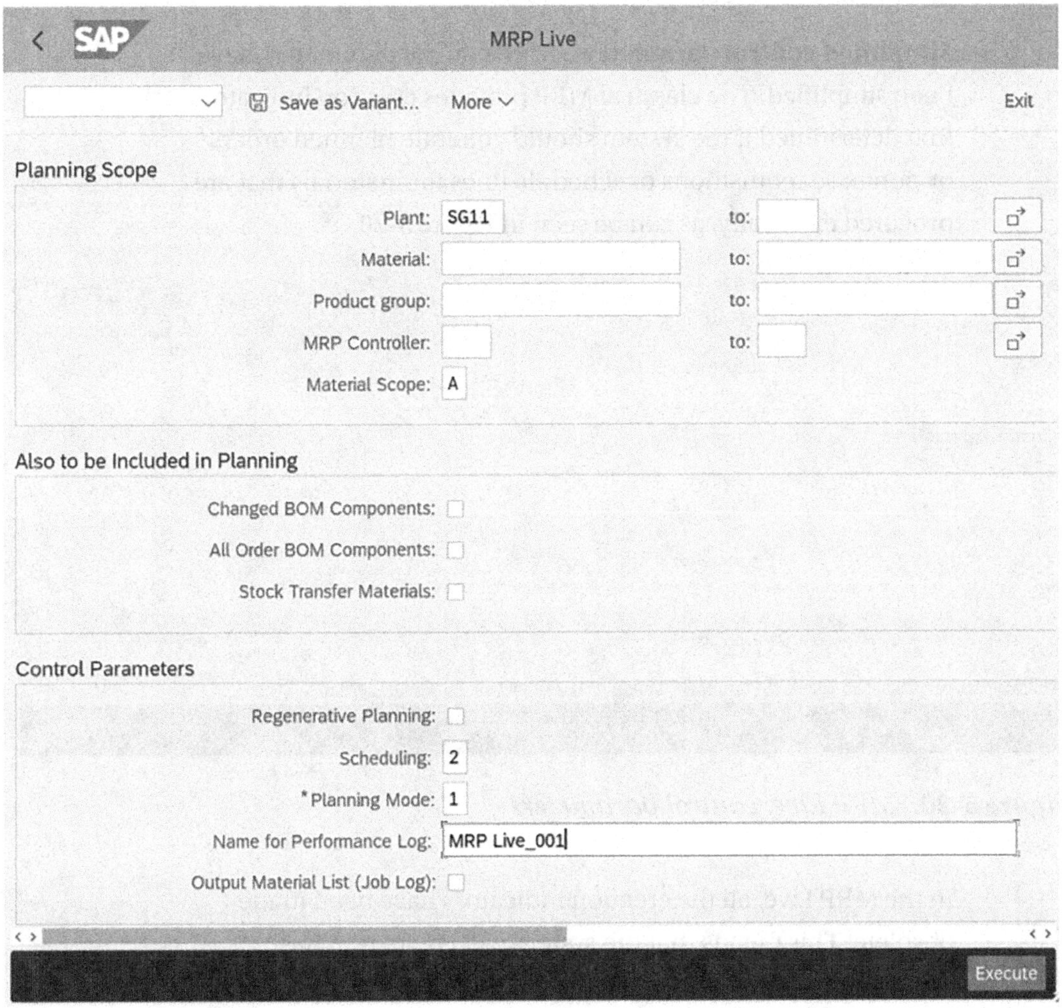

Figure 5-19. *MRP Live*

Some of the major changes implemented in MRP Live are as follows:

> **The MRP list was made redundant:** Classical MRP provided the function to generate the MRP list. The MRP list was a static list that displayed the MRP results when the planning run was last executed. The performance of the planning run has been immensely improved therefore it provides an opportunity to run

MRP more frequently and always work on live data. It made no sense to evaluate results from the last planning run and thus MRP lists are no longer generated in MRP Live.

Simplified control parameters: MRP control parameters have been simplified. The classical MRP provides creation indicators that determined if the system should generate planned orders or purchase requisitions or schedule lines for materials that are procured externally, as can be seen in Figure 5-20.

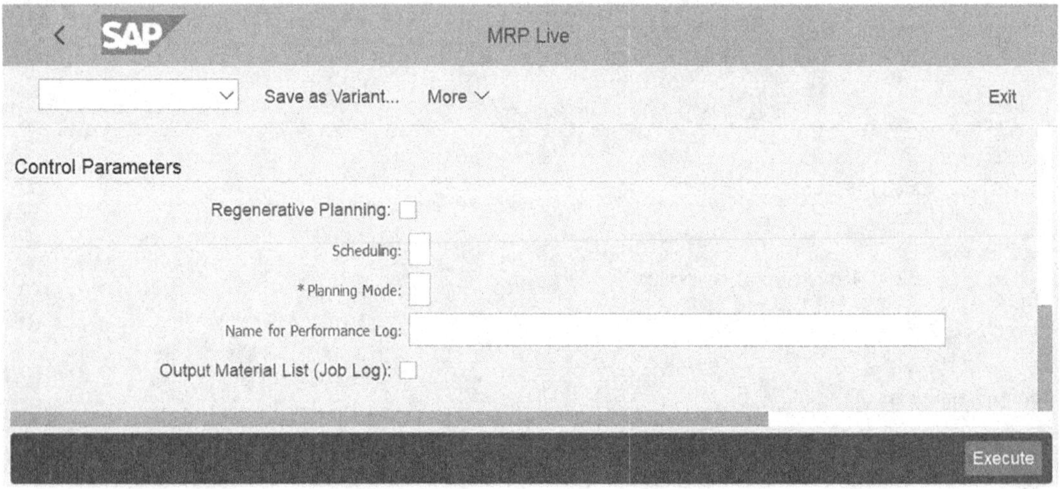

Figure 5-20. *MRP Live: control parameters*

In the MRP Live, all the creation indicators have been made obsolete. This means that the system will create purchase requisitions for the materials that are procured externally. However, if a scheduling agreement exists for the material, scheduling lines are generated.

BAdIs in classical MRP: Classical MRP came with a lot of BAdIs that could be implemented. These BAdIs can no longer work with MRP Live. If there is a need, then the BAdIs used in classical MRP must be translated into new AMDP BAdIs. This is due to the fact that classical MRP was written in ABAP, whereas MRP Live logic has been designed to be executed in SAP HANA.

NETPL is no longer available: It is no longer possible to select the processing key. MRP Live can be executed in a normal mode (i.e., NETCH). You can also choose to run planning in Regenerative mode.

Planning mode is simplified: The planning mode is also simplified. The Re-explode BOM and Routing option is no longer available in MRP Live. MRP Live's planning mode has only two options:

- **Adapt Planning Data:** If an unfirmed procurement proposal exists that fulfills the requirement, the system reuses it. If an unfirmed procurement proposal exists that fulfills the requirements only partially (for example, the requirement quantity is same as of procurement proposal, but the requirement date is different), then the system deletes the existing procurement proposal and creates a new one.

- **Delete and Recreate Planning Data:** As the name suggests, the system deletes all existing procurement proposals and generates new procurement proposals to satisfy the demands (requirements).

You can use Transaction Code MD_MRP_FORCE_CLASSIC to force a material to be planned via classical MRP. You can also determine if you would like to display the material in MRP Fiori Apps. Enter the plant and MRP controller, as shown in Figure 5-21.

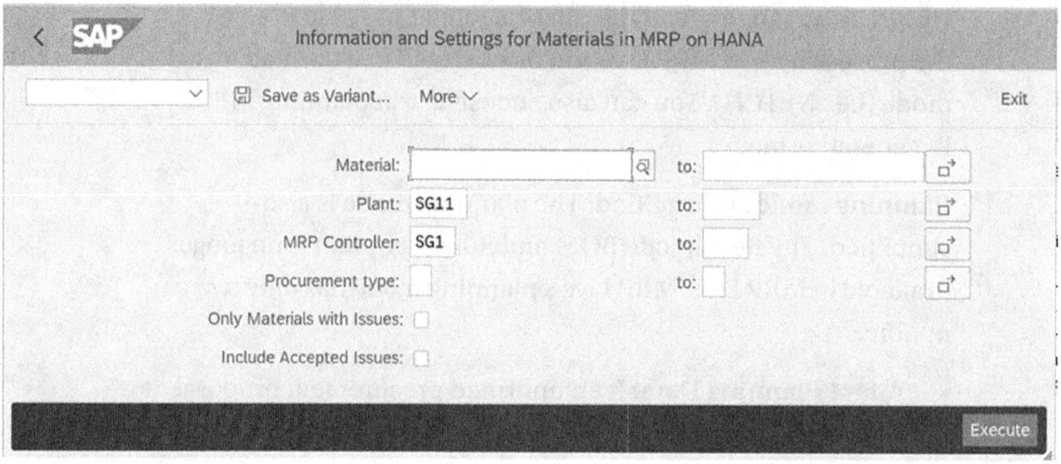

Figure 5-21. *Information and settings for materials in MRP on HANA: initial screen*

Figure 5-22 displays a list of all the materials in the plant SG11, since the report was executed at the plant level. It also shows whether the material is planned via MRP Live or Classical MRP. The report also displays error messages, if there are any.

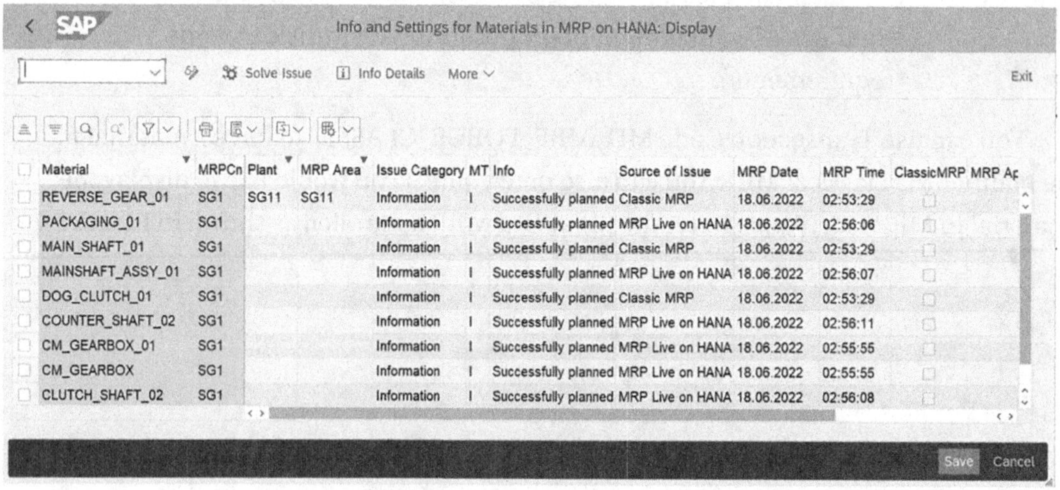

Figure 5-22. *Information and settings for materials in MRP on HANA*

Running MRP Live

You can run MRP Live with Transaction Code MD01N. As compared to classical MRP, MRP Live gives you flexibility to select various parameters for your planning run. You can define your planning scope based on several select options, such as Plants, Material, Product Group, or MRP Controller. You can execute planning for multiple plants or multiple MRP controllers, and so on.

Material Scope: You can determine if you want to execute a planning run for all the materials or restrict your planning run only for MRP materials or MPS materials. As shown in Figure 5-23, I'm executing the report at the plant level.

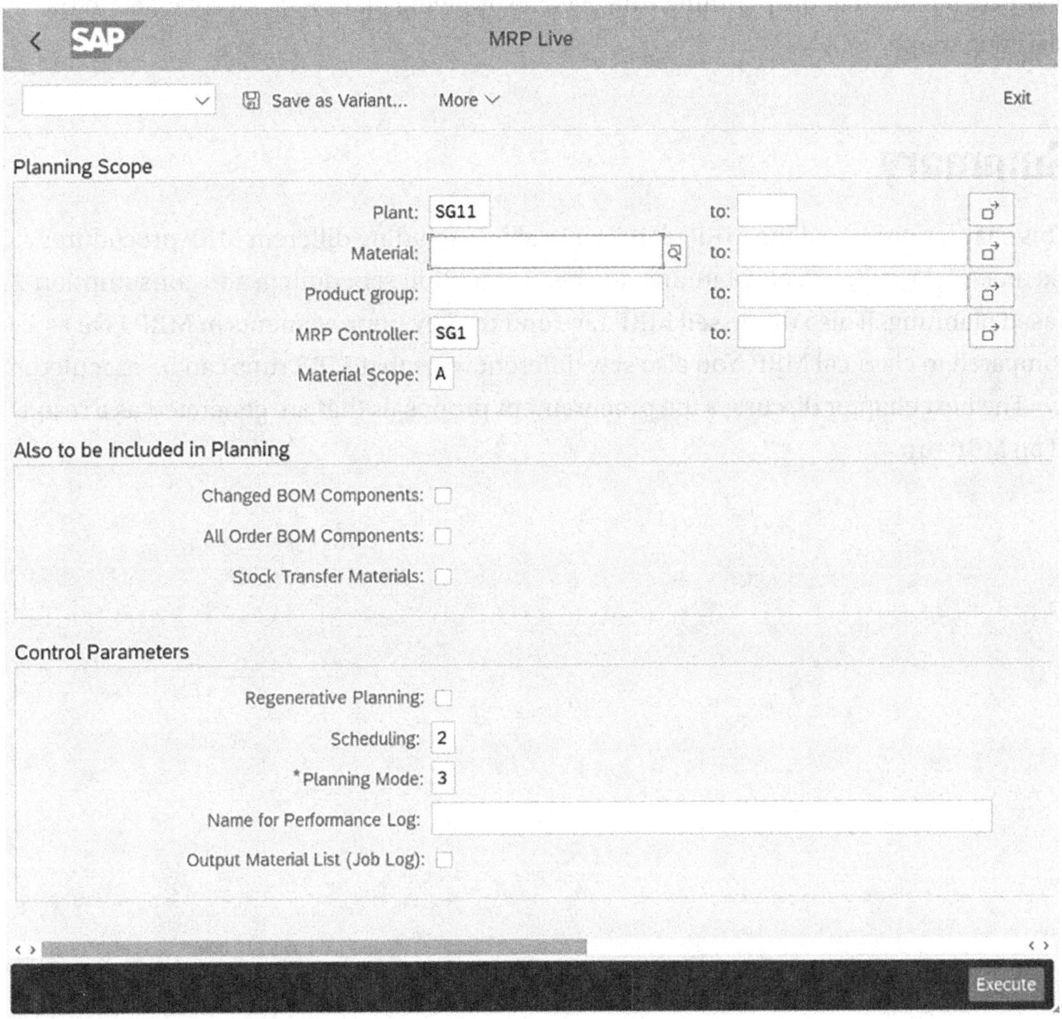

Figure 5-23. MRP Live

Changed BOM Components: You can control if you would also like to plan the BOM components for which the planning situation has changed. The BOM components that aren't impacted by the planning situation are not included in the planning run.

All Order BOM Components: You can run MRP for all the BOM components even if the dependent requirements for the components have not changed. However, the components that have the special procurement key called Withdrawal From Alternative Plant are not considered in the planning run.

Stock Transfer Materials: If a material is procured from a different plant, you can use this indicator to run MRP for the supplying plant as well as the receiving plant. All the materials for which MRP relevant changes have been done in the supplying plant are included in the planning run, even if supplying plant was not specified in the planning scope.

Summary

This chapter discussed the MRP planning engine, including different MRP procedures like material requirements planning, master production scheduling, and consumption-based planning. It also discussed MRP Live and the key improvements in MRP Live as compared to classical MRP. You also saw different ways that MRP runs can be executed.

The next chapter discusses the procurement proposals that are generated as a result of an MRP run.

CHAPTER 6

Procurement Proposals

This chapter covers the procurement element called the planned order. You'll learn how a material availability check can be executed for a planned order and you'll learn about several ways to convert a planned order to a production order.

Procurement proposals are created as a result of an MRP run. The system generates planned orders for materials produced in-house and purchase requisitions for materials procured externally. Planned orders are further converted to production orders for order processing. Purchase requisitions are subsequently converted to purchase orders, which are formal (legal) documents sent to vendors for procuring goods or services. This chapter discusses the planned order, since it is relevant to the production process.

Planned Orders

A *planned order* is a procurement proposal that's usually created by MRP to cover requirements for materials that are produced in-house. A planned order can also be created manually if needed. A planned order contains basic information like the material, quantity, and the production dates, along with some other information. The planned order is only a procurement proposal and thus must be converted to a production order for manufacturing execution.

Note As mentioned, a planned order is only a procurement proposal and is not used for manufacturing execution. This statement is valid for discrete and process industries only. In repetitive manufacturing, planned orders are used for production execution. If the material is flagged to be executed with repetitive manufacturing, then planned orders with the PE Run-Schedule Quantity order type are created. Such planned orders cannot be converted to production orders.

© Himanshu Goel 2022
H. Goel, *Handbook for SAP PP in S/4HANA*, https://doi.org/10.1007/978-1-4842-8566-4_6

As you can see in Figure 6-1, MRP has generated several planned orders to fulfil requirements generated by the planned independent requirements.

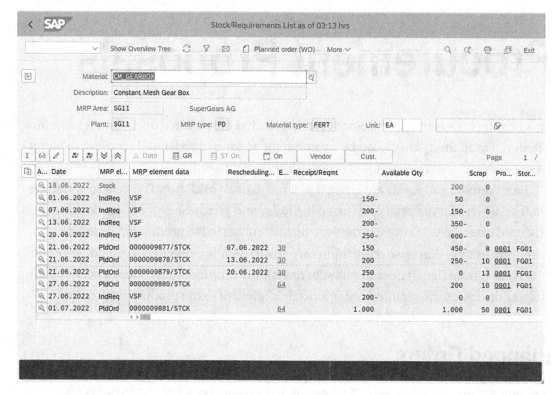

Figure 6-1. *Stock requirement list*

Planned orders can be created manually or automatically as a result of an MRP run.

Manual creation of planned order: A planned order can be generated manually by choosing Logistics ➤ Production ➤ MRP ➤ Planned Order ➤ Create. You can also use Transaction Code MD11 to create a planned order.

You must specify the planned order's profile on the initial screen, as shown in Figure 6-2.

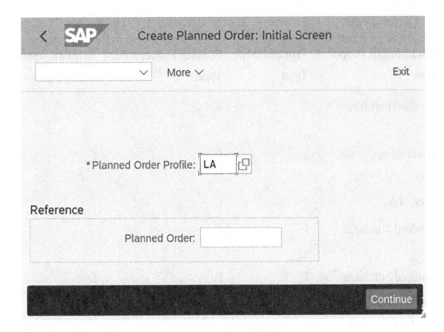

Figure 6-2. *Creating a planned order: initial screen*

A planned order profile uses a unique key that contains several parameters, as shown in Table 6-1:

- Order type (planned order type)

- Procurement type (i.e., in-house procurement or external procurement)

- Special procurement type

- Account assignment category

Table 6-1. *Order Types*

Profile	Procurement Proposal Type	Procurement Type	Special Procurement Type	Account Assignment Category
KB	Standard purchase order	F	K	
KD	Individual customer order	E	E	E
LA	Stock order	E	E	
LB	Standard purchase order	F	L	
LBE	Standard purchase order	F	L	E
NB	Standard purchase order	F		
NBE	Standard purchase order	F		E
PR	Project order	E	E	Q
UL	Standard purchase order	F	U	

The planned order profile called LA Stock Order is used to create standard PP planned orders that are eventually converted to production orders or process orders.

The Planned Order header consists of the planned order number, special procurement type, material number, and so on, as shown in Figure 6-3.

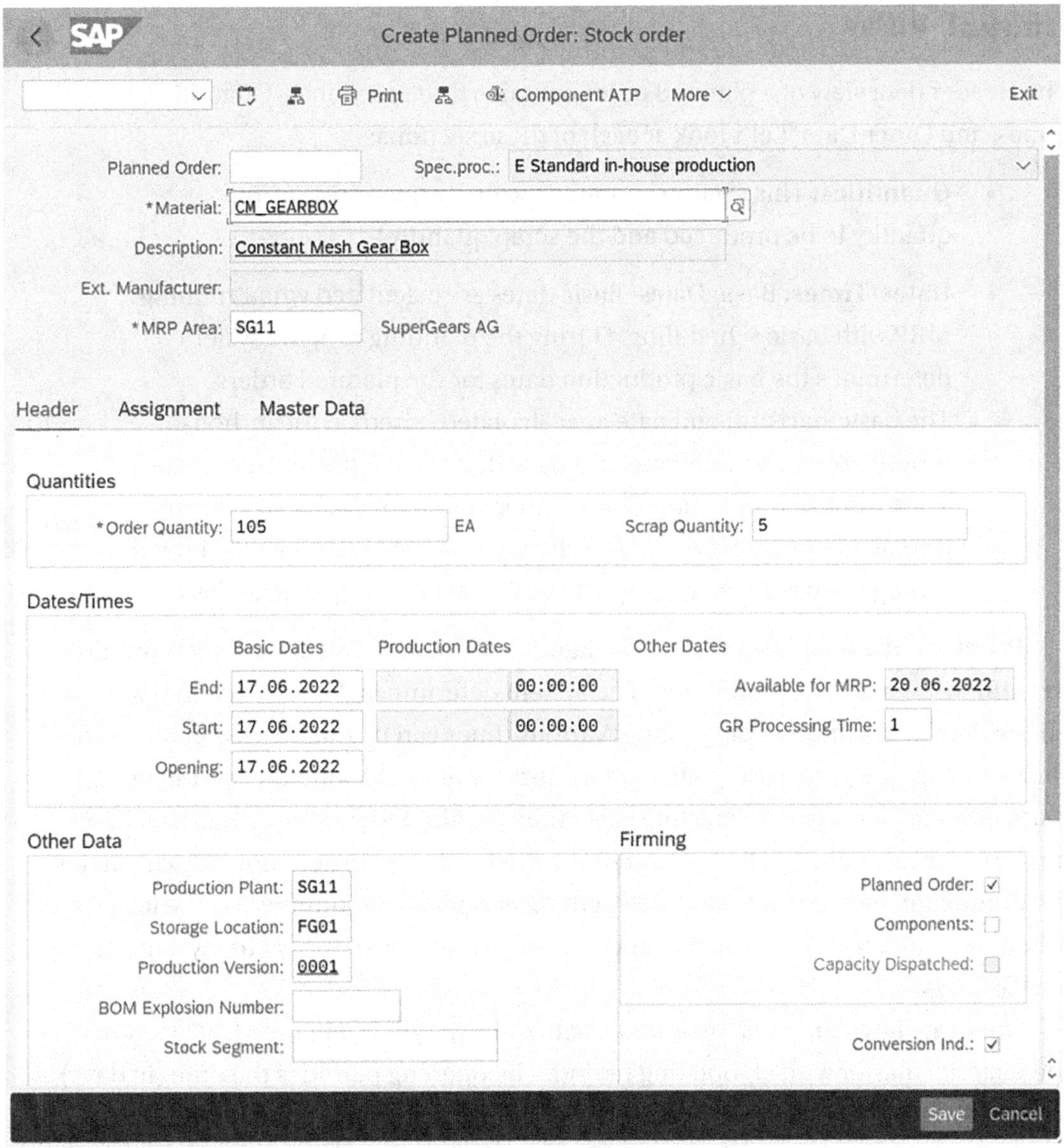

Figure 6-3. *Creating a planned order*

The planned order contains three views—Header, Assignment, and Master Data—each of which contains specific information.

Header View

The Header data view of a planned order contains three sections—Quantities, Dates/Times, and Other Data. Let's look at each of these sections:

- **Quantities:** This section contains the order quantity (i.e., the quantity to be produced and the scrap quantity).

- **Dates/Times:** Basic Dates: Basic dates are calculated when running MRP with basic scheduling. During the planning run, the system determines the basic production dates for the planned orders. The basic start and end date are calculated based on the in-house production time maintained in the MRP2 view of the material master. The in-house production time is independent of the lot size during the calculation of basic dates. Schedule margin key is not considered during the basic scheduling. The basic dates are accurate to days.

Production dates: The production dates and times are calculated when running the MRP with lead time scheduling. The system determines the production dates based on the time maintained in the routing. Various times can be maintained in the routing, such as setup time, processing time, queue time, interoperation time, and so on. All these times are used to calculate the exact time required to produce a material based on the order lot quantity. During lead time scheduling, the system not only calculates the production date and time but also generates capacity requirements. The lead time scheduling calculates the exact production dates and time to the accuracy of minutes and seconds.

Opening date: You must maintain a Schedule Margin key in the MRP2 view of the material master with an opening period. The opening period is the time (in days) to provide the MRP controller with some buffer time to convert planned orders to production orders. The opening date indicates when the planned orders should be converted to production orders.

Available for MRP: This is the date when the material will be available in the warehouse. This is calculated by adding the Goods Receipt processing time to the order finish date.

GR processing time: This is the time needed for inspection and placing the materials in the warehouse once the production is finished.

Other Data

Production plant: The plant where the material is being produced.

Storage location: Where the material produced is stored once the production is finished.

Production version: Let's say there are multiple production versions that can produce the material. You must specify the production version in the planned order.

Firming

Planned Order: If this indicator is active, it means the planned order is firmed. A firmed planned order cannot be changed during the MRP run. The firmed indicator is activated for the planned order when creating the planned order manually or when changing a planned order created by the MRP run.

Components: If this indicator is active, it means the components are firmed and cannot be changed during the next planning run. The firming indicator for a planned order must be activated before activating the firming for components.

Capacity dispatched: This indicator suggests that the capacity requirements for the order have been generated and the capacity has been reserved at the work center for the order to be executed as per scheduled date and time.

Conversion indictor: This indicator determines whether a planned order can further be converted to a production order or a process order or purchase requisition. Planned orders for repetitive manufacturing are created with the PE Run-Schedule Quantity order type, which cannot be converted to production or process orders.

Assignment View

The Assignment view contains two sections—Responsibility and Account Assignment—as shown in Figure 6-4.

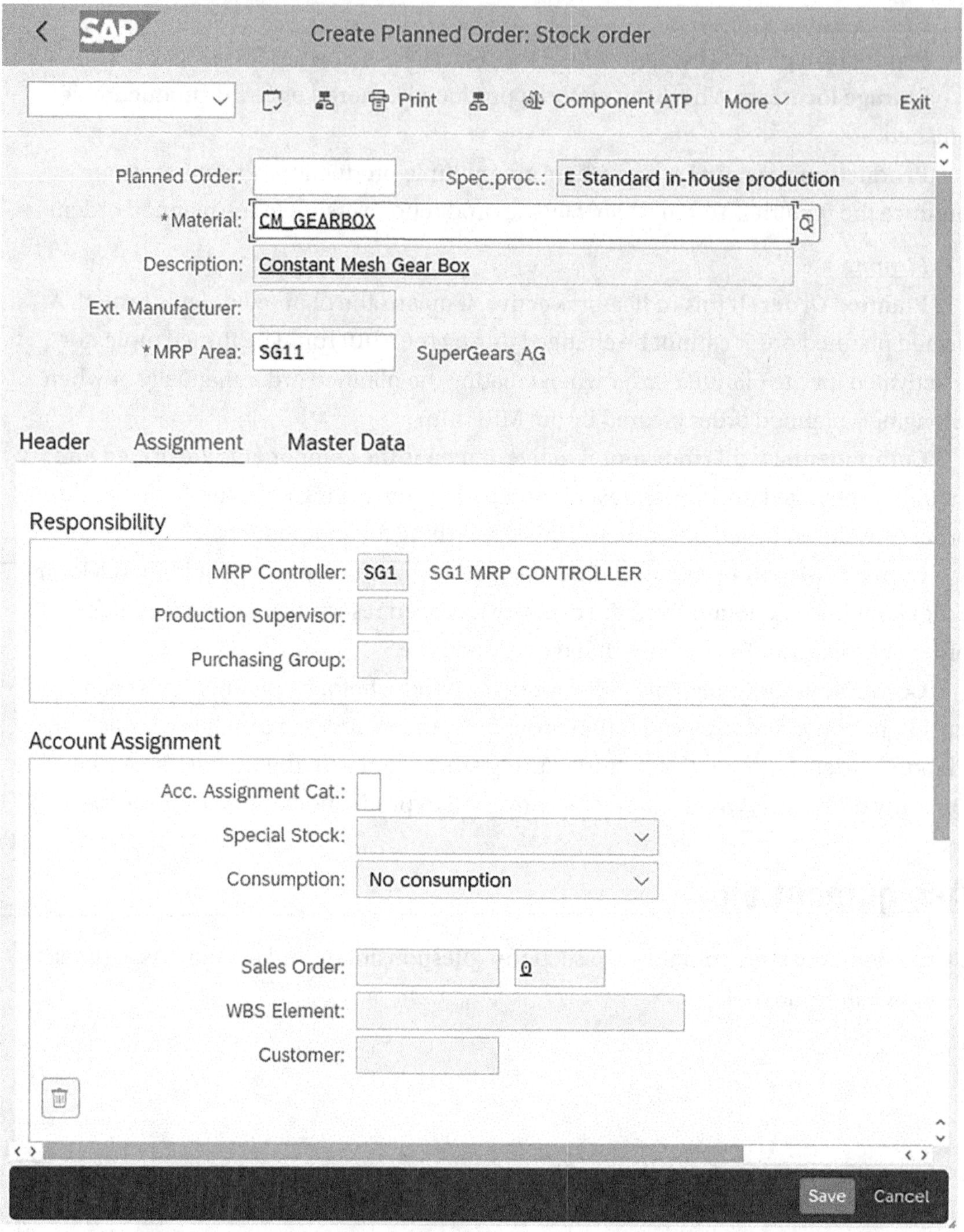

Figure 6-4. *Planned order: assignment view*

- **Responsibility:** The MRP controller, production supervisor, and purchasing group are populated from the material master to specify the responsible person/group of persons in each area.

- **Account Assignment:** Account Assignment category: This field determines the cost object, such as a cost center, order, and so on, where the cost of production should be posted.

Special stock: This field specifies the special stock type for the material—for example, consignment stock.

Consumption: This field specifies if the consumption is to be posted to a consumption account (V) or an asset account (A).

Sales order: In a make-to-order environment, the planned order is generated with reference to a sales order to establish a 1:1 relationship. The reference sales order is populated in the planned order.

WBS element: If you're working in an engineer-to-order environment and the planned orders are generated with reference to a WBS (Work Breakdown Structure) element.

Master Data View

The master data view contains two sections—material master and bill of material. The material master section displays a field from the material master—MRP views and the bill of material (BOM) sections. The BOM is exploded based on the production version in the planned order, as shown in Figure 6-5.

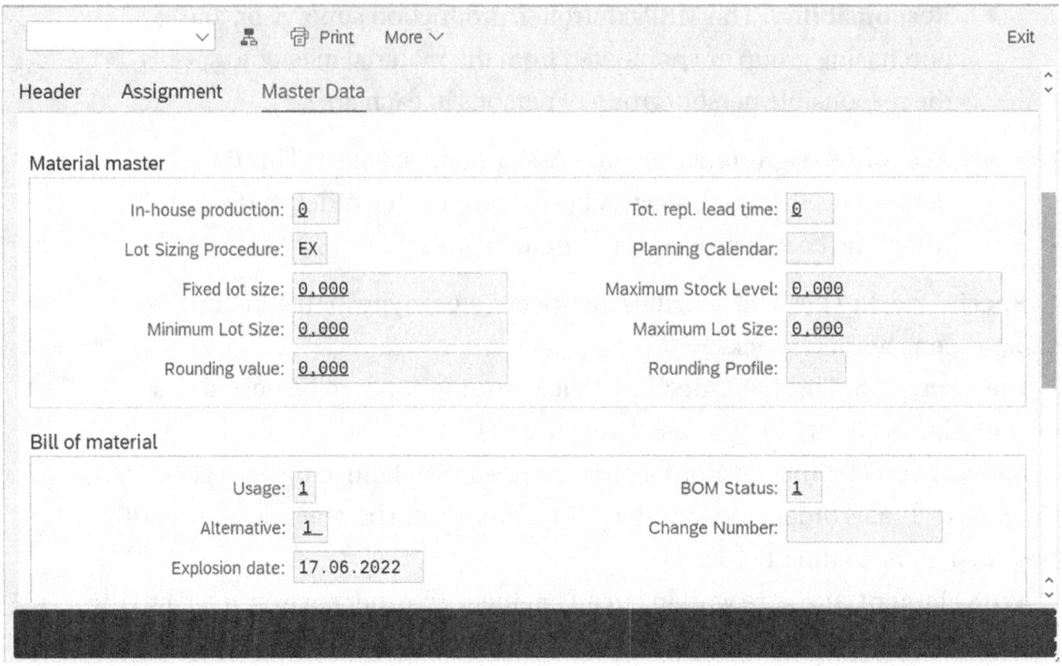

Figure 6-5. *Planned order: master data*

Several functions can be executed on the planned order on the menu bar. The planned order can be deleted by clicking the Delete button.

Schedule Planned Order

If you had run basic scheduling during the MRP run, you can schedule the order by clicking the Schedule Planned Order button. The system will calculate the production date and time based on the routing. The scheduling is the same as the scheduling carried out by lead time scheduling during the MRP run. If the order has been scheduled earlier manually or using the lead time scheduling during the planning run, you can reschedule the planned order manually to calculate the latest production dates.

Component overview: You can display all the components and their needed quantities by clicking the Components Overview button, as shown in Figure 6-6.

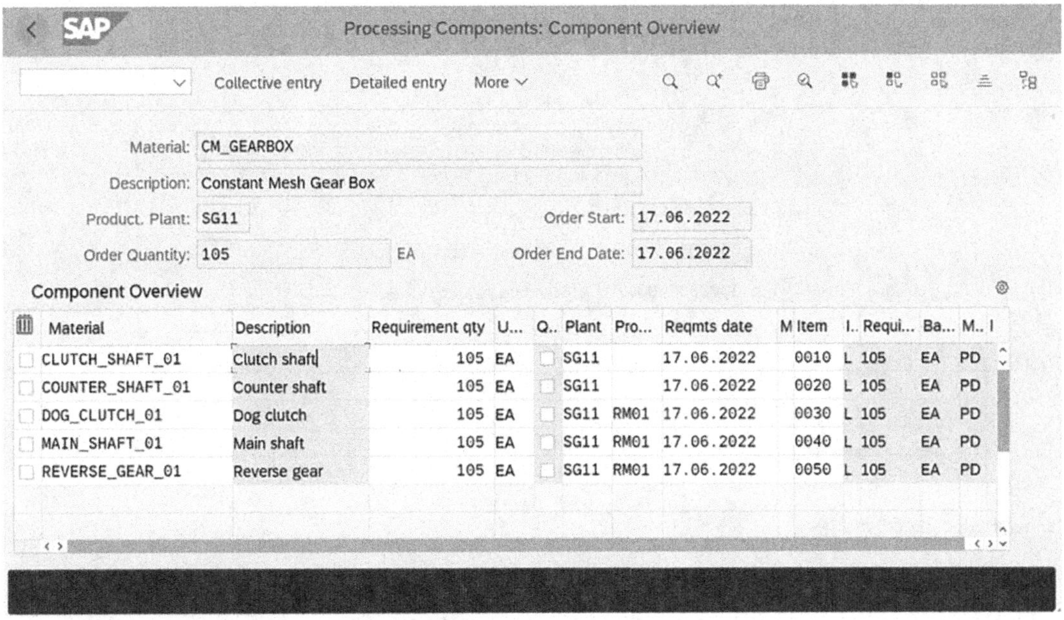

Figure 6-6. *Components overview*

Material Availability Check

You can execute a component availability check to determine if the components are available in the required quantity on the required date. If the component isn't available in the required quantity, the material is flagged with the Missing Part indicator.

The MRP controller can also run a collective availability check by choosing Logistics ➤ Production ➤ MRP ➤ Planned Order ➤ Collective Availability Check. You can also use Transaction Code MDVP.

Enter the selection parameters on the selection screen. For example, the production plant and the MRP controller (see Figure 6-7).

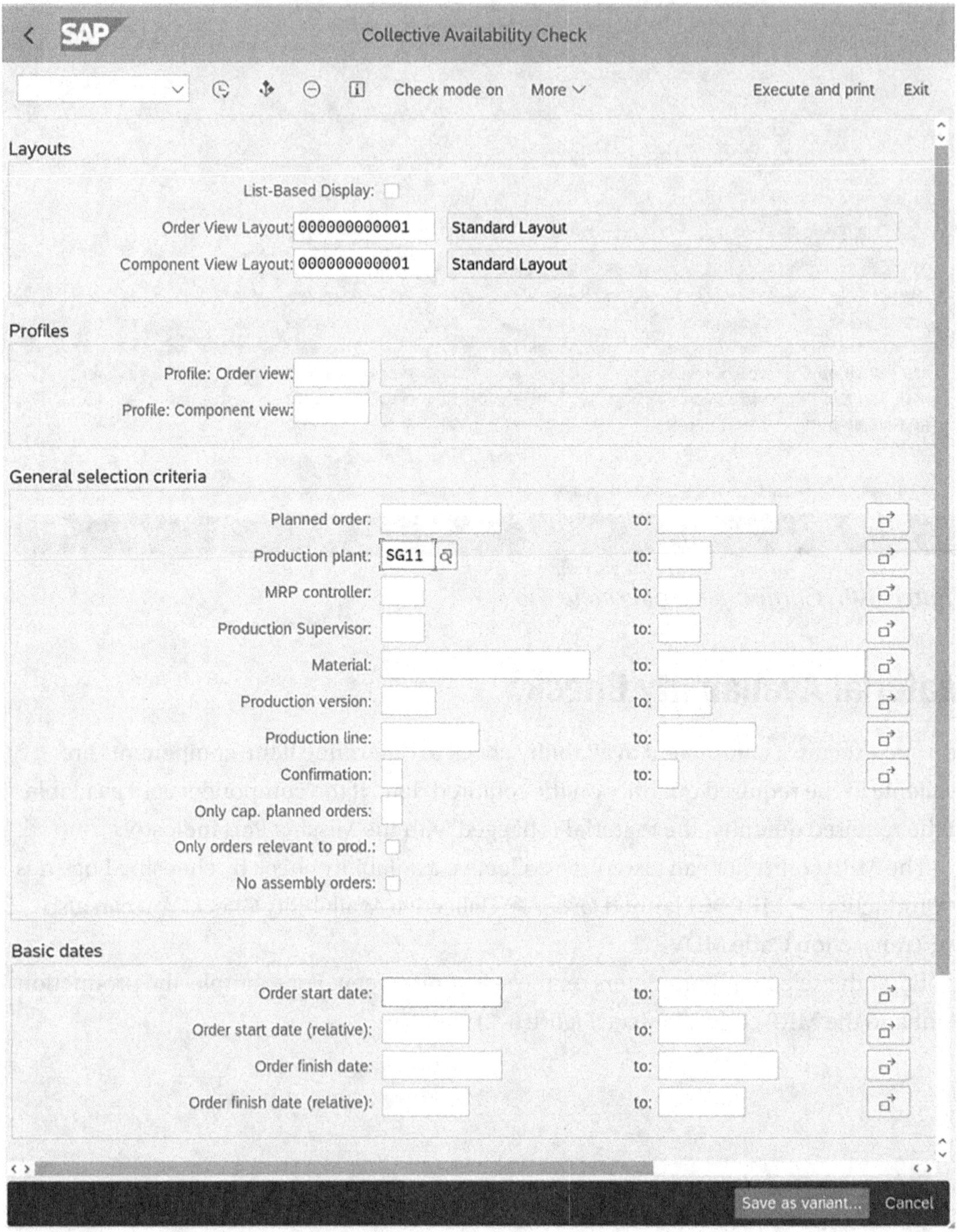

Figure 6-7. *Collective availability check*

Based on the selection parameters, a list of planned orders is displayed, as shown in Figure 6-8.

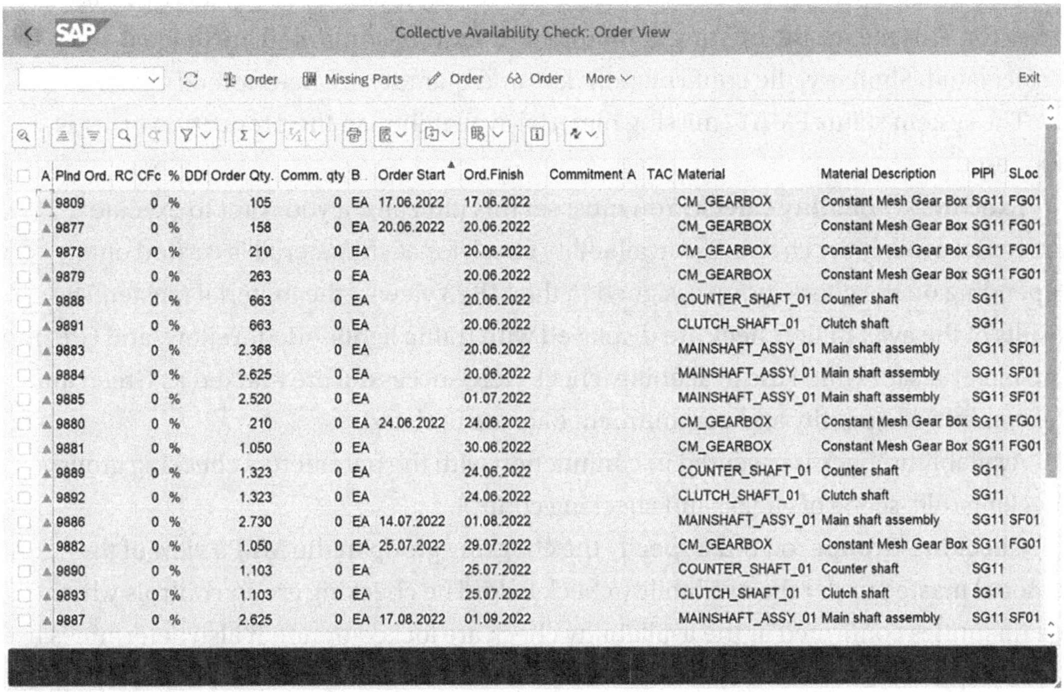

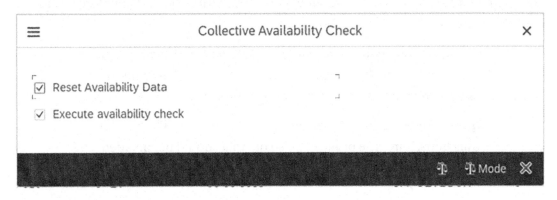

Figure 6-8. *Collective availability: order view*

You can select a few orders manually or click the Select All button to select all the planned orders from the list. Click the Order button to execute the material availability check for the selected orders. A popup window appears, where you must select the Reset Availability Data and Execute Availability Check options, as shown in Figure 6-9.

☰	Collective Availability Check	✕

☑ Reset Availability Data

☑ Execute availability check

Figure 6-9. *Collective availability check*

You can select the indicators to control how the availability check is executed.

Reset Availability Data: If you want to run the material availability check on orders for which the availability check has been executed previously, you may activate this indicator. This means the existing components that were confirmed are deleted and recalculated. Similarly, the confirmation date and quantity are determined again.

The system status FMAT (missing material availability) in the production order is also reset.

Execute Availability Check: You must set this indicator if you want to execute a material availability check. The availability check for each material is carried out depending on the check group assigned in the MRP3 view of the material master. The results of the availability check are displayed with traffic lights—Red, Yellow, and Green. The materials for which the availability check were successful are marked as Green and the committed quantity and commitment date are updated.

Availability check is executed in conjunction with the parameters checking group, checking rule, scope of check, and checking control.

Checking Group: You must specify the checking group in the MRP3 view of the material master, under the availability check field. The checking group controls whether the quantities confirmed in the availability check are locked or not. It also determines if the ATP quantity are added up.

Checking Rule: You can define a checking rule in customization for various application areas like sales and distribution, MRP, production order, inventory management, and so on.

Scope of Check: The scope of check is used to determine the stocks and demand and supply elements that should be considered during the availability check. A scope of check is defined for a unique combination of checking group and checking rule. You can also control if the replenishment lead time is checked during the availability check, as shown in Figure 6-10.

- **Stocks:** You can define which stocks should be considered during the availability check. For example, safety stock, stock in transfer, and quality inspection stocks are included in the scope of check.

- **Supply elements:** You can select the supply elements like purchase requisitions, purchase orders, and so on, that should be included during the availability check.

- **Demand elements:** You can select the demand elements like sales orders, reservations, dependent requirements, and so on, that should be included during the availability check.

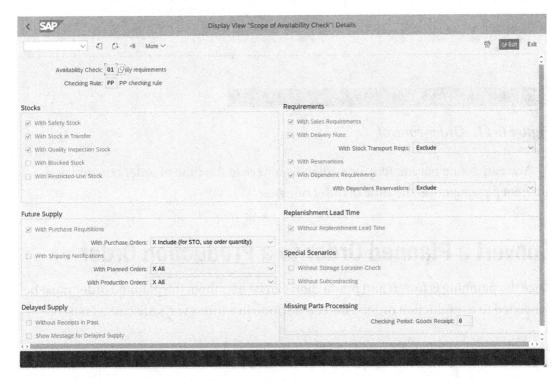

Figure 6-10. *Scope of availability check*

Checking Control: Using a checking control, you can control if the availability check should be carried out while creating or releasing an order, as shown in Figure 6-11. Using the checking control, you can define which checking rule should be used and how material shortage affects order creation/release.

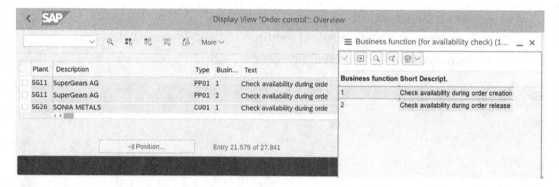

Figure 6-11. *Order control*

You can define parameters for availability check at the time of order creation and different parameters at the time of order release.

Convert a Planned Order to a Production Order

Once the planning is frozen and production can be executed, the planned order must be converted to a production order. This can be done in various ways, discussed next.

Convert in Stock Requirement List

You can convert a planned order to production from the stock requirement list. Double-click the planned order and then click the ➤ Prod. Ord. button, as shown in Figure 6-12, to convert a planned order to a production order.

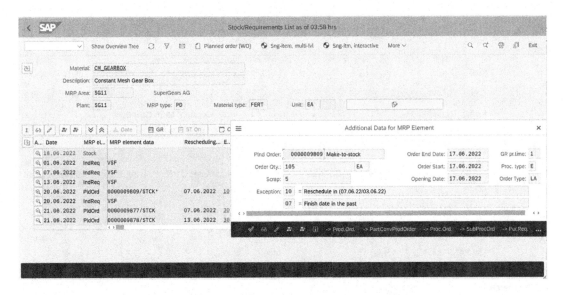

Figure 6-12. *Convert a planned order to a production order*

This function will convert a planned order into a production order. All the details—like material, quantity, production dates, and so on—are automatically copied from the planned order to the production order (see Figure 6-13).

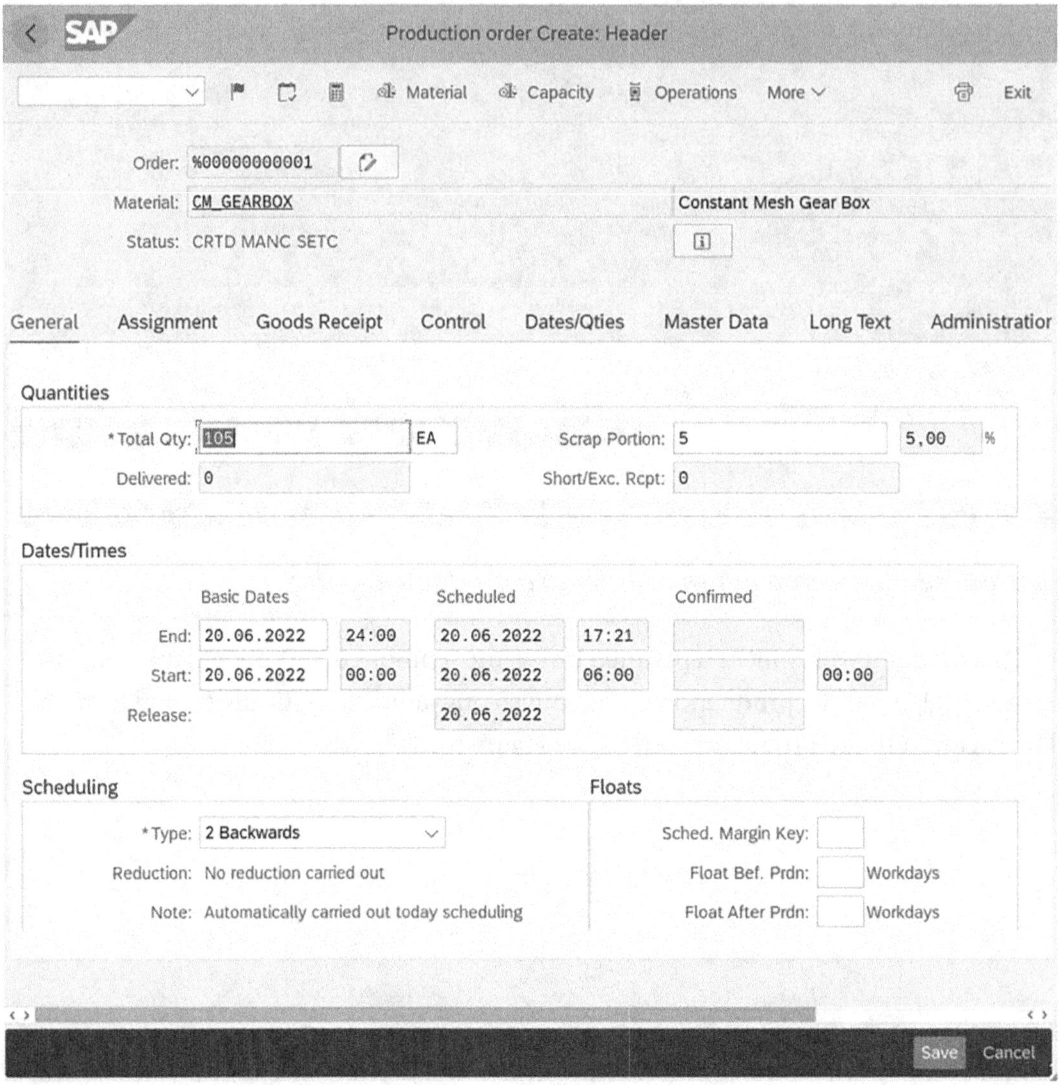

Figure 6-13. *Creating a production order: general*

In the assignments view, the planned order number is stored to establish a 1:1 relation with the production order, as shown in Figure 6-14. However, it must be noted that the moment a planned order is converted, it is permanently deleted from the system. This means the planned order cannot be displayed using the Transaction Codes MD04, MD12, and MD13 or in the planned order PLAF table.

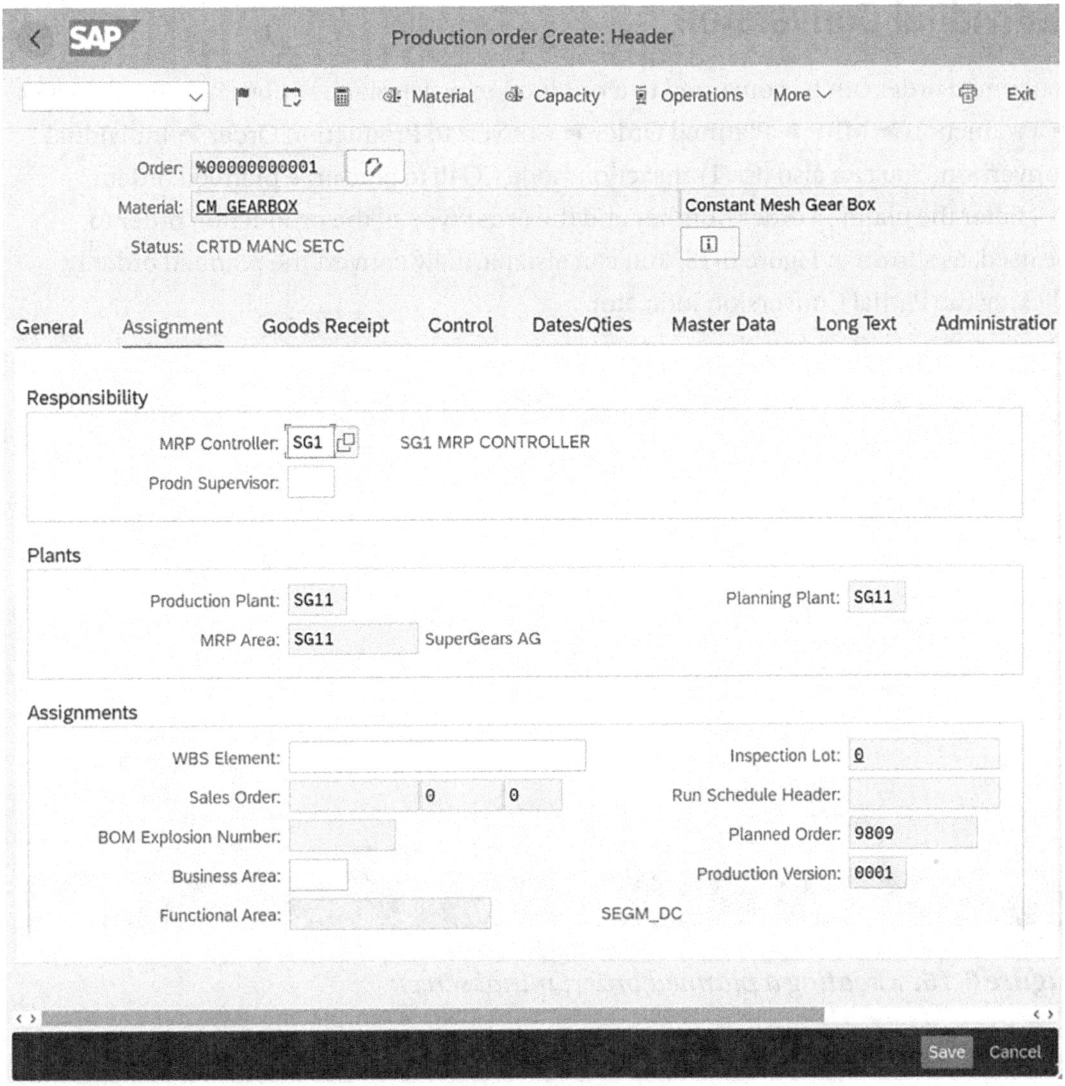

Figure 6-14. *Creating a production order: assignment*

Click the Save button to save the production order; the system will generate a production order number.

Individual Conversion

A planned order can be converted to a production order manually by choosing Logistics ➤ Production ➤ MRP ➤ Planned Order ➤ Convert to Production Order ➤ Individual conversion. You can also use Transaction Code CO40 to convert a planned order.

Enter the planned order number and the order type of the production order to be used, as shown in Figure 6-15. You can also partially convert the planned order by clicking the Partial Conversion indicator.

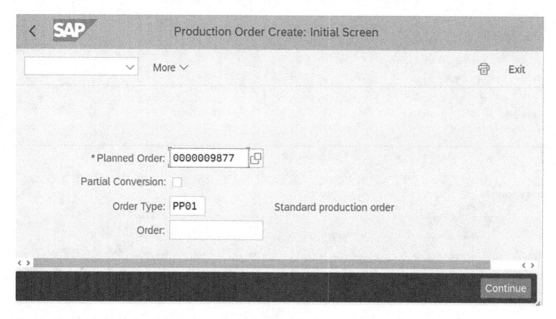

Figure 6-15. *Creating a planned order: initial screen*

Click the Continue button. The system will convert the planned order to a production order and generate a production order number when you save the order.

Collective Conversion

Planned orders can be converted to production orders collectively by choosing Logistics ➤ Production ➤ MRP ➤ Planned Order ➤ Convert to Production Order ➤ Collective conversion. You can also use Transaction Code CO41 for mass conversion.

You can select the parameters on the initial screen for which you would like to convert the planned orders—for example, the planning plant and MRP controller—as shown in Figure 6-16.

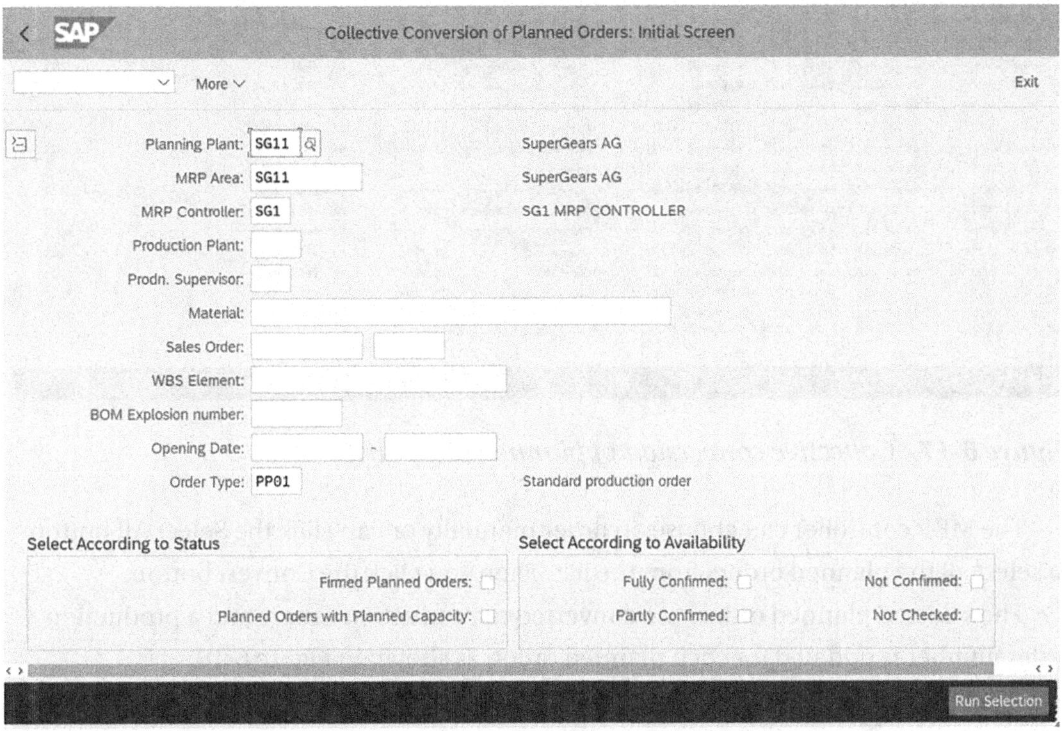

Figure 6-16. *Collective conversion of planned order: initial screen*

Based on the input parameters on the selection screen, the screen in Figure 6-17 is displayed. The output list shows a list of planned orders and other relevant information like material, material description, order quantity, order dates like start data, and end date, as shown in Figure 6-17. The first column shows the opening date, which can help the MRP controller decide whether to convert the planned order or not. The order type for the production order is also populated based on the plant's customization settings.

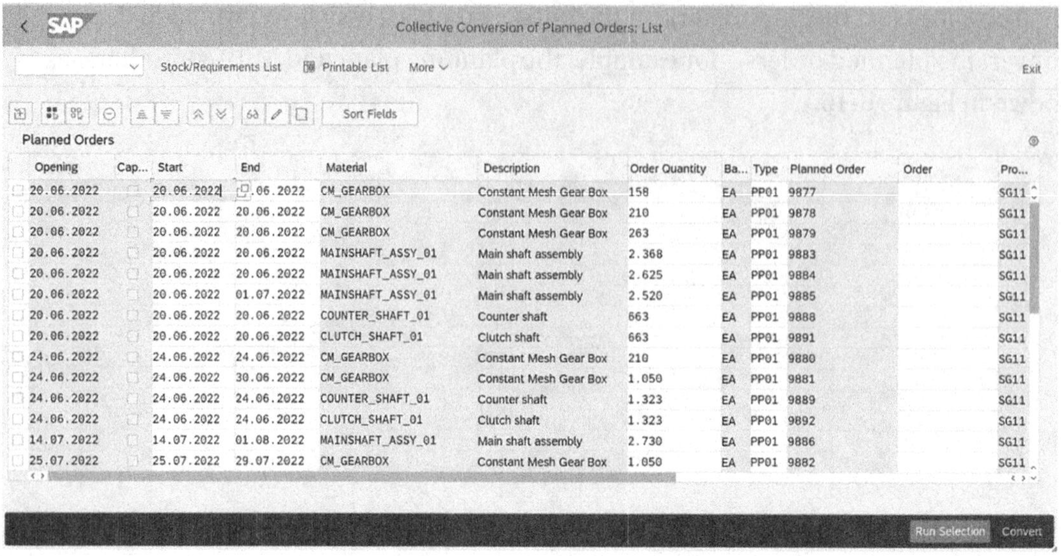

Figure 6-17. *Collective conversion of planned order: list*

The MRP controller can choose an order manually or can click the Select All button to select all the planned orders from the list. Then you click the Convert button.

The selected planned orders are converted to production orders and a production order number is updated for each planned order, as shown in Figure 6-18.

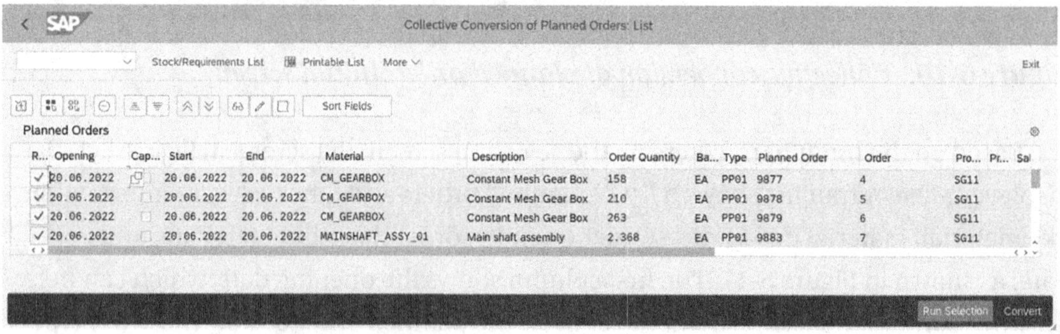

Figure 6-18. *Collective conversion of planned orders: list*

Summary

In this chapter, you learned about the planned order procurement element. The chapter discussed several details about planned orders. It also discussed different ways to convert planned orders to production orders.

Planned orders should be converted to production orders only after the planning process is finished. Once planned orders are generated, you must run:

- Material availability check

- Capacity requirement planning

The system provides the flexibility to run the capacity requirement planning for planned orders as well as production orders. It can be argued if capacity requirement planning should be run for planned orders or production orders. From my point of view, capacity planning should be run for planned orders.

You must identify material shortages using MRP and then dispatch your capacity requirements. Once the shortage situation is dealt with and the capacity is reserved for the planned order, you can convert the planned orders to production orders.

This chapter discussed the material availability check. The next chapter moves to the last step of production planning (Capacity Requirement Planning).

CHAPTER 7

Capacity Requirement Planning

Capacity planning is an integral part of the production planning process. It helps companies determine underload or overload situations for the work center and identify the bottlenecks. This chapter covers several tools available in SAP that can help—capacity evaluation and leveling.

What Is Capacity Requirement Planning?

Capacity requirement planning or simply capacity planning is performed after the MRP run. The purpose of capacity planning is to evaluate the capacity of the work centers in order to ensure that enough capacity is available so that the production can be carried out. It aims at optimizing work center capacity utilization.

> **Capacity Evaluation:** The capacity situation of a work center is assessed to see if all the orders can be produced based on the planned dates.

> **Capacity Leveling:** Distributes orders in a linear fashion based on the work center capacity. If there is a capacity overload, the order dates and quantities must be adjusted.

Before going into capacity evaluation and capacity leveling, you must understand how the total available capacity of a work center is calculated.

© Himanshu Goel 2022
H. Goel, *Handbook for SAP PP in S/4HANA*, https://doi.org/10.1007/978-1-4842-8566-4_7

Availability Capacity

Available capacity is maintained in the Capacity view of the work center. The available capacity of a work center is calculated based on the parameters maintained in the Available Capacity section:

- Operating time (start and end time)

- Duration of breaks

- Capacity utilization

- Number of individual capacities

The factory calendar can be assigned in the work center to determine the working days and thus calculate the capacity of a work center during a day/week. If the factory calendar is not assigned in the work center, then the system uses the factory calendar assigned for the plant. The capacity is valid for an infinite period.

If you want to define your capacity for a fixed period, you can maintain an interval of available capacity. For example, say you typically run three shifts from 6AM to 6AM the next day, with a total break of two hours and 15 minutes, as shown in Figure 7-1.

Figure 7-1. *Availability capacity in a work center*

However, due to reduced demands or maintenance activities, the management has decided to run only two shifts for the month of July 2022. You can define this by clicking the Intervals button. A new screen is displayed, as shown in Figure 7-2.

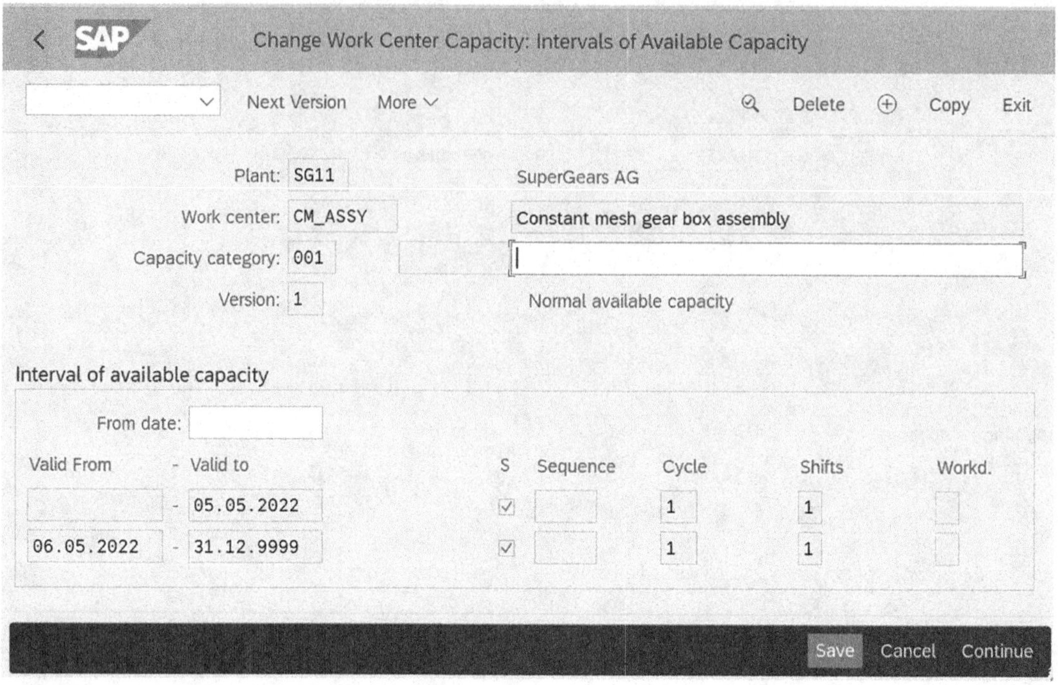

Figure 7-2. *Intervals of available capacity in a work center*

You must choose Edit ➤ Insert to add an interval. Enter valid From and To dates for the interval, as shown in Figure 7-3.

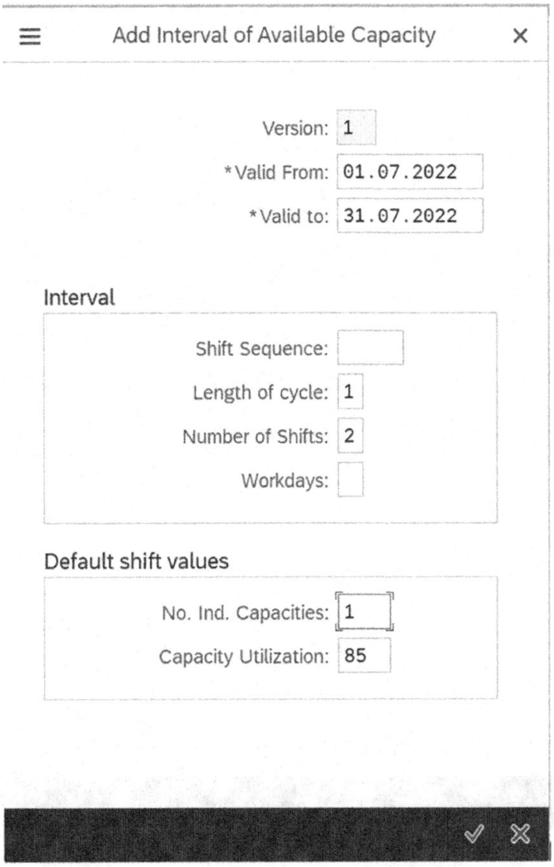

Figure 7-3. *Adding an interval of available capacity*

Now you must define the operating shifts for the month of July, as shown in Figure 7-4. As opposed to standard capacity, where the work center is operating 24 hours from 6AM to 6AM the next day, the work center would be operating for only two shifts— from 6AM to 10PM.

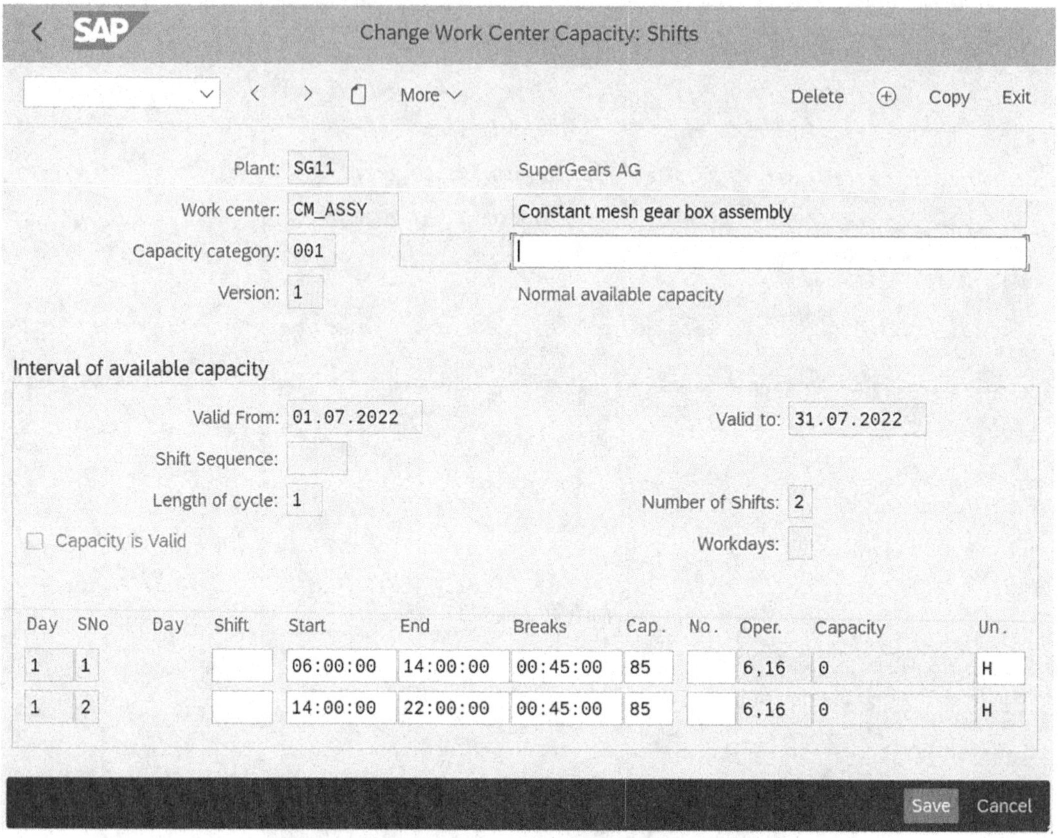

Figure 7-4. *Work center: shifts*

If you go back to the screen intervals of Available Capacity, you'll notice that a new capacity has been added for the month of July, as shown in Figure 7-5.

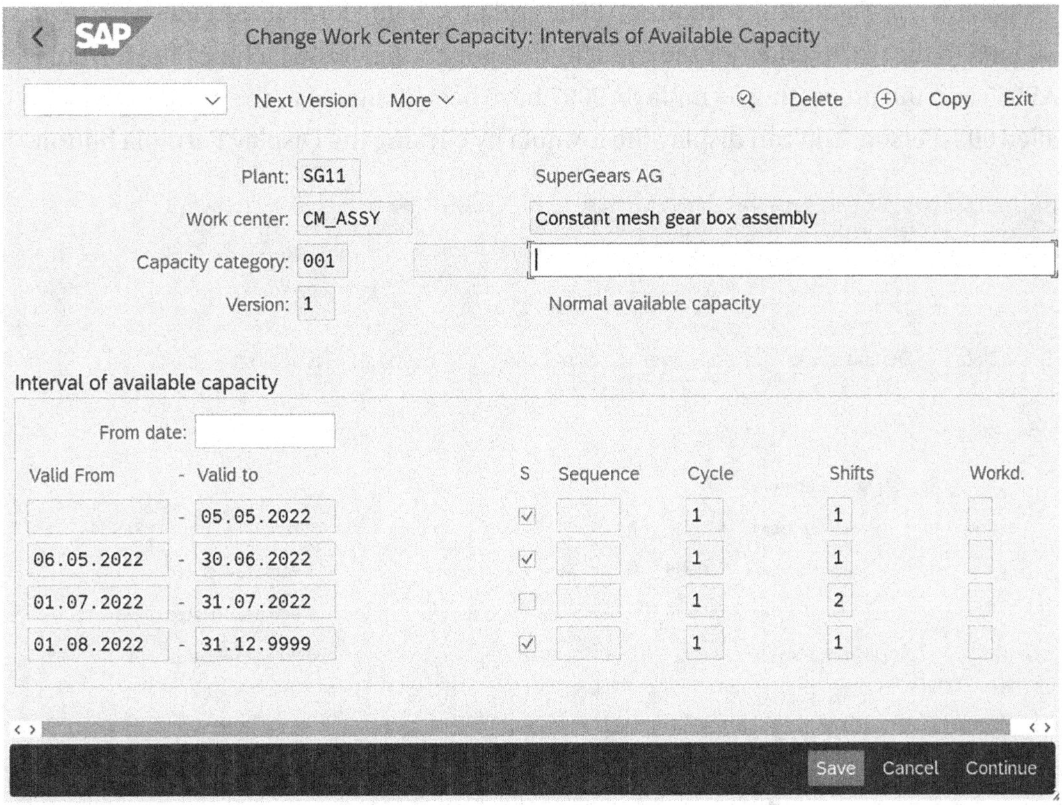

Figure 7-5. *Work center: intervals of available capacity*

You may also maintain the shifts of a work center. If shift is to be maintained, the shift definition and shift sequence can be maintained with a validity date.

Capacity Requirements

Capacity requirements are generated by various orders, including planned orders, production orders, process orders, and so on, which subsequently calculate the load on a work center.

The operation time required to produce a material is maintained in the routing/master recipe/rate routing. The operating time calculates the capacity requirement using the formulas assigned in the work center.

Calculating the capacity requirements to manufacture a material takes place when the order is scheduled and uses the formulas from the work center. Appropriate formulas must be assigned in the work center to calculate the capacity requirements for each operation.

As shown in Figure 7-6, formula SAP005 and processing formula SAP006 have been assigned to the work center for the capacity category called 001-Machine. The formula SAP005 and the processing formula SAP007 have been assigned to the capacity category called 002-Person. You can display the formula by clicking the Display Formula button.

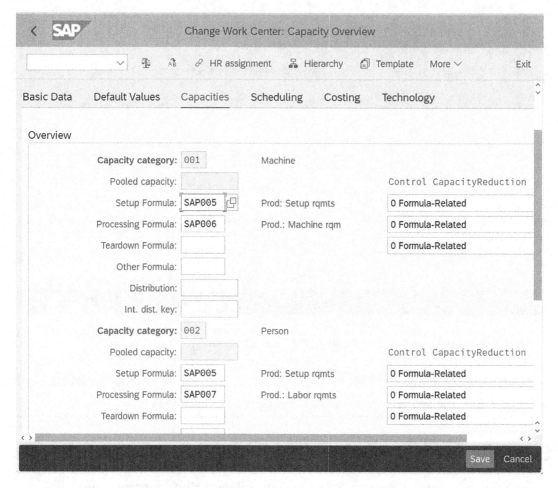

Figure 7-6. *Work center: capacity overview*

Let's look at the standard formulas provided by SAP:

- Setup: SAP005 = Setup * Operation quantity / Base quantity

- Machine: SAP006 = Machine * Operation quantity / Base quantity

- Labor: SAP007 = Labor * Operation quantity / Base quantity

Capacity Evaluation

The orders (planned orders, production orders, or process orders) generate load on the work center. Capacity evaluation analyzes the capacity loads on a work center. Several transactions are available to perform capacity evaluation.

Choose Logistics ➤ Production ➤ Capacity Planning ➤ Evaluation ➤ Work Center View. From this path, you can choose one of the following Transaction Codes to evaluate the capacity situation:

- CM01 - Load
- CM02 - Orders
- CM03 - Pool
- CM04 - Backlog
- CM05 – Overload

CM01 - Load

Go to Transaction Code CM01 to evaluate the capacity load on the work center. Select the General option under the Settings menu to display the default settings for capacity evaluation. You can specify the time in hours or minutes or you can edit the Int. Finish field to update the capacity evaluation horizon based on your requirements. The Int. Finish field is set to 60 days by default. The Periods section represents the evaluation period and is set to Week by default. You can select other time periods, such as Day, Factory Calendar Day, Month, and so on, based on your requirements, as shown in Figure 7-7.

Figure 7-7. *Capacity planning settings*

Enter the work center and plant into the initial screen and then click Standard Overview, as shown in Figure 7-8.

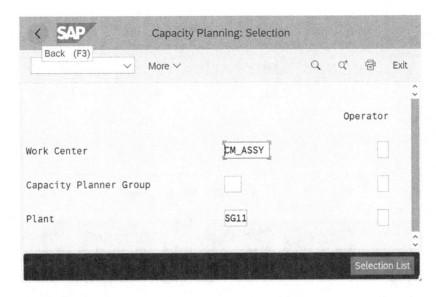

Figure 7-8. *Capacity planning selection*

Standard Overview

In the standard overview, the list displays the following information:

- Period (week or day, per the settings)
- Requirements: Displays the capacity requirements in the evaluation period
- Available capacity in the period
- Capacity load (as a percentage)
- Remaining available capacity in the period

In Figure 7-9, you can see that there is slight overload in weeks 25 and 26. The capacity load stands little above 100%. Whereas the work center is overloaded by 15% in week 27. The available capacity for week 27 is 92,44 hours, while the requirements expect a capacity of 106.33 hours. Similarly, the capacity required for week 26 is 94,50, while available capacity is 92,44 hours.

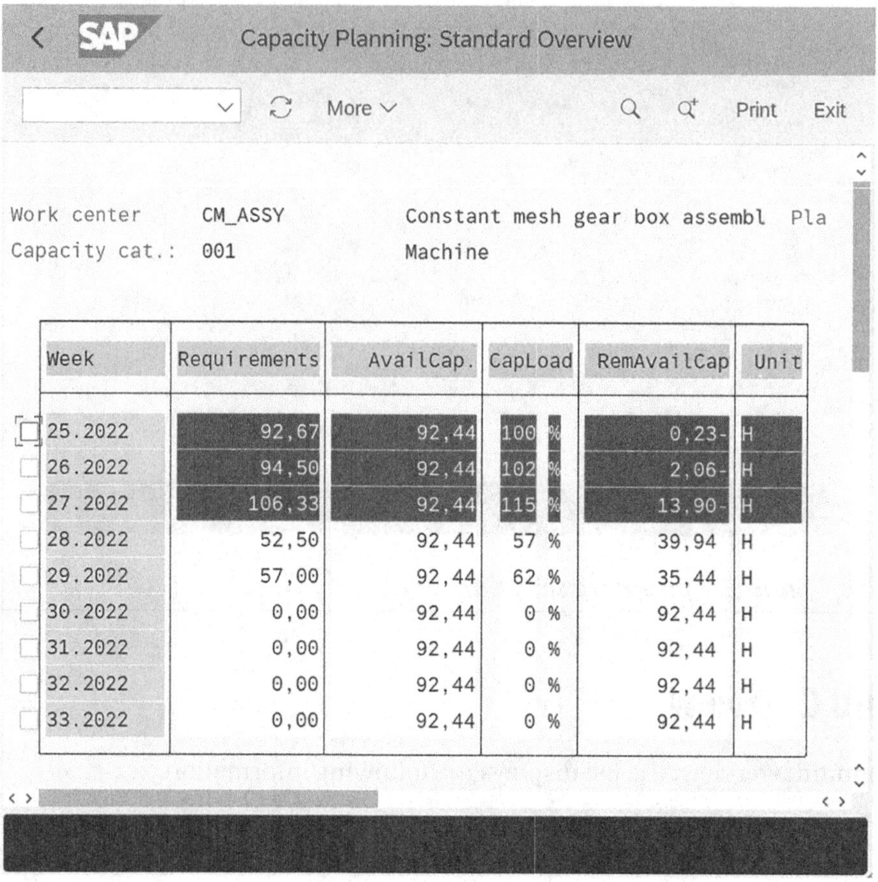

Figure 7-9. *Capacity planning standard overview*

You can select weeks 25, 26, and 27 and click the Capacity Details/Period icon. A list showing capacity requirements for the work center is arranged according to the pegged requirements and displayed per period. For every capacity, the following information is displayed (see Figure 7-10):

- Period

- Order capacity requirements per period

- Other data for the pegged requirements and the capacities

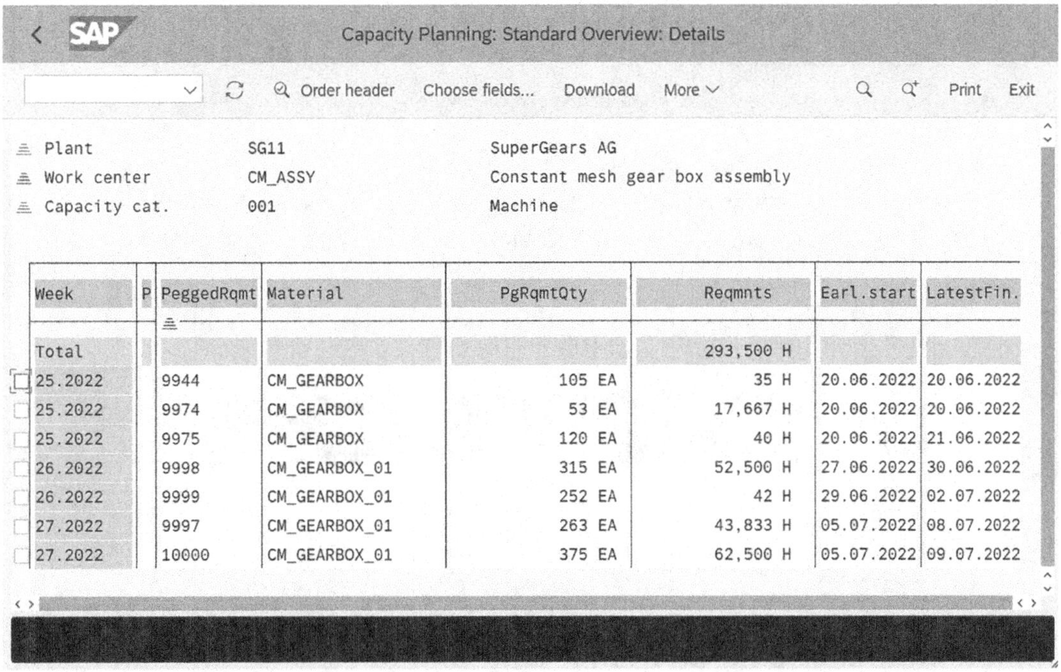

Figure 7-10. *Capacity planning: standard overview: details*

To resolve the overload situation, you may have to make some adjustments to the plan. For example, you can move the order 9997 of 263 EA to the next week. Otherwise, you may have to check if the same material can be produced on an alternate production line. If so, you may change the production version in the planned order. I moved planned order 9997 to the next week. The capacity load for week 27 is now 75%, which is shown in Figure 7-11.

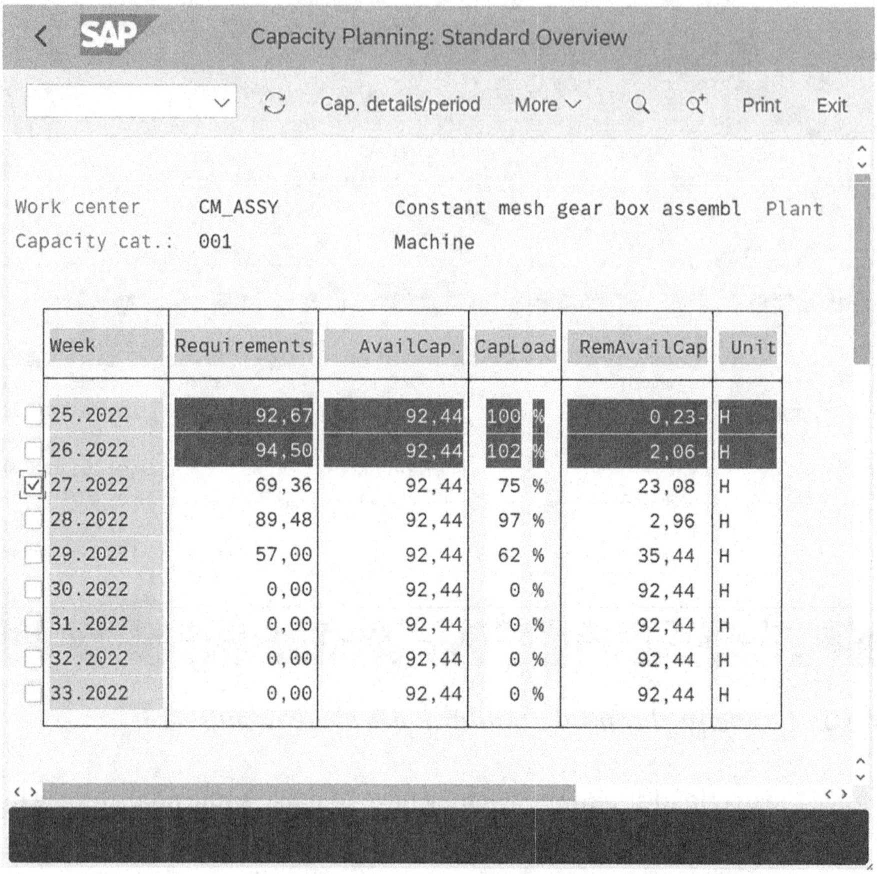

Week	Requirements	AvailCap.	CapLoad	RemAvailCap	Unit
25.2022	92,67	92,44	100 %	0,23-	H
26.2022	94,50	92,44	102 %	2,06-	H
27.2022	69,36	92,44	75 %	23,08	H
28.2022	89,48	92,44	97 %	2,96	H
29.2022	57,00	92,44	62 %	35,44	H
30.2022	0,00	92,44	0 %	92,44	H
31.2022	0,00	92,44	0 %	92,44	H
32.2022	0,00	92,44	0 %	92,44	H
33.2022	0,00	92,44	0 %	92,44	H

***Figure 7-11.** Capacity planning: standard overview*

Based on the capacity evaluation, the production schedule is adjusted as follows:

- Adjust date/quantity in planned independent requirements and rerun MPS or MRP.
- Adjust date/quantity in planned orders and rerun MPS or MRP.
- Adjust date/quantity in Production orders/process orders and rerun MPS or MRP.

CM04 - Evaluate Backlog

You can evaluate backlogs on the work center using Transaction Code CM04. Select the General option under the Settings menu to display the default settings for backlog display. As you can see in Figure 7-12, the evaluation horizon is defined for two days, starting 20.06.2022 and ending 26.06.2022, and the evaluation period is selected as Day.

Figure 7-12. *Capacity planning settings*

Now click Standard Overview to display the backlogs, as shown in Figure 7-13.

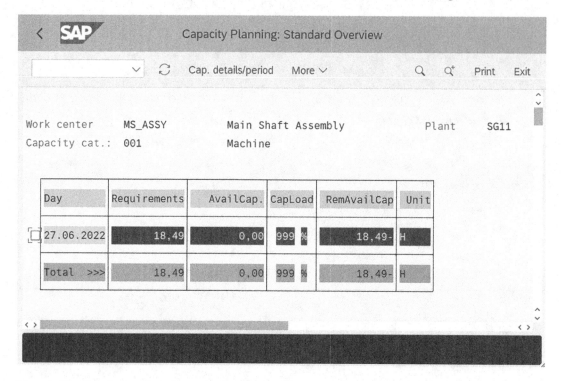

Figure 7-13. *Capacity planning: standard overview*

Figure 7-13 shows a backlog on 27.06.2022. Select the 27.06.2022 and then click Cap. Details/Period. The capacity details display the orders that are in backlog, as shown in Figure 7-14. You must reschedule these orders to be produced on a new date.

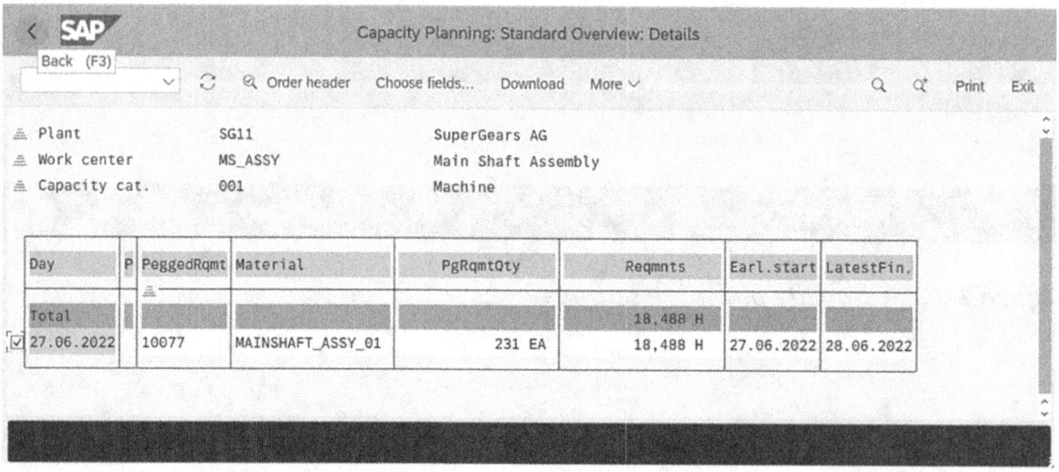

Figure 7-14. *Capacity planning: standard overview: details*

CM05 - Evaluate Overload

You can use Transaction Code CM05 if you are only interested in viewing the overload situation on a work center. Figure 7-15 shows that there is an overload in weeks 26 and 29.

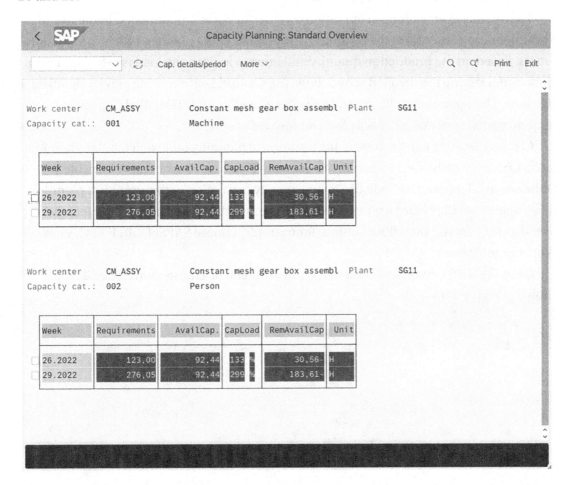

Figure 7-15. *Capacity planning: standard overview*

> **Note**   Several Transaction Codes are available for capacity evaluation. However, I personally prefer CM01, since you can view capacity situation on the work center for several weeks. If there is a capacity overload in a week, you can check the load in other weeks and adjust the production plan to mitigate the overload situation.

Capacity Leveling

Capacity leveling enables detailed planning of capacity requirements. The operations/orders are dispatched to individual capacities to specific points in time and in the sequence in which they are to be processed.

The operating time for each operation on a work center is maintained in the routing. These operating times from the routing are populated in the planned orders/production orders. Based on the production quantity and operation time, the load is calculated on a work center during the detailed scheduling. The Control key in routing plays a significant role here. The operations with control keys Det. Cap. Reqmnts (Detailed Capacity Requirements) generate a capacity load on the work center.

Capacity leveling can be done using a graphical planning table or a tabular planning table. Choose Logistics ➤ Production ➤ Capacity Planning ➤ Leveling ➤ Variable ➤ Online or use Transaction Code CM25 for capacity evaluation with a graphical planning table. Many overall profiles are provided in the standard SAP, and you must select the overall profile for the shop floor control; for example, choose SAPSFCG011: SFC: View Work Center/capacity (3 graf.)

Enter the work center and plant in the initial screen of Transaction Code CM25, as shown in Figure 7-16.

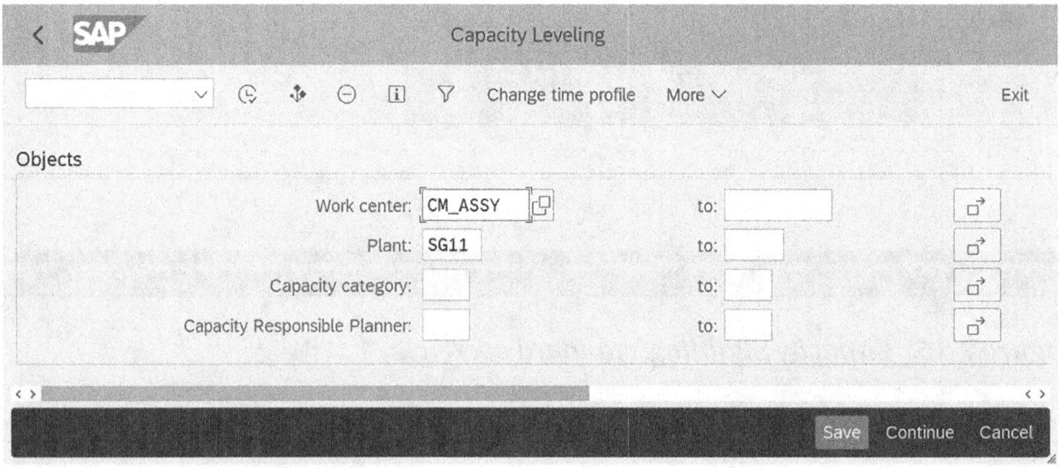

Figure 7-16. *Capacity leveling*

Time Profile: You can select the planning horizon for which you want to run the capacity requirements planning. Click the Change Time Profile icon and the screen in Figure 7-17 will pop up. Based on the current settings for the time profile SAP___Z002, the CM25 planning table has an evaluation and planning period that's three days in the past and 100 days in the future.

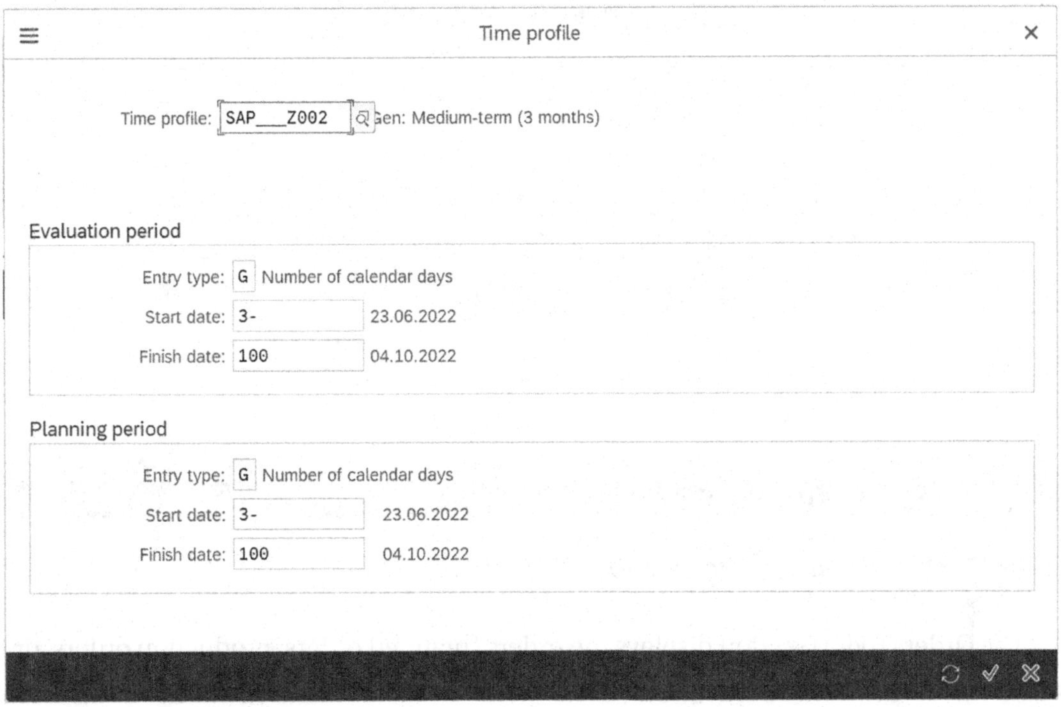

≡	Time profile	✕

Time profile: | SAP___Z002 | 🔍 Gen: Medium-term (3 months)

Evaluation period

Entry type:	G	Number of calendar days
Start date:	3-	23.06.2022
Finish date:	100	04.10.2022

Planning period

Entry type:	G	Number of calendar days
Start date:	3-	23.06.2022
Finish date:	100	04.10.2022

Figure 7-17. Time profile

In Figure 7-18, you can see that the planning table is split into three sections—work centers, orders (dispatched), and orders (pool).

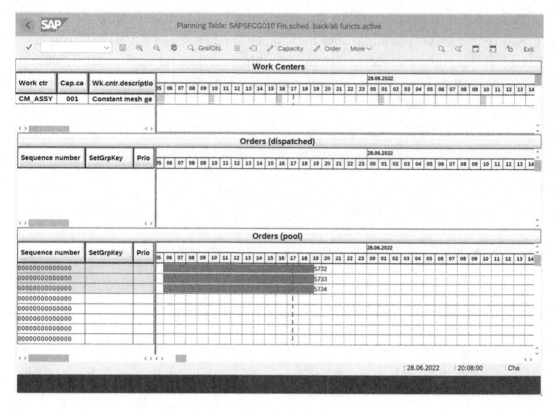

Figure 7-18. *Planning table for capacity evaluation*

The Orders (pool) section displays the orders (planned orders, production orders, or process orders). The orders displayed in this section are yet to be dispatched. As shown in Figure 7-18, several orders are scheduled to run at the same time. It is not feasible to produce multiple orders at a time from the same work center.

Therefore, it is imperative to dispatch the order/operations on the work center. Click the icon to dispatch the orders. As shown in Figure 7-19, the orders are dispatched. Now the order/operation is scheduled in such a way that only one order/operation is loaded in a work center at a time.

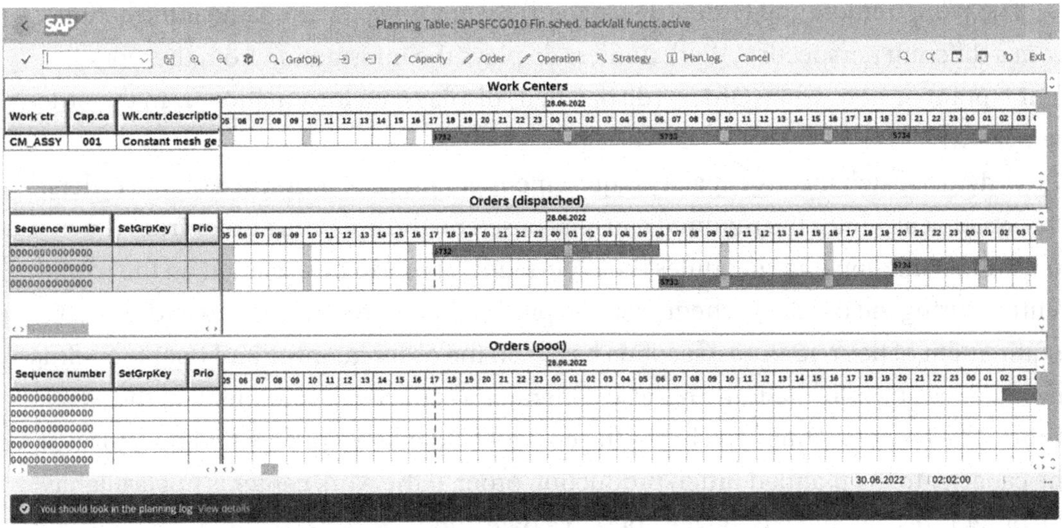

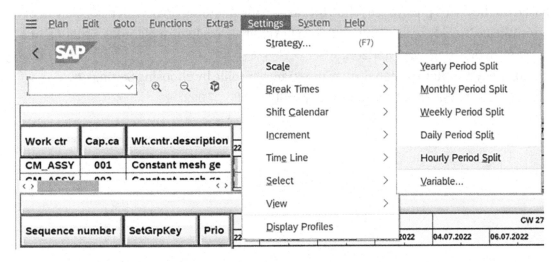

Figure 7-19. *Planning table for capacity evaluation*

Figure 7-20. *Planning table for capacity evaluation: time scale*

The Order (dispatched) section displays all the orders and the timeline on which they are supposed to be produced.

The Work Centers section displays the timeline and all the orders that are planned to be produced.

The Work Centers and Order (dispatched) sections display the same information from a different perspective. Work Centers displays the information from the work center point of view, while Orders (dispatched) displays the information from the order's perspective.

Order Dispatch means capacity requirement planning is performed on the orders. The system calculates the required capacity based on the operating times from the routing information and schedules the orders/operations to be executed on the work center. During the detailed scheduling, the production time is calculated to the exact requirement of hour/minutes/seconds based on the order quantity and operation time from the routing information. This also generates a capacity requirement on the work center. The Dispatch function checks the current load of the work center and allocates the capacity to the planned order/production order. If the work center is not available, the order is rescheduled to the next possible date/time.

Click Settings in the menu bar, and then click Scale.

Time Scales: CM25 offers the option of changing the scale on the planning table based on the user's preference. The Time axis of the planning board can be displayed in hourly/daily/weekly scales. This gives you flexibility to evaluate a planning situation in a short-term or a long-term horizon.

Strategy Profile: You can display the strategy profile by choosing Settings ➤ Strategy. Figure 7-21 displays the strategy profile SAP___T002.

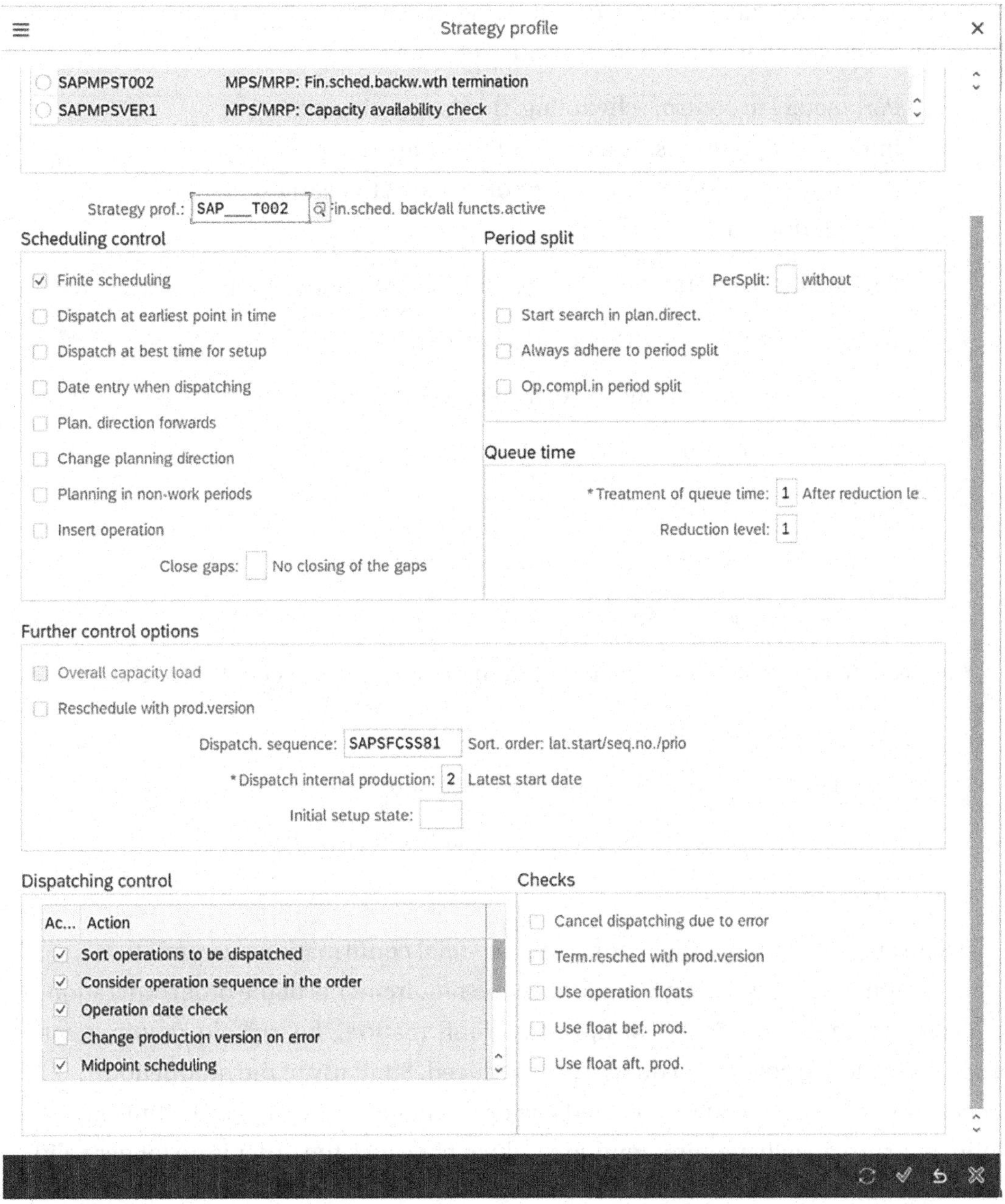

Figure 7-21. *Planning table for capacity evaluation: strategy profile*

You can use the strategy profile to control the dispatching of operations. It gives you flexibility to select various parameters, including:

- Parameters to control scheduling, that is, the dispatching of individual operations. You can control Finite Scheduling and Planning Direction parameters or dispatch at the earliest point in time, and so on.

- Parameters to control data, like period split and queue time.

- Parameters to control dispatching, such as:

    - Sorting of operations to be dispatched

    - Consider operation sequence in the order

    - Operation date check

    - Change production version in event of an error

    - Midpoint scheduling

Capacity Reduction: The capacity requirements on the work center are reduced by

- Order confirmations

- Changing the order status to Technically Complete

- Locking an order (changing the order status to Locked)

- Deletion flag

There are two types of order confirmation—final confirmation and partial confirmation. During final confirmation, all the requirements of the order/operation are reduced from the work center. During partial confirmation, the capacity requirements proportional to the confirmed quantity are reduced. Similarly, if the production/process order is set up with the Deleted flag or the status is assigned to Technically Complete, the capacity requirements are reduced because the order is no longer valid for production.

Summary

This chapter discussed capacity planning, which is the last step in the production planning process. You learned how the available capacity for a work center is calculated. You also learned about several tools that can be used for capacity planning and capacity evaluation.

The next chapters discuss the production execution methodologies. The next chapter specifically covers discrete manufacturing and production order-based production.

CHAPTER 8

Discrete Manufacturing

This chapter covers production order management, which is primarily used in discrete manufacturing. You'll learn about the entire production execution cycle and how each step is executed in SAP. You'll also learn how other processes, such as Rework, Scrap, Joint Production, and more, are handled in production order-based manufacturing.

What Is Discrete Manufacturing?

Discrete manufacturing is a production methodology used to produce materials or assemblies that can be disassembled, completely or partially, into the original state of their components. In discrete manufacturing, the products are produced in low volumes with high complexity or high volumes with low complexity. The methodology uses complex, multi-level BOMs and products change frequently from order to order. A lot of different products can be produced on the same production line with a little variation of machine parameters/settings. The products are manufactured using processes like assembly, welding, machining, punching, stamping, and so on. Industries like automotive, electronics, medical devices, and heavy machinery all use discrete manufacturing to produce products like bicycles, cars, computers, mobile phones, forklifts, bulldozers, and so on.

Discrete manufacturing is executed using production orders. This chapter discusses production order management.

The production order cycle consists of the main activities shown in Figure 8-1. However, there can be many more processes in the production order cycle:

- Create a manual production order/convert a planned order into a production order

- Release a production order to the shop floor to begin production

- Issue components to a production order

© Himanshu Goel 2022
H. Goel, *Handbook for SAP PP in S/4HANA*, https://doi.org/10.1007/978-1-4842-8566-4_8

- Confirm a production order (time booking)

- Goods receipt for a production order

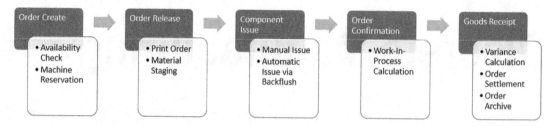

Figure 8-1. *Production order cycle*

Production Orders

A production order specifies the material that should be manufactured, in what quantities, and when. It is a comprehensive document that contains key information like components needed for production and sequence of operations for the production process. It also captures the costs of production. A production order regulates the manufacturing in an organization and captures the end-to-end manufacturing process, including the production status, capacities, and production costs.

A production order can be created in the following ways:

- Create a production order manually

- Convert a planned order to a production order

- Sometimes a production order is created without materials to capture the material and activity, such as with a rework order

Create a Production Order Manually

Choose Logistics ➤ Production ➤ Shop Floor Control ➤ Order ➤ Create ➤ With Material. You can also use Transaction Code CO01 to create a production order. Enter the material number of the finished/semifinished material to be produced, the production plant, and the order type on the initial screen.

The order type determines the master data that should be populated in the order when the production order is created, and it also governs which parameters are relevant for controlling. SAP comes preconfigured with the following production order types:

- PP01 Standard Production Order
- PP02 Standard Production Order (external NA)
- PP04 Assembly orders

You can define new order types based on your requirements. More than one production order type can be defined; for example, there can be one order type for standard production and another for rework orders.

Convert a Planned Order to a Production Order

Planned orders are generated as a result of an MRP run. The planned orders are then converted to production orders to initiate the manufacturing cycle. There are multiple ways to do this:

Using MD04: Double-click a planned order that should be converted to a production order, as shown in Figure 8-2.

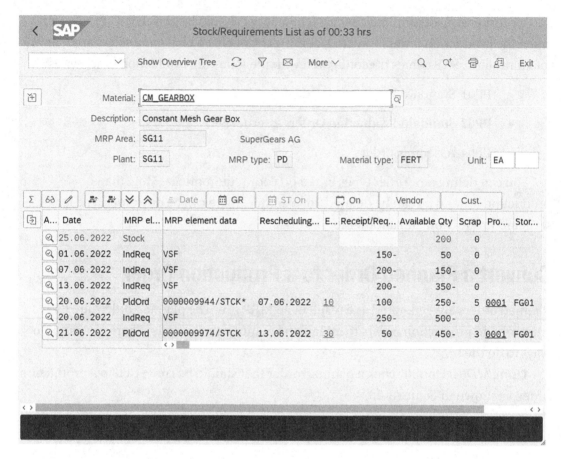

Figure 8-2. *Stock requirement list*

Click the ➤ Prod. Ord. icon to convert the planned order to a production order, as shown in Figure 8-3.

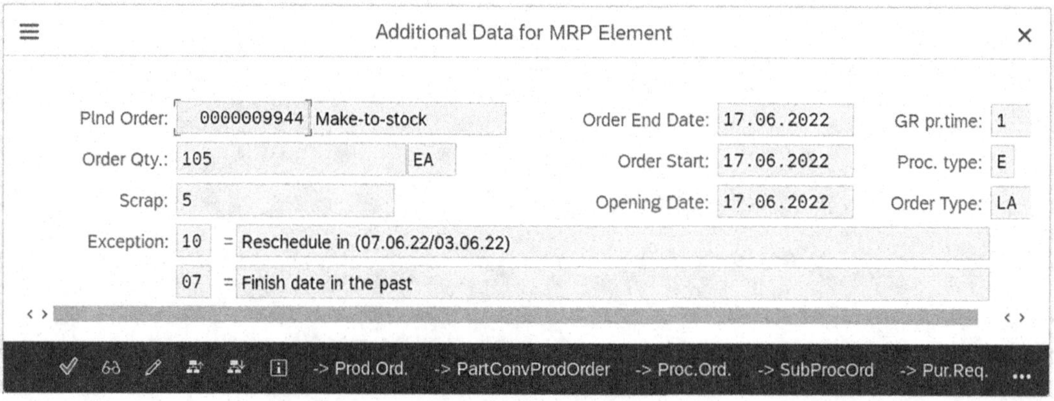

Figure 8-3. *Stock requirement list: additional data for MRP element*

Once you click the ➤Prod. Ord. icon, the system will take you to the screen in Figure 8-4. Here you can see that the production order details like material, plant, quantity, production dates, and so on, have been populated automatically from the planned order, as shown in Figure 8-4.

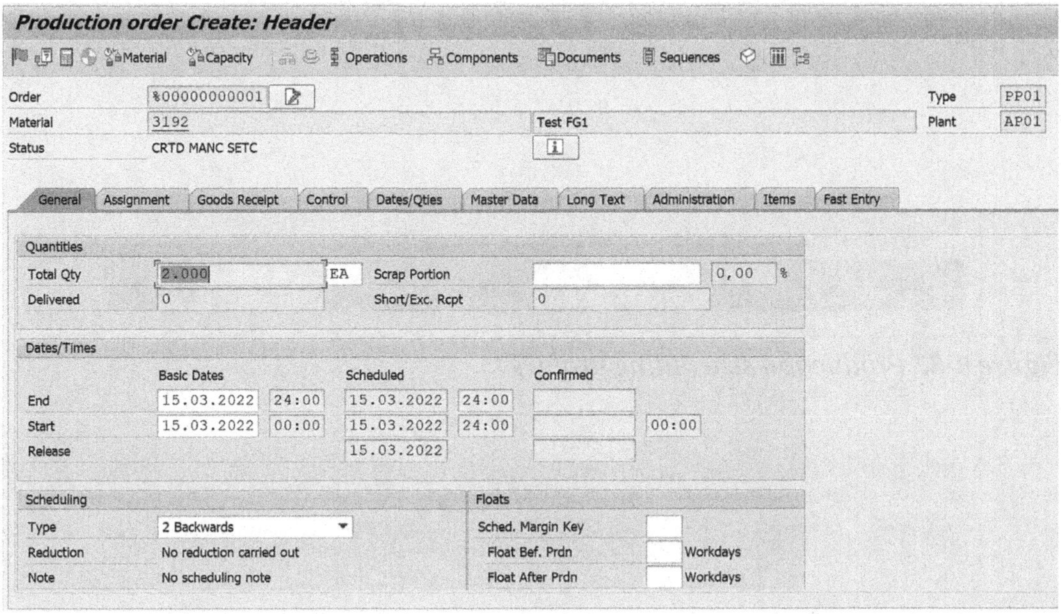

Figure 8-4. *Creating a production order*

Are you wondering how the order type populated automatically in the production order? Well, the order type is determined by the Production Scheduling Profile setting, which is assigned in the Work Scheduling view of the material master. You can check/ configure the Production Scheduling profile using Transaction Code OPKP. Figure 8-5 shows the configuration setting of the order type assignment to the production scheduling profile.

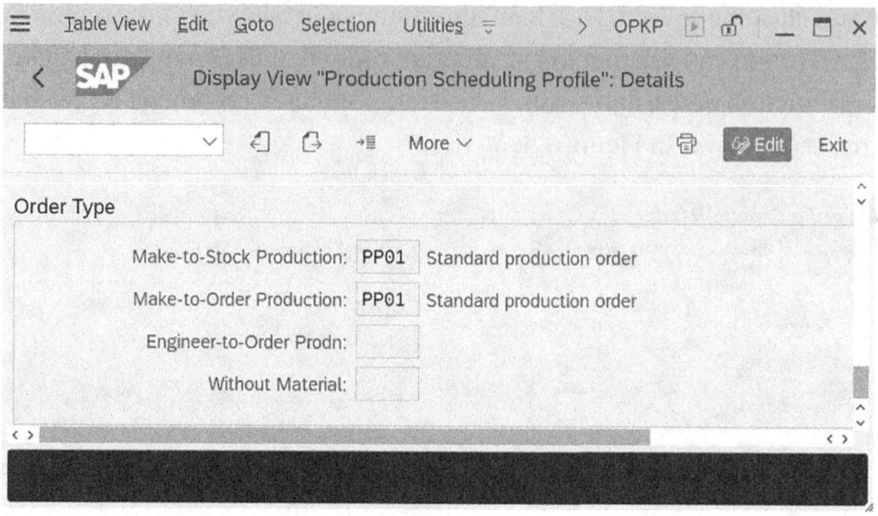

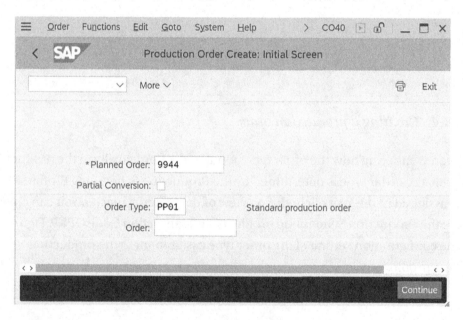

Figure 8-5. *Production scheduling profiles*

Figure 8-6. *Production order create: initial screen*

You can also convert a planned order to a production order using Transaction Code CO40 or CO41.

Choose Logistics ➤ Production ➤ Shop Floor Control ➤ Order ➤ Create ➤ From Planned Order. You can also use Transaction Code CO40 to convert a single planned order to a production order.

Enter the planned order's number and order type and press Enter to convert the planned order to a production order.

Choose Logistics ➤ Production ➤ Shop Floor Control ➤ Order ➤ Create Collective Conversion of Planned Orders. You can also use Transaction Code CO41 to convert many planned orders at once.

Enter the input parameters on the selection screen. There is a wide range of selection parameters, including Planning Plant, MRP Area, MRP Controller, Production Plant, Material, and so on, as shown in Figure 8-7.

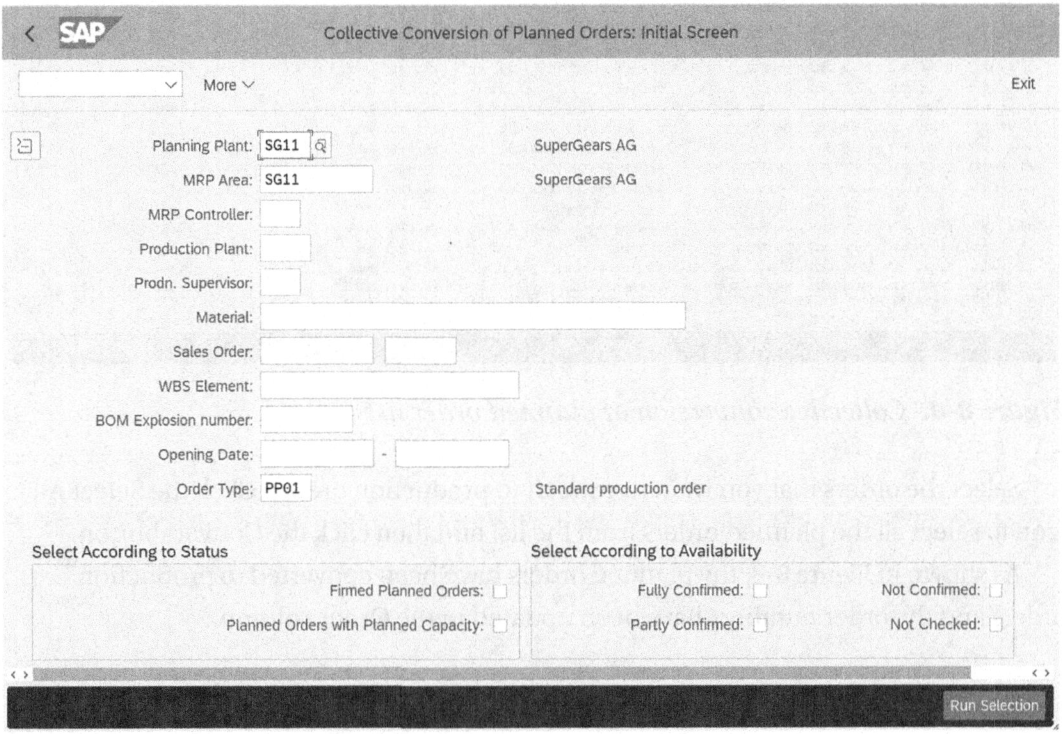

Figure 8-7. *Collective conversion of planned order*

I entered the Production Plant; however, it is recommended to enter as much selection parameters as possible to get the best filtered results. Click Execute to display the list of planned orders, as shown in Figure 8-8. The list displays a lot of information, like the Planned Order number, Material, Start Date, End Date, Order Quantity, Order Type, and so on. You can also see that some columns are in white, which means they are editable. You are allowed to change to order quantity and dates as well as the order type.

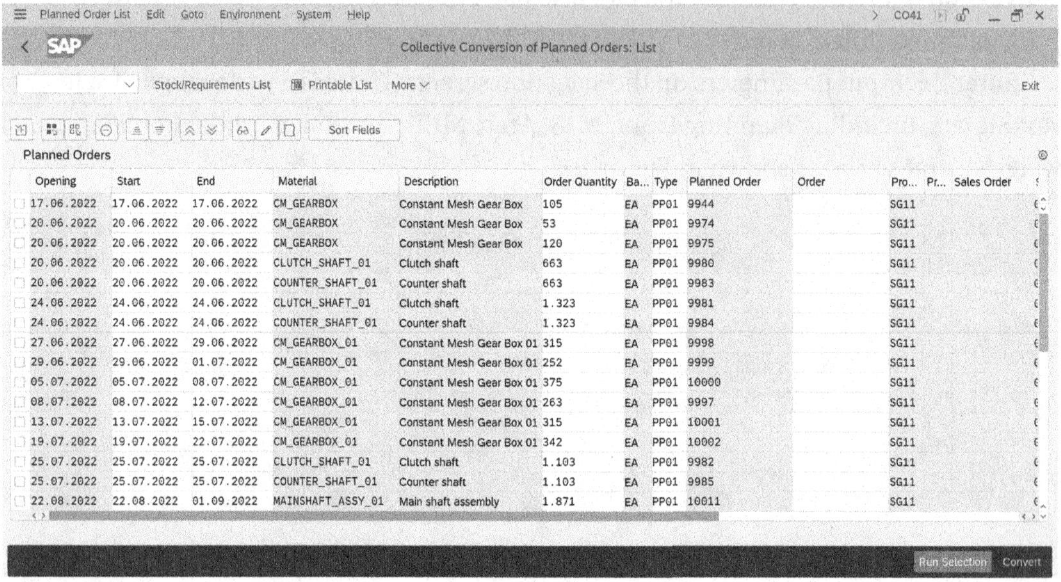

Figure 8-8. *Collective conversion of planned order list*

Select the orders that you want to convert to production orders. Click the Select All icon to select all the planned orders from the list and then click the Convert button.

As shown in Figure 8-9, the planned orders have been converted to production orders and the order numbers have been updated in the Order column.

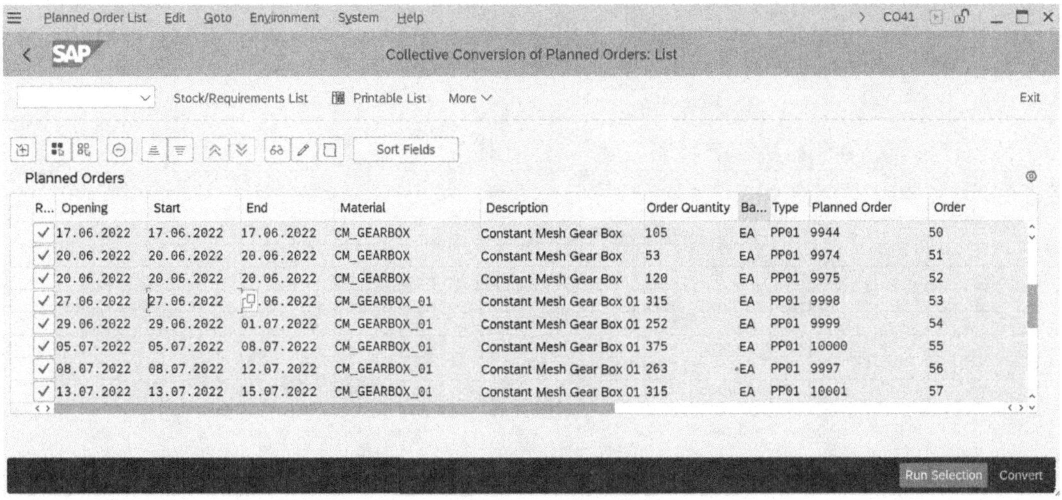

Figure 8-9. *Collective conversion of a planned order list*

Note   Once a planned order is converted to a production order, the planned order is deleted from the database. The planned order number is set in the assignment view of the production order for traceability purposes. However, it is not possible to display the planned order in MD13 since it is permanently deleted.

Now that you have seen several approaches to creating production orders, you are ready to look at production orders in detail.

Change/Display Production Order

Choose Logistics ➤ Production ➤ Shop Floor Control ➤ Order ➤ Create ➤ With Material. You can also use Transaction Code CO01 to create a production order.

You can use Transaction Code CO02 to change a production order and CO03 to display a production order.

Enter the material number of the finished/semifinished material to be produced, the production plant, and the order type on the initial screen, as shown in Figure 8-10.

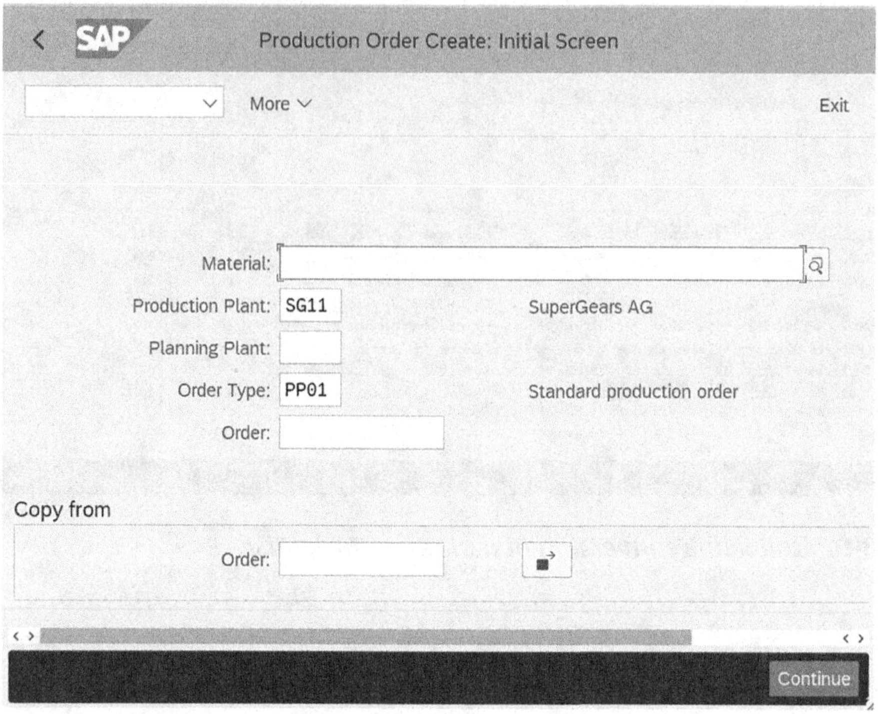

Figure 8-10. *Production order create: initial screen*

Press Enter. The Production Order header screen appears, as shown in Figure 8-11, where you can see information for the order header. Let's look at the Production Order header:

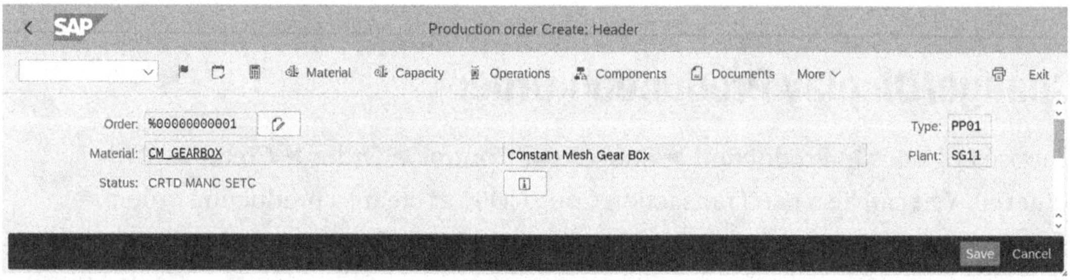

Figure 8-11. *Production order create: header screen*

Order: Currently blank since the production order has not been created and therefore the order number has not been generated yet.

Material: The finished/semifinished material that should be manufactured. This field is set up automatically based on the input from the initial screen.

Type: This field displays the production order type that was entered in the initial screen.

Plant: This field displays the production plant where the material should be produced. It is also displayed based on the input from the initial screen.

There are many views in the production order, as shown in Figure 8-12. Let's look at these views and consider the most important fields:

- General

- Assignment

- Goods Receipt

- Control

- Dates/Quantities

- Master Data

- Long Text

- Administration

- Items

- Fast Entry

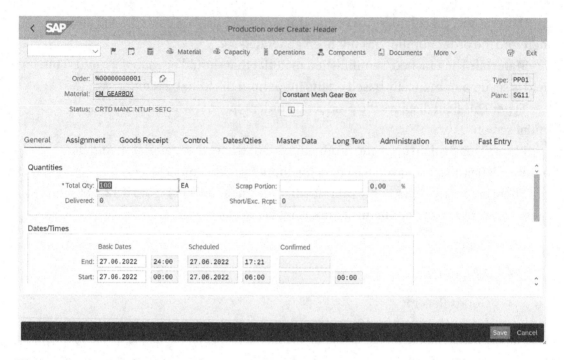

Figure 8-12. *Production order create: header screen*

General View

This view contains generic information about the production order. This view has four sections—Quantities, Dates/Times, Scheduling, and Floats.

Total Quantity specifies the total parts that should be produced, including scrap.

Scrap Portion specifies the expected scrap during the production process. Scrap percentage can be maintained as Assembly scrap % in the MRP1 view of the material master, as shown in Figure 8-13.

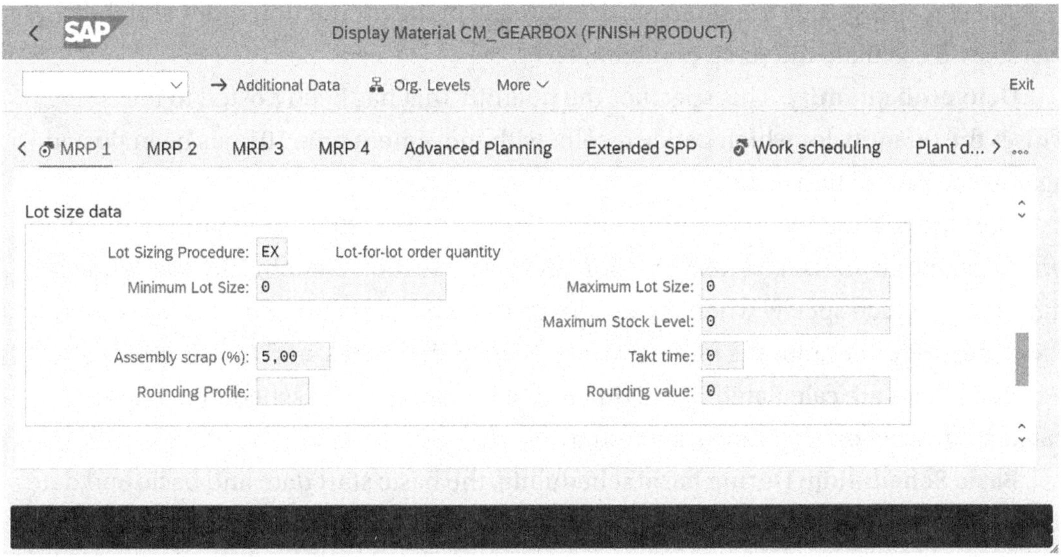

Figure 8-13. *Display material: lot size data*

If the assembly scrap % is maintained in the material master, the total quantity in the production order is increased automatically considering the scrap percentage, as shown in Figure 8-14. The system also issues a warning message that the order quantity is increased due to scrap.

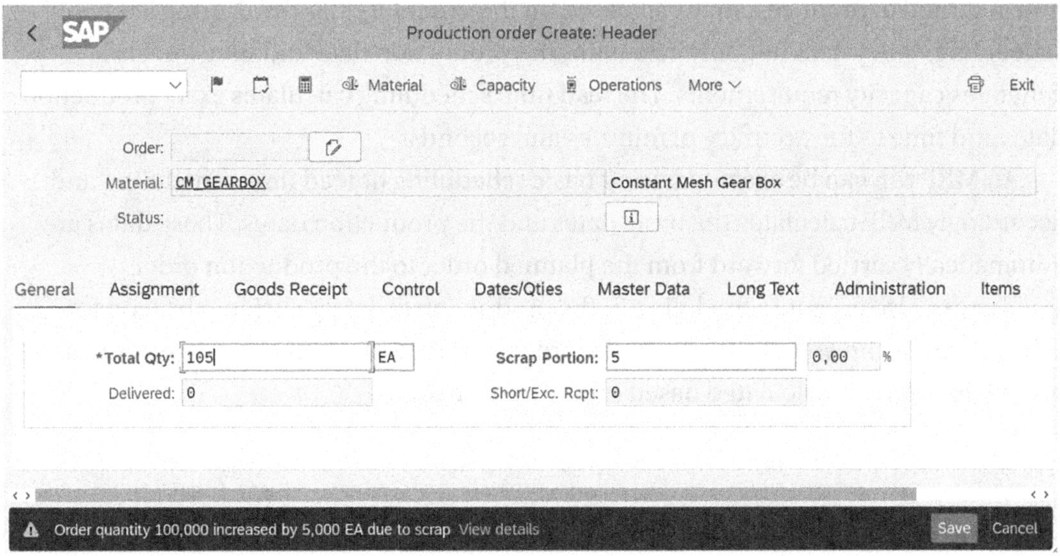

Figure 8-14. *Production order: general*

You can also specify the scrap portion directly in the production order and the system will calculate the scrap percentage.

Delivered quantity: This specifies the quantity that has been posted to the stock. This is the quantity for which goods receipt with movement type 101 has been posted against the production order.

The **Dates/Times** section specifies the dates and times that the material should be produced based on the given production order. The section contains the start and end date/times, which specify when the production should start and end. In this section, there are also three columns for Basic Dates, Scheduled Dates, and Confirmed Dates.

Basic dates are calculated based on basic scheduling, while scheduled dates are calculated based on lead time scheduling.

Basic Scheduling: During basic scheduling, the basic start date and basic end date are calculated based on the in-house production time maintained in the MRP2 view of the material master. The inhouse production time is independent of lot size during the calculation of basic dates. The schedule margin key is not considered during the basic scheduling. The basic dates are accurate to the day.

Lead time scheduling: During lead time scheduling, the system calculates the production dates based on the time maintained in the routing. Various times can be maintained in routing, like Setup Time, processing Time, Queue Time, Interoperation Time, and so on. All these times maintained in routing are used to calculate the exact time required to produce a material based on the order lot quantity. During lead time scheduling, the system not only calculates the production date and time but also generates capacity requirements. The lead time scheduling calculates exact production dates and time to the accuracy of minutes and seconds.

An MRP run can be executed using basic scheduling or lead time scheduling and accordingly MRP calculates the basic dates and the production dates. These dates are automatically carried forward from the planned order to the production order.

You can also execute scheduling in the production order by clicking the icon for scheduling. As shown in Figure 8-15, the order start date/time and end date/time of the production order is calculated based on the routing time.

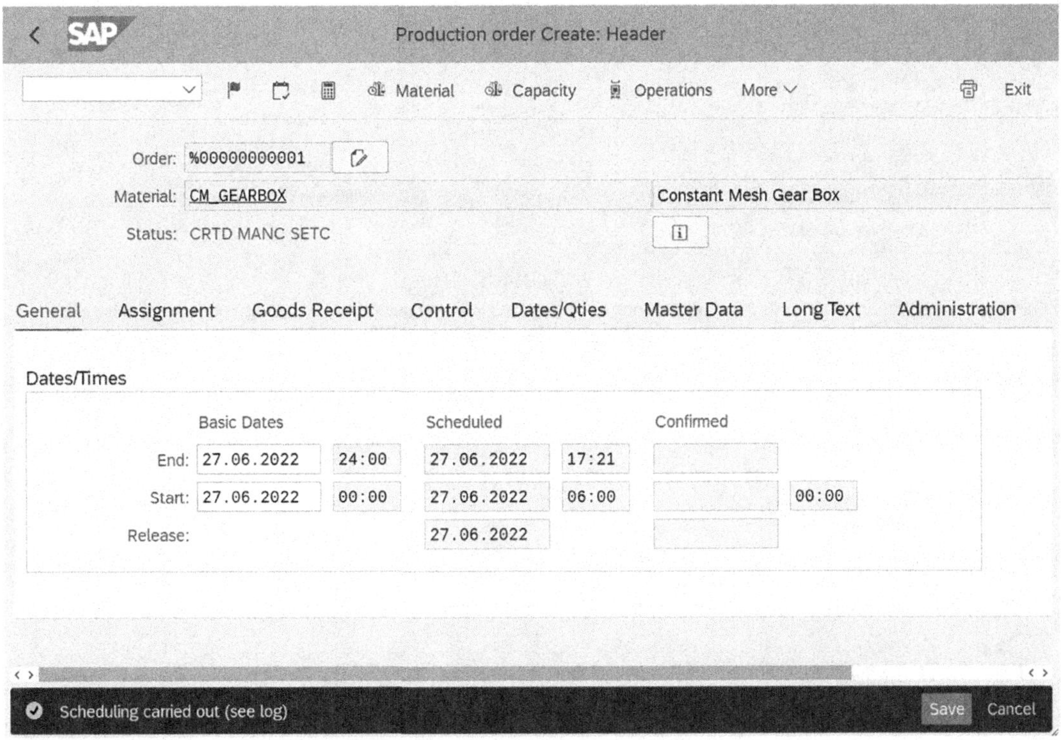

Figure 8-15. Production order: scheduling

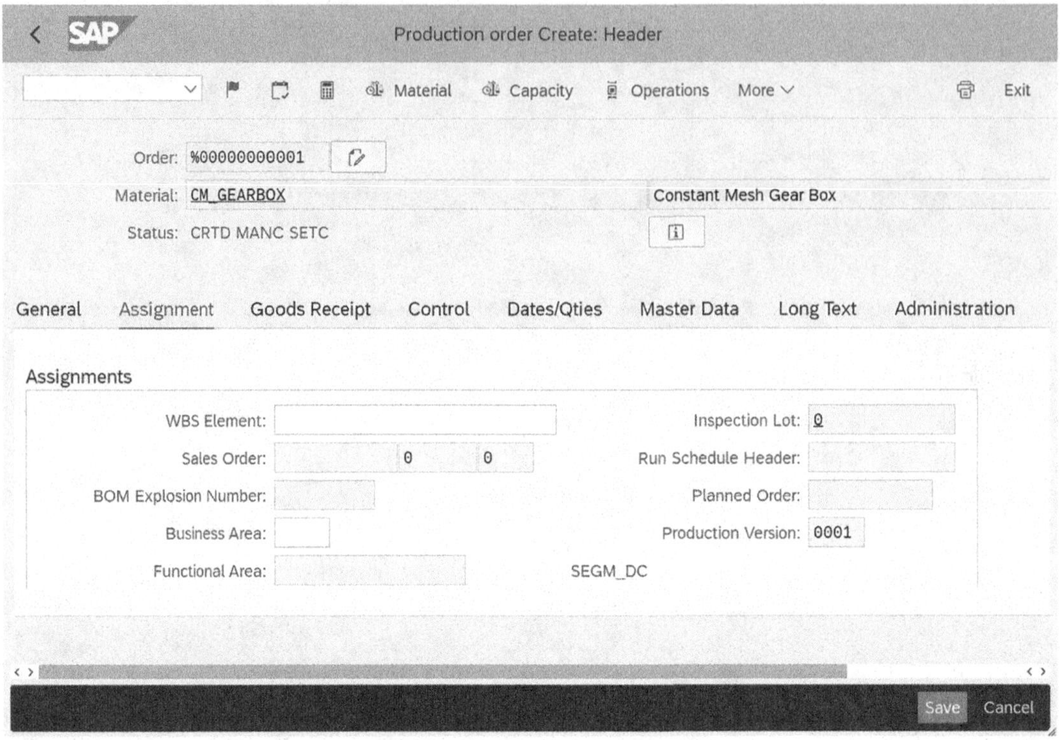

Figure 8-16. *Production order: assignment*

The Confirmed Date column specifies the exact dates when the production was started and finished. These dates are set automatically by the system based on the confirmation dates.

Scheduling: In the scheduling section, you can specify the scheduling type, which determines how the order should be scheduled. You may schedule the order backward or forward. If you like to run backward scheduling, you must enter the end date and the system will calculate the start date. If you like to run forward scheduling, you must enter the start date and the system will calculate the end date.

With the Only Capacity Requirements scheduling type, you must specify the start as well as the finish dates of the production order. The scheduled start and finish dates of the order are calculated based on the floats and the schedule margin key in the MRP2 view of the material master. Scheduling is not carried out for the individual operations of the order.

With the Current Date scheduling type, the start date is set as the current date and the finish date is calculated in forward mode.

Floats: Based on the schedule margin key, floats are calculated for the order and the start date and end dates for the order are adjusted.

Assignment View

The assignment view contains key information with regards to assignment with various objects, for example WBS Element, Inspection Lot, Sales Order, Planned Order, and so on. If the production order is created with reference to a project, the field WBS element is updated automatically with the project number. In a make-to-order scenario, the production order is created with reference to a sales order and the sales order number is updated automatically in the production order. If quality management is active, then an inspection lot is generated for each production order, which specifies how the produced material should be inspected to adhere to quality standards. If a planned order is converted to a production order, the planned order number is also updated in the production order.

Upon saving the production order, a reservation number is generated and stored in the Reservation field. A *reservation* is a formal request or notification to the warehouse to reserve the components required for the production order. A reservation created against a production order can be displayed using Transaction Code MB23, as shown in Figure 8-17. A reservation can also be created manually using Transaction Code MB21.

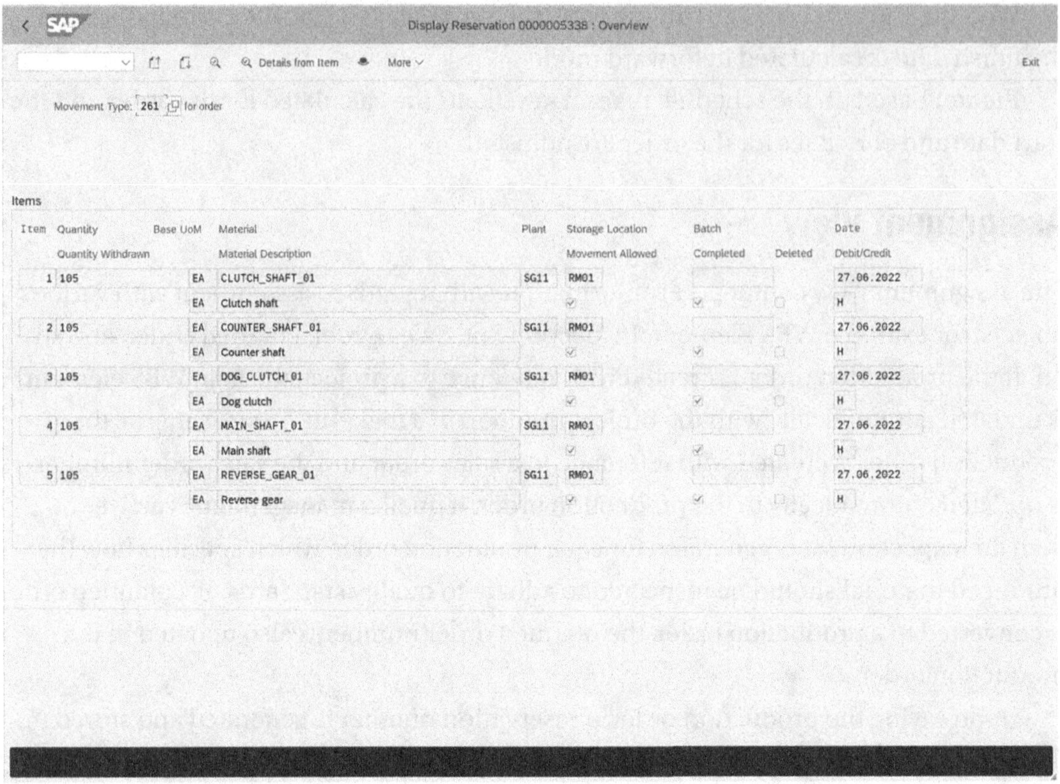

Figure 8-17. *Display a reservation*

Goods Receipt View

The Goods Receipt view contains information that specifies how the goods receipt should be posted. Figure 8-18 shows the Control section of the Goods Receipt view.

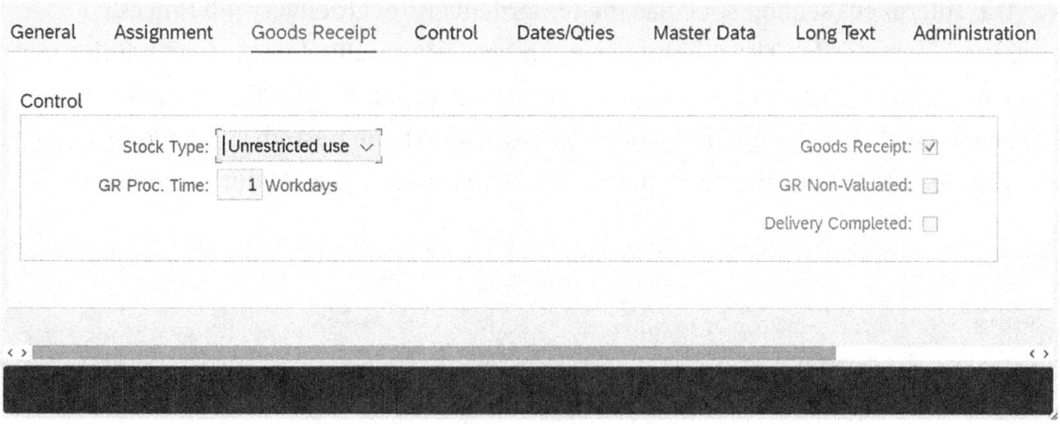

| General | Assignment | Goods Receipt | Control | Dates/Qties | Master Data | Long Text | Administration |

Control

Stock Type:	Unrestricted use ∨				Goods Receipt:	☑
GR Proc. Time:	1 Workdays				GR Non-Valuated:	☐
					Delivery Completed:	☐

Figure 8-18. *Production order: goods receipt: control*

The **Stock Type** specifies where the stock should be posted once the goods receipt is done. The stock can be posted in Unrestricted, Blocked Stock, or Quality Inspection.

GR Processing Time specifies the time needed for inspection and placing the materials into the storage location once the goods receipt has been posted.

The **Goods Receipt** indicator specifies if a goods receipt is allowed for the production order. The indicator is set as active automatically if the settlement receiver is material or a sales order. If the production order is created for a project (WBS element), then the goods receipt indicator is not activated, which means stock is not posted. This is because the settlement receiver for such orders is a WBS element.

The **Delivery Completed** indicator is set automatically by the system when the goods receipt is completed. This means the order can be referred to as complete.

Figure 8-19 shows the Tolerances section of the Goods Receipt view.

| General | Assignment | Goods Receipt | Control | Dates/Qties | Master Data | Long Text | Administration |

Tolerances

| Underdelivery: | 0,0 | % | | | | | |
| Overdelivery: | 0,0 | % | | | Unlimited Overdelivery: | ☐ |

Figure 8-19. *Production order: goods receipt: tolerances*

The Tolerances section specifies the underdelivery/overdelivery tolerances permitted for the order. The tolerance percentages are specified in work scheduling view of the material master and are populated automatically in the production order.

The Receipt section specifies where the stock should be posted, as shown in Figure 8-20. The storage location species where the stock is posted during goods receipt.

| General | Assignment | Goods Receipt | Control | Dates/Qties | Master Data | Long Text | Administration |

Receipt

Stor. Loc.: FG01   Batch:

Distribution: Stk Seg.

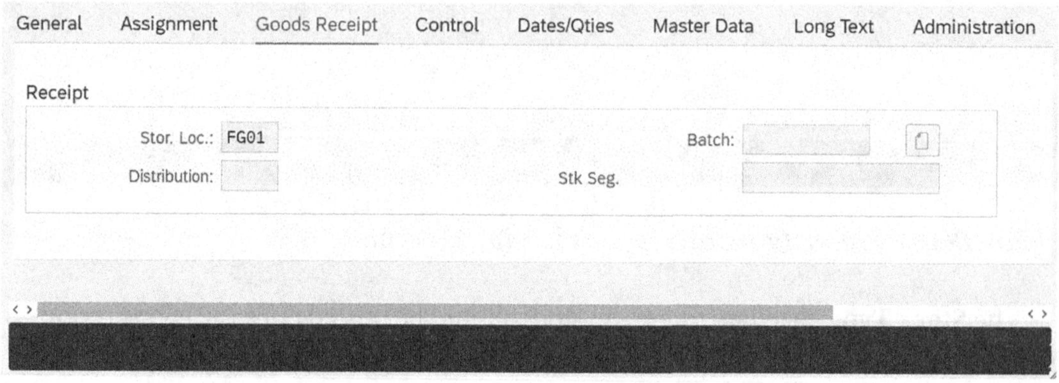

Figure 8-20. Production order: goods receipt: receipt

The goods receipt posted will create/update the stock of the batch specified in the production order. If multiple goods receipts are posted, then the stock for the batch is updated each time.

How a batch is created is determined by the Customization setting of the production scheduling profile. Batches can be created in the production order at the time of order creation or order release. This would mean there would be one batch per production order. Batches can also be created during goods receipt. In such a case, a new batch number is generated each time a goods receipt is posted against the production order.

Control View

Control view contains various sections—Order, Costing, Scheduling, and Production Scheduling Profile.

This view controls lots of important parameters, like how a reservation or purchase requisition should be generated, costing variant for planned costs, costing variant for actual costs, results analysis key, variance key, production scheduling key, and so on.

Dates/Quantities View

The Dates/Quantities view contains two sections—Dates/Times and Quantities.

The Dates/Times sections contains all start/end dates and times relevant for the production order, such as Planned Order, Basic Dates, Scheduled, Committed, and Confirmed (see Figure 8-21).

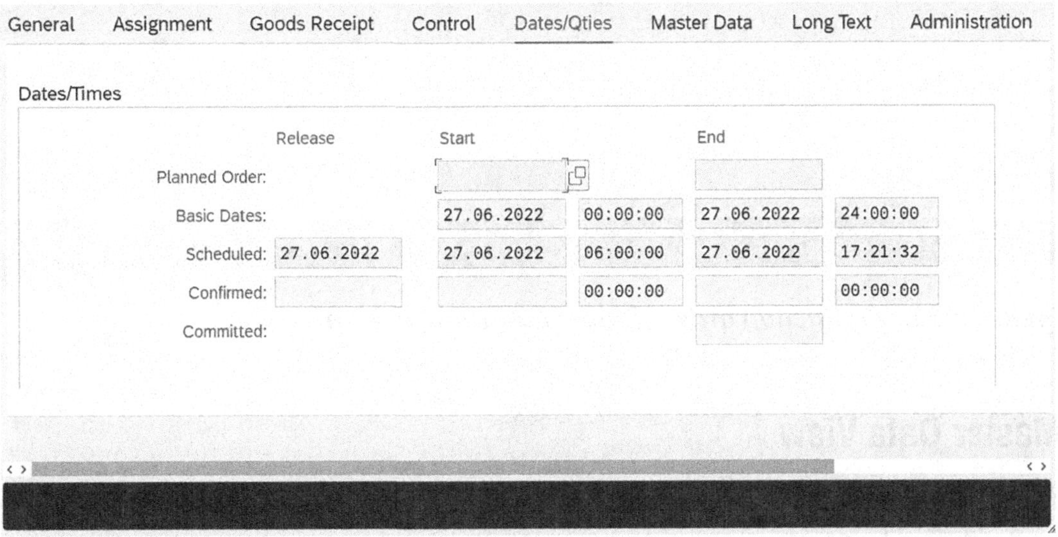

Figure 8-21. *Production order: dates/quantities: dates/times*

The quantities sections contain the Quantity or Scrap for the Planned Order, Order, Delivered, and Committed (see Figure 8-22).

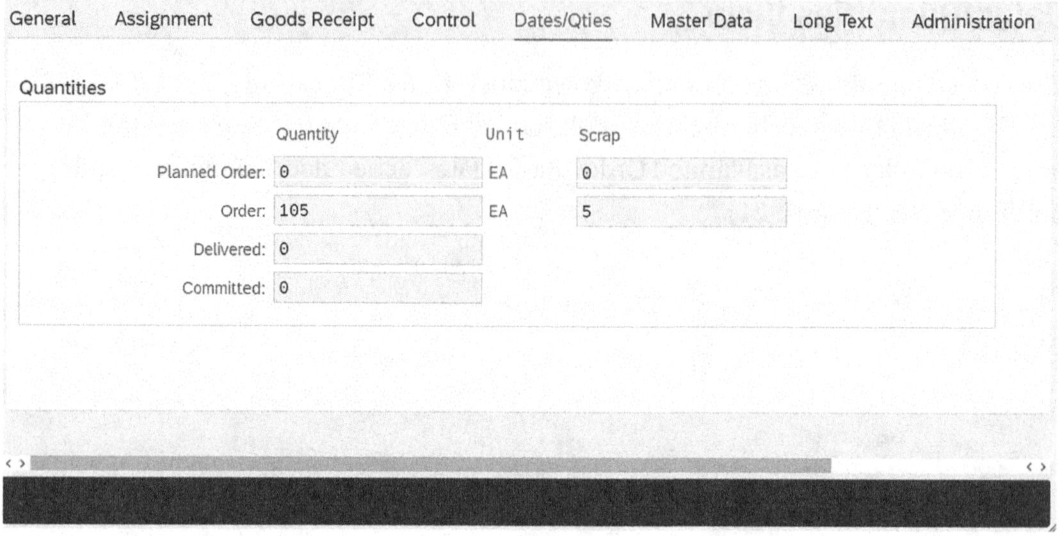

| General | Assignment | Goods Receipt | Control | Dates/Qties | Master Data | Long Text | Administration |

Quantities

	Quantity	Unit	Scrap
Planned Order:	0	EA	0
Order:	105	EA	5
Delivered:	0		
Committed:	0		

Figure 8-22. *Production order: dates/quantities: quantities*

Master Data View

The Master Data view contains information regarding the master data used for the production order. The first section is the production version. Based on the production version selected in the order, the routing header details and BOM header details are displayed in the Routing and BOM sections.

Figure 8-23 displays the production version and routing details like Group, Valid from Date, Lot Sizes, Explosion Dates, and so on.

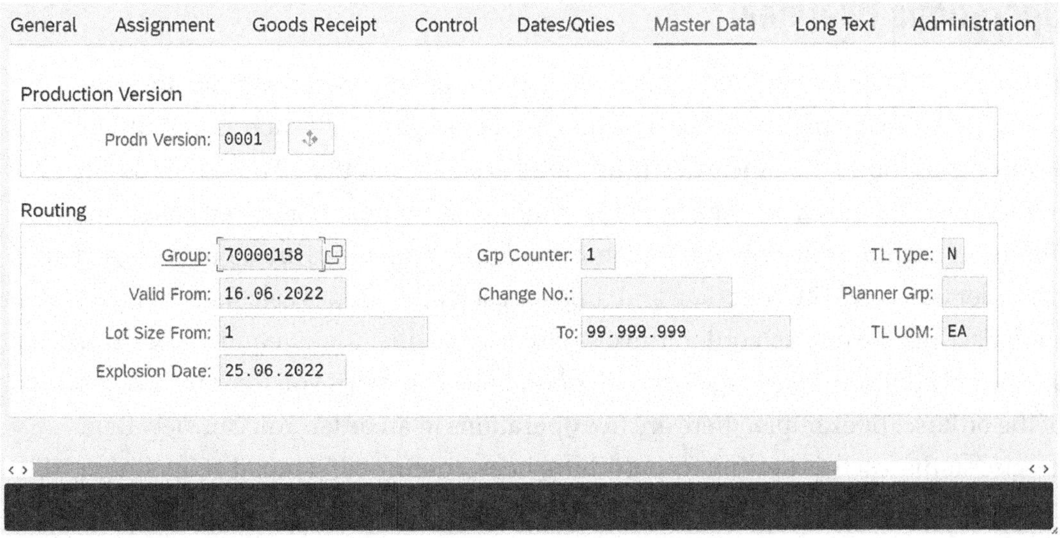

General	Assignment	Goods Receipt	Control	Dates/Qties	Master Data	Long Text	Administration

Production Version

Prodn Version: `0001` ⟡

Routing

Group: `70000158` 🗗		Grp Counter: `1`		TL Type: `N`
Valid From: `16.06.2022`		Change No.:		Planner Grp:
Lot Size From: `1`		To: `99.999.999`		TL UoM: `EA`
Explosion Date: `25.06.2022`				

⟨ ⟩   ⟨ ⟩

Figure 8-23. *Production order: master data: routing*

Figure 8-24 displays the Bill of Material details, like BOM number, BOM Usage, Valid from Date, Lot Sizes, Explosion Dates, and so on.

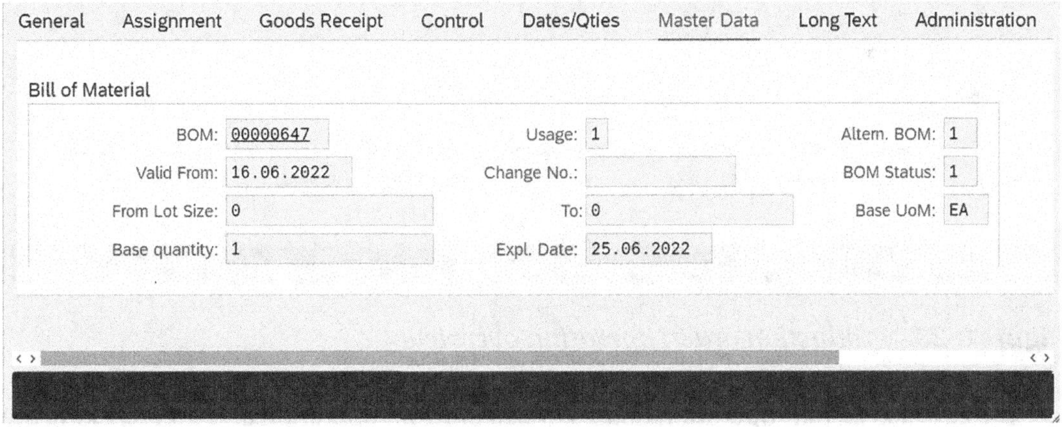

General	Assignment	Goods Receipt	Control	Dates/Qties	Master Data	Long Text	Administration

Bill of Material

BOM: `00000647`		Usage: `1`		Altern. BOM: `1`
Valid From: `16.06.2022`		Change No.:		BOM Status: `1`
From Lot Size: `0`		To: `0`		Base UoM: `EA`
Base quantity: `1`		Expl. Date: `25.06.2022`		

⟨ ⟩   ⟨ ⟩

Figure 8-24. *Production order: master data: bill of material*

The administration view contains the information regarding the user and dates on which the order was created and last changed.

Now that you have learned about all the views of the order and the important fields across all views, it's time to move on to the operations overview. Click the Operations icon in the menu bar to display the operations overview.

Operations Overview

The operations overview (see Figure 8-25) displays all the operations that are required to manufacture the material. The data in operations overview—such as operations, work center, control key operation times, and so on—is populated from the routing information. However, the data from the routing information is adopted based on the order. For example, the operation quantity and operation times are adjusted based on the order quantity. The start data and time for each operation is calculated, and a system status is available for each order. You can also see the operation quantity, confirmed scrap, and confirmed yield against each operation. This helps you track the exact status of the orders. For example, there are five operations in an order. You can view their precise status, such as how many parts have been confirmed/scraped at operation 10, 20, 30, and so on.

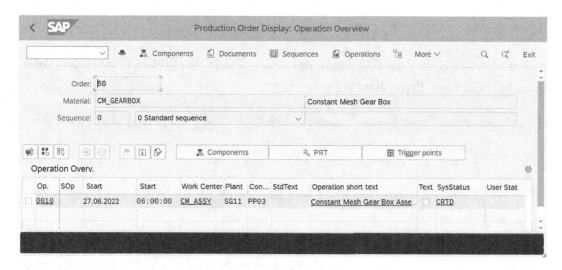

Figure 8-25. *Production order: operation overview*

You can also display operation details by selecting an operation and then clicking the Operation Details icon.

Figure 8-26 displays the operation details. Most of the data on the header screen comes from the routing information, like operation number, work center, operation short text, control key, and so on. Note that a unique confirmation number is generated for each operation. You can use the confirmation number for posting operation confirmation for the production order.

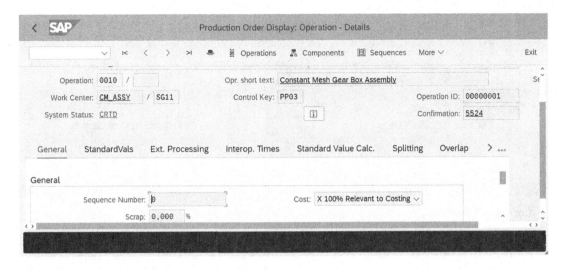

Figure 8-26. *Production order: operation details*

The operation details contains a lot of views, like General, Standard Values, External Processing, Interoperation Times, and so on.

The Standard Values section displays important data from routing, like the activities and the time for each operation.

The External Processing view contains all the information of an operation if the operation is subcontracted. For a subcontracted operation, a Purchase Requisition is created automatically based on the Purchase Info Record.

There is also lot of other information stored for each operation in the operation details. Go back to the operations.

Components Overview

Click the Components icon to display the Components Overview. Here you can see all the components required to produce a material. As shown in Figure 8-27, you can view all the components, the component description, the quantity needed of each component, the unit of measure, the operation on which the component is required, and the item category of the component (stock item, non-stock item, issue storage location, batch number, and so on). The component data is populated from the BOM (Bill of Materials) and adjusted based on the order quantity.

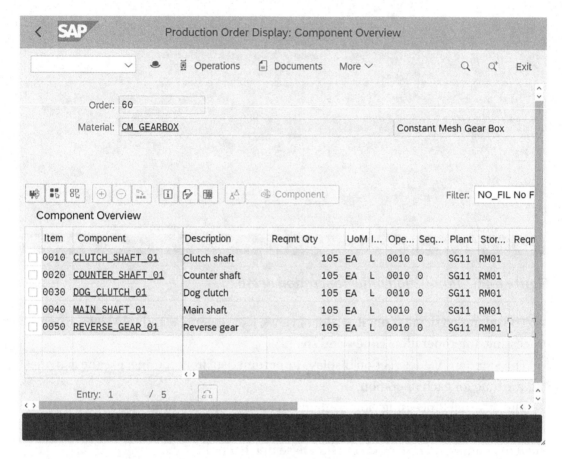

Figure 8-27. *Production order: components overview*

You can also see other important information in the component overview table, like committed quantity, quantity withdrawn, requirements date, purchase requisition number, and so on. The Purchase Order Exists check box indicates whether a purchase order has been created for the component.

Let's check the other functions on the menu bar. Click Header to go back to the order header.

Material Availability Check

You must ensure that all the components required for the production order are available based on the required quantity on the requirement dates. In order to do this, you must run a material availability check for the order. The availability check can be run manually or automatically. Click the Check Material Availability icon to run the check manually.

The availability check can also be executed automatically based on the Checking Control customization, where you define Checking Rule at order creation and order release. This means you can execute an automatic availability check based on different checking rules at the time of order creation and order release. Note that the system runs the material availability check for components that are stock items (i.e., they have the item category L).

The material availability check includes four customization objects:

- **Checking Group:** This is assigned to each material and together with Checking Rule determines how the availability check should be executed. The checking group is assigned in the Availability Check field in the MRP3 view of the material master.

- **Checking Rule:** These are defined for different application areas, like Sales and Distribution, Material Resource Planning, Production Order, Maintenance Order, Inventory Management, and so on.

- **Scope of Check:** This is defined for a combination of Checking Group and Checking Rule. A Scope of Check controls various parameters:

  - Which demand and supply elements—like Purchase Requisitions, Purchase Order, Planned Order, Production Order, Sales Order, Reservation, Dependent Requirements—should be included in the availability check.

  - Which stocks—like safety stock, quality stock, blocked stock, and stock in transfer—should be considered in the availability check.

  - If the replenishment lead time should be considered.

- **Checking Control:** This is used to determine if material availability check should be executed when an order is created or released. You specify the checking rule to be used for a combination of Plant, Order Type and Business Function (i.e., Order Create or Order Release) and how the material shortfall could impact the order creation or release.

If there is a shortage of components during the material availability check, a list of missing components is generated. You can check missing parts by choosing Goto ➤ Missing Parts ➤ Missing Parts Overview or Goto ➤ Missing Parts ➤ Missing Parts List.

Capacity Availability Check

Like material availability check, you must execute a capacity availability check to ensure the capacity is available at the work center for all operations of the order. The system checks the total available capacity of the work center and the capacity consumed by other orders to determine the free capacity. Then the system checks the capacity required for the order against the free capacity on the work center.

Order Costing

When you create a production order, the system calculates the planned costs for the order. The total costs usually consist of three elements: component costs, production costs, and overheads. The planned costs are assigned to cost elements.

Settlement Rule

When a production order is created, the system automatically assigns a settlement rule to the order based on the customization settings. Choose Header ➤ Settlement Rule.

As you can see in Figure 8-28, a settlement rule contains various important parameters relevant to order settlement.

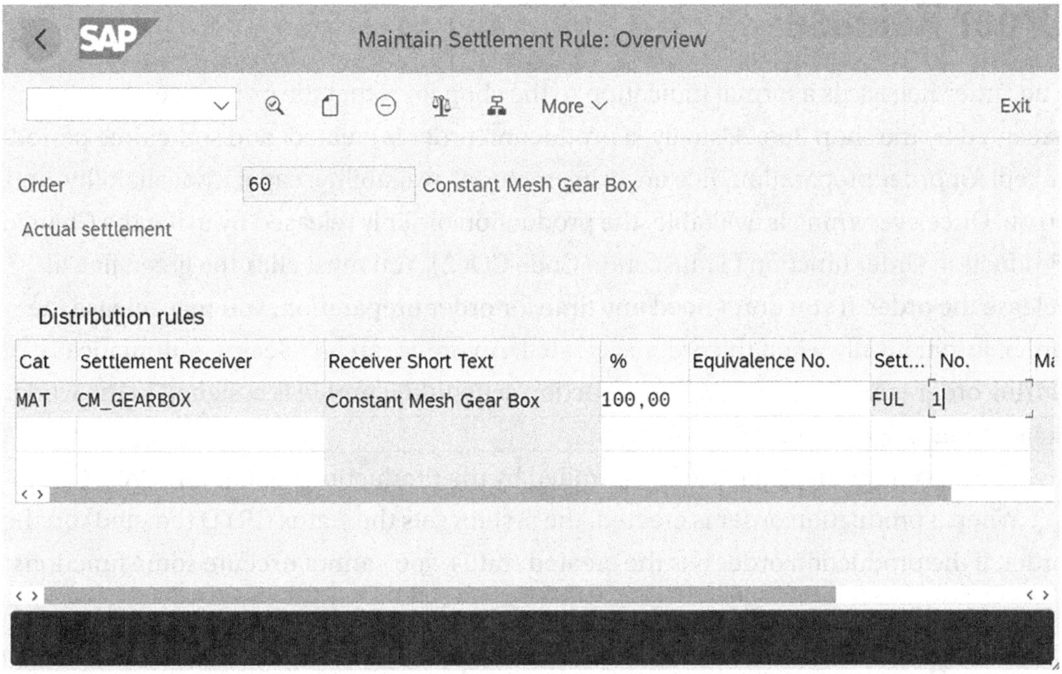

Figure 8-28. *Settlement rule*

Account assignment category specifies the object type for the settlement receiver like Material, Order, Cost Center, WBS Element, and so on. Usually, the settlement receiver is Material for make-to-stock scenarios and Sales Order for make-to-order scenarios.

Settlement receiver specifies the cost object on which the actual costs of the production order should be settled.

Settlement Percentage Rate: If you want to allocate the cost of the order to multiple cost objects, you can specify the percentages in settlement percentage rate.

The settlement type determines how the costs are settled; for example, you can settle the order in full or periodically.

Now save the order. The system will create an order and provide a success message with the order number.

The first step of the order execution cycle—creating a production order/converting a planned order to a production order—is complete.

Let's move to the next step of order execution—the release production order.

Order Release

The Order Release is a formal indication to the shop floor that the order is ready to be executed by the shop floor. Usually, a production order is created, and some time period is kept for order preparation, like ensuring material availability, capacity availability, and so on. Once everything is available, the production order is released by using the Change Production Order function (Transaction Code CO02). You must click the green flag to release the order. If you don't need any time for order preparation, you may release the order automatically when the order is created. An order can be released automatically during order creation if a relevant production scheduling profile is assigned in the work scheduling view of the material master.

The automatic order release is controlled by the Production Scheduling Profile.

When a production order is created, the system sets the status CRTD (created) on the order. If the production order has the created status, you cannot execute some functions:

- Shop floor papers cannot be printed.

- Order confirmations cannot be executed.

- Goods movements like goods issue and goods receipt cannot be executed.

You can execute these functions only when the production order is released with the status REL (released).

Goods Issue to a Production Order

Before starting the production on the shop floor, it is necessary to issue the components required for the production process. The components must be issued from the warehouse to the production based on a reservation. When a production order is created, the system generates a reservation which is a list of all the components and their quantities required for production. Goods issue to a production order can only be posted once the order is released.

Choose Logistics ➤ Production ➤ Shop Floor Control ➤ Goods Movements ➤ Goods Issue/Goods Receipt. You can also use Transaction Code MIGO_GI to post goods issue. Otherwise, you can simply use Transaction Code MIGO to post any goods movement.

While using MIGO, you must select the executable action as Goods Issue and it is selected as default if you're using MIGO_GI. Select the Reference Document as Order or Reservation and enter the relevant document number, as shown in Figure 8-29.

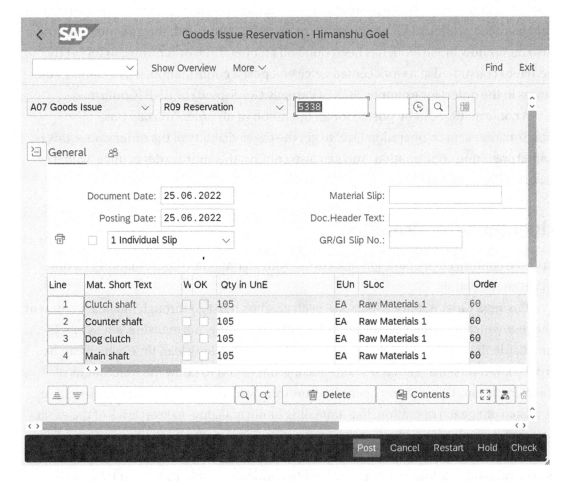

Figure 8-29. *Goods issue reservation*

Based on the reference document, all the relevant components are displayed in the table. Click Check. If the data is correct, you must post the goods issue by clicking the Post button.

Confirmation

An order confirmation is a document used to report completion (partial or full) of an operation or an order. While posting a confirmation, you can report the yield or scrap that has been produced for an operation or an order. Along with the quantity, you can also report how much work has been done on an operation/order. You can report the activities consumed at a work center. Once you post a confirmation, it also updates the status in the order; for example, PCNF (Partially Confirmed) or CNF (Confirmed).

A confirmation can be posted for an operation or an order. You can post confirmation at each operation level to get the exact visibility of the order status, this is called operation confirmation. You can also confirm the entire order at once, which is called order confirmation.

Operation Confirmation

You can confirm each operation of an order with an operation confirmation or a time ticket confirmation.

Business Case: At SuperGears AG, each gearbox must go through the heat treatment process, which includes several operations like annealing, normalizing, stress relief and hardening, and so on. Each of these processes has a long lead time, which can be from a few hours to a few days. Therefore, it is important to know the exact status of each operation. That's where operation confirmation is used. Operation confirmation is posted after each operation, like annealing or normalizing, to keep track of the exact status of the order.

Choose Logistics ➤ Production ➤ Shop Floor Control ➤ Confirmation ➤ Enter ➤ For Operation ➤ Time Ticket. You can also use Transaction Code CO11N to post operation confirmation or time ticket confirmation.

Figure 8-30 shows the first section of the Enter Time Ticket for Production Order screen.

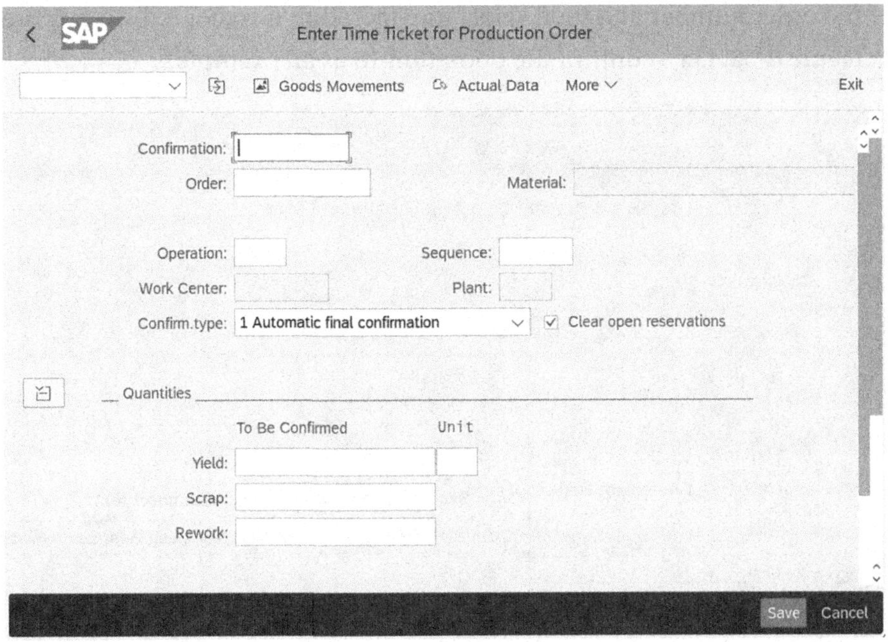

Figure 8-30. *Time ticket for production order*

You can post a confirmation for a confirmation or a combination of order and operation. A unique confirmation number is generated for each operation of an order. You can find it in Operation Details in the order, as shown in Figure 8-31.

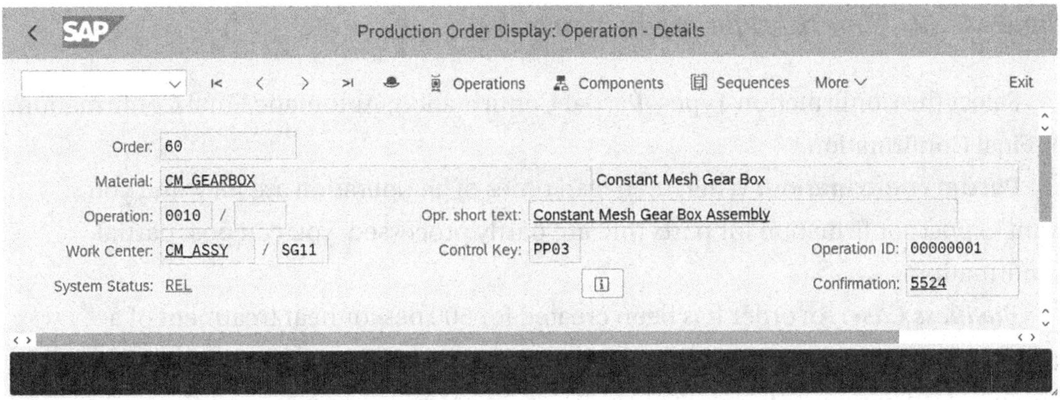

Figure 8-31. *Production order: operation details*

Enter the order number and then select the operation number to be confirmed, as shown in Figure 8-32. Let's confirm the operation 10 as an example.

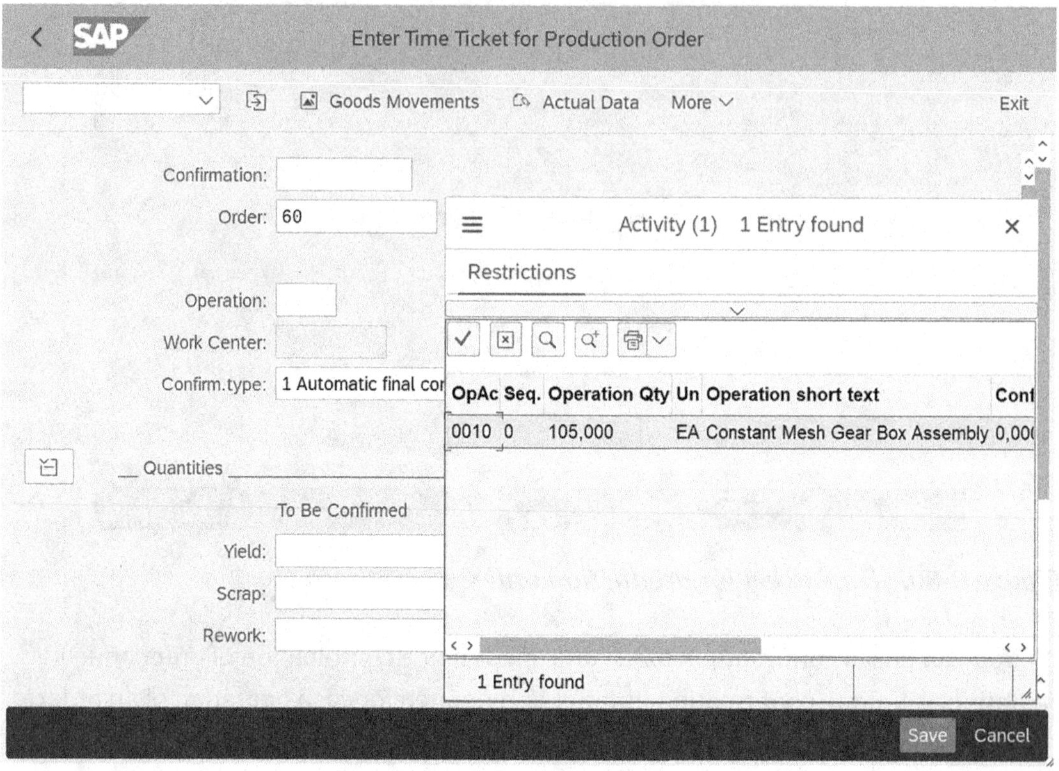

Figure 8-32. *Time ticket for production order*

Select the Confirmation Type—Partial Confirmation, Automatic Final Confirmation, or Final Confirmation.

Partial confirmation: When then lead times of an operation are long and you want to post confirmation for parts that are partly processed, you can post partial confirmation.

Business Case: An order has been created for 500 pcs for heat treatment of a gearbox. The first process (Annealing) takes six hours for 100 pcs. You can use Partial Confirmation to report 100 pcs every six hours to get real-time status on the order.

Once you post a partial confirmation for an operation, the system updates the status as PCNF (Partially Confirmed) for the operation, as shown in Figure 8-33.

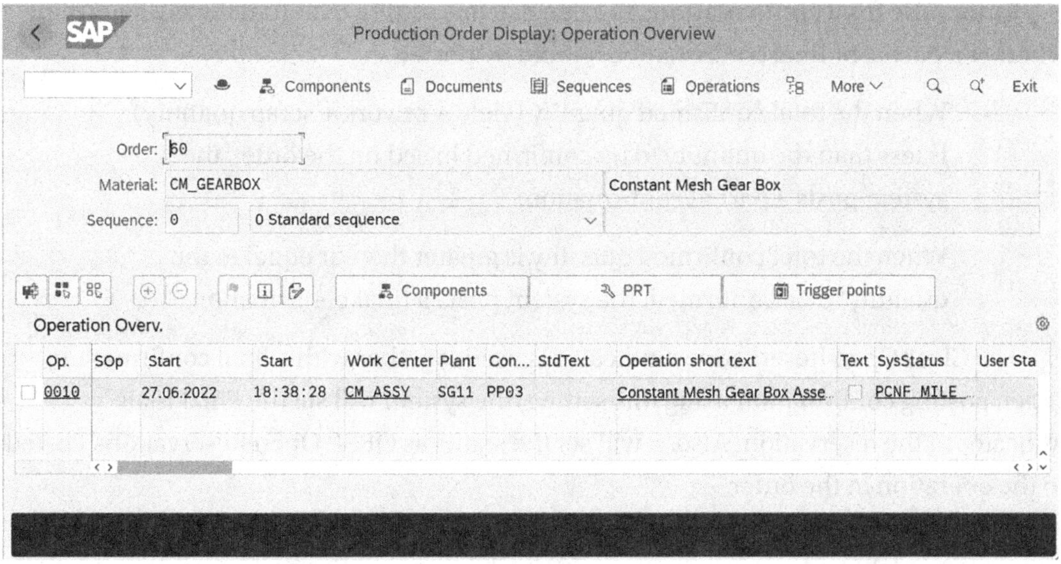

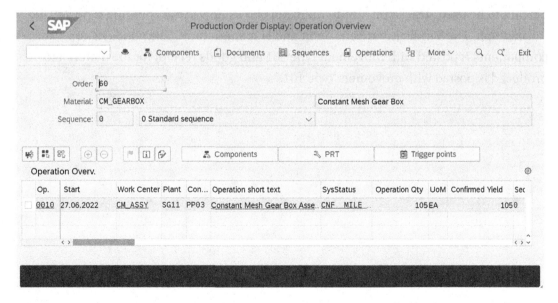

Figure 8-33. *Production order: operation overview*

Final confirmation: When the operation is processed completely and there is no work left to be performed for the order, you must select Final Confirmation. Once you post a final confirmation for an operation, the system updates the status as CNF (Confirmed) for the operation in the order. You can also check Operation Quantity, Confirmed Quantity, and so on, as shown in Figure 8-34.

Figure 8-34. *Production order: operation overview*

Automatic final confirmation: You can use this setting to automatically determine whether a partial or final confirmation should be posted.

- When the total confirmed quantity (yield + rework + scrap quantity) is less than the quantity to be confirmed based on the order, the system posts a partial confirmation.

- When the total confirmed quantity is greater than or equal to the quantity to be confirmed, the system posts a final confirmation.

The Clear Open Reservations indicator is used together with a final confirmation. When posting confirmation using this setting, the system will set the Final Issue indicator in the reservation. Also, it will set the status as ORSP Open Reservations Posted to the operation in the order.

If you click the Actual Data icon, the system will propose the data to be confirmed; for example, yield and activities to be confirmed as planned.

In the Quantity section, you must specify the quantity to be confirmed—for example Yield, Scrap, or Rework. You can enter Reason for Variance when there is a deviation from the quantity planned; for example due to scrap.

You can click the Goods Movement button to display all the materials for which a goods movement should be posted. The list shows all the materials for which goods issue and Goods receipt should be posted, as shown in Figure 8-35. The list contains information like material, quantity, plant, storage location, and so on. You can select the batches to be used. The Debit/Credit indicator shows how the accounting is posted for the material. The S indicator means debit and H means credit. The goods issue for the components is posted with movement type 261 and goods receipt for the material to be produced is posted with movement type 101.

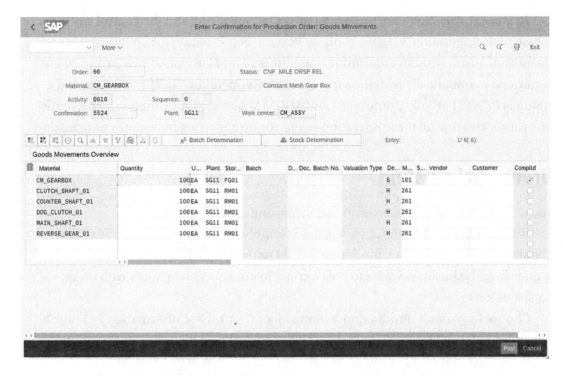

Figure 8-35. *Enter confirmation for production order: goods movements*

Once you have specified all the details for all the material/components, you can post the confirmation by clicking the Save button.

Milestone Confirmation: The milestone confirmation is a special form of confirmation used to report only critical operations and all preceding operations are confirmed automatically by the system. The milestone operations are defined in the Control key and then assigned to the operations in the routing information. The following table shows the type of confirmations available. Confirmation type 1 means Milestone Confirmation. The control key PP03 comes preconfigured with Milestone Confirmation.

Confirmations	Short Description
1	Milestone confirmation (not PS/PM)
2	Confirmation required
3	Confirmation not possible
	Confirmation possible but not necessary

Business Case: There are three operations in the routing and the control key PP03 is assigned to operation 30 in the routing. Post the confirmation for operation 30 for a quantity of 50 pcs without confirming operations 10 and 20. Operations 20 and 30 are confirmed automatically with the same quantity as operation 30. The system sets the status as PCNF (Partially Confirmed) and MILE (Milestone Confirmation). The status MILE indicates that all these operations were confirmed using milestone confirmation.

Order Confirmation

You can confirm the whole order in one step using order confirmation.

Business Case: At SuperGears AG, the assembly process for each gearbox takes about five minutes; i.e., they produce about 24 parts every hour. Since the lead time is quite low, the business wants to post a confirmation every two hours with order confirmations.

Choose Logistics ➤ Production ➤ Shop Floor Control ➤ Confirmation ➤ Enter ➤ For Order. You can also use Transaction Code CO15 to post an order confirmation.

Enter the order number on the initial screen, as shown in Figure 8-36.

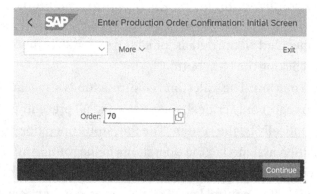

***Figure 8-36.** Production order confirmation: initial screen*

Enter the quantity (i.e. Yield, Scrap, or Rework) to be confirmed. Select the Confirmation type—Partial Confirmation, Final Confirmation, or Automatic Final Confirmation. Enter the execution dates/times—execution start date/time, execution finish date/time and posting date—as shown in Figure 8-37.

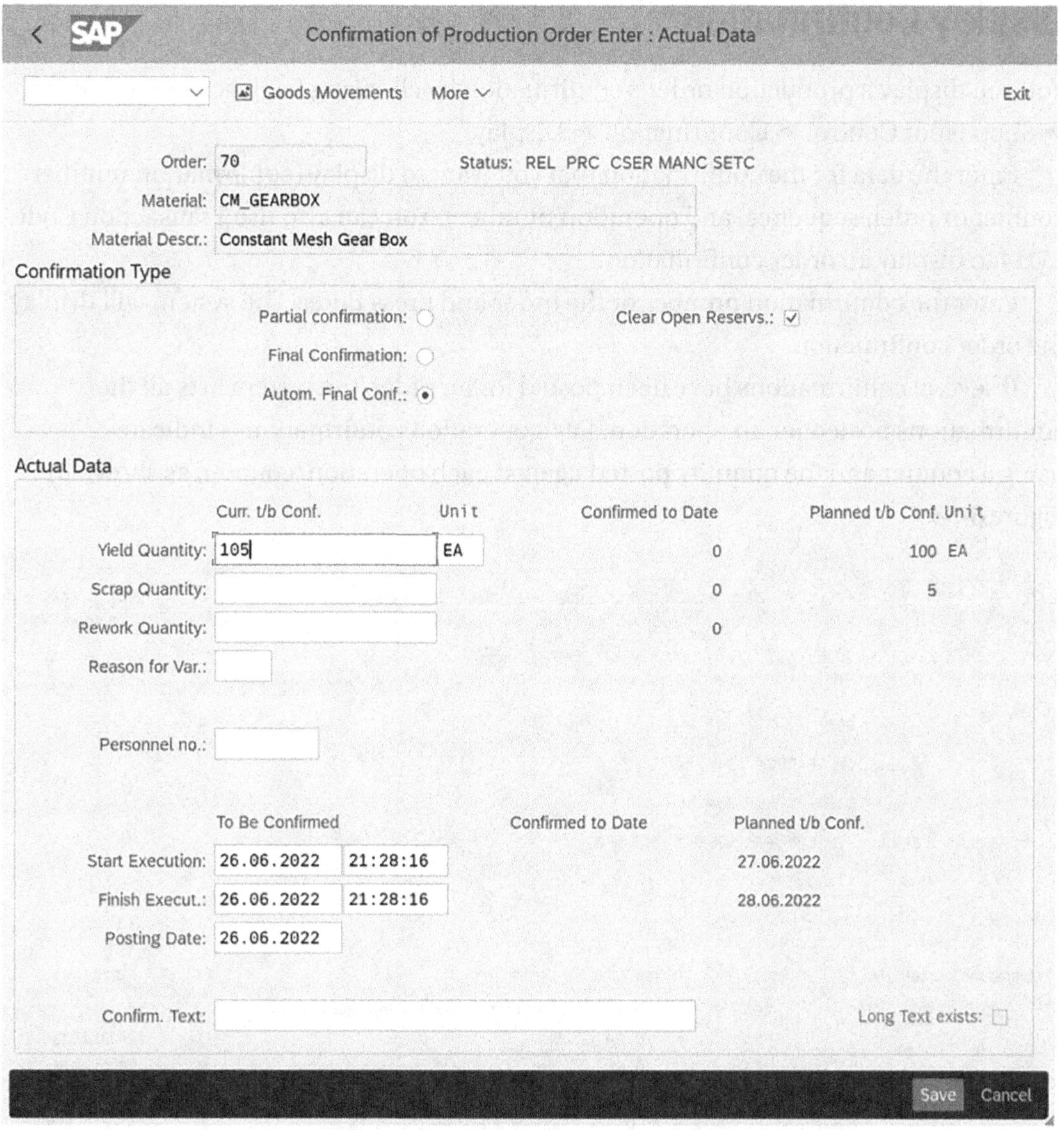

Figure 8-37. *Production order confirmation: actual data*

Click the Save icon to save the confirmation. Once the confirmation is posted, the system updates the status of the order to PCNF (Partially Confirmed) or CNF (Confirmed).

Display Confirmation

You can display a production order's confirmation by choosing Logistics ➤ Production ➤ Shop Floor Control ➤ Confirmation ➤ Display.

Enter the data for the confirmation that you want to display (confirmation number/counter or order, sequence, and operation number). You can also use Transaction Code CO14 to display an order confirmation.

Enter the confirmation number or the order and press Enter. The system will display the order confirmation.

If several confirmations have been posted for an order, the system lists all the confirmations posted for an operation. Each operation confirmation is indicated using a counter and the quantity posted against each operation/counter, as shown in Figure 8-38.

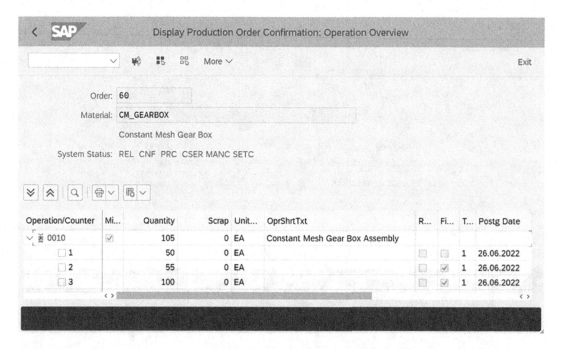

Figure 8-38. *Display production order confirmation: operation overview*

You can select the operation/counter and then click the Details icon to display the confirmation.

Cancel Confirmation

If you entered a confirmation by mistake or want to cancel the confirmation for any other reason, you can cancel it by using Transaction Code CO13 or choosing Logistics ➤ Production ➤ Shop Floor Control ➤ Confirmation ➤ Cancel. Enter the confirmation number or the order that you want to cancel.

If several confirmations have been posted for an order, the system lists all the confirmations posted for an operation. You can select the confirmations you want to cancel, similar to Figure 8-38.

Click the Save button to save the confirmation cancellation.

Goods Receipt for Production Order

Once the production is finished, you must post the goods receipt for the production order. The goods receipt is posted with movement type 101 and the stock of the material is debited or increased.

Choose Logistics ➤ Production ➤ Shop Floor Control ➤ Goods Movements ➤ Goods Issue/Goods Receipt. You can also use Transaction Code MIGO to post goods receipt.

Select the executable action as Goods Receipt and the Reference Document as Order. Enter the production order number. Based on the order number, the system populates all the information from the production order, like the material, quantity, storage location, and so on, as shown in Figure 8-39.

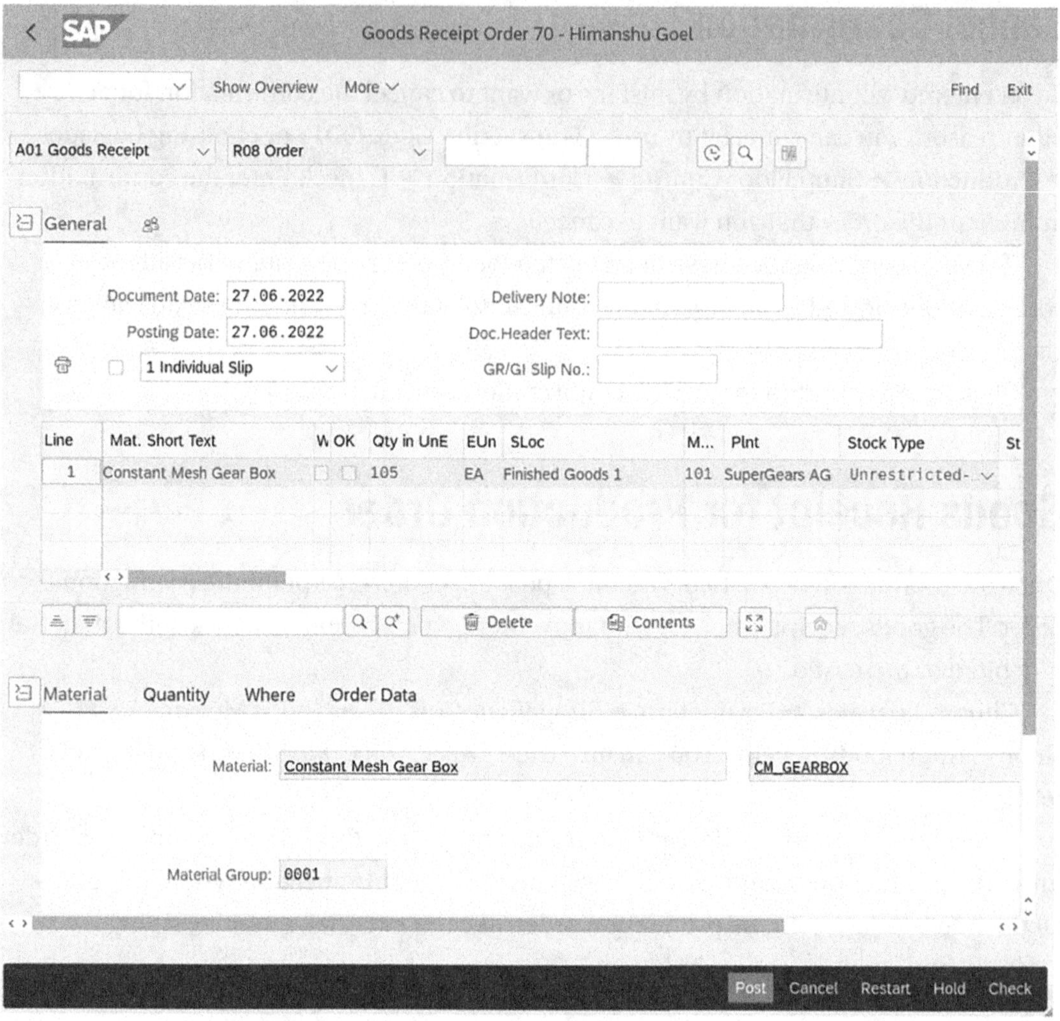

Figure 8-39. *Goods receipt order*

Check the material, quantity, plant, storage location, and so on. The goods receipt will be posted with movement type 101. Select the Item OK indicator. Click the Check icon to ensure there are no errors in the document. If everything is fine, click the Post button. The system will post goods receipt and then generate a material document number.

Status Management

A status documents the entire lifecycle of an order and specifies its current processing status. Whenever a business transaction is posted, the status of the order changes accordingly. The order status also controls or influences which business transactions can be performed on the order.

The production order allows two types of statuses—the System status and the User Status.

System Status

Whenever a business transaction is performed, the system status is set automatically by the system. For example, when an order is created, the system status is set as CRTD (created). Likewise, when the order is released, the system automatically assigns the status as REL (released). These statuses inform the users of the current stage of the order and which particular business function was performed on the order. The system status is set by the system automatically and the user cannot change the status manually. The system status can only be set or changed by posting a business function or a transaction.

User Status

In addition to the system status, it is possible to assign additional statuses, which can be used to control several business functions. User statuses are defined in the Status Profile in the customizing area. A status profile is created based on the order type, which can have as many statuses as needed.

- A status profile is used to define user statuses and document their function in long texts.

- The sequence of user statuses can be assigned using a "status number" for each user status.

- Initial status can be defined and set automatically when the order is created.

- A user status can be set automatically when a business transaction is posted.

- User status can be used to control (allow or forbid) certain business transactions.

269

Technical Completion of a Production Order

Technical completion means that the production order is finished from a logistics point of view. This function should be used when you want to terminate any further logistics business function. It can be used when the order is finished, or an order must be stopped prematurely, and no further business transaction should be performed. This will allow the system to delete open reservations, capacities, and purchase requisitions for external operations. The system status TECO (Technical Complete) is restricted to execute any logistics activity on the order. However, activities like confirmation, goods movements, settlement, and variance calculation can still be posted. The order is not relevant for MRP planning. An order cannot be changed if it has the TECO status.

If you want to set the TECO status on an order, use Transaction Code CO02: Change Order. Then choose Functions ➤ Restrict Processing ➤ Technically Complete. You can also use mass processing transaction COHV to set the TECO status on several orders.

The system status technical completion can be reversed by changing the order in Transaction Code CO02: Change Order. Then choose Functions ➤ Restrict Processing ➤ Revoke Technical Completion.

Close a Production Order

The closed (CLSD) status means the order is finished from a logistics as well as a financial point of view. You cannot post any goods movements or confirmation to the order. An order cannot be changed if it has a closed status. To set a closed status, the order must have a Released (REL) or Technically Completed (TECO) status and there cannot be any open purchase requisitions or purchase orders.

If you want to set a closed status on an order, use Transaction Code CO02: Change Order. Then choose Functions ➤ Restrict Processing ➤ Close. You can also use mass processing transaction COHV to set the CLSD status on several orders.

The closed status can be reversed by changing the order in Transaction Code CO02: Change Order. Then choose Functions ➤ Restrict Processing ➤ Undo Close/Complete.

Co-Products and By-Products

In some special production process, a secondary product is also produced in conjunction with the primary product. The secondary product produced can be either a co-product or by-product. Although both of them are produced as a secondary product, they are conceptually different.

A *co-product* is produced as a secondary product alongside the main product. This means while producing the primary product, a secondary product is produced as a co-product. The cost of the production is split between the member of the joint production (co-products).

Business Case: On the machining line in SuperGears AG, a lot of steel chips or swarf is generated while running operations like machining, drilling, and boring. These chips can be treated as co-products or by-products, depending on how the cost is shared.

The product must be activated as a co-product in the material master, as shown in Figure 8-40.

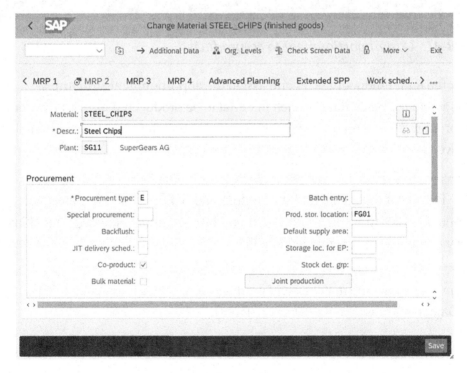

Figure 8-40. *Material master: MRP2 view*

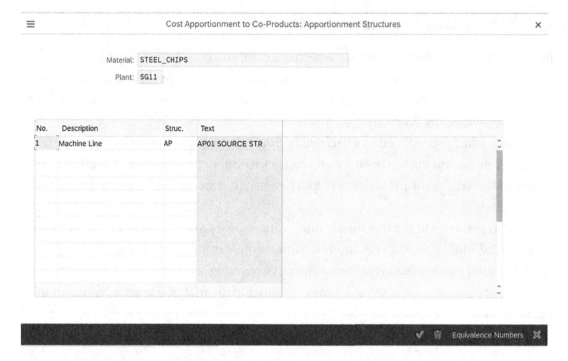

Figure 8-41. *Cost apportionment to co-products*

Click the Joint Production icon and assign the apportionment structure.

Now assign the percentage of each material to be produced (i.e., primary product and co-product). Based on the apportionment structure, the costs of the production is split between the primary product and the co-product.

Note   To explain the concept of co-product, the STEEL_CHIPS are assigned as a co-product to CM_GEARBOX, which is a gearbox assembly. However, the chips are actually generated at the machining line.

Figure 8-42 shows the major cost of production (i.e., 95% is assigned to CM_GEARBOX and 5% is assigned to STEEL_CHIPS).

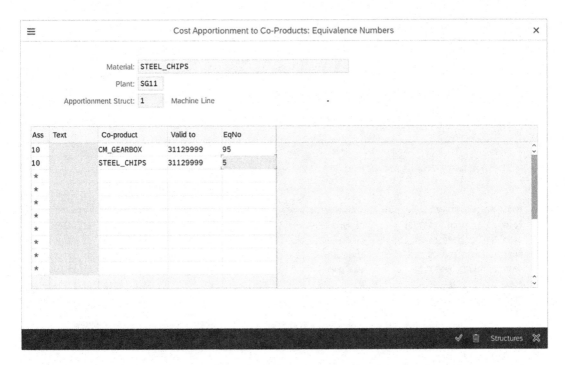

Figure 8-42. *Cost apportionment to co-products: equivalence numbers*

The co-product is then assigned as a BOM component of the primary product. The co-product should be maintained as a negative quantity, as shown in Figure 8-43.

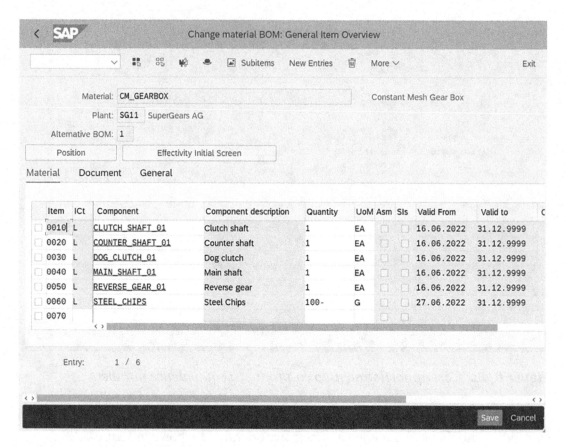

Figure 8-43. *Change material BOM: assign co-product*

Now go to the item detail and activate the Co-Product field, as shown in Figure 8-44.

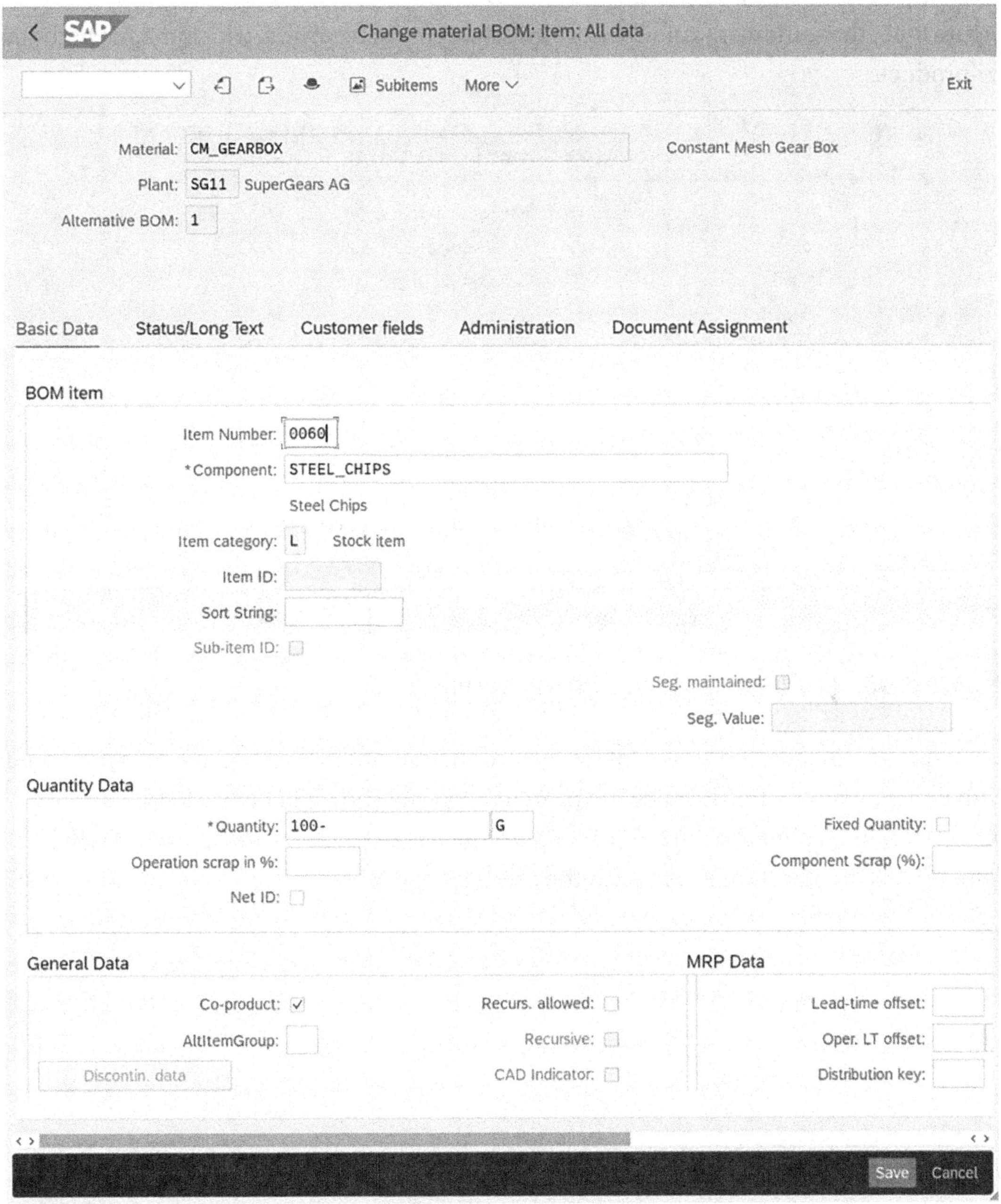

Figure 8-44. *Change material BOM: activate co-product*

When creating a production order for the main material or the primary material, the system will generate a separate order item for the co-product. As you can see in Figure 8-45, the settlement rule contains two settlement receivers, which means both the co-products.

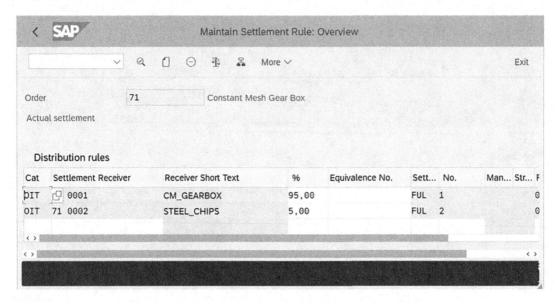

Figure 8-45. *Production order: settlement rule*

While posting the goods receipt for the production order, the co-product is produced with movement type 101, just like the primary material shown in Figure 8-46. The cost of production is split between the primary product and the co-product based on the Apportionment Structure assigned in the material master.

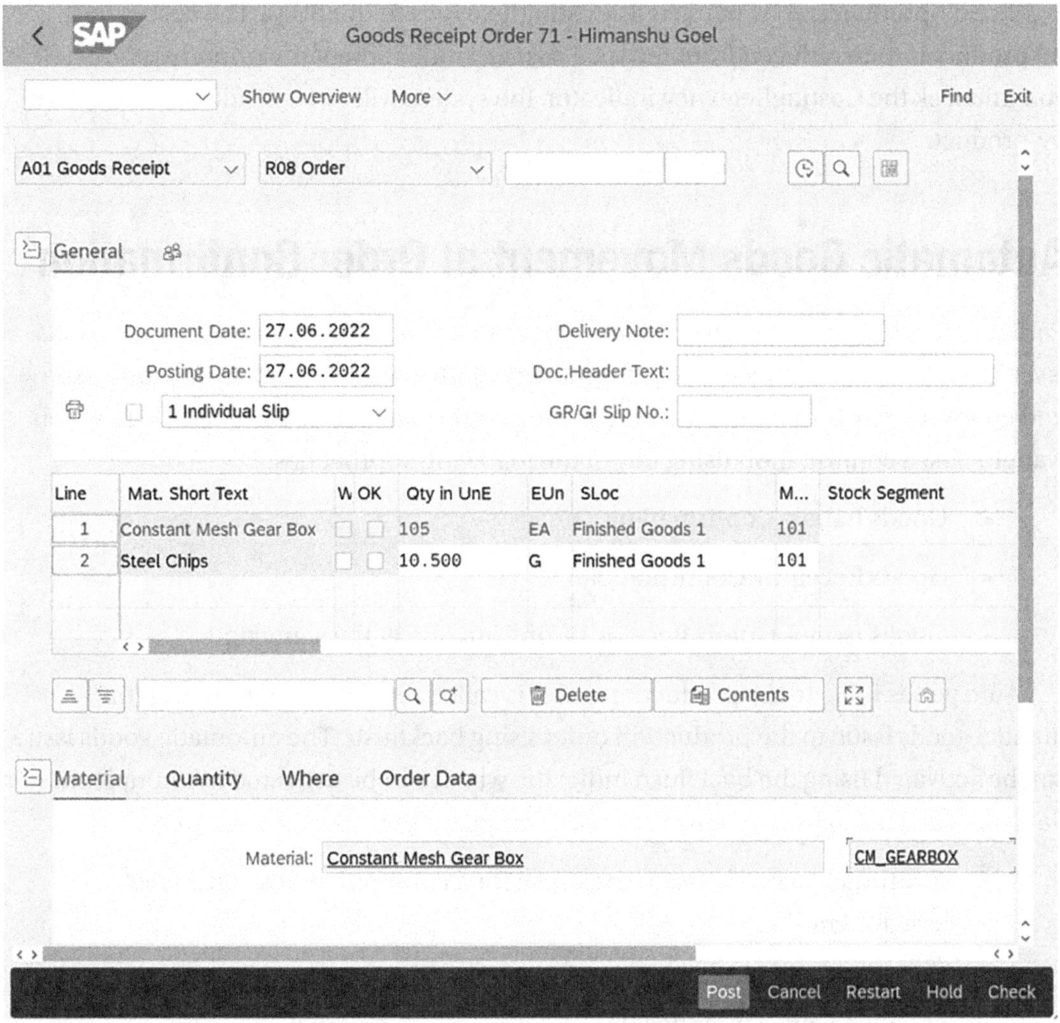

Figure 8-46. *Goods receipt order*

A by-product is produced as a secondary product alongside the main product. However, it is different from a co-product due to the fact that a separate order item is not created for a by-product. Also, the valuation of a by-product is based on the price defined in the Accounting view of the material master.

The by-product is specified as a component in the BOM of the primary material with a negative quantity similar to the co-product. However, during the goods receipt of the production order, the by-produced is produced with movement type 531.

The by-product can be marked as CostingRelevncy in the BOM. The cost of the by-product is then reduced from the total cost of production of the primary product. If you uncheck the CostingRelevncy indicator, the system will not consider the cost of the by-product.

Automatic Goods Movement at Order Confirmation

Earlier in this chapter, you learned how to post goods movement manually (i.e., goods issue to the order and goods receipt for the order). However, you can post goods issue and goods receipt automatically when posting confirmations. You can decide how you want to post a confirmation using any of the following approaches:

- Goods Issue + Confirmation

- Goods Receipt + Confirmation

- Goods Issue + Goods Receipt + Confirmation at the same time

Auto goods issue to the production order is called *backflush*. You can skip the manual goods issue to the production order using backflush. The automatic goods issue can be activated using the backflush indicator, which can be activated in multiple master data objects. The highest priority is checked based on the following hierarchy:

- **Routing:** You can activate backflush for a component in a component assignment.

- **Material master:** You can activate backflush in the material master or let the work center decide.

- **Work center:** If you opted for the work center to decide in the material master, you can activate the backflush in the work center. This provides an advantage if you want to backflush all the components that are consumed in this work center and thus do not need to activate backflush for each material in the material master.

Once backflush has been activated on any of these objects, you can see that the backflush indictor is reflected for the component in the production order, as shown in Figure 8-47. The goods issue of the component that has backflush indicator is posted automatically during order confirmation.

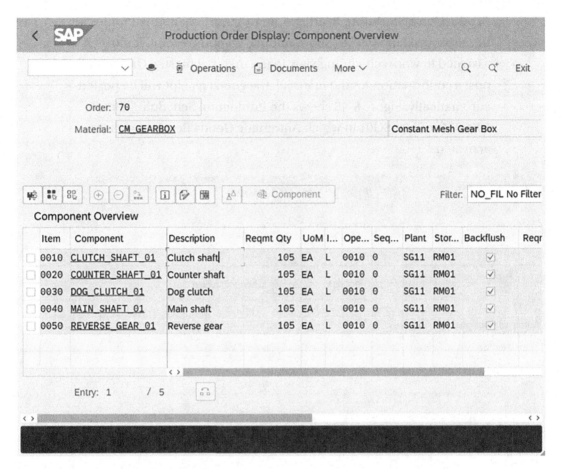

Figure 8-47. *Display production order: component overview*

Auto goods receipt to the production order can be controlled in two ways:

- **Control Key:** Goods receipt can be posted automatically during order confirmation when confirming an operation with a control key that has Automatic GR active. The heat treatment process for the gearbox has four operations—Annealing, Normalizing, Stress Relief, and Hardening. The last operation (Hardening) is assigned with Control key PP03, which comes preconfigured with Automatic GR active. When posting confirmation for operation 40, the system will also post goods receipt automatically.

- **Production Scheduling Profile:** A Production Scheduling Profile can be customized in SPRO to allow automatic goods receipt. It must be assigned to work scheduling view in the material master. Once you post a confirmation for the material, the goods receipt will be posted automatically. Figure 8-48 shows the Production Scheduling Profile 000001 for Plant SG01 in which Automatic Goods Receipt has been activated.

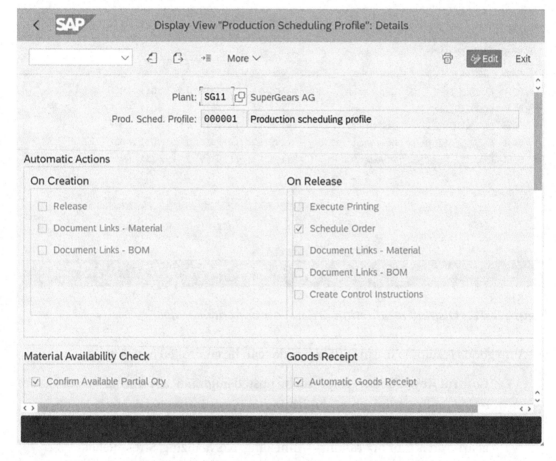

Figure 8-48. *Production scheduling profile*

Rework Order

During quality inspection, some of the gear assembly were found to be "Not OK" and thus they need to be reworked. The production planner should create a rework order to rework these faulty materials.

Choose Logistics ➤ Production ➤ Shop Floor Control ➤ Order ➤ Create ➤ Without Material. You can also use Transaction Code CO07 to create an order without material or a rework order.

On the initial screen, enter the production plant and order type. Enter the quantity to be reworked. Press Enter. In the popup window that appears, you must assign the Reference Operation Set. Usually, a task list with task list type S Reference Operation Set is created for rework orders. The operations from the reference operation set are assigned to the Operation tab in the order.

In the Component tab, you must assign the defective material to be reworked. This defective material is consumed as a component in the rework order.

Go to Settlement Rule and assign the rework cost center as the settlement receiver.

Release the rework order by clicking the Release icon. Click the Save icon and the system will generate a rework order. The rework order is confirmed and the goods receipt with movement type 101 is posted like normal a production order.

Scrap

During production, some products were found defective and they cannot be reworked. Therefore, these products must be scrapped. There are two possibilities to post scrap:

During production: If products are found defective during the production process, they must be scrapped during confirmation. This way you would post the loss of components and the activity costs.

After production: Once the production process has been finished and goods receipt has been posted, the quality inspection is carried out. During the quality inspection some of the products can be found to be faulty. These products must be scrapped using Transaction Code MIGO with movement type 551.

Summary

This chapter discussed the entire production order management process, which is mostly used in discrete industries. It discussed the production order document in detail and all the steps involved in manufacturing execution using production order-based manufacturing.

The next chapter discusses manufacturing executing using repetitive manufacturing.

CHAPTER 9

Repetitive Manufacturing

This chapter covers production execution using repetitive manufacturing in SAP. You'll learn about master data for REM, costing objects like the product cost collector, and so on. You'll learn about the planning table and REM backflush and scrap.

What Is Repetitive Manufacturing?

Repetitive manufacturing is a simplified manufacturing execution methodology. There is a common misconception that repetitive manufacturing is implemented only in repetitive industries or continuous industries. Although, this is not true. Manufacturing industries are classified into two industry types—discrete industry and process industry. Repetitive manufacturing can be implemented in discrete as well as repetitive industries, where you want to keep the manufacturing lean.

Repetitive manufacturing can be implemented in industries where similar products are produced over a period. It is not required to produce material in lots. The production process (routing/rate routing) is similar for materials and the setup time is shorter. The biggest strength of repetitive manufacturing lies in the simplified manufacturing execution process. The steps required in the manufacturing execution cycle are reduced to an absolute minimum. This is also called lean manufacturing.

Repetitive manufacturing can be implemented in make-to-stock as well as make-to-order environments.

Repetitive Manufacturing with Make-to-Stock

It is very common to implement repetitive manufacturing in make-to-stock environments. Production is carried out based on the run schedule header. The production plan is created using demand management and then the planned orders with Order Type PE, also called a run schedule quantity, are created by the MRP.

© Himanshu Goel 2022
H. Goel, *Handbook for SAP PP in S/4HANA*, https://doi.org/10.1007/978-1-4842-8566-4_9

The production execution is performed using backflush and the requirement for the sales orders are delivered from the stock.

The cost of production is accumulated and settled by the product cost collector. A product cost collector is created from a unique combination of material, plant, and production version.

Business case: Repetitive manufacturing with make-to-stock can be implemented for automotive suppliers, like SuperGears AG, who produce similar parts over and over. The production process is similar and the same gears can be shipped to multiple customers.

Moreover, repetitive manufacturing can also be implemented in process industries, such as the beverage industry, where similar products are produced over and over.

Repetitive Manufacturing with Make-to-Order

Repetitive manufacturing can be implemented to produce materials in make-to-order environments. The demands are derived from the sales orders and the planned orders are created by the MRP to meet the customer's demands. Each planned order is created with reference to a sales order. The parts are backflushed and placed into stock with reference to the sales orders.

The cost of production is accumulated and settled by the product cost collector.

Business case: Repetitive manufacturing with make-to-order can be implemented in the automotive industry (OEM). The vehicles can be produced based on customer specifications (using configurable materials). However, there is no need to capture the costs of production against each sales order. Consequently, product cost collectors are used for capturing and settling production costs.

Master Data for Repetitive Manufacturing

At SuperGears AG, the production of the main shaft assembly is a continuous process and thus is produced using repetitive manufacturing. Let's create the master data for the main shaft assembly in the REM environment.

Material Master

The material should be created with the REM indicator in MRP4 view. Also, a REM profile must be assigned to the material, as shown in Figure 9-1.

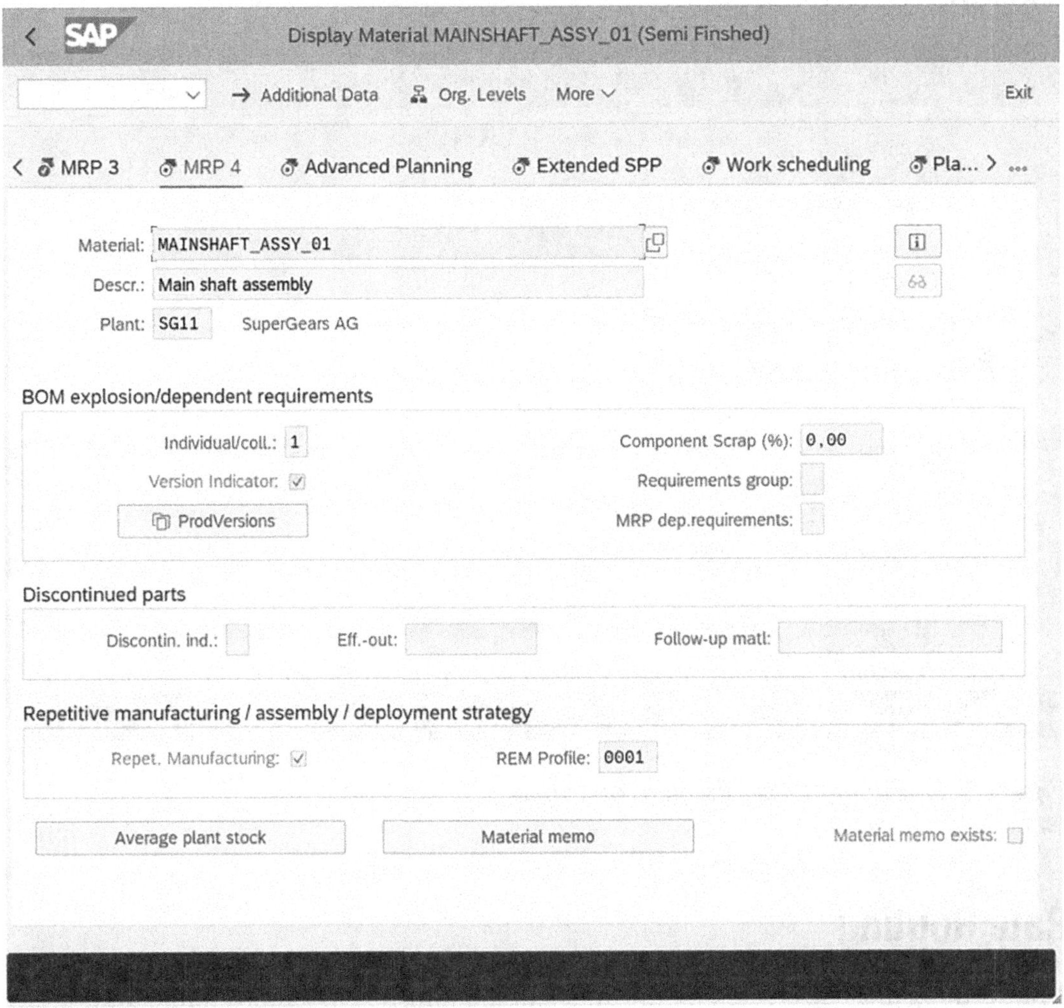

Figure 9-1. *Material master: MRP 4 view*

Bill of Materials

A bill of materials should be created for finished/semifinished materials, similar to discrete manufacturing. Figure 9-2 shows the bill of materials for the main shaft assembly.

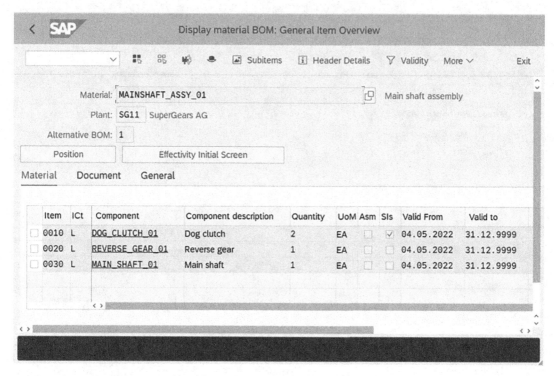

Figure 9-2. *Bill of materials: item overview*

Rate Routing

A rate routing must be created for the finished/semifinished assembly. A rate routing is a task list with type R, which is similar to routing.

Choose Logistics ➤ Production ➤ Master Data ➤ Routings ➤ Rate Routings ➤ Create. You can also use Transaction Code CA21 to create a rate routing. Figure 9-3 shows the operations overview of the rate routing for the main shaft assembly.

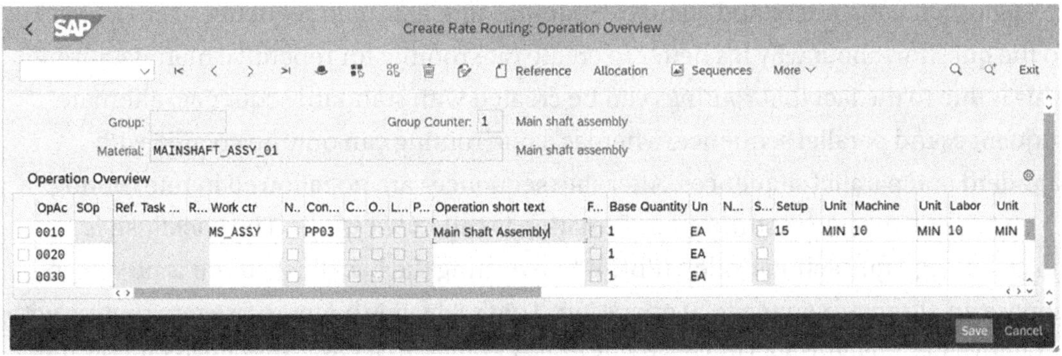

Figure 9-3. *Create rate routing: operation overview*

Standard routings with task list type N can also be used in repetitive manufacturing. Yet, it is recommended to use rate routing with repetitive manufacturing. You might wonder why.

A routing can be created with three types of sequencing—standard sequence, parallel sequences and alternative sequence.

Standard sequence: When you create a task list (a routing or a rate routing) that defines all the operations needed to produce the material, it is created as a standard sequence.

Parallel sequence: More than one operation can be processed at the same time. You must specify parallel operations. For example, there is a machining line that consists of several CNCs. However, the grinding operation is performed on a lathe machine, which is a bottleneck operation. Thus, two lathe machines are installed to overcome the capacity constraints. Therefore, a standard sequence is created with Lathe01, and a parallel sequence is created for the grinding operation with work center Lathe02.

Alternate sequence: Alternate sequences contain operations or series of operations that are supposed to be alternative to standard operations or series of operations in the standard sequence. For example, a machining operation is performed on CNC1. However, if the batch is bigger, CNC2 is used. For a batch size of 1 to 100 pieces, CNC1 is used while for a batch size of more than 100 pieces, CNC2 is used. This business scenario is captured in the routing information using alternate sequences for the machining operation.

Now that you understand standard, parallel, and alternate sequences, let's go back to the question about why it's better to create rate routing for repetitive manufacturing. This is due to the fact that routings can be created with standard sequence, alternate sequence, and parallel sequence, whereas a rate routing can only be created with standard and parallel sequences. Alternate sequences are not allowed in rate routing.

In repetitive manufacturing, confirmation is called *backflush*. The backflush is posted using Transaction Code MFBF. While posting the backflush, there is no way to choose an alternate sequence of operation. That's why it is better to use rate routing with repetitive manufacturing. However, this doesn't mean that you cannot use rate routing with repetitive manufacturing. You must ensure that alternate sequences are not defined in the routing when used with repetitive manufacturing.

Production Version

A production version must be created and you must activate the REM Allowed indicator, as shown in Figure 9-4.

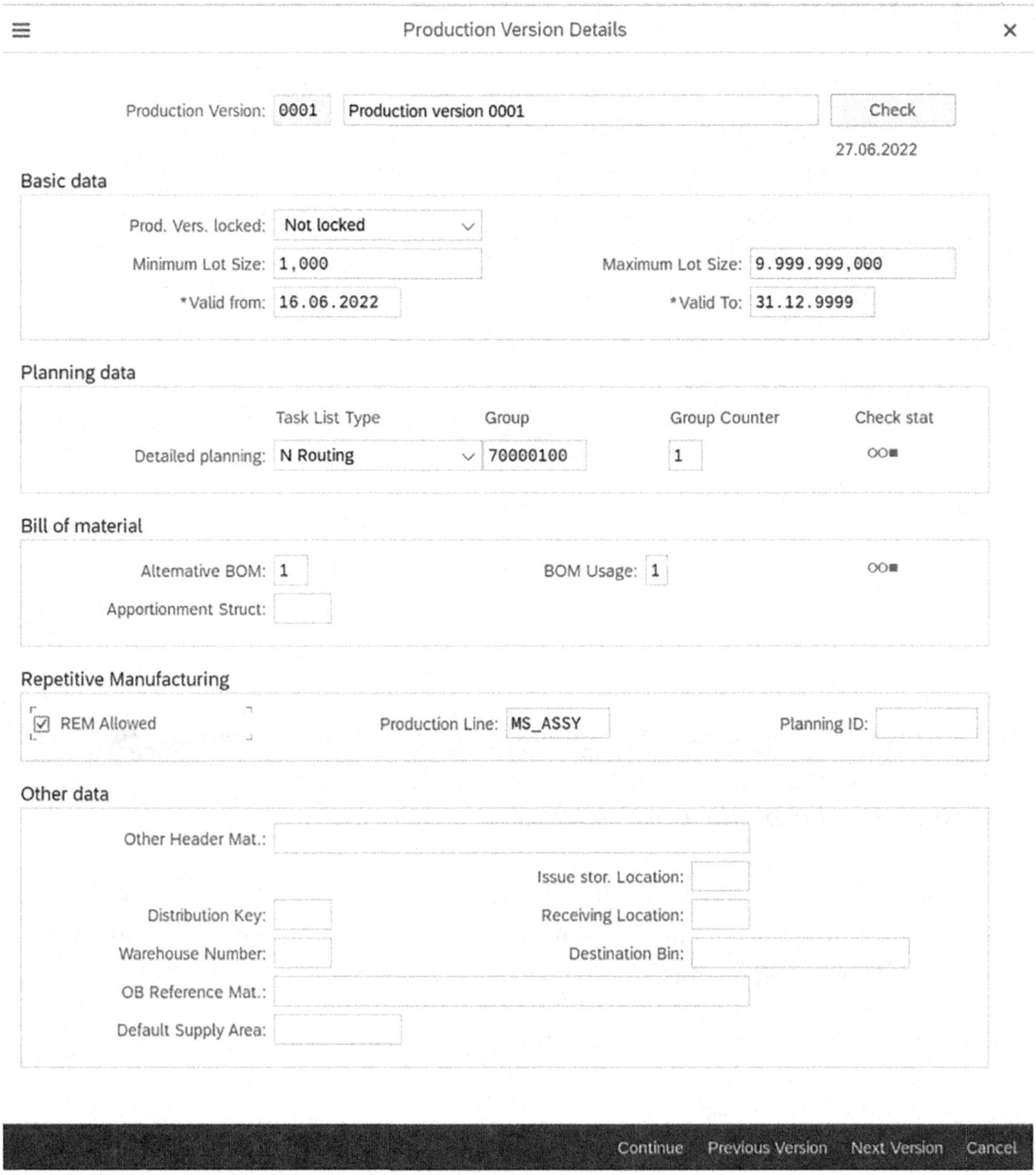

≡   Production Version Details   ✕

Production Version: `0001`   Production version 0001   [Check]

27.06.2022

Basic data

Prod. Vers. locked: Not locked ⌄

Minimum Lot Size: `1,000`   Maximum Lot Size: `9.999.999.000`

*Valid from: `16.06.2022`   *Valid To: `31.12.9999`

Planning data

	Task List Type	Group	Group Counter	Check stat
Detailed planning:	N Routing ⌄	70000100	1	○○■

Bill of material

Alternative BOM: `1`   BOM Usage: `1`   ○○■

Apportionment Struct:

Repetitive Manufacturing

☑ REM Allowed   Production Line: `MS_ASSY`   Planning ID:

Other data

Other Header Mat.:

Issue stor. Location:

Distribution Key: Receiving Location:

Warehouse Number: Destination Bin:

OB Reference Mat.:

Default Supply Area:

Continue   Previous Version   Next Version   Cancel

Figure 9-4. *Production version details*

Product Cost Collector

A *product cost collector* must be created for each material. It is a costing object that's used to collect the actual costs of materials production and settle these costs periodically.

Choose Logistics ➤ Production ➤ Repetitive Manufacturing ➤ Product Cost Collector ➤ Process Product Cost Collector. You can also use Transaction Code KKF6N to create a product cost collector.

Enter the material and plant and then click the Create icon to create a product cost collector, as shown in Figure 9-5.

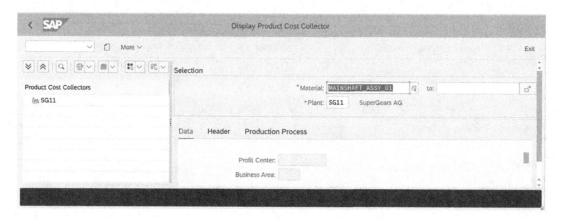

Figure 9-5. *Display product cost collector*

A popup window, as shown in Figure 9-6, is displayed. You must specify Order Type RM01 and the production version of the main shaft assembly to create this product cost collector, as shown in Figure 9-6.

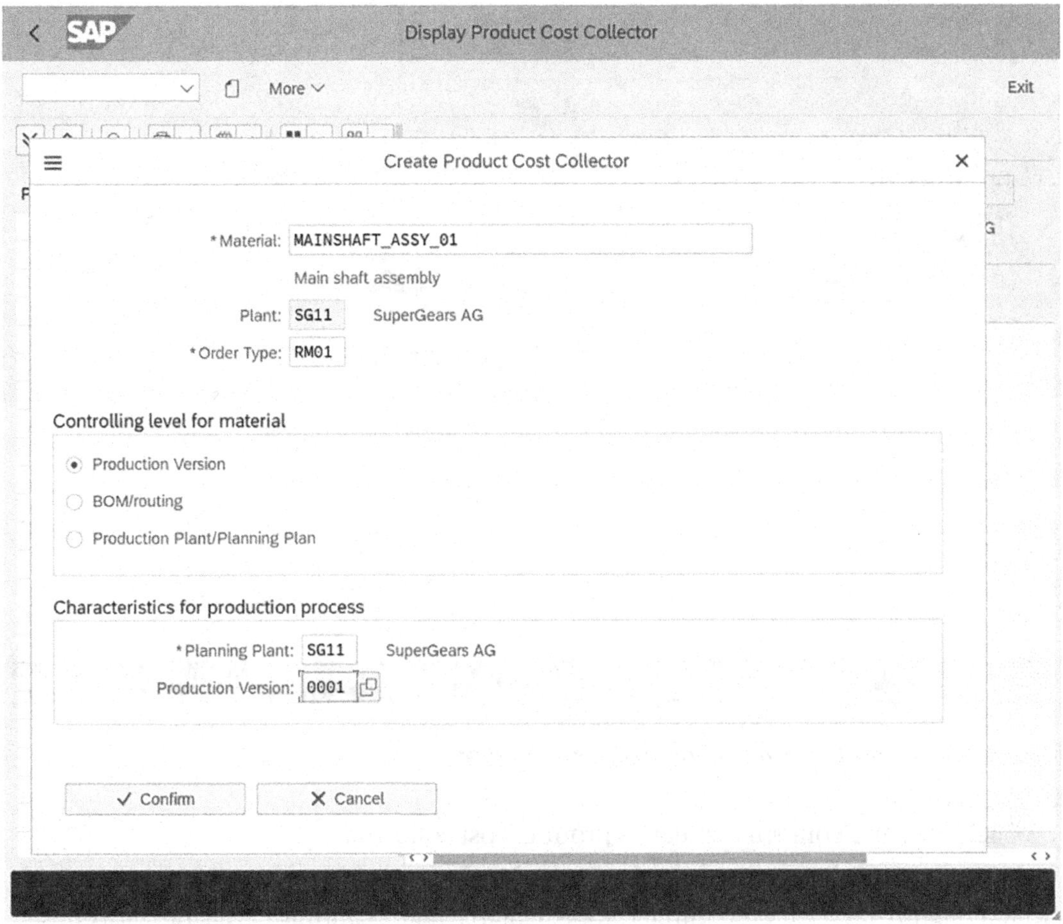

Figure 9-6. *Create a product cost collector*

Now click the Header tab. Here you can see that an internal order with the order number 700062 has been created with Order Type RM01 Product Cost Collector, as shown in Figure 9-7. An internal order can also be displayed using Transaction Code KO03.

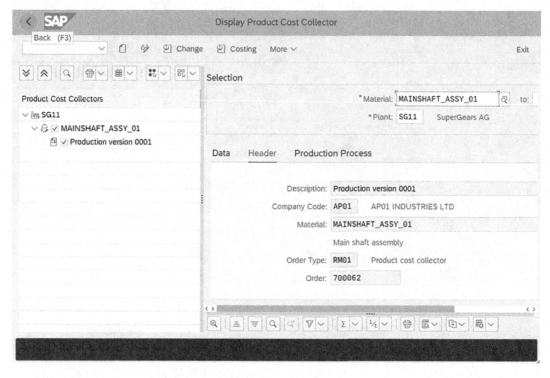

Figure 9-7.   *Create product cost collector header*

Click Save and confirm to create a product cost collector.

Product cost collectors can also be created in mass using the mass Transaction Code KKF6M. Figure 9-8 shows the initial screen, called Create Multiple Cost Collectors for Production Versions. You can enter the plant and order type. You can also enter a range of materials on the selection screen.

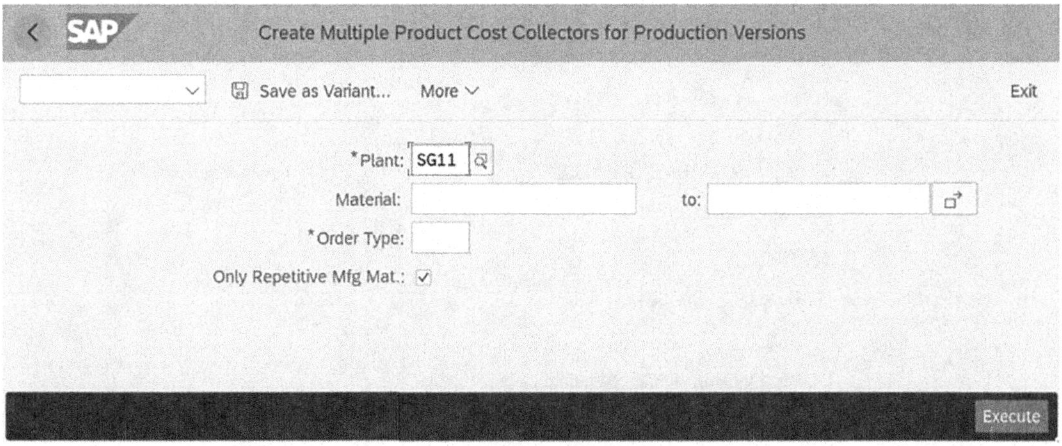

Figure 9-8. Create Multiple Cost Collectors for Production Versions screen

The master data for repetitive manufacturing has been created. Now you see how to create a standard cost estimate.

Standard Cost Estimate

A *standard cost estimate* is created to calculate the standard price of a material. The materials produced in-house usually have price control S in the Accounting 1 view of the material master. The standard cost estimate calculates the price of finished goods, and it takes into account product structure, production costs, and overheads.

Choose Logistics ➤ Production ➤ Product Cost Planning ➤ Material Costing ➤ Cost Estimate with Quantity Structure ➤ Create. You can also use Transaction Code CK11N to create a standard cost estimate.

Enter the material, plant, and costing variant. The appropriate costing variant must be selected based on the configuration settings, as shown in Figure 9-9.

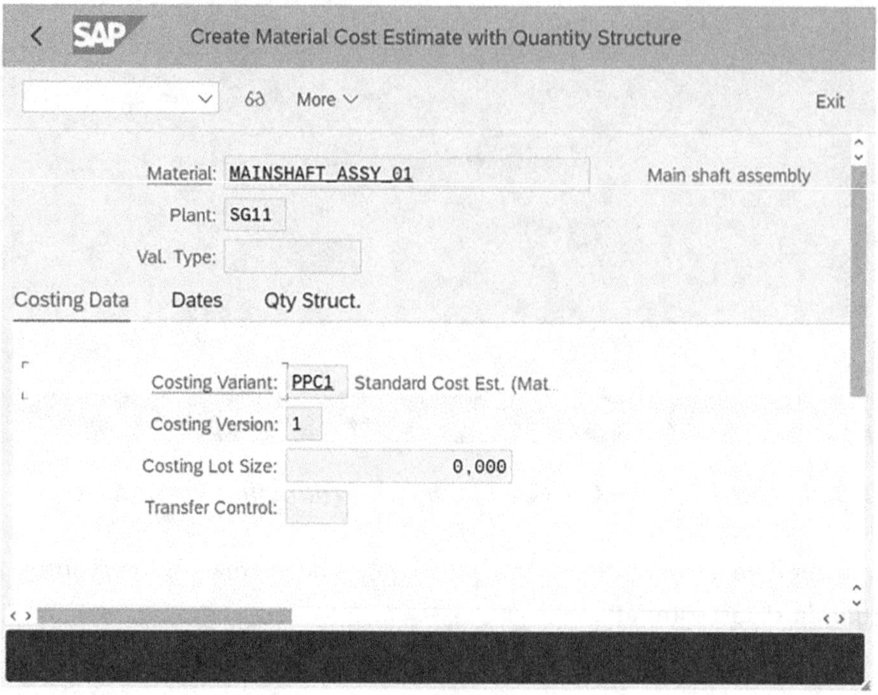

Figure 9-9. *Create Material Cost Estimate with Quantity Structure screen*

Once you have entered the data, click Enter. The system will take you to the next tab—Dates. Here you must enter the Costing Date From, Costing date to, Quantity Structure Date, and Valuation Date. The Costing Date To defaults to the end of the year, while the other three dates set the current date as the default. These dates can be changed.

A standard cost estimate contains the total cost of production of a material, which contains all the costs like component costs, production cost, and overheads. The cost of components is calculated based on the quantities from the BOM, and the cost of production activities is taken from the routing, The overhead costs are taken from the costing sheet and overhead key, as shown in Figure 9-10.

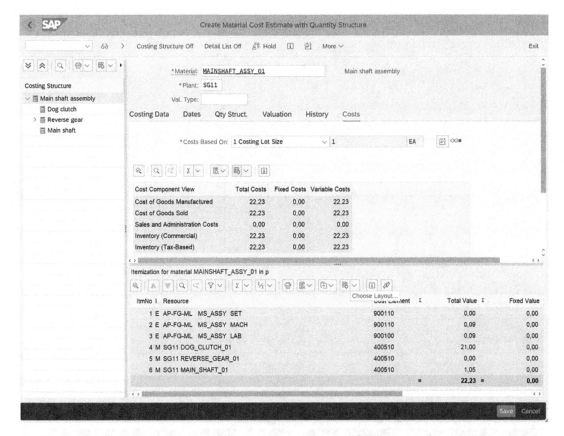

Figure 9-10. *Create Material Cost Estimate with Quantity Structure screen*

Now that the standard cost estimate has been created, it is time to update the calculated price in the material master.

Choose Logistics ➤ Production ➤ Product Cost Planning ➤ Material Costing ➤ Price Update. You can also use Transaction Code CK24 to update the price in the material master.

Enter the posting period, plant, and material code. It is not mandatory to enter the company code since it is filled in automatically based on the configuration, as shown in Figure 9-11.

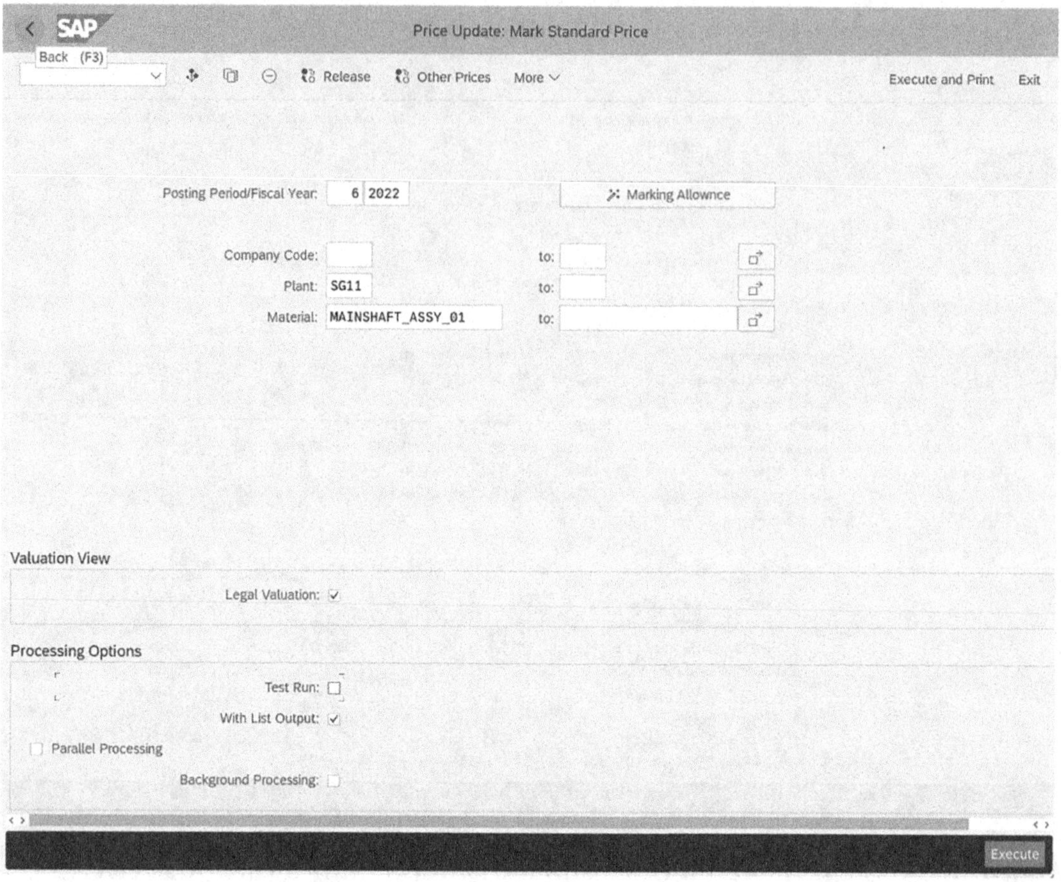

Figure 9-11. *Mark and release standard cost estimate*

When you mark the standard cost estimate, the costs of the finished good calculated by the cost estimate are updated as the future standard price in the costing view of the material master.

When you release the standard cost estimate, the costs of the finished good calculated by the cost estimate is updated as the current standard price in the costing view of the material master. This price is used for valuation in Financial Accounting until the next time the standard cost estimate is released.

Planning Table

The planning table is used in repetitive manufacturing to plan production quantities for a planning period. The planning table is a very powerful tool that's used by production planners to check and adjust production quantities. The tool lets the planner monitor the production line capacities. It also provides real-time overviews of availability situations of the products.

Choose Logistics ➤ Production ➤ Repetitive Manufacturing ➤ Planning ➤ Planning Table ➤ Change Mode. You can also use Transaction Code MF50 to plan your production in repetitive manufacturing.

Enter the MRP area or plant into the initial screen of the planning table.

The planning table can be executed based on several selection parameters. The tool provides flexibility in planning production for a production line or a product group. You must select the relevant selection parameter using the radio button.

- Production Line

- Work Center Hierarchy

- Material

- Product Group

- Class

- MRP Controller

Production Line: You can run the planning table for a production line, and it will display all the materials that are assigned on the production line. The table gives you a holistic overview of the capacity situation of the production line and thus helps you plan production considering the capacity constraints.

Based on the selection parameters, the planning table displays the planning situation for the materials assigned to the production line.

Material: The planner can review and adjust the production plan of a material by using this option. Enter the plant and material, as shown in Figure 9-12.

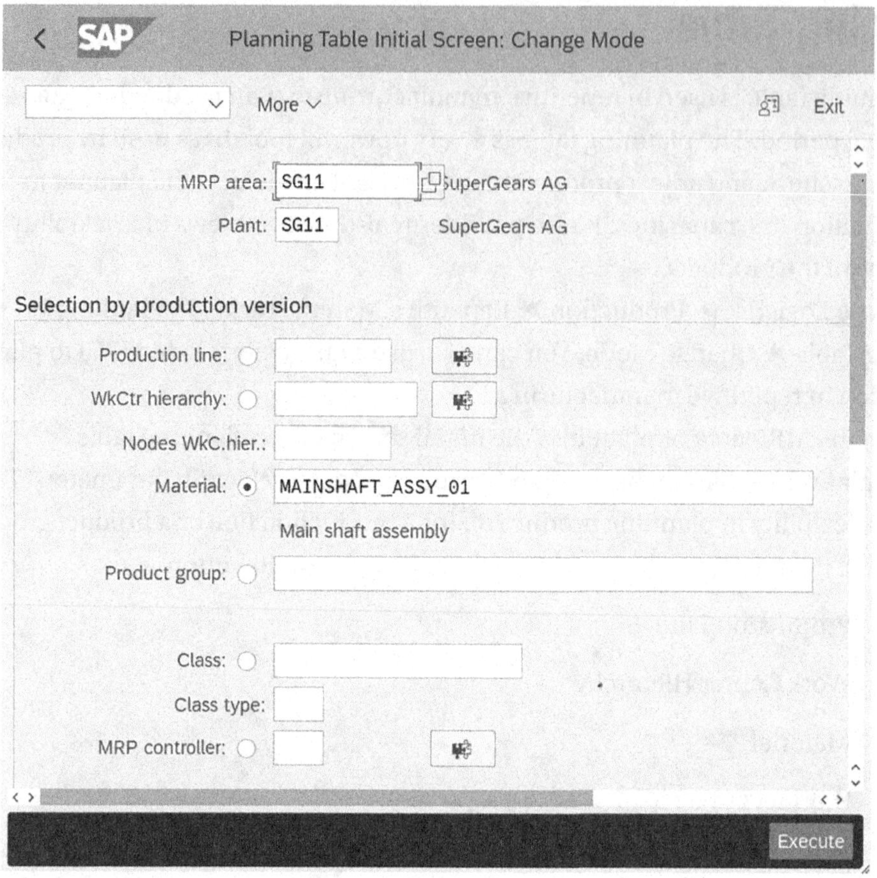

Figure 9-12. Planning table: initial screen

Product group: Several products can be grouped together using a product group. You can run the planning table for a product group, and it'll display the planning situation for all the members assigned in the group.

MRP group: The planning table can be executed for an MRP controller. The MRP controller will be able to plan all the materials, which falls in their responsibility area in a single screen.

Execute the planning table with Transaction Code MF50 for a material, as shown in Figure 9-13.

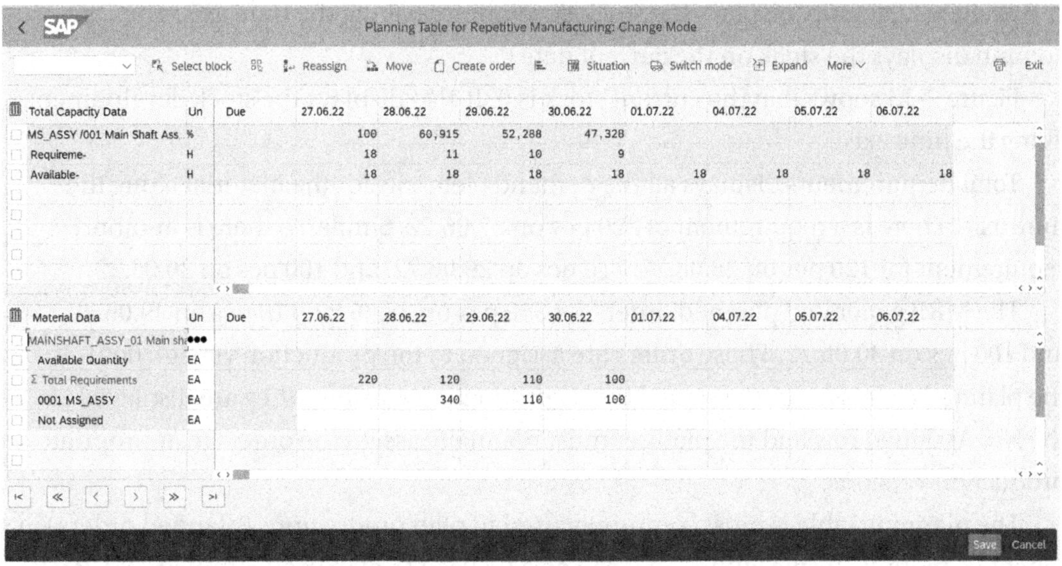

Figure 9-13. *Planning Table for Repetitive Manufacturing*

You may notice that the planning table has the look and feel of Microsoft Excel. This provides the planner an excellent user experience.

The screen contains two sections—Total Capacity Data and Material Data. The Total Capacity Data section displays information from the work center's point of view and displays the required capacity versus the available capacity. The Material Data section contains information from the material's perspective.

On the X-axis, the planning table shows the planning periods based on the planning period selected on the initial screen. The planner can select any of the planning periods for planning purposes:

- Shift

- Day

- Week

- Month

- Planning Calendar

On the Y-axis, the planning table has several parameters, including Available Quantity, Requirements, and so on.

The first column displays the material information (the material number).

Available Quantity displays the stock development along the time axis. The Due column displays the stock on the current date.

Figure 9-13 shows that the current stock is 0. It also displays the stock development along the time axis.

Total Requirements displays all the demand elements for the material along the time axis. There is a requirement of 220 pcs on 27.06.22. Similarly, there is another requirement for 120 pcs on 28.06.22, 110 pcs on 29.06.22, and 100 pcs on 30.06.22.

The MRP generated planned orders for 340 pcs on 28.06.22, 110 pcs on 29.06.22, and 100 pcs on 30.06.22. These orders are assigned to the production version 0001. If the planned orders are not assigned to any production versions, they are displayed in the Not Assigned row and the planner must manually assign the orders to appropriate production versions.

The planning table is most commonly used to plan productions (planned orders) in repetitive manufacturing, although it can also be used to plan production orders. If you want to use the planning table for planning, you must ensure that a valid production version exists for the material master record.

Create a Planned Order Using the Planning Table

A production planner can also create planned orders directly in the planning table. All that a planner must do is enter the quantity of the material that they want to produce on a given date, such as 125 pcs on 01.07.2022.

Double-click the 125 pcs and a popup screen appears, as shown in Figure 9-15. Here you can see that a planned order with an order number has been created for a quantity of 125 pcs to be produced on 01.07.2022. Isn't that great?

Figure 9-14 shows the available quantity as 125 from 01.07.2022 onward, due to the fact that there is no requirement.

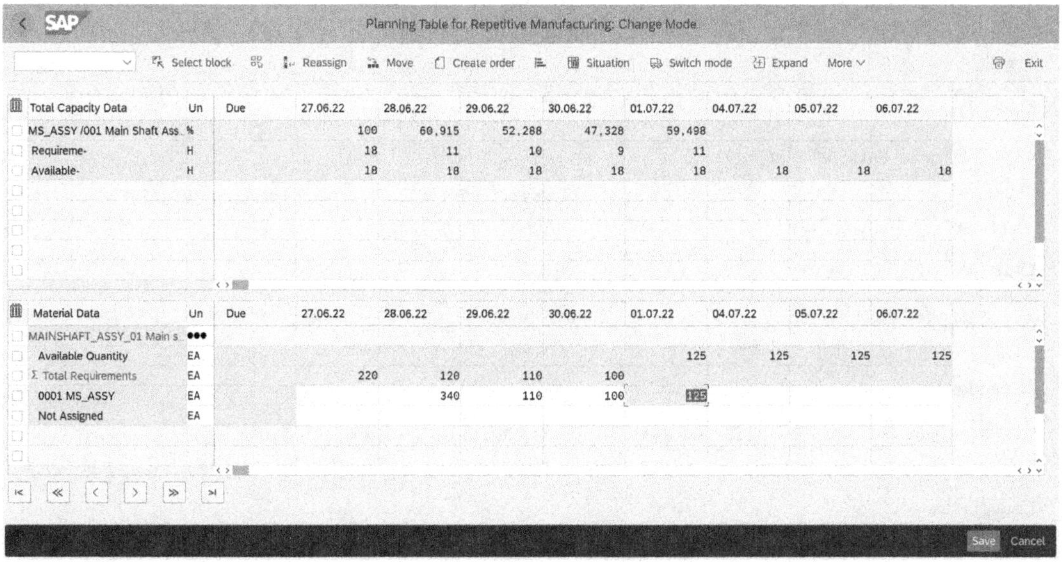

Figure 9-14. *Planning Table for Repetitive Manufacturing screen*

The planning table provides a lot of options; for example, Convert a Planned Order to Production Order/Process Order or to Move Quantities Along Time Axis, or Download the Data into Microsoft Excel.

Convert Quantities to Production/Process Orders

You can convert a planned order directly into a production order or a process order by clicking to the Quantity Change option in the menu bar. Click Convert Quantities. The system provides you with two options—In Production Order and In Process Order.

Move Quantities Along the Time Axis

You can allocate production quantities along the time axis, in partial or full. For example, there is an order of 125 pcs on 01.07.2022, as shown in Figure 9-14. To move this time order, click the Move icon and a new screen appears, as shown in Figure 9-15.

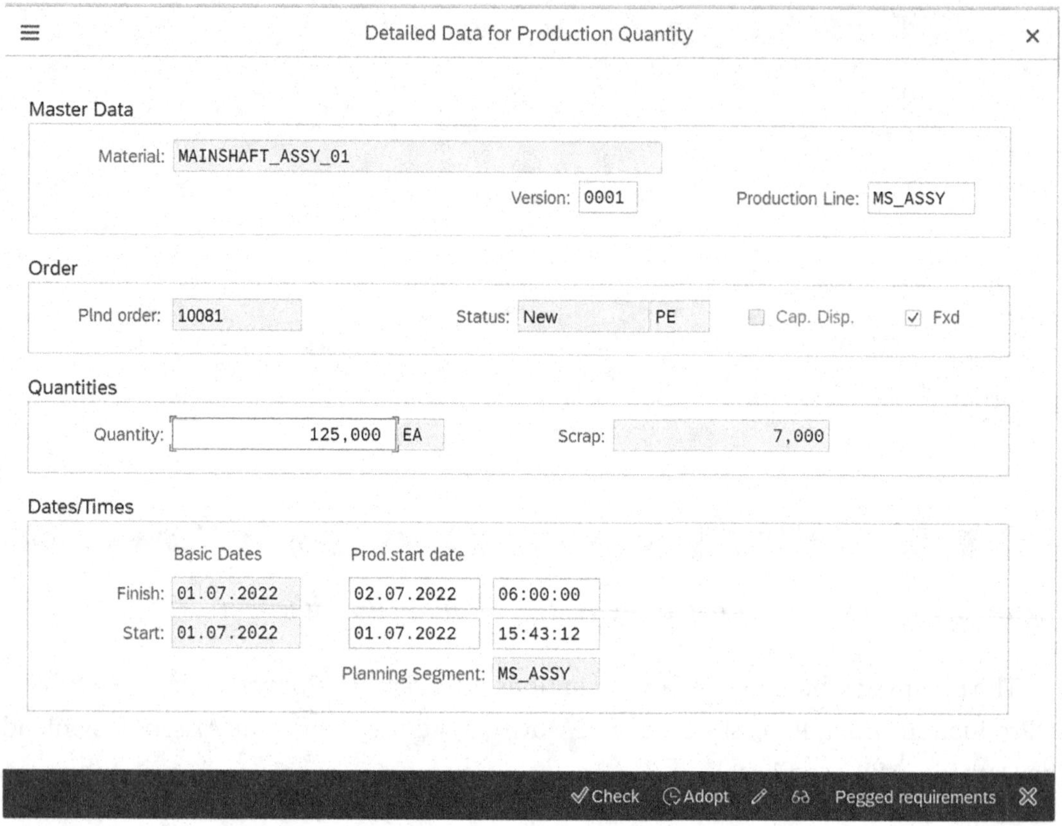

Figure 9-15. *Planning table: detailed data for production quantity*

Now, click the Select Periods icon to specify the period for which you would like to move the planned order. Enter the start and end dates to move the order, as shown in Figure 9-16.

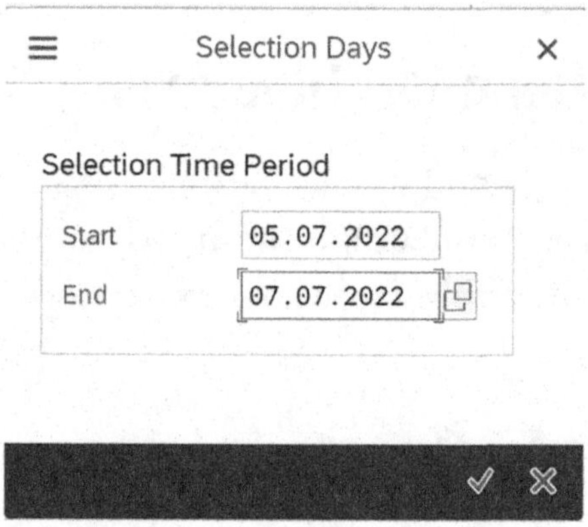

Figure 9-16. *Planning table: selecting days*

The order has been moved/split based on the selected periods. As shown in Figure 9-17, the order with quantity 125 pcs has been split into three orders of 42 pcs, 42 pcs, and 41 pcs for the dates 05.07.2022, 06.07.2022, and 07.07.2022, respectively.

Total Capacity Data	Un	28.06.22	29.06.22	30.06.22	01.07.22	04.07.22	05.07.22	06.07.22	07.07.22	08.07.22
MS_ASSY /001 Main Shaft Ass.	%	60,915	52,288	47,328			20,283	19,834	19,38	
Requireme-	H	11	10	9			4	4	4	
Available-	H	18	18	18	18	18	18	18	18	18

Material Data	Un	28.06.22	29.06.22	30.06.22	01.07.22	04.07.22	05.07.22	06.07.22	07.07.22	08.07.22
MAINSHAFT_ASSY_01 Main sh●●●										
Available Quantity	EA						42	84	125	125
Σ Total Requirements	EA	120	110	100						
0001 MS_ASSY	EA	340	110	100			42	42	41	
Not Assigned	EA									

Figure 9-17. *Planning table: move function*

Pull List

The components required to produce finished goods should be moved from the warehouse to the production storage location (PSL). The process of transferring the materials to PSL is called *material staging*.

Choose Logistics ➤ Production ➤ Repetitive Manufacturing ➤ Material Staging ➤ Pull List ➤ Trigger Replenishment. You can also use Transaction Code MF60 for material staging.

Material staging can be triggered on various levels, like Inventory Management, Warehouse Management, Kanban, and Extended Warehouse Management. It can also be triggered for planned, production, and process orders.

Enter the planned order number in the Planned Orders section, as shown in Figure 9-18.

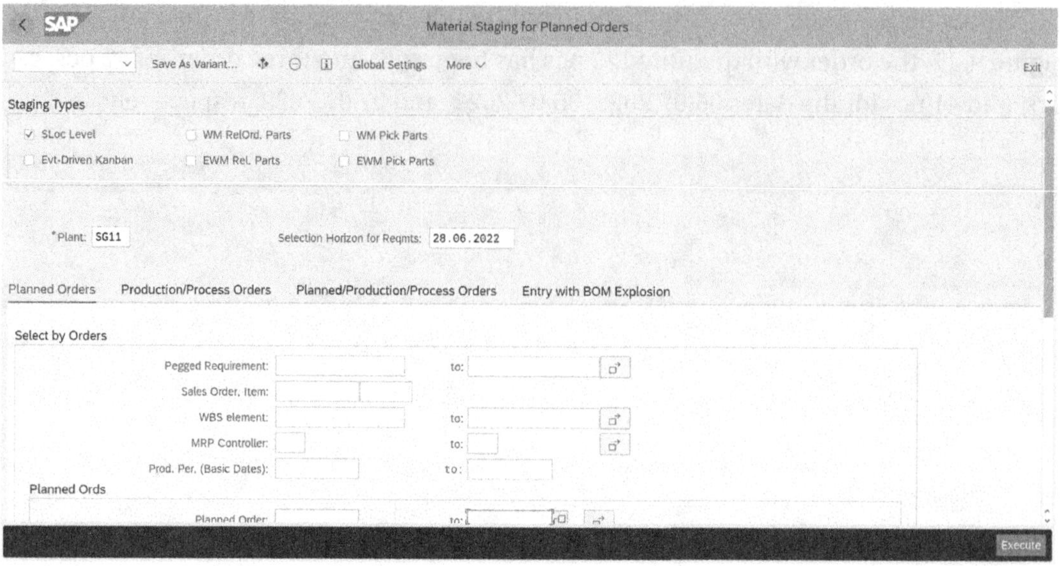

Figure 9-18. *Material Staging for Planned Orders: initial screen*

The pull list (see Figure 9-19) is split into two sections—Total Requirements and Replenishment Elements. The pull list checks the requirements and the available stock of the components at the production storage location. Based on this data, the pull list calculates the quantities of missing components.

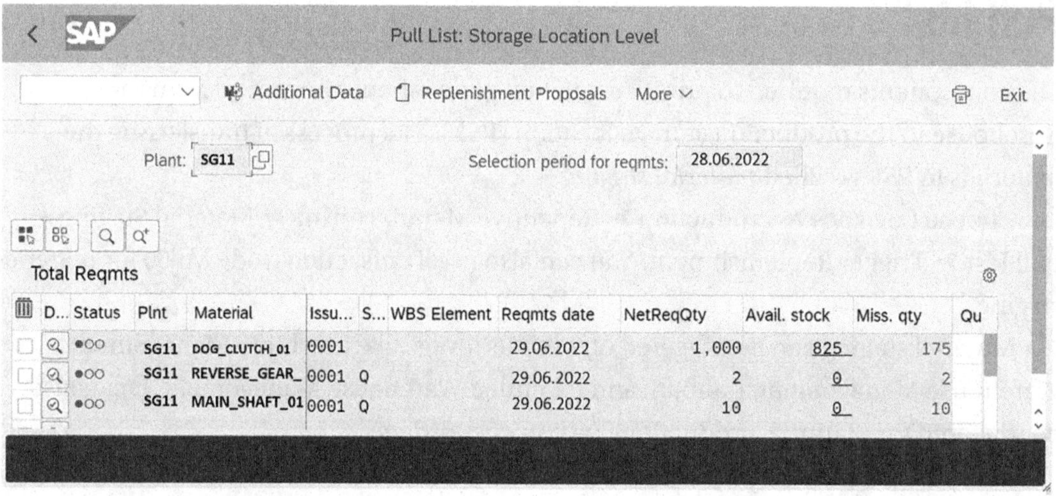

Figure 9-19. *Material staging for planned orders: output list*

You can create replenishment elements for the missing parts by clicking the Replenish Proposals icon.

REM Confirmation

The confirmation process in repetitive manufacturing is commonly known as backflush. In discrete manufacturing, the term backflush refers to automatic goods issue during the order confirmation process. This means there is no need to execute the goods issue separately. Whereas, in repetitive manufacturing, the term backflush is used for order confirmation which may or may not include goods issue, activity posting, and goods receipt.

Choose Logistics ➤ Production ➤ Repetitive Manufacturing ➤ Data Entry ➤ Repetitive Manufacturing Confirmation. You can also use Transaction Code MFBF to post order confirmations for repetitive manufacturing, as shown in Figure 9-12.

Transaction Code MFBF gives you an option to post three types of backflush (confirmations)—Assembly Backflush, Component Backflush, and Activity Backflush.

- **Assembly Backflush:** This is the most commonly used backflush type and it's used to post goods issue, activity confirmation, and goods receipt. While producing materials using repetitive manufacturing, it is common to post assembly backflush periodically: say every hour or two. Assembly backflush indicates that the finished good is produced and the components consumed is posted at the same time. The activities consumed during the production process is also posted together with goods issue of components and goods receipt of finished goods.

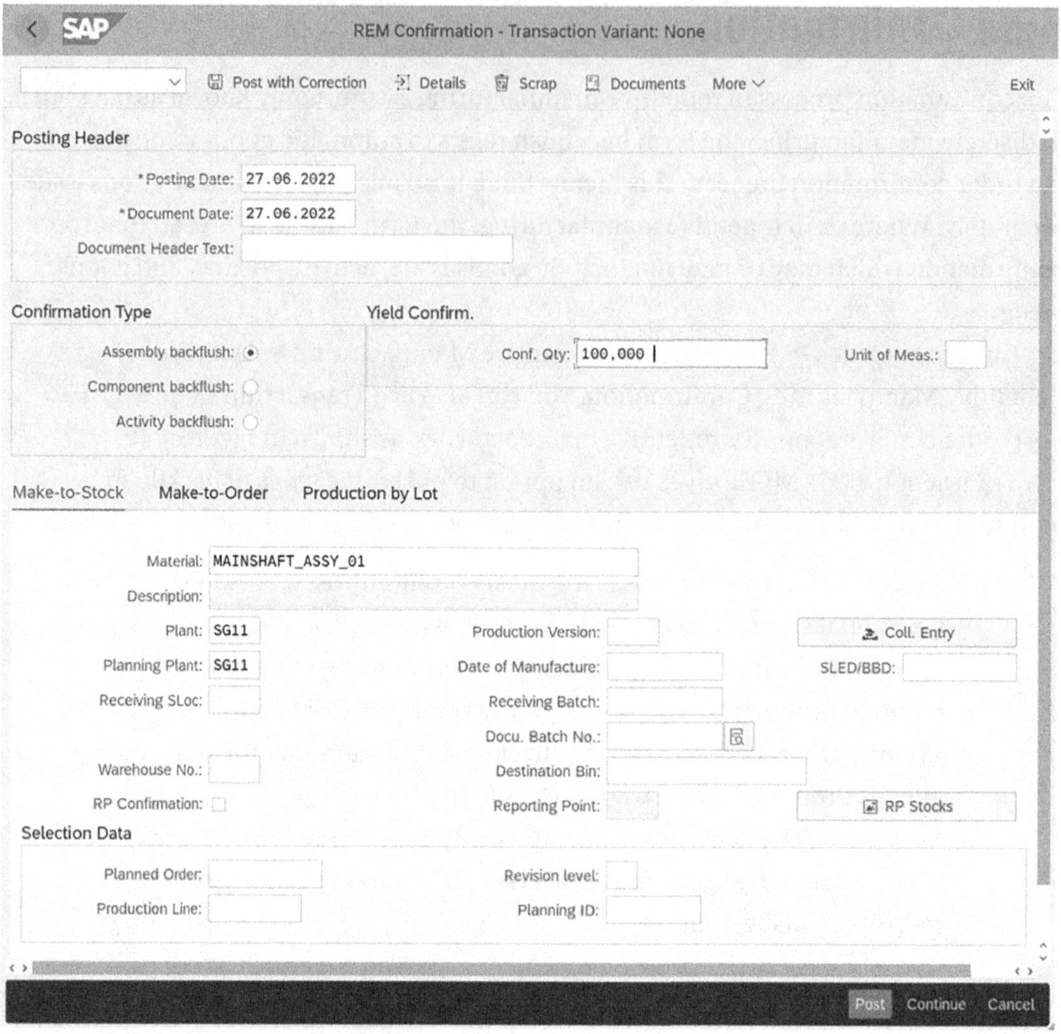

Figure 9-20. *REM confirmation*

If you click the Post with Corrections icon, a new screen appears which shows all the materials (i.e., the finished goods and all the components needed to manufacture the product). The goods receipt for the finished goods is posted with movement type 131 and the goods issue for the components is posted with movement type 261.

- **Component Backflush:** You can use Component Backflush only to report the goods issue of components during the confirmation process. While using Component Backflush, the goods receipt for finished goods and confirmation for activities are not posted. For example, you may use Component Backflush to report excess consumption of components.

- **Activity Backflush:** You can use Activity Backflush only to post activities consumed during the confirmation process. While using Activity Backflush, the goods receipt for finished goods or goods receipt for components are not posted.

Reporting Point Backflush

Reporting point backflush is similar to milestone confirmation in discrete manufacturing. It is used to reflect the progress of an order. For example, there are several operations in the routing of a material. Some of these operations are critical and the lead time for the production is several days, whereas other operations have shorter lead times and no additional components are consumed. You may define the critical operations as reporting points to keep track of the status of the work in progress and to note when components are consumed.

Reporting points can be confirmed by selecting the RP Confirmation check box and selecting the reporting point (the operation number).

You can also display the reporting point information by choosing Logistics ➤ Production ➤ Repetitive Manufacturing ➤ Evaluations ➤ Reporting Point Overview or using Transaction Code MF26.

Enter the plant and material, as shown in Figure 9-21.

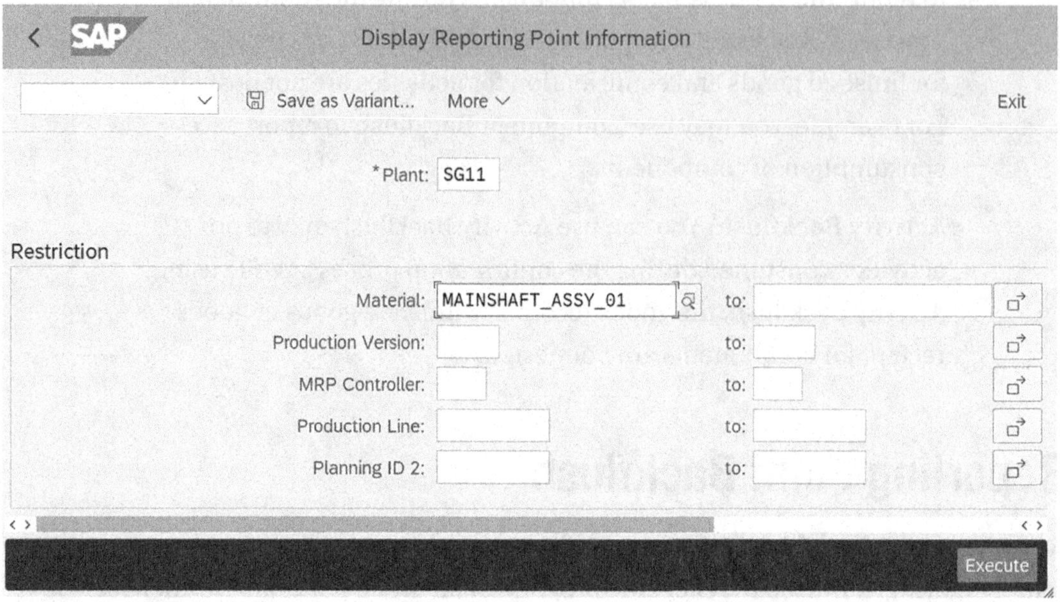

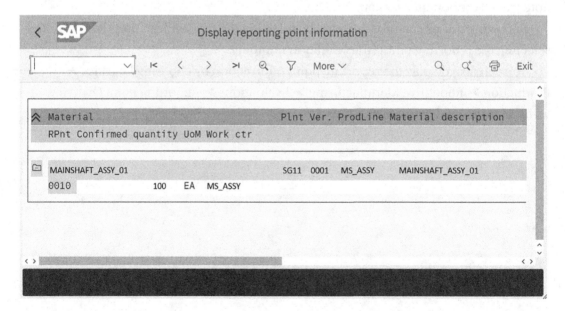

Figure 9-21. *Display Reporting Point Information: initial screen*

The reporting point information is displayed, as shown in Figure 9-22. The report displays the material and quantity reported for each reporting point.

Figure 9-22. *Display Reporting Point Information: output list*

Scrap in Repetitive Manufacturing

You can post scrap incurred during the production process using Transaction Code MFBF. You must click the Scrap icon. The screen looks almost similar to the Backflush screen, except the Yield Quantity field disappears and the Scrap Quantity field is displayed. You can also specify the reason for the scrap and the scraped quantities.

Just like with backflush, you can post scrap for Assembly Backflush, Component Backflush, and Activity Backflush.

Post-Processing of Error Records

Some activities might fail during posting REM backflush. For example, insufficient stock of the component may lead to failure of goods issue document posting. Or a material was being processed by another user, so the goods movement of the material could be posted. The backflush process should not stop due to such errors. Therefore, all such errors are recorded and then can later be reprocessed.

Choose Logistics ➤ Production ➤ Repetitive Manufacturing ➤ Data Entry ➤ Postprocess ➤ Postprocessing List. You can also use Transaction Code MF47 to post-process error records.

Enter the plant on the initial screen. You can also enter other selection parameters to filter the output, as shown in Figure 9-23.

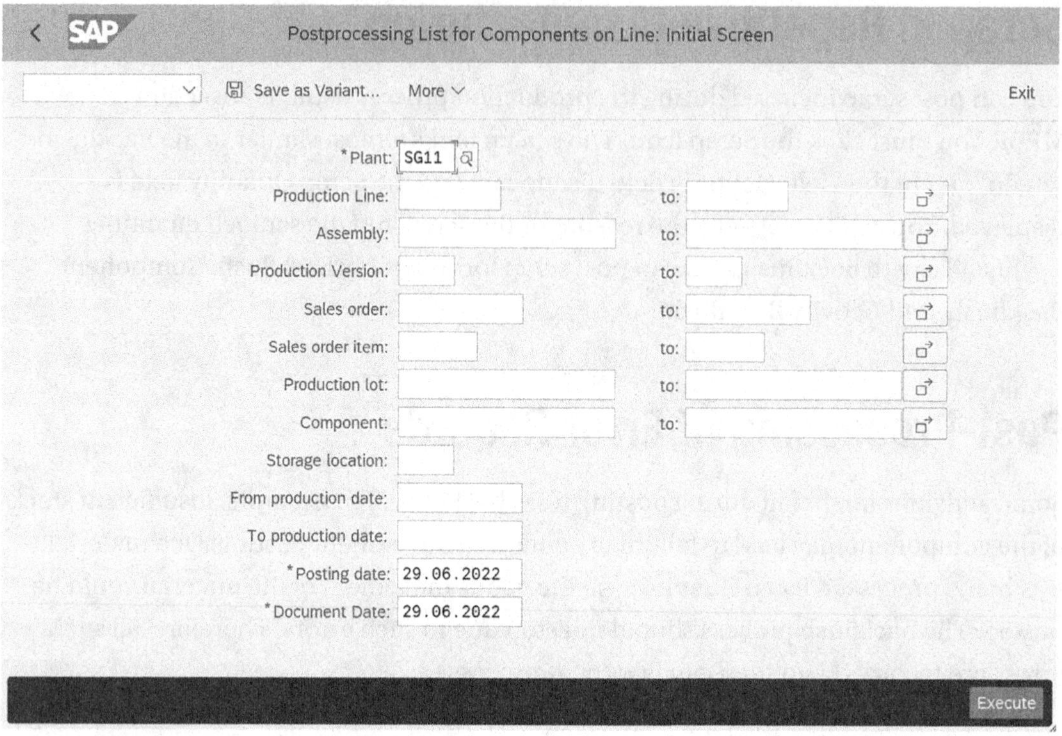

Figure 9-23. *Postprocessing List for Components on Line: initial screen*

The postprocessing list is generated and displays information like Assembly, Material, Material Description, Plant, Quantity, and so on.

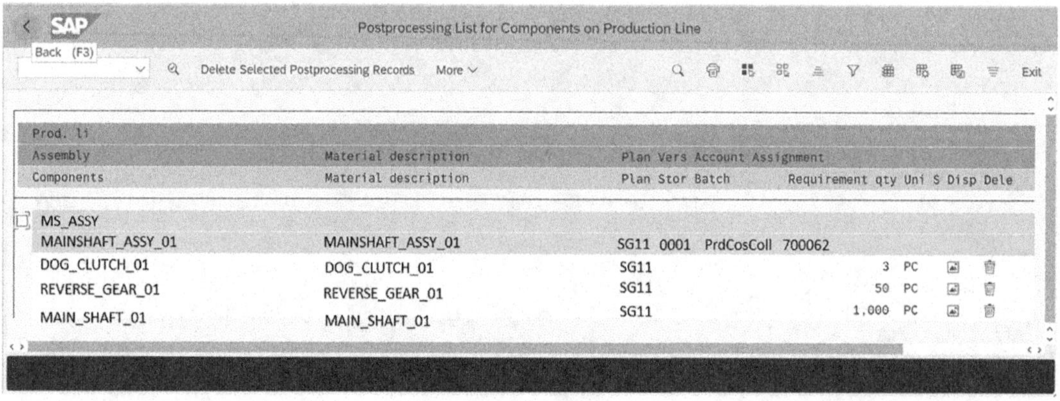

Figure 9-24. *Postprocessing List for Components on Production Line: output list*

You must select the error by clicking the check box and then clicking the Postprocess Selected Postprocessing Recs icon.

Summary

This chapter covered repetitive manufacturing, which is used for serial production or continuous production. It discussed the master data needed for REM, different costing objects, backflush in repetitive manufacturing, scrap posting, post-processing of error records, and so on.

In the next chapter, you'll learn about process order-based manufacturing, which is primarily used in process industries.

CHAPTER 10

Process Order Management

In this chapter, you learn about manufacturing execution using process order management, which is primarily used in process industries. The chapter discusses master data objects and other functions in SAP PP-PI. Special attention is paid to process management, which includes PI-sheets and control recipes.

What Is Process Order Management?

Process order management is used in batch-oriented process manufacturing. Process manufacturing is a production methodology where the production involves special processes that transform the ingredients into a totally new product. The production process is intricate and usually involves formulas or recipes. This production is used with highly composite processes like casting, grinding, blending, boiling, and so on. Pharmaceutical, petroleum, plastics, rubber, paper, textile, metal, and food products go through such chemical processes. Industries like Chemical, Pharma, FMCG (Fast-moving consumer goods), and Food and Beverages use process manufacturing to manufacture products like chemicals, medicines, shampoo, soaps, cheeses, juices, and so on.

Unlike with discrete manufacturing, the finished goods cannot be disassembled into their original raw materials.

The process industry is executed using process orders. This chapter discusses process order management.

© Himanshu Goel 2022
H. Goel, *Handbook for SAP PP in S/4HANA*, https://doi.org/10.1007/978-1-4842-8566-4_10

Master Data for the Process Industry

The following master data is required for process order management:

- Material master

- Bill of materials

- Production version

- Resources

- Master recipes

Material Masters

Material masters should be created for all materials, similar to the discrete industry. In the process industry, it is quite common to execute orders in batches or, in other words, batch management is used quite extensively here.

A material is created called Fruit Juice – Apple, as shown in Figure 10-1.

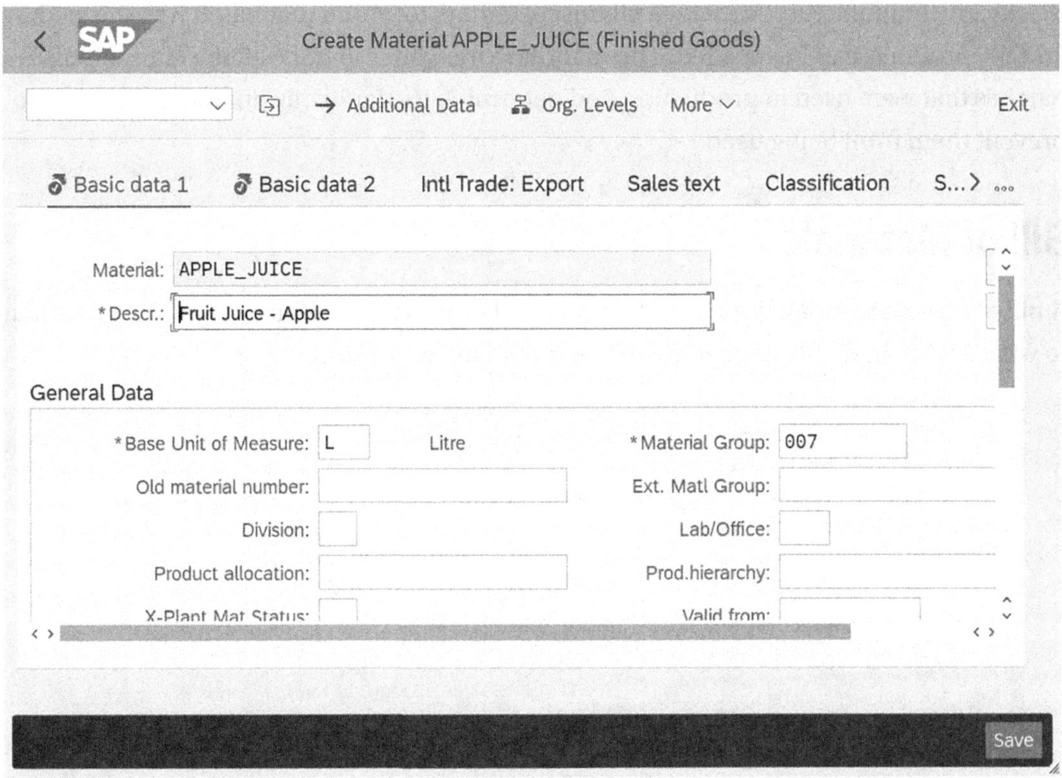

Figure 10-1. *Material master*

A *batch* represents a lot produced in one go. All the materials produced during this production run should have the same characteristics and specifications. For instance, a process order is created to produce 1000 liters of fruit juice. Usually, the production line produces 250 liters of fruit juice in four hours in one production run. Since 250 liters of juice is produced in one go, it means that the entire batch will contain the same specifications, including Calories, Vitamin C, Protein, Sugar, and so on. To meet the process order requirement, four batches should be produced. Although the product is the same, different batches can have different characteristics that fall within the allowed thresholds. For such materials, inventory is managed at the batch level. Batch management is critical in process industries, as it helps with end-to-end traceability. A batch contains all the information about the raw material/batches consumed as well as the resources used to produce the batch. You can see batch numbers or lot numbers on soft drinks and packaged foods that you buy. If a batch is found to be faulty for some reason, the manufacturer can trace all the customers to whom that batch was shipped, and the products can be recalled. The manufacturer can also trace all the component/batches that were used in production and determine the faulty raw materials/batches to prevent them from being used.

Bill of Materials

A bill of materials should be created for finished products/semifinished products, similar to what's done in the discrete industry, as shown in Figure 10-2.

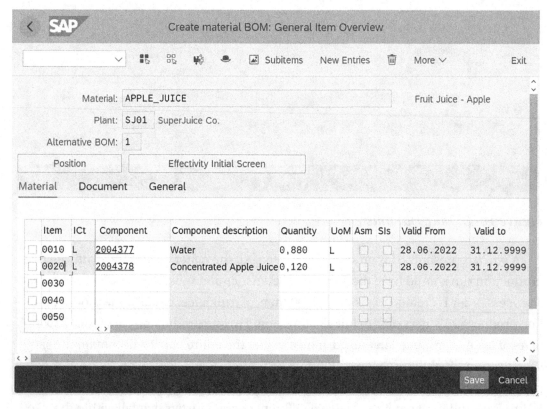

Figure 10-2. *Bill of material*

Resources

This refers to a place or a workstation where an activity or an operation is performed during the production process. A resource performs the same function as a work center in production order management.

The work center and resources are differentiated by the work center category. Each work center category is assigned to an application area in customization. Figure 10-3 displays the application areas of the work center category 0001- Machine and 0008-Processing Unit. The 0001 – Machine category can be used in routings, while 0008-Processing Unit can be used in recipes.

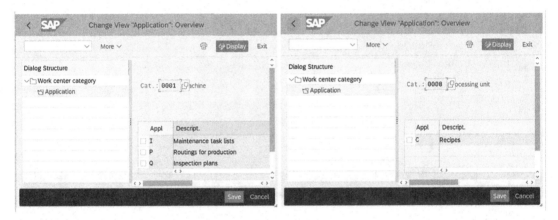

Figure 10-3. *Work center category: application*

You can create a resource using Transaction Code CRC1 or choosing Logistics ➤ Production-Process ➤ Master Data ➤ Resources ➤ Resource ➤ Create. A processing unit has been created for the juice processing line, as shown in Figure 10-4.

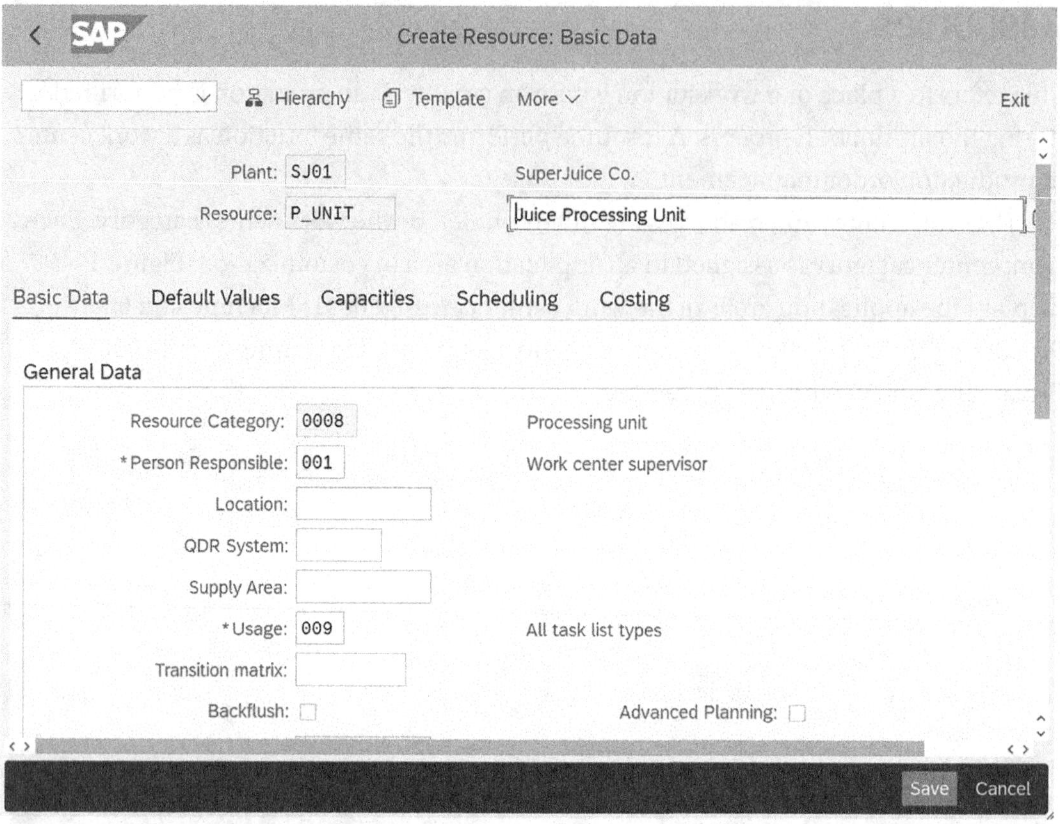

Figure 10-4. *Resource: process industry*

Production Version

The production version defines a unique production technique for producing a material. In other words, this is a unique combination of alternative BOMs and the master recipe. The process of creating a production version is a bit different in the process industry as compared to discrete manufacturing. In PP-PI, the production version is created with BOM details, as shown in Figure 10-5, and it is later assigned to the master recipe when the master recipe is created. A production version can be created using Transaction Code MM02 or C223.

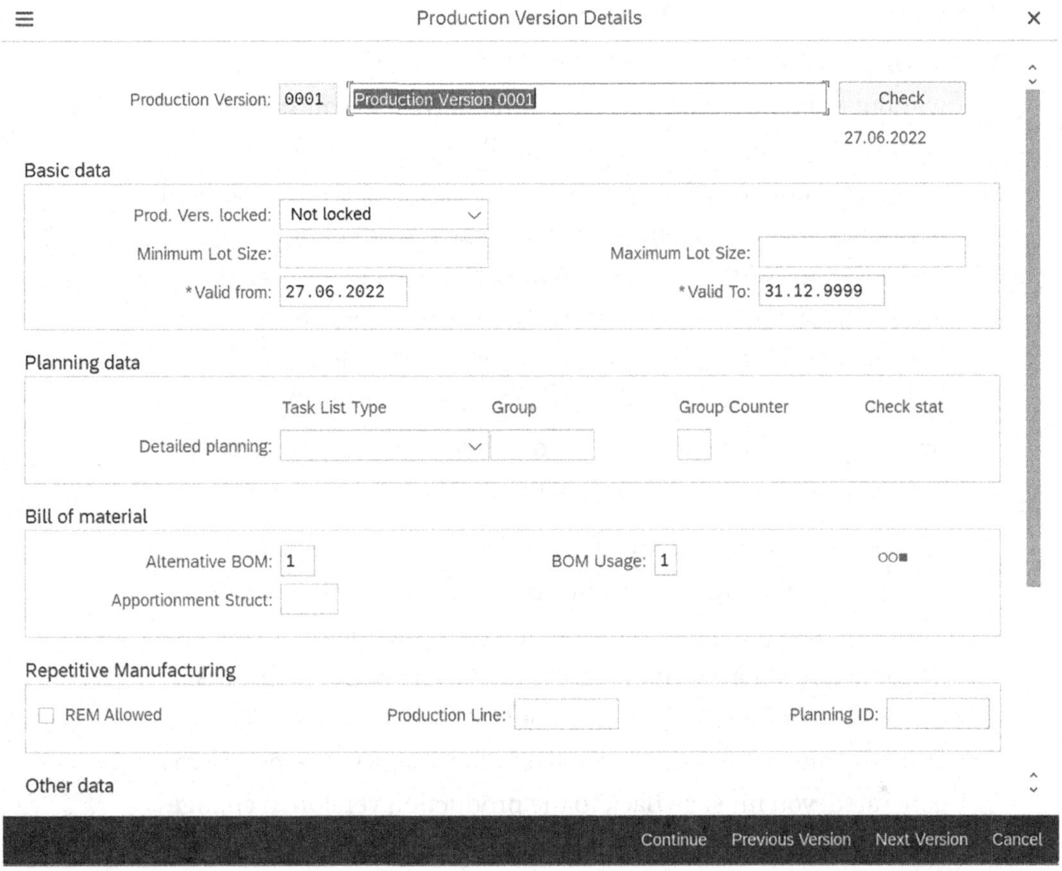

Figure 10-5. Production version

Master Recipes

The master recipe outlines the production process or a series of operations that transform raw materials to finished products in a process industry. The master recipe is similar to routing in discrete industries, with Task List Type 2.

You can create a master recipe by using Transaction Code C201 or by choosing Logistics ➤ Production-Process ➤ Master Data ➤ Master Recipes ➤ Recipe and Material List ➤ Create.

A master recipe can be created in two ways:

1. **Without reference to a material:** You can create a master recipe without reference to the material or plant. When a master recipe is created, a unique recipe group number and recipe is generated, which are similar to the routing group number and group counter in discrete manufacturing. You can create a production version and enter the BOM and recipe details. Now that the production version has been created, you can go back to the master recipe in change mode (Transaction Code C202) and assign the header material in the material assignment. You must also assign the production version, since it is mandatory to assign a production version to a master recipe so that the BOM can be exploded.

2. **With reference to a material/plant:** A master recipe can be created for a material and plant. However, a production version must be created as a prerequisite, since it is mandatory to assign a production version when creating a master recipe. In this case, the production version is created only with the BOM details. Once the master recipe is created and the recipe group number is generated, you must go back to the production version in change mode and assign the recipe details.

To create a master recipe, enter the material, plant, production version, and profile. The profile is created in customization and it controls several functions, including increment for process instruction number, usage of X-Steps as optional or mandatory, and so on.

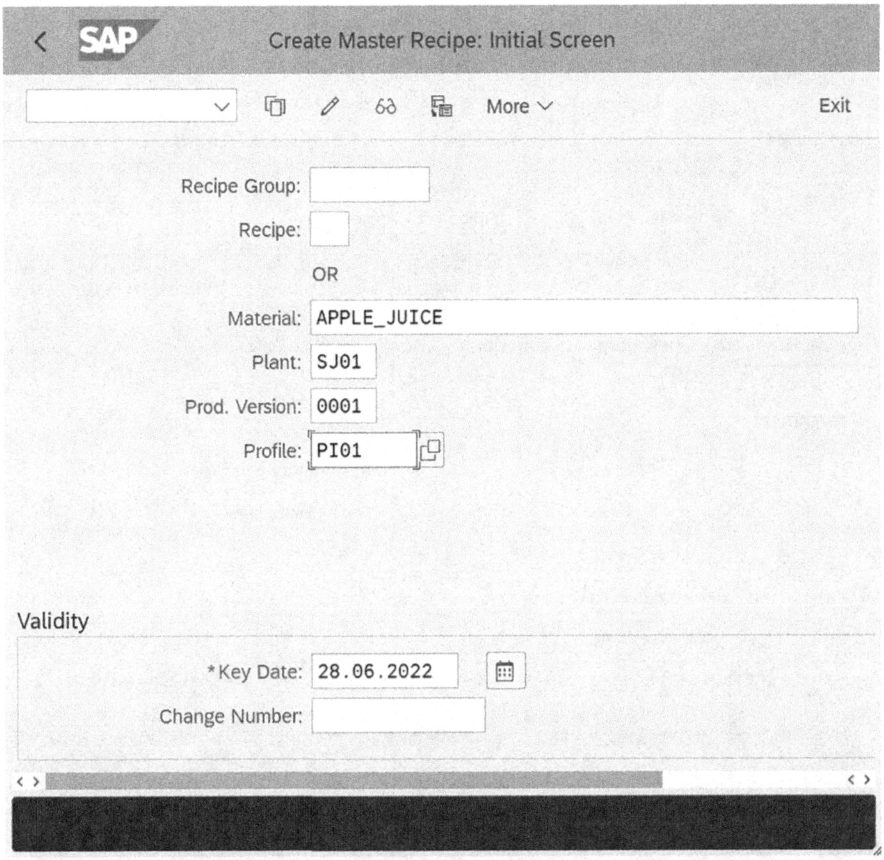

Figure 10-6. *Create Master Recipe: initial screen*

Master Recipe Header

On the Recipe Header screen, you must enter the Status, Usage, and so on. These fields are similar to the ones found in routing.

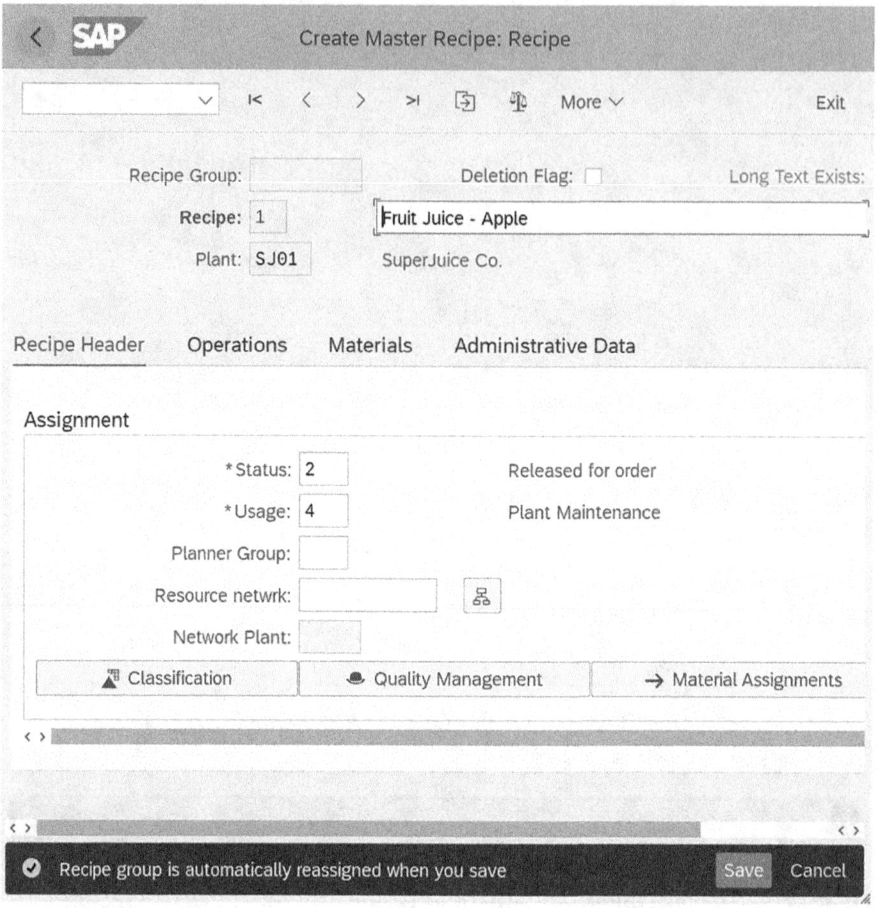

Figure 10-7. *Create Master Recipe: header*

One interesting feature with the master recipe is Charge Quantity. The unit of measure of a recipe is pieces, while the unit of measure for operations is kilogram. The total weight of two pieces is three kilograms, which means that each piece is 3/2 kgs. You can specify the Charge Quantity as 2 while the operation quantity will be 3.

This relationship is maintained directly in the operations details in routing or rate routing.

Operations and Phases in a Master Recipe

A master recipe contains two objects—Operations and Phases. An operation is used to define the general production process and the resource on which the operation will be processed. An operation can be split into various phases describing the process in more detail. A resource and a control key are assigned to the operation and the same resource is adopted by the phases, since phases acts similar to sub-operations, as shown in Figure 10-8. The components from the BOM are assigned to phases and not to operations. Activities like Setup, Machine Time, and so on, are assigned to each phase. This is different than discrete manufacturing, since activities are maintained at the operation level in routing or rate routing. An operation can be branched into multiple phases and the time required to process an operation is the total of the activities of the phases. Since the activities are maintained at the phase level, this implies that the operations confirmed are performed at the phase level as opposed to the operation level in discrete manufacturing. The inspection characteristics can be assigned to operations as well as to the phases.

First, you must create an operation, assign the resource and control key, and enter the operation details. Then you can activate the Phase check box and assign the operation to link the phase to an operation. You can specify the relation between phases as start-finish, finish-start, finish-finish, or start-start. This means the phases can be executed in parallel or in an overlapping sequence. The relationship between phases can be defined by choosing Goto ➤ Relationships in the Operations tab of the master recipe.

The control recipe destination and process instructions should be assigned to the phases. The process instructions can be assigned to the control recipe destination in the customization, or they can be assigned directly to the master recipe as master data. The process instructions can be assigned to the phases in the operations view of the master recipe by choosing Goto ➤ Process Management ➤ Process Instructions.

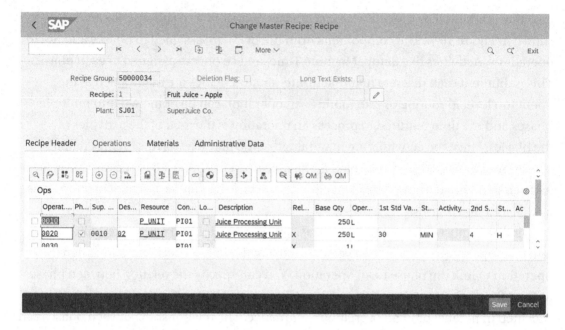

Figure 10-8. *Create Master Recipe: operations*

Once the operations and phases have been created, click the Materials tab.

Bill of Materials in Master Recipes

The bill of material is exploded in the master recipe with the help of the production version. As explained earlier, a production version is created with only the BOM details and then the master recipe is created with reference to the production version. All the components of the BOM are exploded to the master recipe in the Materials view of the master recipe, as shown in Figure 10-9. The BOM in the master recipe is used for Material Quantity Calculations, which is another unique feature of the master recipe. The master recipe details (Recipe Group and Recipe) should be updated in the production version once the master recipe is created.

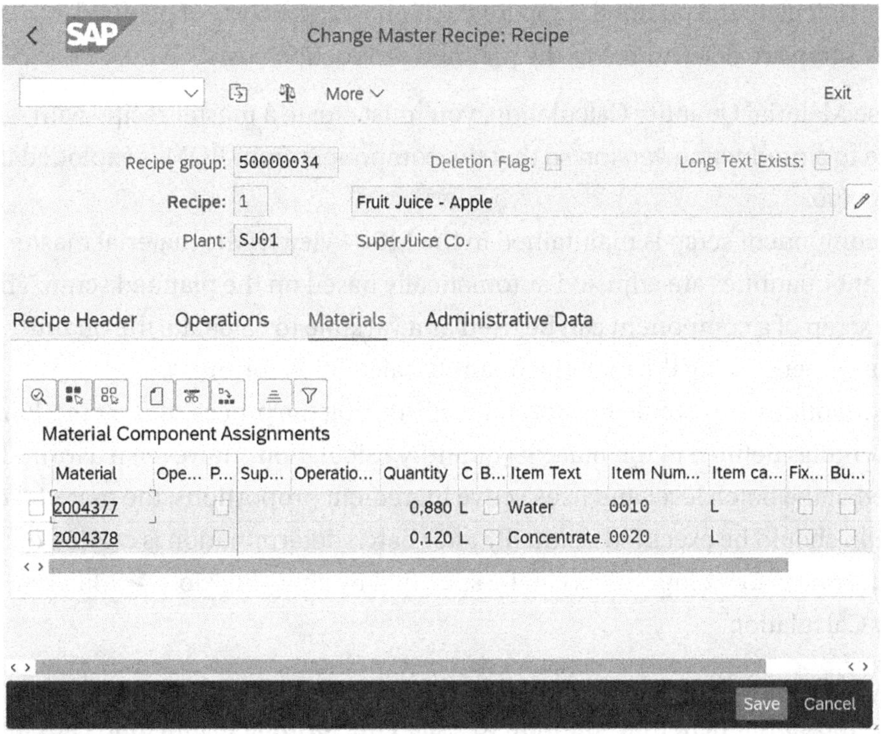

Figure 10-9. *Create Master Recipe: materials*

Material Quantity Calculations

The quantity of the component to be used in a process order is calculated based on the order quantity. However, in process industries, it may happen that you need to change the order quantity since it was needed to consume the entire batch of the raw material or change the component quantities due to a change in the amount of another component. This can be accomplished by using Material Quantity Calculations.

Material Quantity Calculations is a unique feature of the process industry and it provides the following functions:

- Change the production quantity of the header material in proportion to the component quantities or the active ingredient proportions.

- Change the quantities of the component in proportion to a change to the quantity of other components or the header product or with reference to active ingredient proportions.

- Calculate the planned scrap for each phase. The costs of planned
  scrap are determined in the planned production costs.

To use Material Quantity Calculation, you must create a master recipe with reference to a production version so that the component from BOM is exploded in the master recipe.

The component scrap is maintained in the MRP4 view of the material master. The component quantities are adjusted automatically based on the planned scrap. The planned scrap of a component can be used as a variable to calculate the quantity of other components using the material quantity calculation formulas.

The quantities are calculated automatically during the process order creation, based on the formulas defined in the material quantity calculation. However, if a formula is processed at the batch level and uses active ingredient proportions, the material quantity calculation should be executed manually after batch determination is carried out.

The formulas for components can be specified by choosing Goto ➤ Material Quantity Calculation.

- Figure 10-10 shows the Material Quantity Calculation screen. Select
  the component that you want to assign the formula to and then click
  the Select Formula button in the menu bar.

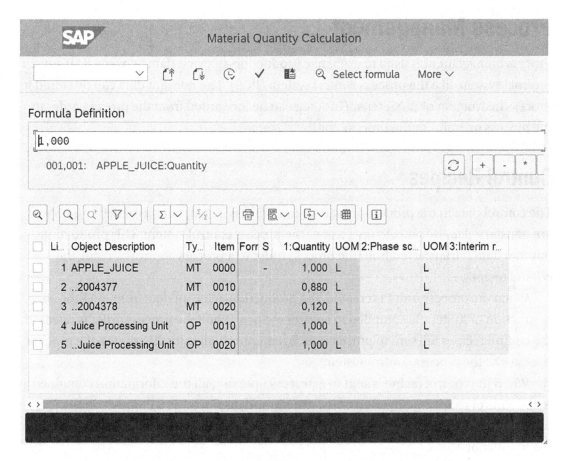

Figure 10-10. *Material Quantity Calculation screen*

- Enter the formula or equation that should be used to derive the output.

- You can easily include the variables in the formula. Double-click the variable that you want to include in the formula or place your cursor on the variable and click the Insert in Formula button in the menu bar.

Various operators, including +, -, *, /, DIV, and MOD, can be used in the formulas. You can also use functions like Exponential, absolute values (ABS), rounding (ROUND), truncation (TRUNC), square root (SQRT), IF THEN ELSE conditions, IF THEN NOT conditions, and EXP, LOG, SIN, COS, and TAN.

Process Management

Process management is used to exchange production-relevant data between SAP and an external system, like the process control system (PCS). The relevant data can be stored in Process Instruction or in X-Steps. This data can be forwarded from the process order to the process operator or the process control system.

Control Recipes

The control data in the process order (such as process instructions assigned to a phase) are transferred to the process operator or the process control system. This production relevant data is transferred from the process order to a process control by using the control recipes.

When the process order is created, the production-relevant data from the Process Instruction or X-Steps is compiled in control recipes. When the process order is released, the control recipes are sent to process management, which is further sent to the process operator or the process control system.

When the control recipe is sent to a process operator, all the information contained in the control recipe is converted into a text file and displayed as a PI-Sheet on the operator's screen. The PI-Sheets provide instructions to the operator on how to execute the production steps.

When the control recipe is sent to an external process control system (PCS), the information specified in the control recipe is transferred as parameters via the PI-PCS interface. These parameters are used to monitor and regulate the production process by the process control system.

The process operator or process control system can report the production to SAP by sending the process messages via a PI-Sheet or the process control system.

Figure 10-11 explains the various elements and the process flow in process management.

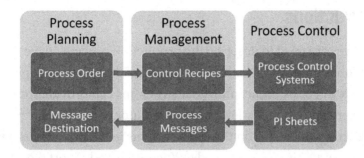

Figure 10-11. *Process flow in process management*

The process management component of PP-PI supports the following functions:

- It receives control recipes once the process order is released and then sends the control recipes to process operators or process control systems.

- Process instructions are converted to texts, which are then displayed on the operator's computer screen.

- Process messages can be received with actual production data from the process control system. The data is verified and sent to SAP.

- Process messages and control recipes are monitored, and manual creation of process messages is also supported.

Control Recipe Destinations

The control recipe destination can be defined in customization to specify who receives and processes information from the control recipe. The destination could be a process operator, a group of operators, or a process control system. While creating the process order, one control recipe should be created for each control recipe destination.

Control recipe destination could be defined for one of the following types:

- Transfer to ABAP list-based PI-Sheet

- Download to external system, initiated by SAP process management

- Download to external system, initiated by process control

- Transfer to browser-based PI-Sheet

Process Instructions

Process instructions are used to describe the production process, in part or in full. The process instructions contain comprehensive details of the production process that the operator must follow. For example, process instructions can provide specifications like the temperature and humidity level for an operation. The operator must ensure the operation is processed based on the specifications in the process instructions. Not just that, but the operator is also supposed to document and report the specifications. The data must be communicated and exchanged between the plant operator and process control system (PCS). This ensures that the products are produced with the correct specifications, as this is quite critical to process industries. Any deviation to the process beyond the specified thresholds could result in the material being scraped. Communication between SAP and the PCS (Process Control System) can be established by defining the type of control recipe destination.

The process instructions are assigned in the master recipe and the process order. SAP allows two types of process instructions:

- **Characteristic-Based Process Instructions:** The process instructions can be created for a phase using characteristics and their characteristics value.

- **X-Step Process Instructions:** The X-Step or Execution Step is created using the context menu in the X-Steps Editor. Although X-Steps are based on characteristics and their values, the knowledge of characteristics structure is not needed. X-Steps are not created with reference to a phase; rather, they are assigned to a phase with reference to a context.

The process instructions are assigned to the phase in the operation view of the master recipe. Select the phase that you would like to assign the process instructions to, as shown in Figure 10-12. Then choose Goto ➤ Process Management ➤ Process Instructions from the menu bar.

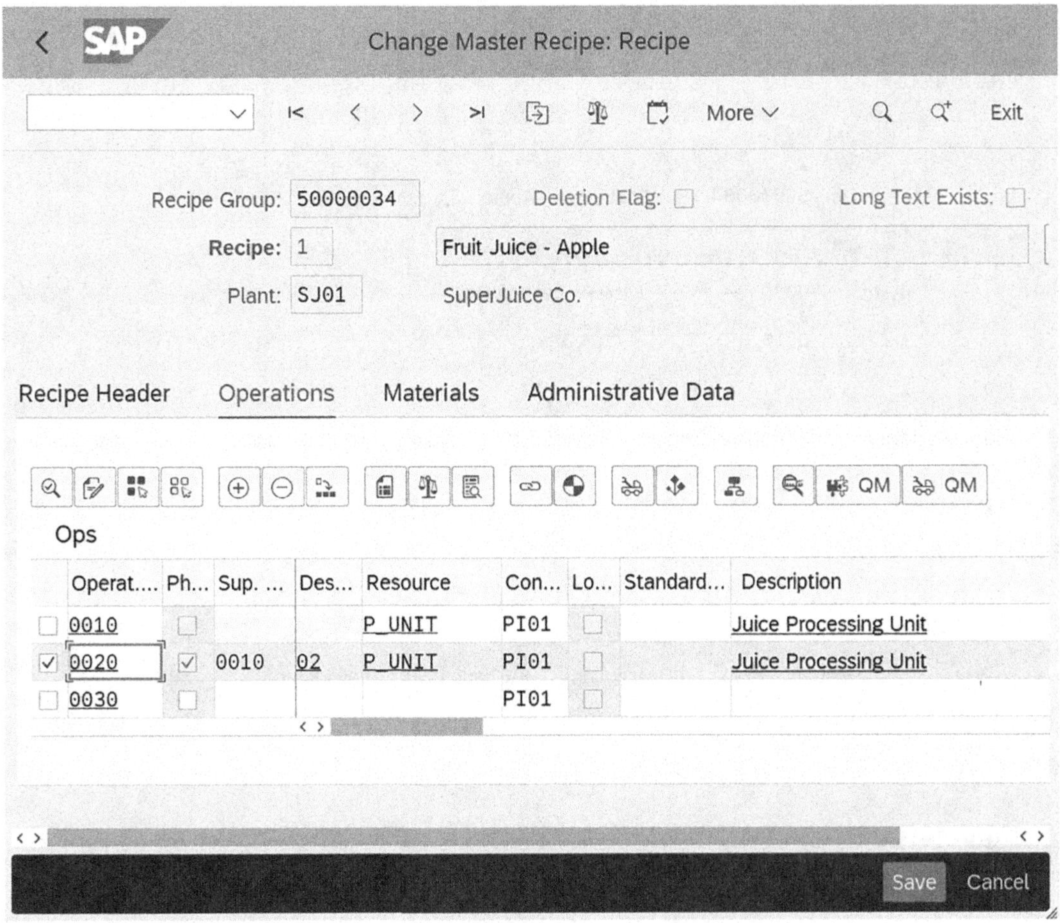

Figure 10-12. *Change Master Recipe: recipe*

You can assign the process instruction categories in the next screen, as shown in Figure 10-13. You can also simulate the PI-Sheet by choosing Goto ➤ Process Management ➤ Simulate PI Sheet for phases. This will enable you to display the output format of the PI-Sheet.

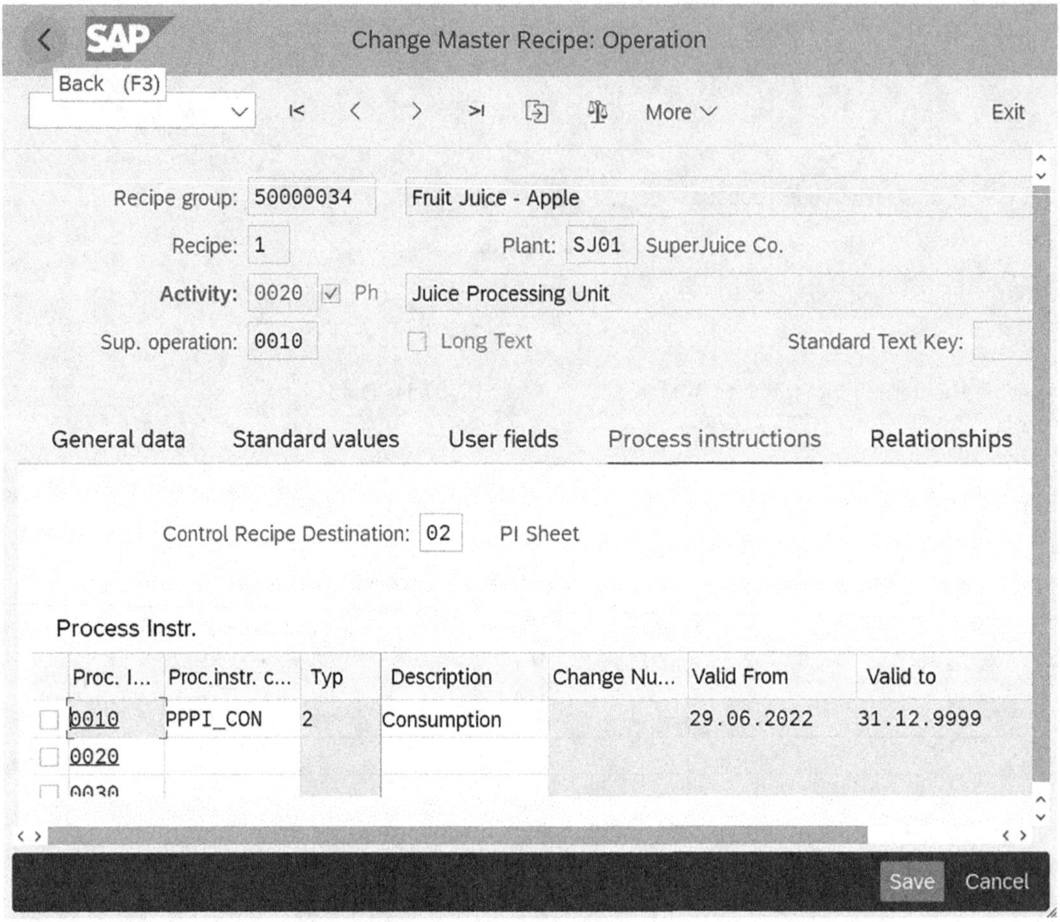

Figure 10-13. *Change Master Recipe: Operation: process instructions*

All the master data required for PP-PI is created. The production planning part is the same as with discrete manufacturing. All the steps in the production planning, including S&OP, Demand Management, Material Requirement Planning, and Capacity Requirement planning, are the same as in discrete manufacturing. The next section discusses process order management.

Manufacturing Execution with Process Order Management

Most of the manufacturing execution process in a process order is similar to discrete manufacturing; however, there are a few differences. There are some functions that are unique to process orders, including Releasing Control Recipe, Executing Material Quantity Calculations, and Batch Allocation.

Create Process Order

You can create a process order by choosing Logistics ➤ Production-Process ➤ Process Order ➤ Process Order ➤ Create ➤ With Material or you can use Transaction Code COR1. Enter the material number of the finished/semifinished material to be produced, the production plant, and the process order type on the initial screen, as shown in Figure 10-14.

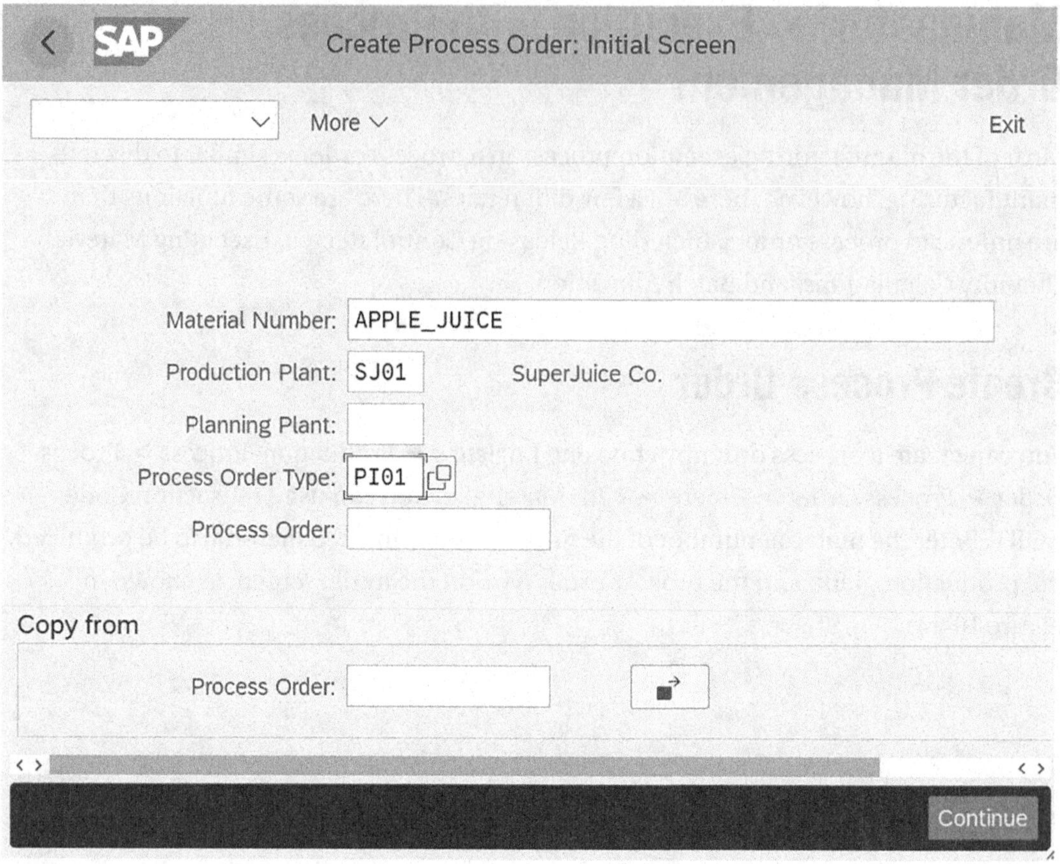

Figure 10-14. *Create Process Order: INITIAL SCREEN*

Order Type determines the master data that should be populated in the order when the process order is created, and it also governs which parameters are relevant for controlling. SAP comes preconfigured with the process order types listed in Table 10-1.

Table 10-1. *SAP Process Order Types*

Order Type	Description
PI01	Process order (internal number assignment)
PI02	Process order (external number assignment)
PI04	Filling/packaging with "assembly order"

When the process order is created, all the master data (such as the material master, the BOM, and the master recipe data) is populated in the process order. The material quantity calculation data is also taken into account.

Click the Generate Control Recipe icon, as shown in Figure 10-15. The control recipe can also be generated automatically when the process order is released. A control recipe is generated for each control recipe destination in the process order.

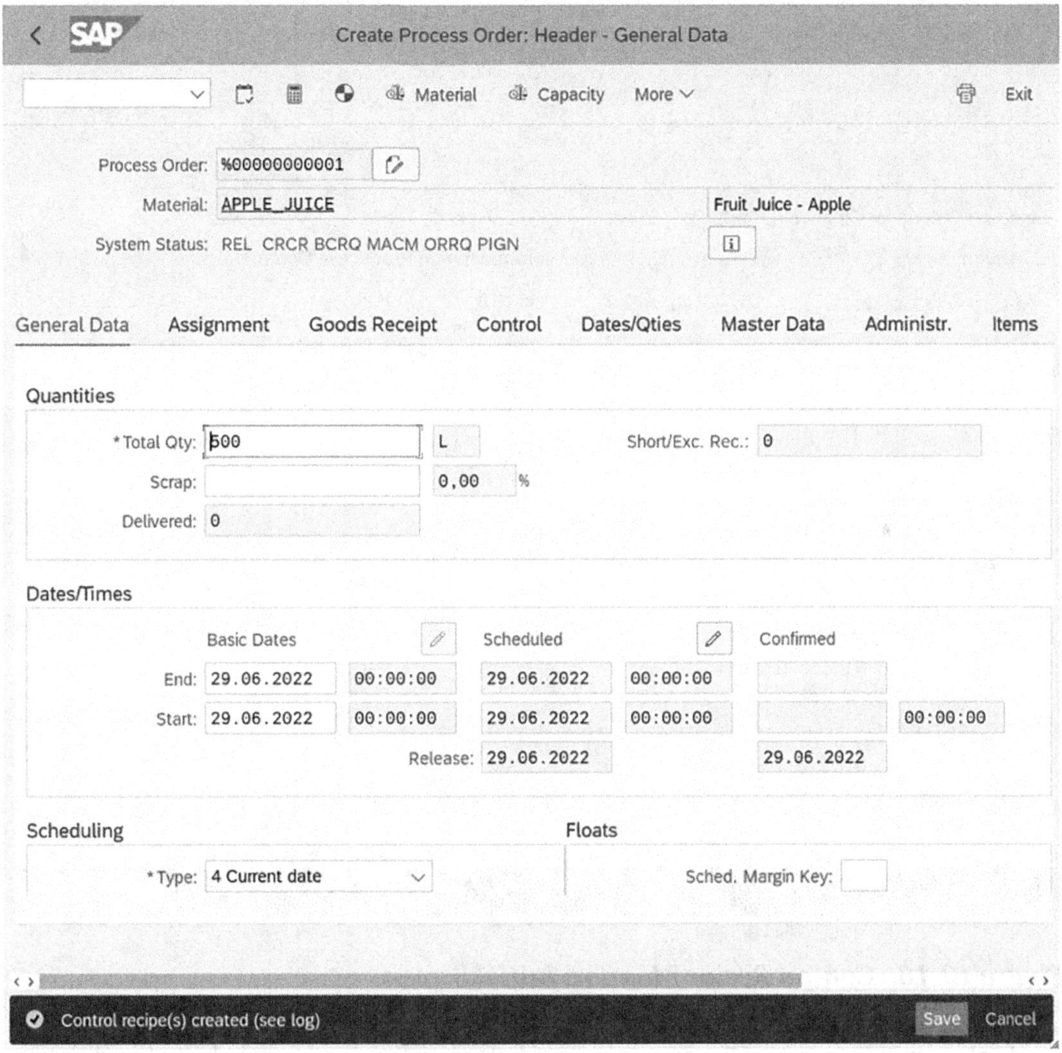

Figure 10-15. *Create Process Order: header*

Control Recipe Monitor

Once the control recipes have been generated, you can use the Control Recipe Monitor (Transaction Code CO53) to generate PI-Sheets from the control recipe. Enter the process order number and click the Display button.

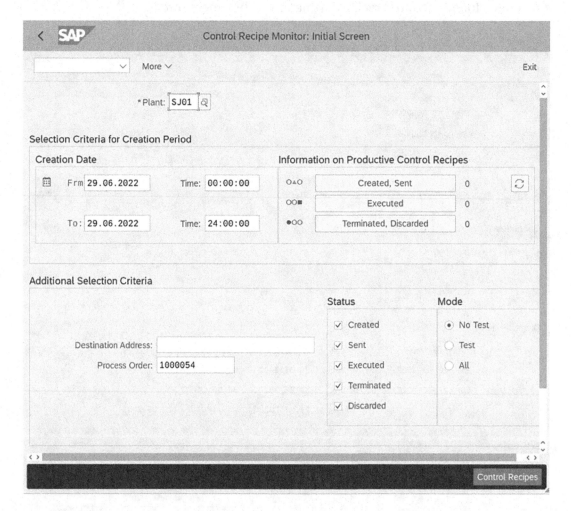

Figure 10-16. *Control Recipe Monitor: Initial Screen*

As shown in Figure 10-17, you can select the control recipe and click the Send button to generate PI-Sheets.

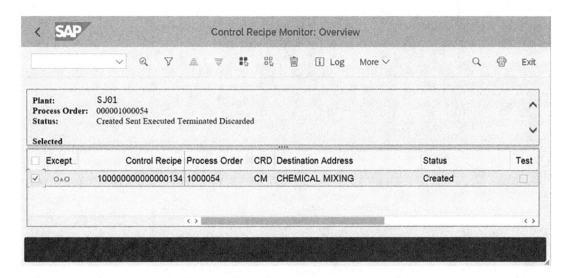

Figure 10-17. *Control Recipe Monitor: Overview screen*

You can display the PI-Sheet using Transaction Code CO60, which has been generated. You can display the PI-Sheets for a combination of the plant and control recipe, or you can enter the process order number, as shown in Figure 10-18.

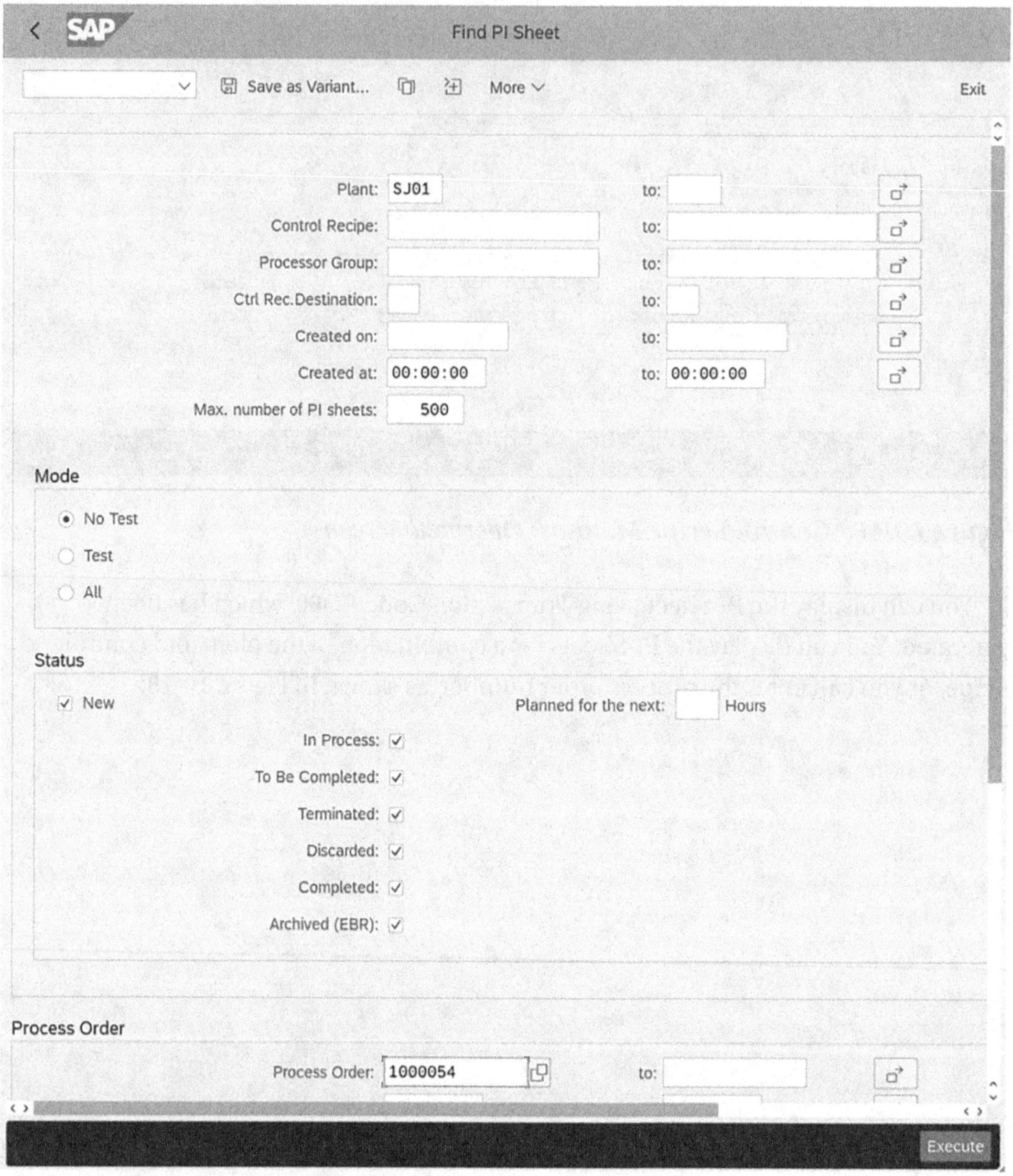

Figure 10-18. *Find PI-Sheet: initial screen*

The output list displays all the PI-Sheets and their status based on the selection criteria, as shown in Figure 10-19.

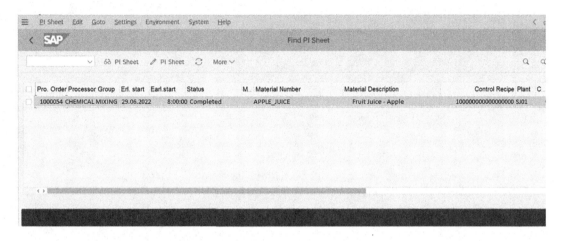

Figure 10-19. *Find PI-Sheet: output*

The next section discusses how you can display and change the PI-Sheets.

Maintain PI-Sheets

You can maintain the PI-sheets by choosing Logistics ➤ Production Process ➤ Process Management ➤ PI Sheet ➤ Work List -Maintain. You can also use Transaction Code CO55. You can enter the selection parameters on the selection screen, like the new or in-process PI-Sheets, as shown in Figure 10-20. You can also specify the resource or materials for which you want to display PI-Sheets.

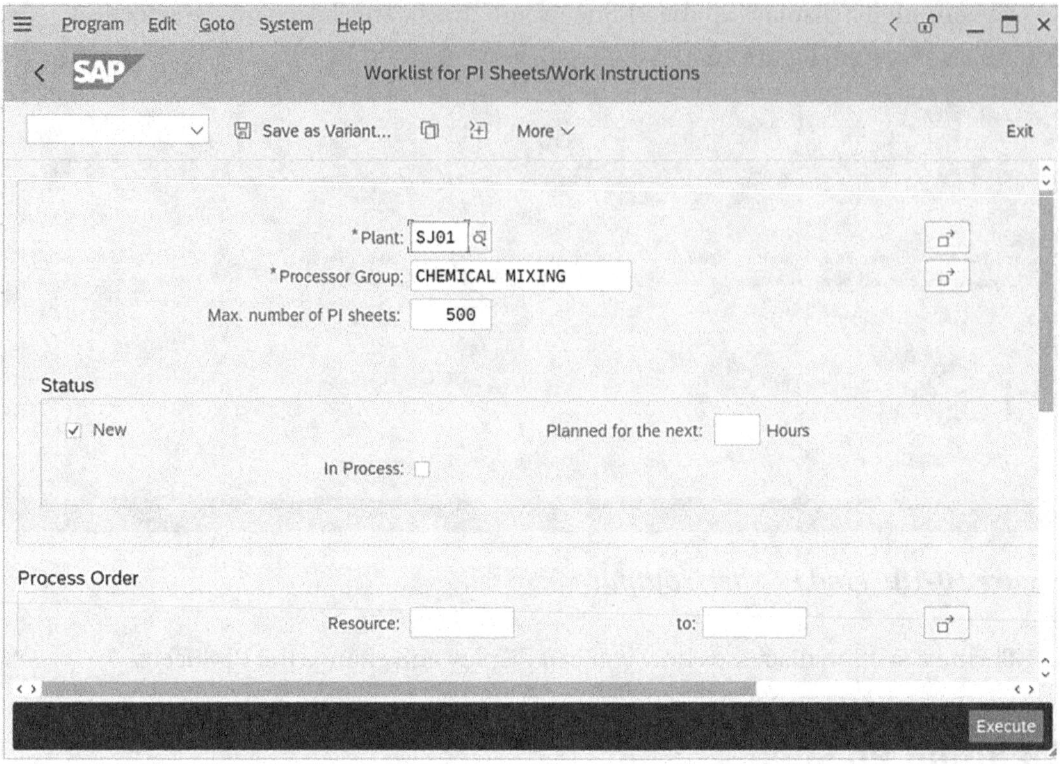

Figure 10-20. *Worklist for PI-Sheets/Work Instructions*

The output screen displays all the PI-sheets, which are relevant based on the selection criteria.

Select the PI-Sheets and click Maintain PI-Sheet. Figure 10-21 displays all the fields that can be maintained/changed in the PI-Sheet. A PI-Sheet is assigned to each phase.

A wide range of functions can be performed using a PI-Sheet:

- Standard operating procedure can be assigned to a phase to inform the operator how the process should be executed and which parameters should run.

- Drawings or other PDFs can be assigned to a PI-Sheet using thing the document management system.

- You can call another transaction, like MIGO, by clicking GO TO MIGO.

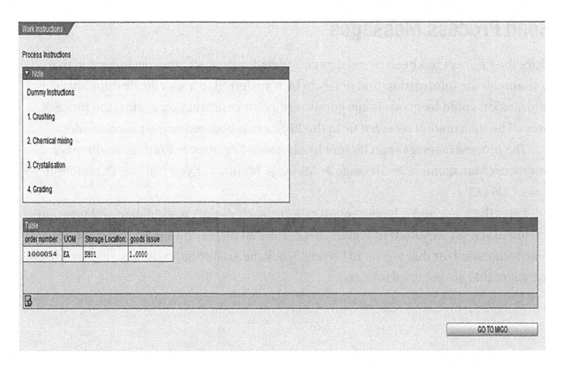

Figure 10-21. *Work instructions*

- Goods issue/goods receipt for the process order can be posted.

- Special parameters can be recorded, like temperature, pressure, viscosity, and so on.

- Digital signatures can be incorporated to track which user updated the fields in the PI-Sheet.

- QM results recording can be executed by using the Call Transaction function.

These are the fields that must be maintained by the operator. Once all the fields have been maintained in the PI-Sheet, it can be marked as completed. If the operator wants to save the PI-sheet without completing it, they can simply click Save so that the field values are not lost. Once all the fields have been maintained, the operator can click the Complete button. Once the PI-Sheet has been marked as complete, it's no longer possible to make changes to it.

Send Process Messages

Once the PI-Sheet has been marked as completed, a process message is created that contains all the information that needs to be transferred to a specific destination. This information could be goods issue, goods receipt, or confirmation against the process order. The information received from the PI-Sheet is updated in the process order.

The process messages can be sent by choosing Logistics ➤ Production-Process ➤ Process Management ➤ Message ➤ Message Monitor or you can use Transaction Code CO54XT.

Enter the plant and other selection criteria, such as the creation date and time, on the initial screen, as shown in Figure 10-22. You can display messages that have been sent, terminated, or that are yet to be sent. Click the To Be Sent button to display a list of messages that are yet to be processed.

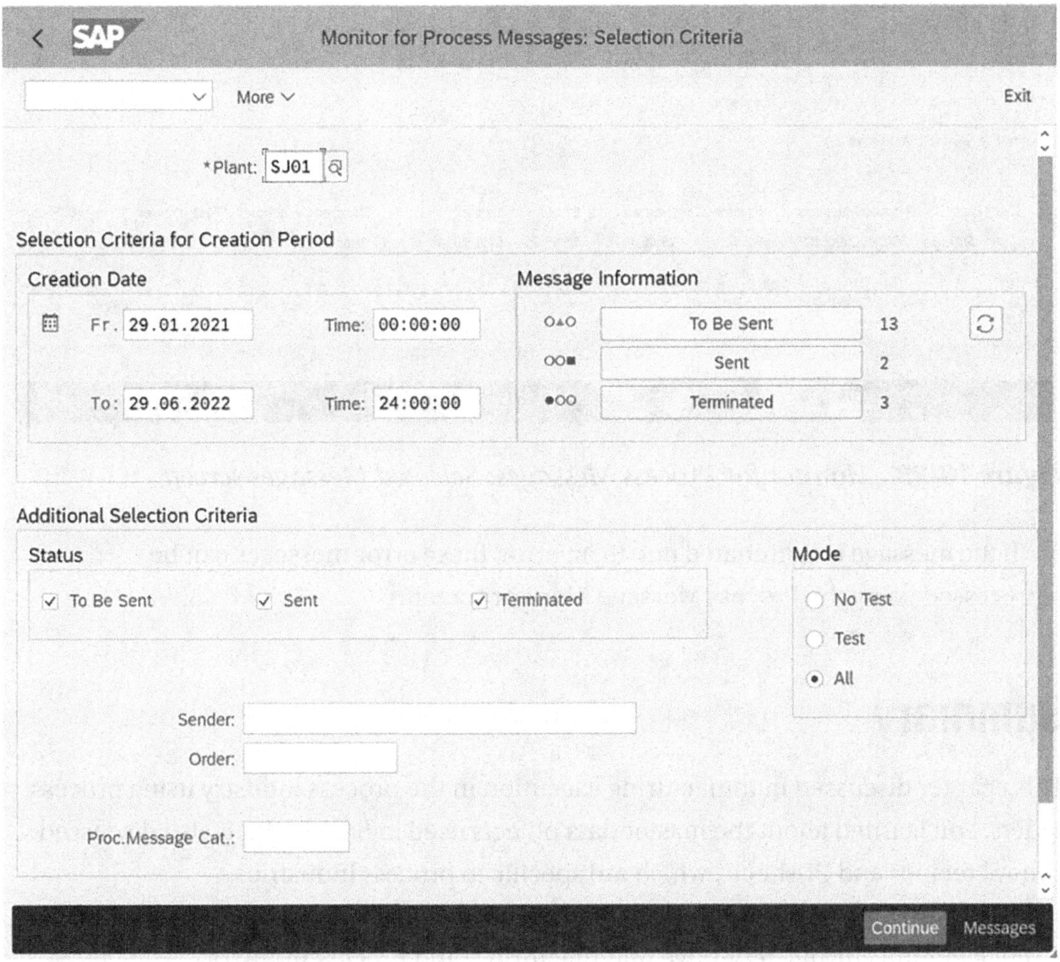

Figure 10-22. *Monitor for Process Messages: Selection screen*

The output list displays all the messages with their status, like To be Sent, Sent, or Terminated, as shown in Figure 10-23. Select the message that you want to send and then click the Send button.

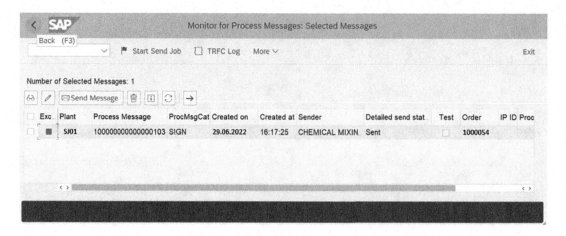

Figure 10-23. *Monitor for Process Messages: Selected Messages screen*

If the message is terminated due to an error, these error messages can be reprocessed using the Process Message Monitor screen.

Summary

This chapter discussed manufacturing execution in the process industry using process orders. You learned about the master data objects used in SAP PP-PI. It also discussed control recipes and PI-sheets, which are specific to process industries.

So far you have learned about all the manufacturing execution methodologies—discrete manufacturing, repetitive manufacturing, and process industry.

The following chapters cover the latest innovations in SAP S/4HANA. Let's start with SAP PP/DS in the next chapter.

CHAPTER 11

PP/DS in S/4HANA

Production planning and detailed scheduling (PP/DS) in SAP S/4HANA aims at maximizing production efficiency and reducing costs of production. In this chapter, you'll learn about tools like Heuristics, the PP/DS Optimizer, and the Detailed Scheduler, which are available in SAP S/4HANA PP/DS.

What Is Production Planning and Detailed Scheduling?

Before the S/4HANA era, SAP offered a product called SAP Advanced Planning and Optimization or simply SAP APO, which was a specialized supply chain planning tool. SAP APO was comprised of several modules, including demand planning, supply network planning, production planning, and detailed scheduling. The production planning and detailed scheduling (PP/DS) module was designed to provide advanced features that were not available in SAP ERP, including:

- Materials planning with finite capacity planning

- Planning with exact times

- Forecast consumption with descriptive characteristics

- Planning runs with multiple steps

- Dynamic pegging (assignment of receipt elements across the bill of material levels)

- Planning with custom heuristics (planning algorithm that executes the planning on selected objects)

© Himanshu Goel 2022
H. Goel, *Handbook for SAP PP in S/4HANA*, https://doi.org/10.1007/978-1-4842-8566-4_11

SAP APO was a standalone system, and it was needed to exchange data from SAP ERP. It was also needed to send master data from SAP ERP to SAP APO using a tool called the CORE Interface (CIF).

With the launch of SAP S/4HANA, the PP/DS module was integrated within the S/4HANA suite. The other modules (such as demand planning and supply network planning) have been launched in a cloud-based product called SAP Integrated Business Planning (IBP).

Master Data for PP/DS

This section discusses the master data that should be set up to run PP/DS in S/4HANA:

- Locations

- Material master

- Work centers and resources

Locations

A location can be used to represent a plant, a business partner (i.e., a customer or vendor), a shipping or receiving point, or an MRP area. You can create a location by executing the report /SAPAPO/CREATE_LOCATION. Go to Transaction Code SE38 and enter the program name /SAPAPO/CREATE_LOCATION. Then specify the business object that you want to create as a location in SAP APO. In Figure 11-1, I create the location for Plant 1105.

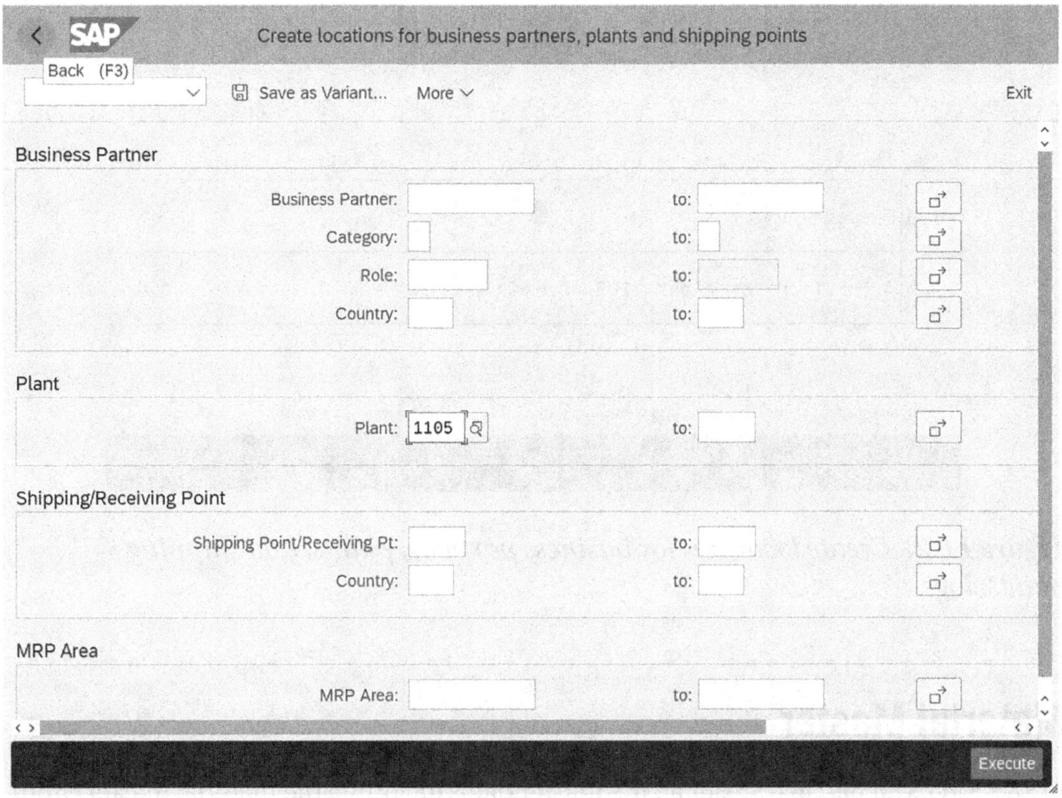

Figure 11-1. *Create locations for business partners, plants, and shipping points*

The system will generate the location 1105 in PP/DS for the specified plant 1105. If the location already exists in the APO, the system will show a message, as shown in Figure 11-2.

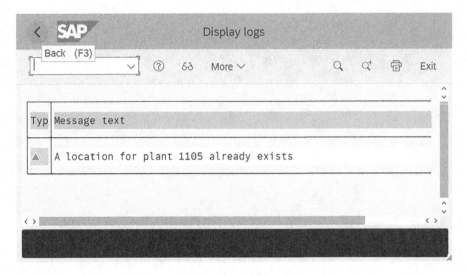

Figure 11-2. *Create locations for business partners, plants, and shipping points: logs*

Material Master

In SAP APO, you had to transfer all the master data (including the material master) from SAP ERP to SAP APO via the Core Interface (CIF). This process has been simplified in SAP S/4HANA. Now that PP/DS is embedded into the S/4HANA suite, you don't have to transfer materials to SAP APO PPDS. You can simply activate PP/DS in the material master in the new view called Advanced Planning.

Advanced Planning View

The Advanced Planning view contains six sections: General, Procurement/PP-DS, Demand, Lot Size, Goods Receipt/Goods Issue, and Location-Dependent Shelf Life. Let's look at these fields. If you want to use PP/DS in SAP S/4HANA, you must activate the Advanced Planning indicator, which supports advanced live cache-based planning and scheduling, as shown in Figure 11-3.

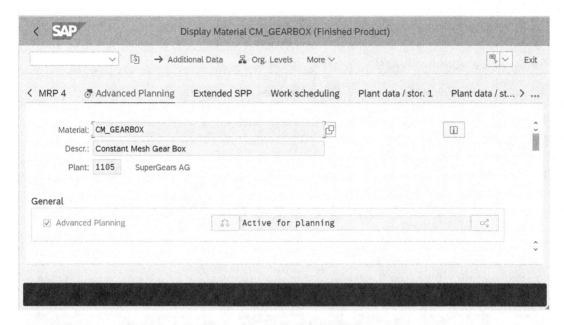

Figure 11-3. *Material master: advanced planning view*

Procurement/PP-DS

This section covers the Proc./PPDS section of the Advanced Planning view of the material master, as shown in Figure 11-4.

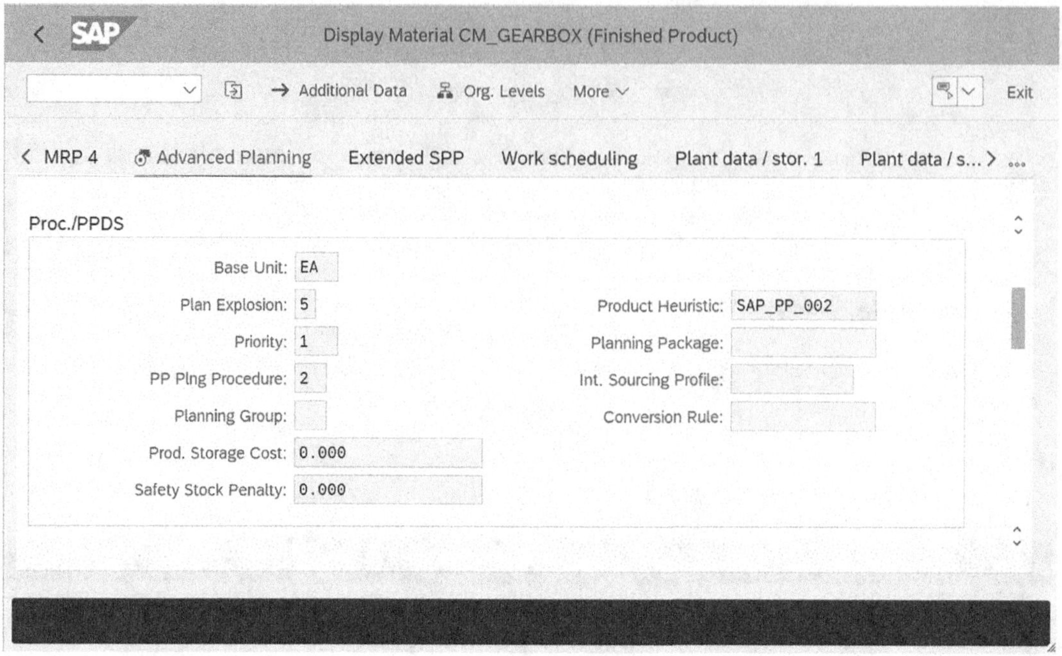

Figure 11-4. Material master: advanced planning view: proc/PPDS

Plan Explosion: This specifies the task list type that the system should use to create receipts in PP/DS. In PP/DS, a task list type is a combination of the bill of materials (BOM) and the routing (production version in SAP ERP ECC) that can be transferred from SAP ERP ECC as a Production Data Structure (PDS) in PP/DS. See Table 11-1.

Table 11-1. Plan Explosion

Plan Explosion	Short Description
	The default value from customizing is used
3	Single explosion of iPPE
4	Matrix explosion of iPPE
5	PDS generated from R/3

Product Heuristic: In PP/DS, a *heuristic* is a planning function that executes planning for selected objects, such as products, resources, operations, or line networks, depending on the planning focus.

A product heuristic is used for procurement planning, which is used in the following scenarios:

- If it automatically and immediately plans a product after a planning-relevant event occurs

- If you plan the product in an MRP planning run

Table 11-2 shows the standard heuristics available in the standard SAP S/4HANA PP/DS system.

Table 11-2. *Heuristics*

Heuristic	Description
SAP_LEN_001	Length-based heuristic
SAP_MOP_001	Multiple output planning heuristic
SAP_PP_002	Planning of standard lots
SAP_PP_004	Planning of standard lots in three horizons
SAP_PP_005	Part period balancing
SAP_PP_006	Least-unit cost proc.: ext. procurement
SAP_PP_007	Reorder point planning
SAP_PP_013	Groff procedure
SAP_PP_017	Plan standard lots for co-products
SAP_PP_C001	Planning of standard lots for conti- I/O
SAP_PP_Q001	Quota heuristics
SAP_PP_SL001	Planning of std lots with shelf life

- **Priority:** The system can determine the priority of the order based on the priority of the product. You can assign values from 0 to 255 for the priority, 1 being the highest and 255 being the lowest. A value 0 or no value means the lowest priority.

- **Planning Package:** This key can be used to group location products that should be planned together in the procurement planning run with an MRP heuristic.

- **PP Planning Procedure:** You can select the strategy to determine the actions to be triggered when a certain event occurs. The production planning (PP) planning procedure can also determine if the desired quantity or confirmed quantity of a schedule line is relevant for pegging for customer requirements. The system immediately executes automatic planning for products that have a relevant planning procedure. This setting is mandatory if you want to run planning with PP/DS.

- **Interactive Sourcing Profile:** The Production Planning (PP) heuristic is equipped with an option for interactive sourcing that allows you to interactively choose the sources of supply for each procurement proposal. An interactive sourcing profile lists the key components and key resources at each location. The information provided in the interactive sourcing profile can be used to determine the availability of key components and resources at the linked product location.

- **Planning Group:** You can use the planning group to restrict the selection of products that you plan in the processing step of the production planning run. The planning group specifies if the product is relevant for planning with heuristics that plan products—for example, for procurement planning heuristics and for the MRP heuristic.

- **Conversion Rule:** You can specify a conversion rule to perform checks during the conversion of planned orders to production orders and purchase requisitions into purchase orders.

- **Product-Dependent Storage Costs:** You can specify the costs to store the product in the warehouse per the base unit of measure and per day.

- **Safety Stock Penalty:** You can use this field to specify the penalty cost if the safety stock is violated or if the stock level falls below the safety stock.

Demand

This section discusses the Demand section of the Advanced Planning view of the material master, as shown in Figure 11-5.

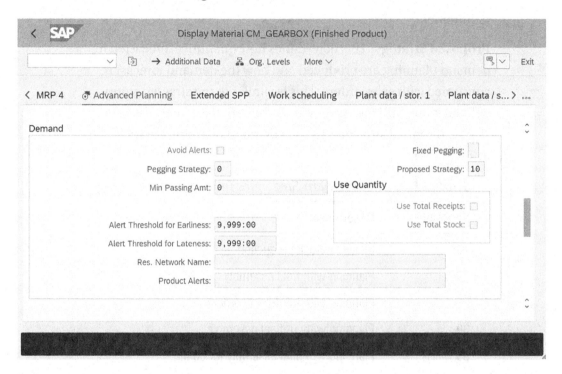

Figure 11-5. *Material master: advanced planning view: demand*

Avoid Alerts in Pegging: If this indicator is selected, the system will attempt to create the pegging relationships between requirements and receipts, if possible, without the quantity or date alerts. First, the system links receipts and requirements that are compatible on a time and quantity basis, and then links the remaining receipts and requirements in a second step.

> **Fixed Pegging:** You can use this indicator to specify if you want to retain fixed pegging for the product even after a document change (for example, after converting a planned order into a production order).

Pegging Strategy: This is used to determine the time sequence in which the system should cover requirements for the product with dynamic pegging and in which time sequence the system should use the product receipts in the pegging interval to cover a requirement.

Proposed Strategy: This determines how quantities forecasted in demand planning are produced and how the demand forecast is consumed with sales orders. This is similar to the strategy group defined in the MRP3 view; however, they are not exactly the same. The requirement strategies used in demand planning are shown in Table 11-3.

Table 11-3. *Requirement Strategies in Demand Planning*

Strategy	Description
10	Make-to-stock production
20	Planning with final assembly
21	Planning with third-party orders
30	Planning without final assembly
35	Planning w/o final assembly for config.
40	Planning product

Figure 11-6 shows a comparison between planning strategies in SAP S/4HANA production planning and SAP S/4HANA PP/DS.

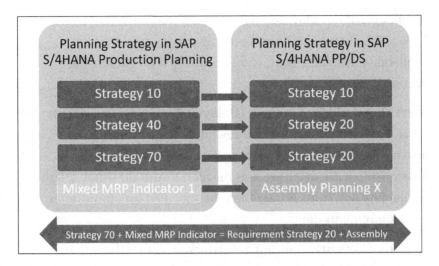

Figure 11-6. *Planning strategy in SAP S/4HANA PP and SAP S/4HANA PP/DS*

Minimum Passing Amount: This field specifies the minimum passing amount for a continuous input/output node. The system splits the receipt element into factors of the value specified in this field.

Use Total Receipts: This indicator specifies if the system should consume the entire quantity of a receipt element. The system may assign a receipt element to just one requirement element for the product during dynamic pegging. The requirement element must thus completely consume the receipt element.

Use Total Stock: This indicator specifies that the system may assign a stock element for the product to just one requirement element in dynamic pegging. The requirement element must thus completely consume the stock element.

Alert Threshold for Earliness (Receipts): The system creates a date/time alert for a fixed or a dynamic pegging relationship if the earliness exceeds the alert threshold—that is, if the availability date/time is earlier than the specified timeframe before the requirements date. To specify the time frame, use the format HHH.HHH:MM (Hours: Minutes). For example, 1000:10 means 1,000 hours and 10 minutes, while 20:20 means 20 hours and

20 minutes. If no value is specified, the system uses the value 100000:00. Therefore, the system only creates an alert if an availability date/time is more than 100,000 hours before the requirements date.

Alert Threshold for Lateness (Delayed Receipts): The system creates an alert similar to the threshold for early receipts. It also creates a date/time alert for a fixed or a dynamic pegging relationship if the delay exceeds the alert threshold—that is, if the availability date/time is later than the specified timeframe after the requirements date.

Resource Network: A resource network describes the physical links between the resources in a plant, such as processing units, reactors, vessels, and so on, which are used to explain the flow of the materials through a plant.

Product Alerts: You can use this field to specify if the system should determine direct alerts for a requirement or a receipt of a product, or if the product is relevant to network alerts. If a product is relevant to network alerts, the system evaluates the direct alerts for this product for receipts or requirements at the higher levels of the pegging structure, as well. Alerts for less critical components can be hidden and thus increase the clarity and transparency of network alerts and improve system performance.

Lot Size

This section discusses the Lot Size section of the Advanced Planning view of the material master, as shown in Figure 11-7.

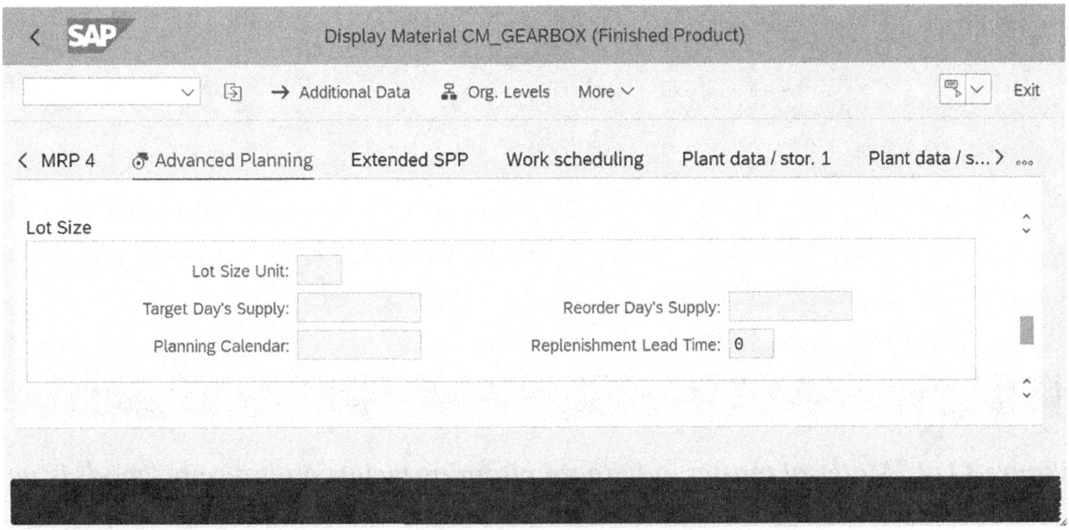

Figure 11-7. *Material master: advanced planning view: lot size*

Lot Size Unit: This field indicates the valid unit of measure for the lot size. If no lot size unit is maintained, the system considers the base unit of measure. If you are specifying the lot size unit, you must also maintain the conversion in an alternate unit of measure.

Target Day's Supply: The PP-DS standard heuristic SAP_PP_002 (planning of standard lots) considers the target day's (in workdays) supply to plan location products using target stock level methods.

Reorder Day's Supply: Specify the reorder day's supply if the Reorder Point Method 2 is defined for the location product.

Goods Receipt/Goods Issue

This section discusses the GR/GI section of the Advanced Planning view of the material master, as shown in Figure 11-8.

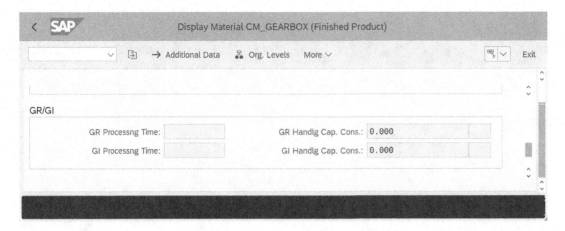

Figure 11-8. *Material master: advanced planning view: goods receipt/goods issue*

GR Processing Time: This is the time required for inspection and placing it in the stock once the stock is received. Goods receipt processing time is also considered in the total replenishment lead time.

Goods Receipt Handling Capacity Consumption: This field is used to specify how much of the handling capacity is consumed by the product during goods receipt for a specific plan.

GI Processing Time: This is the time required for inspection and placing it in the stock between issuing the product from storage and transporting it. Goods issue processing time is also considered in the total replenishment lead time.

Goods Issue Handling Capacity Consumption: This field is used to specify how much of the handling capacity is consumed by the product during goods issue for a specific plan.

Location-Dependent Shelf Life

This section explains the Location Dependent Shelf-Life section of the Advanced Planning view of the material master, as shown in Figure 11-9.

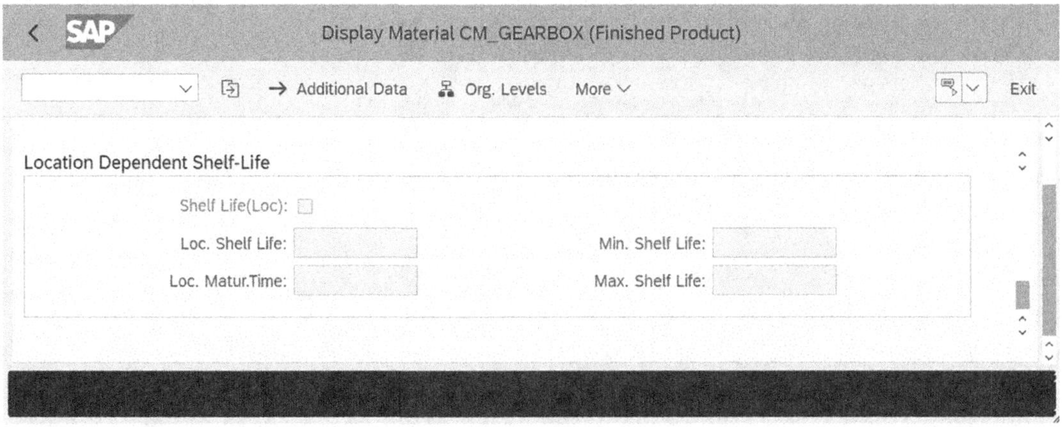

Figure 11-9. *Material Master: advanced planning view: location-dependent shelf life*

This indicator specifies if the system should consider the resource location-dependent shelf life of a product when planning.

If you are using location-dependent shelf life, you must maintain the standard shelf life, minimum shelf life, maximum shelf life, and maturation time, which are location-dependent. In PP/DS, a location can be a plant, a distribution center, a storage location, an MRP area, a transportation lane, or a business partner (customer or vendor).

Product Master in APO

Product master is used in APO to represent the materials or services that are sold by any organization. Similar to the material master in SAP ECC, a product master in SAP APO contains attributes that are global as well as location specific. Once the Advanced Planning is activated in the material master in SAP ECC, the system creates a product master in APO and all the relevant fields are mapped to the corresponding fields in the product master in SAP APO.

You can display the product master using Transaction Code /SAPAPO/MAT1. Enter the product and plant in the initial screen, as shown in Figure 11-10.

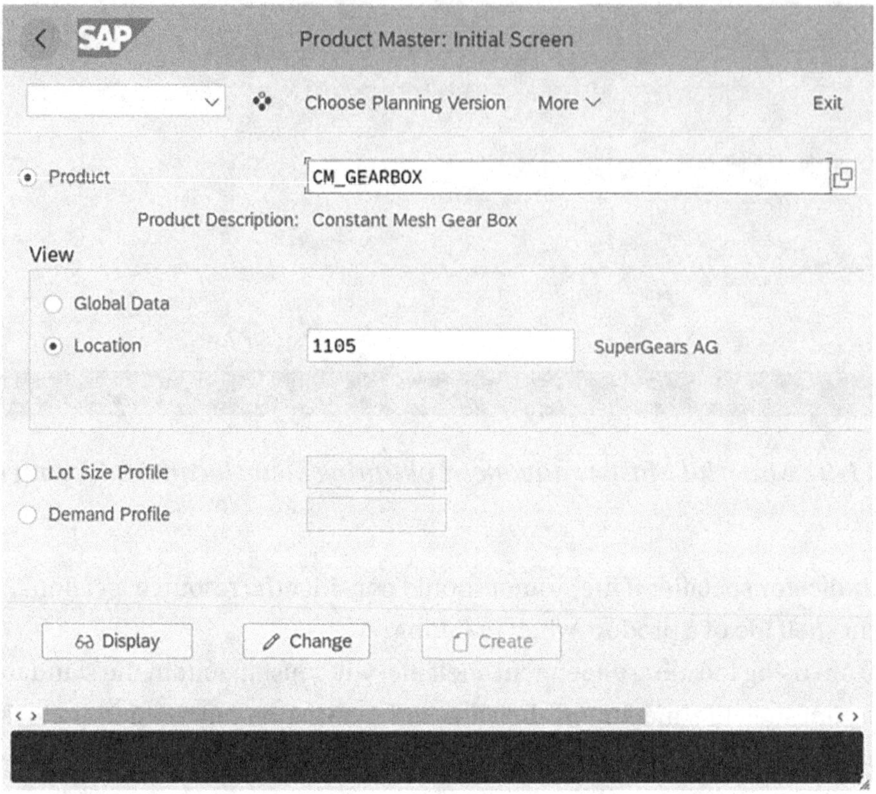

Figure 11-10. *Product master: initial screen*

Go to the PP/DS view of the product master to review the fields shown in Figure 11-11.

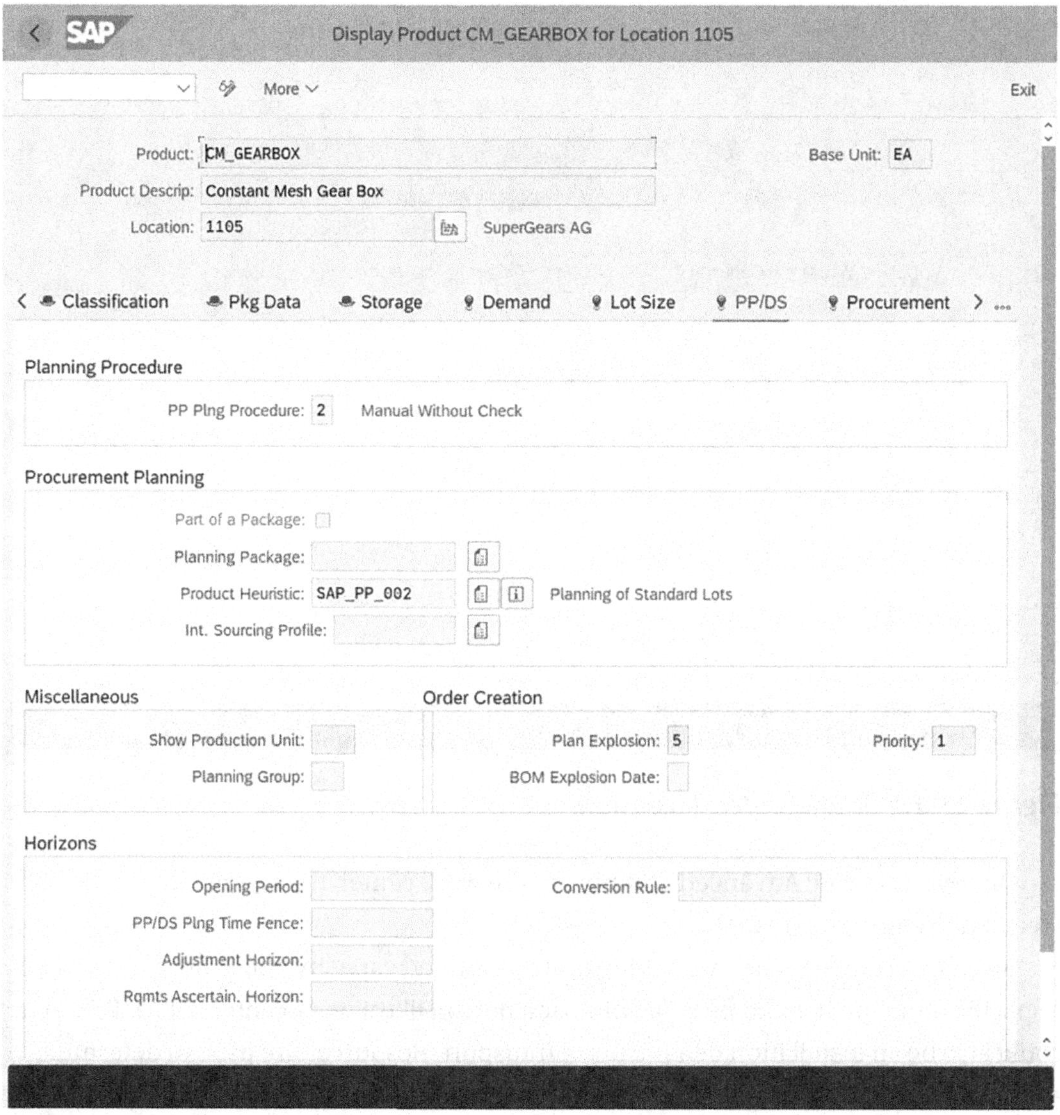

Figure 11-11. *Product master: PP/DS view*

Work Center/Resource

A work center in SAP ERP is called a *resource* in SAP APO. Earlier, it was needed to create a work center in SAP ERP and then transfer it to SAP APO using CIF. However, it is not needed anymore. Similar to material master, you can simply activate Advanced Planning in the Basic Data view of the work center, as shown in Figure 11-12.

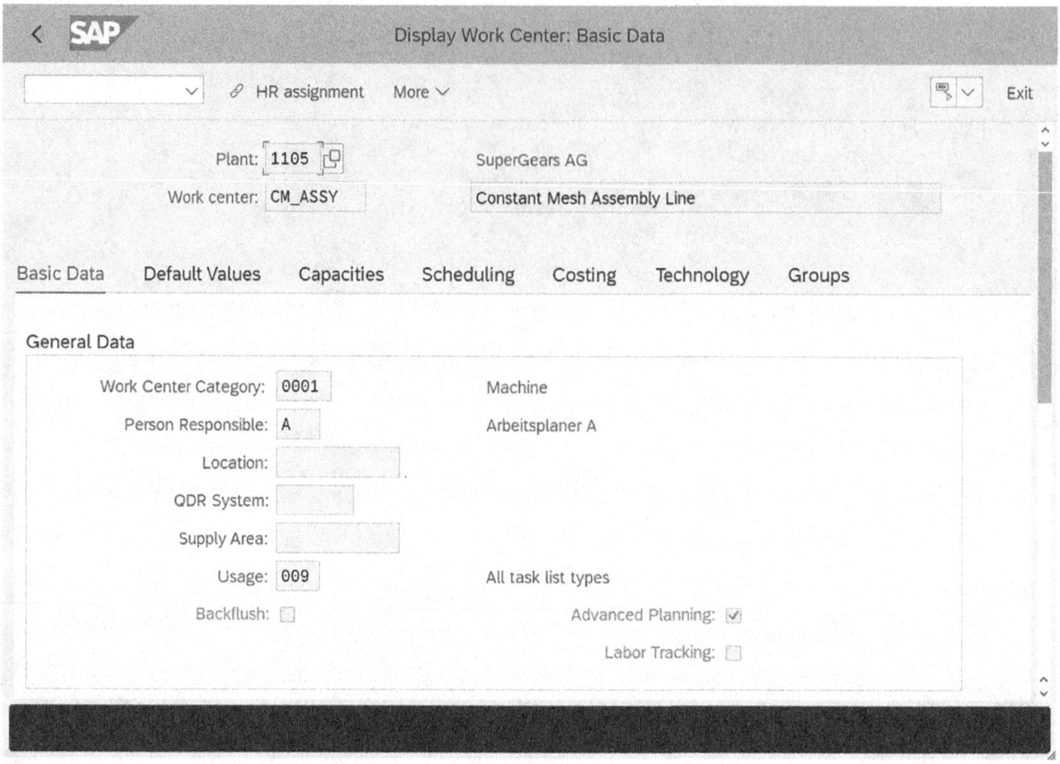

Figure 11-12. *Work center: basic data*

Once you activate Advanced Planning in the work center, the system automatically creates a resource in the APO.

An APO resource refers to anything that has limited capacity and is used to carry out a specific function. It could be a machine or a person like a work center in SAP PP but it could also be an installation or a means of transport. Resources are used to determine available capacity. You can display a resource using Transaction Code /SAPAPO/RES01.

Note   A resource is created using nomenclature other than the work center. You can find the resource by searching for work center name followed by the plant; for example, CMASSY_1105, as shown in Figure 11-13.

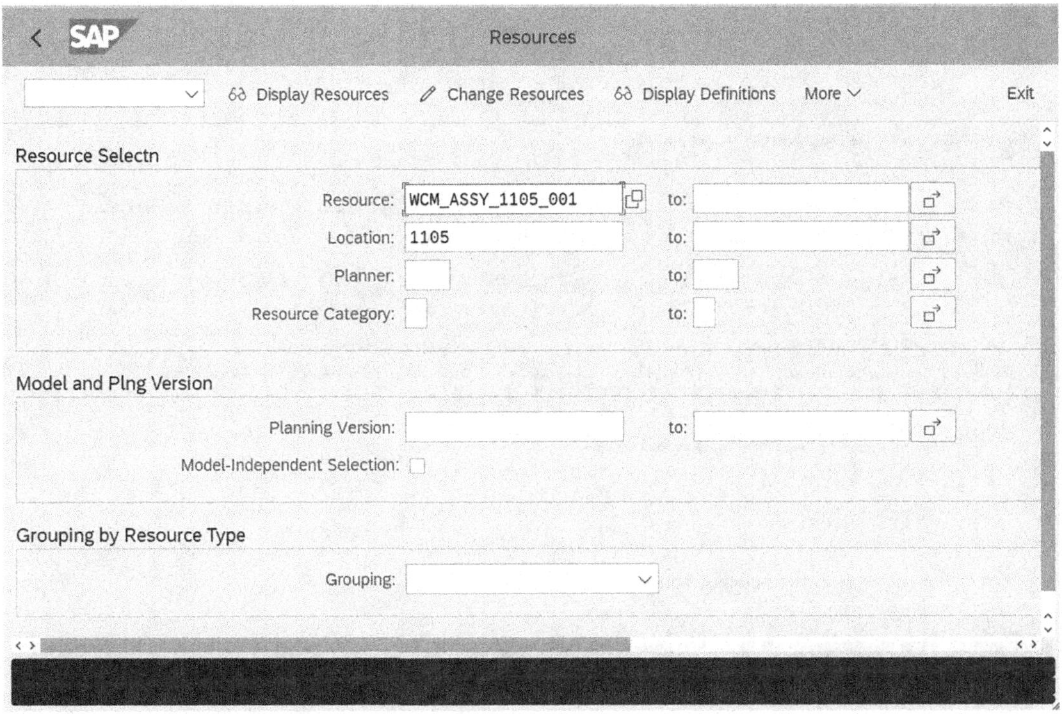

Figure 11-13. *Resources: initial screen*

Figure 11-14 shows the resources in SAP APO. It contains several views, such as General Data, Time-Cont. Capacity, PP/DS Bucket Capacity, External Capacity, Downtimes, Block Planning, Short Texts, and so on.

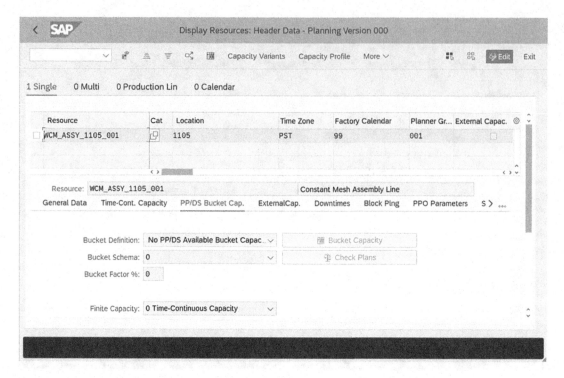

Figure 11-14. *Resources: header data*

Production Data Structure

A production data structure (PDS) is used to determine the BOM and routing for the product. A production version in SAP ERP is used as a basis for creating a production data structure in SAP APO. A PDS can be created using Transaction Code CURTOADV_ CREATE. In the selection screen, enter the selection parameters like Plant, Material, Production Version, and so on, as shown in Figure 11-15.

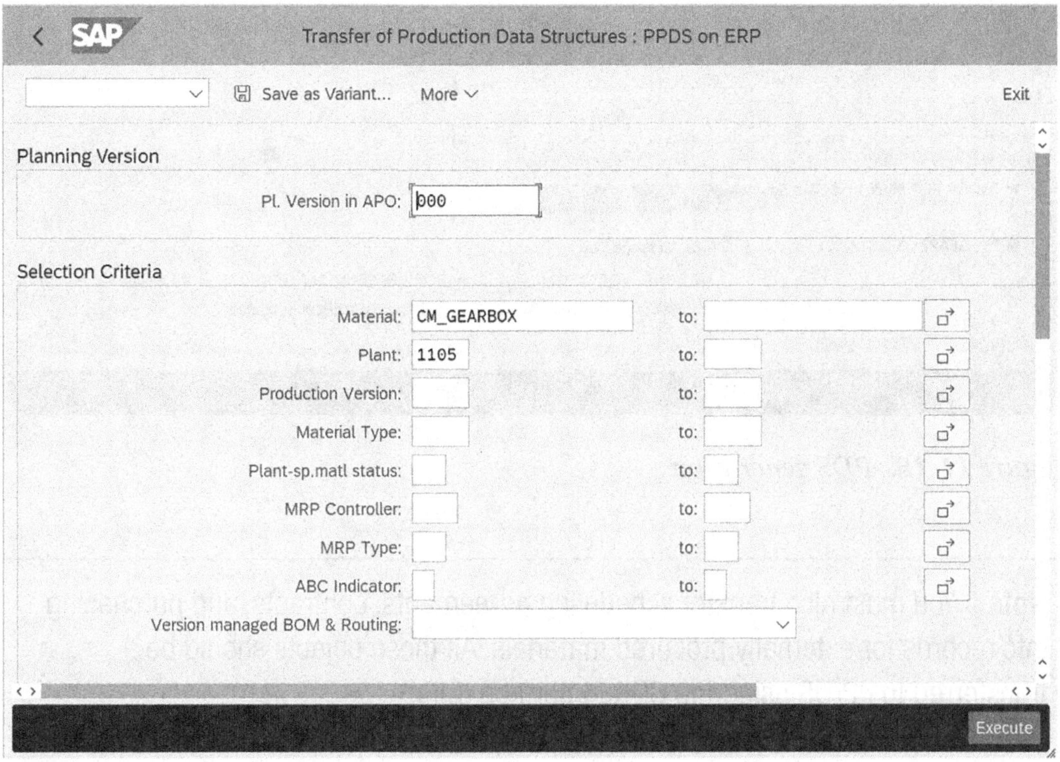

Figure 11-15. *Transfer of product data structures: PPDS on ERP*

You can select one of the transfer modes (i.e. Absolute Transfer, Absolute Transfer (Delta Mode), or Change Transfer). Absolute transfer is used to transfer all the objects and change transfer is used to transfer only the objects that have changed since the last time.

The system will generate logs messages and will display the success or error messages, as shown in Figure 11-16. A PDS has been created for the CM_GEARBOX in Plant 1105.

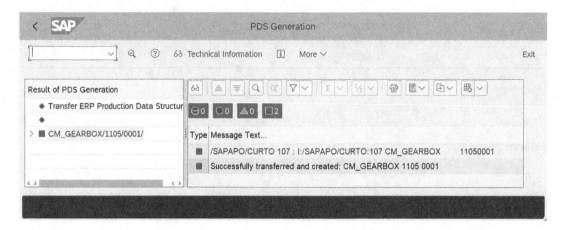

Figure 11-16. *PDS generation*

Note   You must also transfer scheduling agreements, contracts, and purchasing info records for externally procured materials. All these objects should be transferred to PP/DS using the CORE Interface (CIF).

Planning Run with MRP Live

MRP Live can be used to plan materials that are planned with PP/DS heuristics as well as materials that are planned with classic MRP. MRP Live is executed using Transaction Code MD01N or it can also be scheduled to run in the background using the program PPH_MRP_START. Define MRP Type X0 in the MRP1 view of material master for the materials that should be planned with the PP/DS heuristics. You must also ensure that if a semifinished material is to be planned with PP/DS heuristics, the parent material is also planned with PP/DS heuristics.

Production Planning Run

The production planning run can be executed using Transaction Code /SAPAPO/CDPSB0. If you're running the planning for huge set of materials, it is always recommended to run it in the background.

You can execute the planning run for one of the following functions:

- Heuristics

- PP/DS optimization

- Detailed Scheduling (DS)

You must specify the parameters in the Global Settings section, as shown in Figure 11-17.

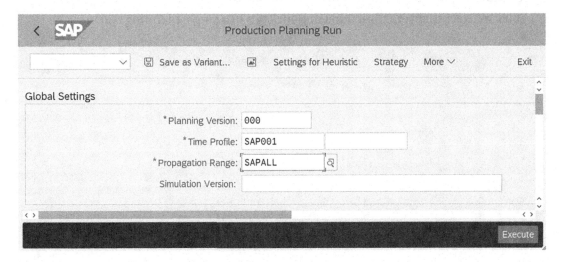

Figure 11-17. *Production planning run*

Planning Version: You can have multiple planning versions, however, only one version is active. The active planning version is 000.

Time Profile: The time profile specifies the planning horizon for the planning run. You may select one of the time profiles that comes preconfigured in standard SAP, as shown in Table 11-4. If needed, new time profiles can be created in customization.

Table 11-4. *Time Profiles*

SAP001	Planning period -2 to +3 months
SAP002	Planning period -1 to +14 days
SAP003	Planning period -1 to +28 days
SAPREM	Test profile for REM heuristic

Propagation Range: Specifies the products or resources that can be planned in PP/DS.

367

A *heuristic* is an algorithm used to execute the planning procedure in a certain way. SAP has delivered several heuristics (or algorithms) that can influence the characteristics of the planning procedure. You can execute the production planning for several heuristics in several steps. For example, you can execute heuristic SAP_PP_002 Planning of Standard Lots in Step one and then run heuristic SAP001 Schedule Sequence. You must specify the appropriate planning object. For example, the planning object for heuristic SAP_PP_002 Planning of Standard Lots should be products, whereas the planning object for Schedule sequence should be operations or resources, as shown in Figure 11-18.

You can execute several functions or heuristics in a single planning run.

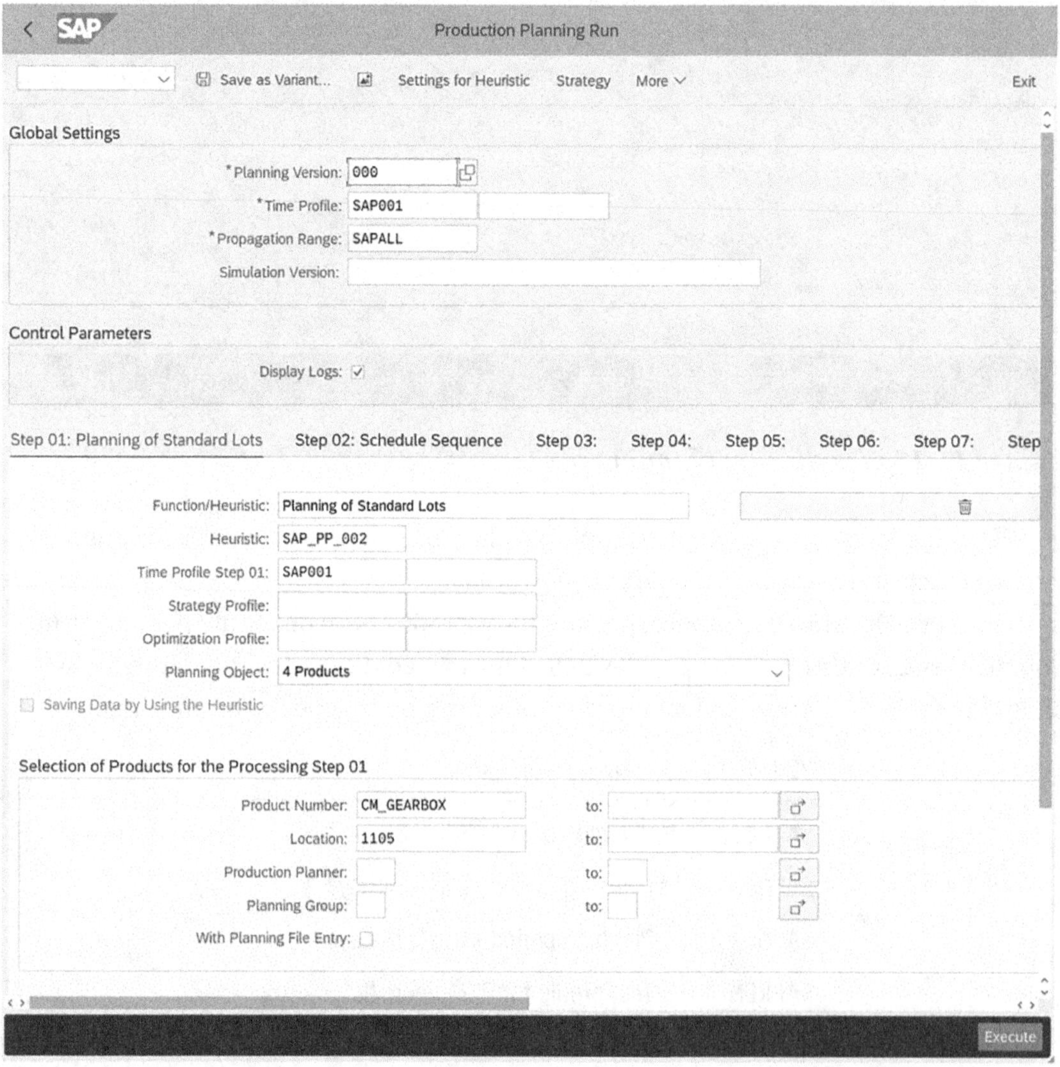

Figure 11-18. Production planning run

Once the planning run has been executed, the logs can be assessed immediately. You can also use the transaction /SAPAPO/RRPLOG1 to check the logs generated during the planning run, as shown in Figure 11-19.

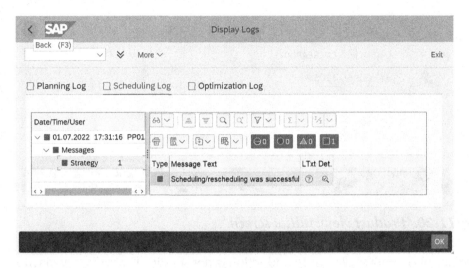

Figure 11-19. *Production planning run: display logs*

Now that the planning run has been executed, the system will create planned orders for in-house produced materials and purchase requisitions for externally procured materials. Go to Transaction Code MD04 to display the stock requirement list.

Product View in PP/DS

Just like Transaction Code MD04 Stock Requirement list in SAP ERP, you can display the demand and supply situation in the product view in PP/DS. However, the product view offers much more functionality than the stock requirement list. You can use Transaction Code /SAPAPO/RRP3 to display the product view. Enter the planning version, product, and location on the initial screen, as shown in Figure 11-20.

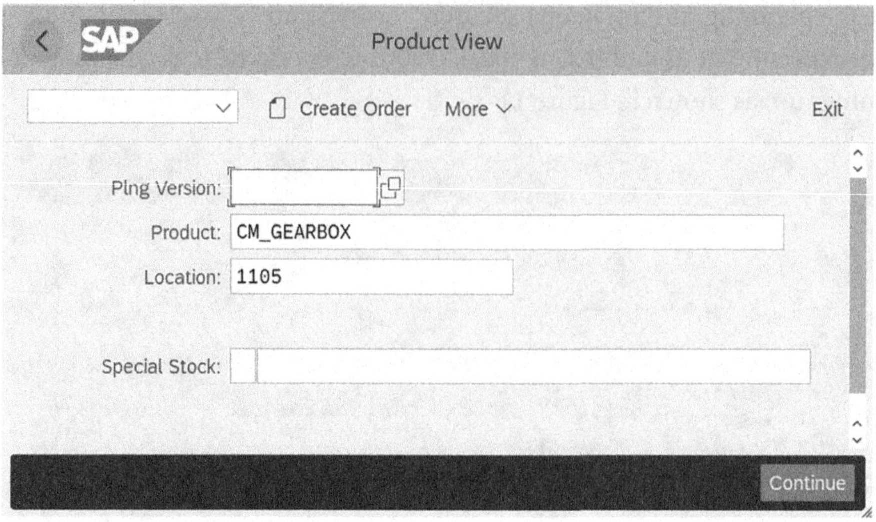

Figure 11-20. *Product view: initial screen*

The supply element (planned/production order) in PP/DS are displayed with dates and times due to the fact that PP/DS runs with finite capacity and can plan the production with the exact time, as shown in Figure 11-21.

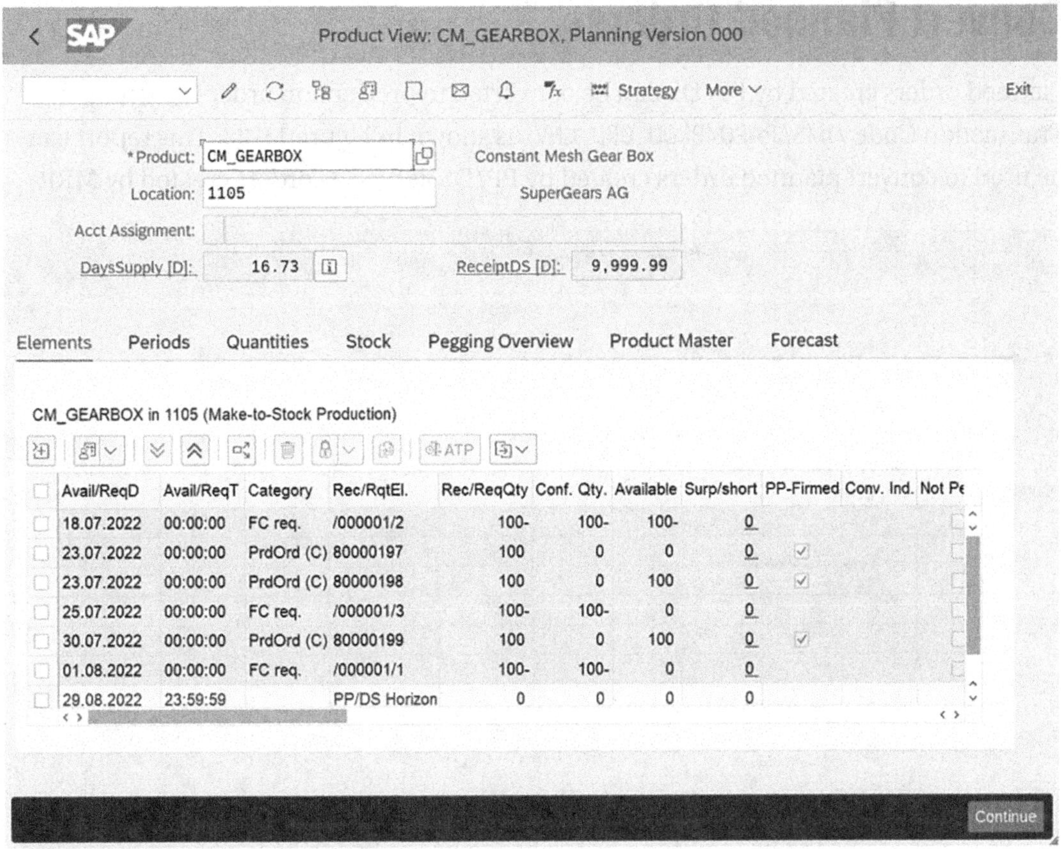

Figure 11-21. *Product view*

There are several tabs in product view (Periods, Quantities, Stock, Pegging Overview, Product Master, and Forecast). These views provide detailed information about the planning situation from a different point of view.

The product view in PP/DS can also be used to execute multiple functions other than displaying demand and supply elements, such as:

- Creating forecasts

- Create planned orders

- Execute product heuristics

- Change the planning strategy of the product

- Display logs and alerts

Convert Planned Orders

Planned orders created by PP/DS can be converted to production orders by using Transaction Code /n/SAPAPO/PROD_ORD_CNV, as shown in Figure 11-22. This report can be used to convert planned orders created by PP/DS as well as orders created by MRP.

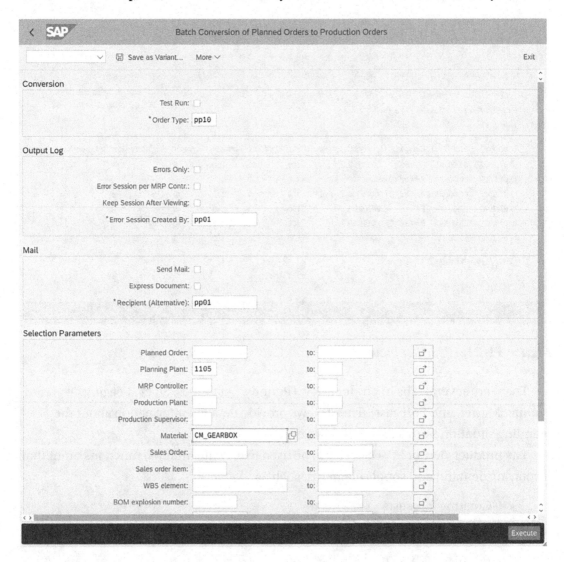

Figure 11-22. Batch conversion of planned orders to production orders: initial screen

The program converts the planned orders to production orders and displays the logs. The report displays the planned order number and the production order number.

It also displays the error messages generated during the conversion; for example, Error calculating costs, as shown in Figure 11-23.

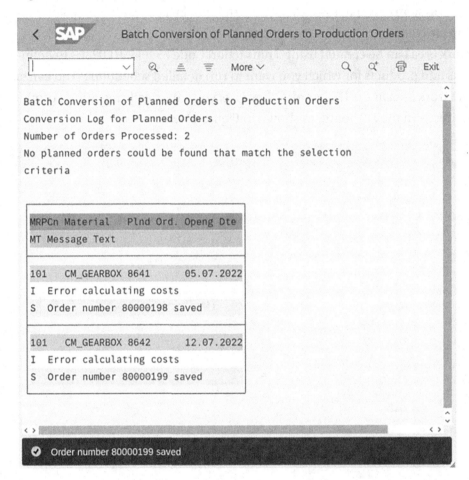

Figure 11-23. Batch conversion of planned orders to production orders: logs

PP/DS stands for production planning and detailed scheduling. So far, you have seen production planning using PP/DS. The next section looks at detailed scheduling.

Detailed Scheduling Board

Detailed scheduling is used for scheduling operations of an order taking into account the capacity constraints as well as component availability. The scheduling board is used for scheduling or rescheduling the operations. You can also deallocate an operation on the resource. You can choose the scheduling direction—forward or backward.

The DS planning board can be accessed via Transaction Code /SAPAPO/CDPS0. Specify the planning version and time profile on the initial screen. Based on the time profile, the system calculates the Display Start, End of Display, Planning Start, and Planning End dates.

A work area can be created using Transaction Code /SAPAPO/CDPSC3 to define the resources and products for which you want to run detailed scheduling. You can simply enter the work area in the DS board. Otherwise, you can specify resources, products, and orders directly in the DS board, as shown in Figure 11-24.

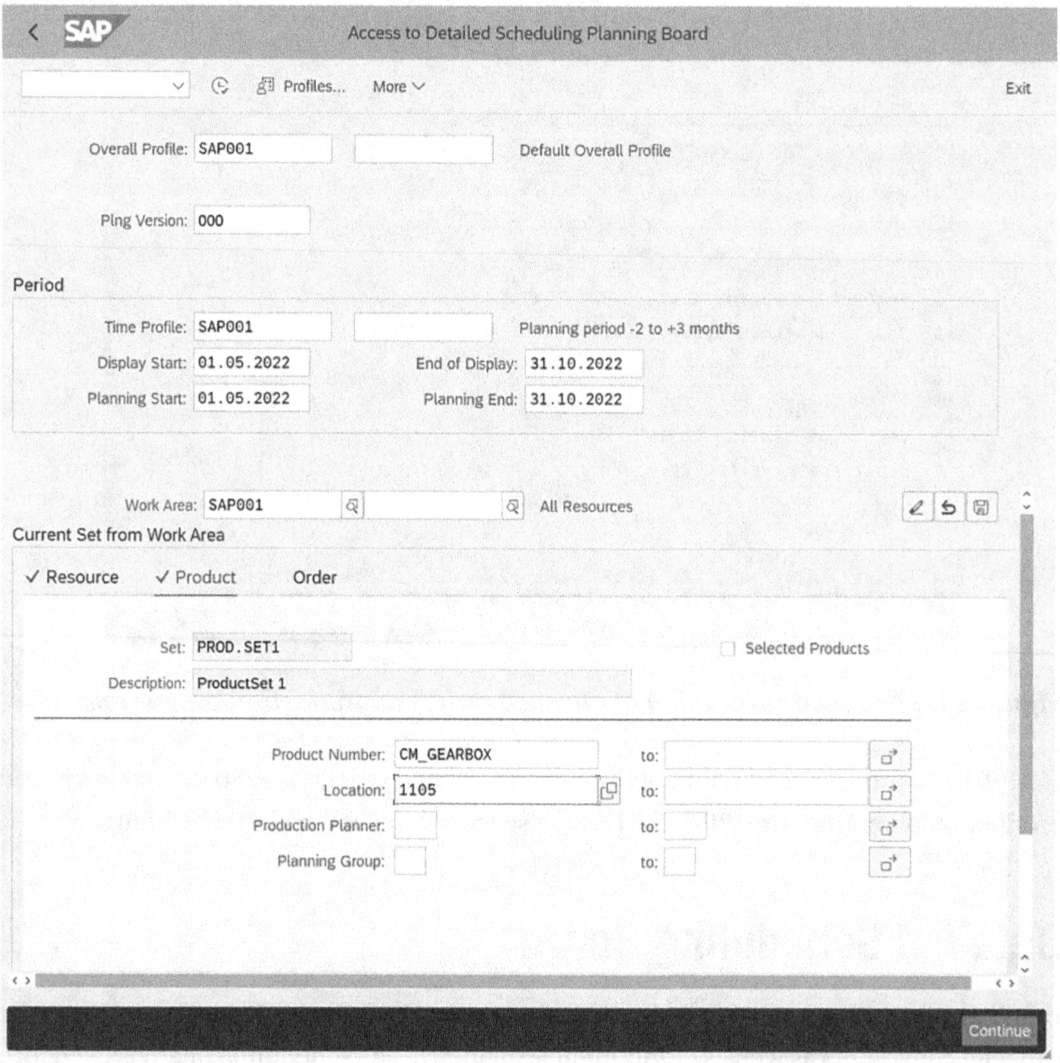

Figure 11-24. *Detailed scheduling planning board: initial screen*

As shown in Figure 11-25, the DS board is split into three sections—the Resources Chart, the Product Chart, and the Product Stock. As you can see, the DS board looks similar to the capacity levelling board (Transaction Code CM25) and provides a graphical representation of the orders, as shown in Figure 11-25.

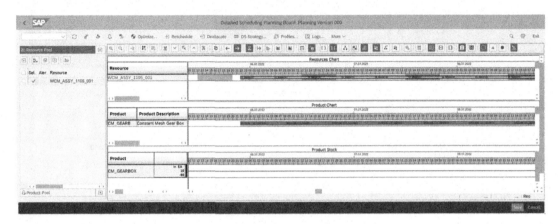

Figure 11-25. *Detailed scheduling planning board*

The DS strategy profile is used to control scheduling parameters, including the Scheduling Sequence, Scheduling Mode, Planning Direction (forward or backward), and so on (see Figure 11-26).

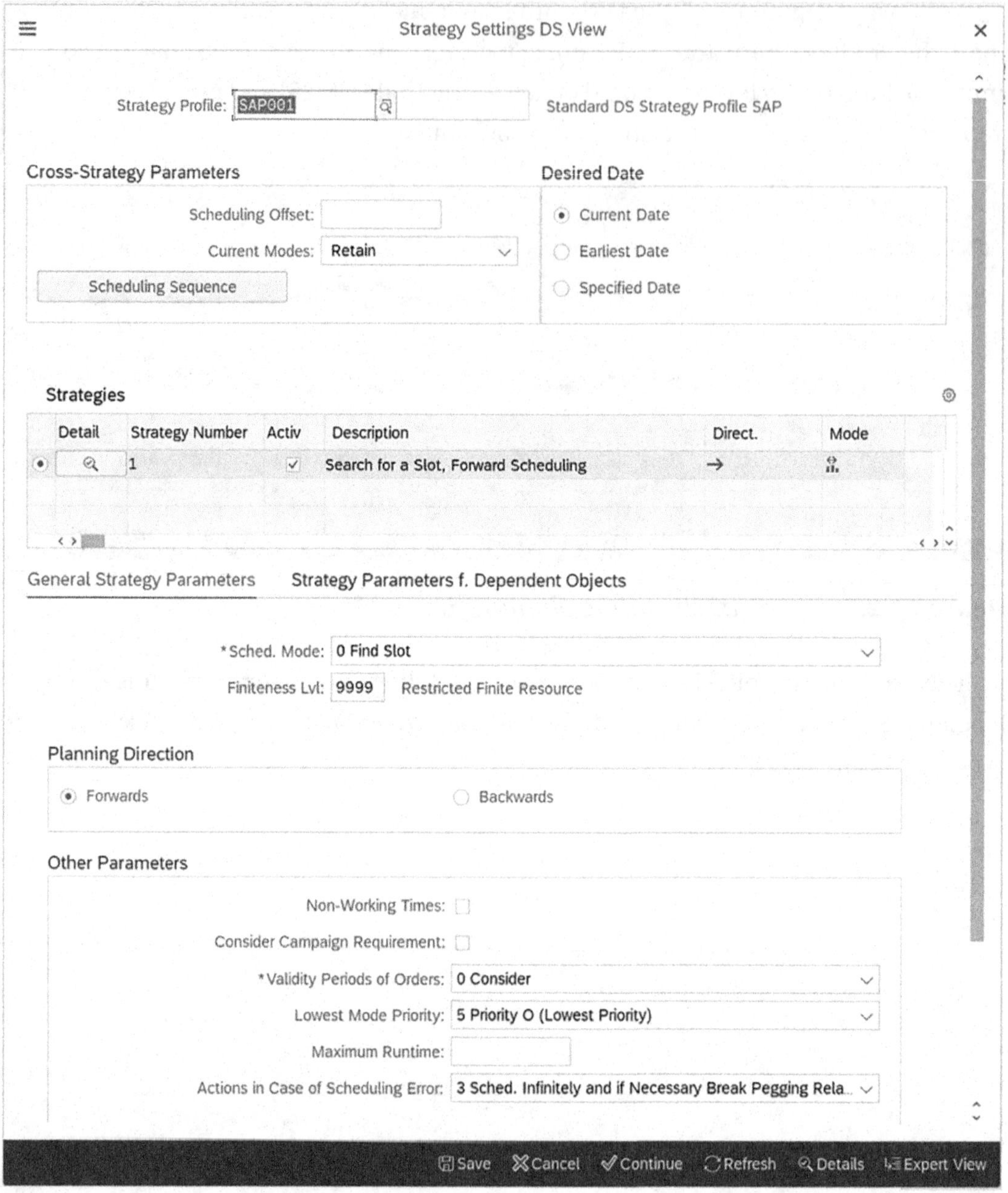

Figure 11-26. *Strategy settings: DS view*

SAP has provided the following heuristics that can be used with a production scheduling board:

- SAP001 – Schedule Sequence

- SAP002 – Remove Backlogs

- SAP003 – Schedule Sequence Manually (Fiori UI Popup Supported)

- SAP004 – Minimize Runtime

- SAP005 – Schedule Operations

- SAP_DS_01 – Stable Forward Scheduling

- SAP_DS_02 – Enhanced Backward Scheduling

- SAP_DS_03 – Change Fixing/Planning Intervals

- SAP_DS_04 – Activate Seq.-Dependent Setup Activities

PP/DS Optimizer

You can also run PP/DS optimizer to create the most cost-effective plan. PP/DS optimizer checks for all possible plans and optimizes the plan by checking the following aspects:

- Costs, such as production, procurement, transport, and storage costs.

- Costs for increasing the production capacity.

- Penalties for violating the stock below the permissible safety stock level.

- Penalties for late delivery.

PP/DS optimizer can be executed via the transaction /SAPAPO/CDPSB1 or directly from the DS board. Enter the optimization horizon, as shown in Figure 11-27.

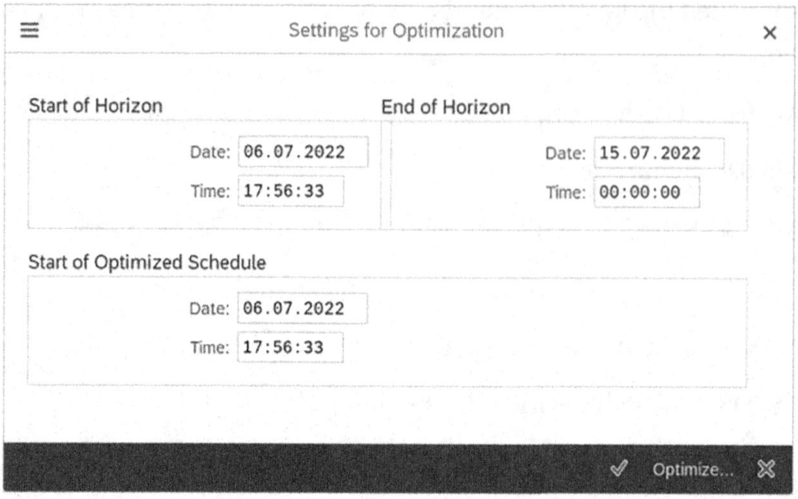

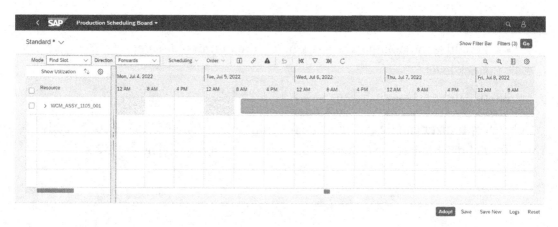

Figure 11-27. *Setting for optimization*

Fiori Application for Production Scheduling Board

A Fiori application is also available for the Production Scheduling Board. You can access the Production Scheduling Board either by using SAP GUI or a Fiori App. One big advantage of Fiori-based apps is that the Production Scheduling Board can be displayed on a monitor and each production line displays the production schedule, as shown in Figure 11-28.

Figure 11-28. *Production scheduling board: Fiori app*

Resource Planning Table

This is used to determine scheduling and sequencing order, similar to the DS planning board. The scheduling data is displayed in tabular format in the resource planning table as opposed to a graphical format in the DS Scheduling board. A resource planning table can be used to execute the following planning functions:

- Sequencing

- Backlog rescheduling

- Capacity leveling

You can use quick drag-and-drop functions to sequence operations. The resource planning table uses the scheduling heuristics assigned to the heuristics profile. You can access the resource planning table with Transaction Code /SAPAPO/RPT. You can also access different applications, including Alert Monitor, Plan Monitor, and Optimizer directly from the resource planning table, as shown in Figure 11-29.

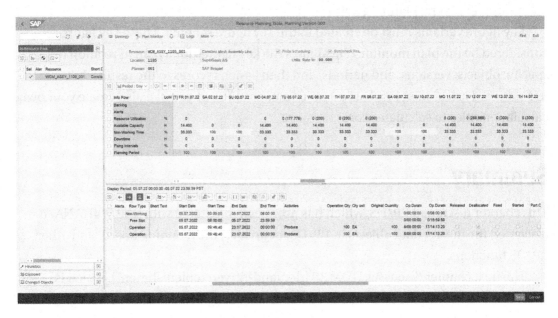

Figure 11-29. *Resource planning board*

Alert Monitor

You can create alert profiles for each application in PP/DS. Based on the alert profile, the system will generate an alert or notification to report a problem. This enables you to monitor the system and make sure the system is running smoothly. The alert monitor is used to display all the alerts that have arisen and allows you to navigate directly to the relevant application in order to resolve the problem. You can access the alert monitor using Transaction Code /SAPAPO/AMON1. It can also be accessed via the product view (Transaction Code /SAPAPO/RRP3) or the planning board (Transaction Code / SAPAPO/CDPS0).

Plan Monitor

The plan monitor can be used to determine the quality of the current planning situation. You can also compare several plans and simulation versions, or you can also compare planning over several planning periods.

Key figure variants must be created in the key figure schema. These key figures are considered by the plan monitor. It evaluates the key figures for a plan in relation to specific objects, versions, and periods, and then assigns scores to the results. You can a use standard calculation (such as a sum or mean value), or you can also create your own calculation rules to calculate scores.

Summary

This chapter discussed PP/DS, which has now been integrated with SAP S/4HANA. It discussed the master data objects in PP/DS, heuristics, the planning board, and other PP/DS functions.

The next chapter discusses DDMRP (demand-driven replenishment), which is another latest innovation in SAP S/4HANA.

CHAPTER 12

Demand-Driven Material Requirements Planning (DDMRP)

In this chapter, you learn about demand-driven replenishment (DDMRP), which is a new approach to classical MRP that reacts more quickly to demand and supply fluctuations. The chapter discusses how DDMRP can be executed in SAP S/4HANA using the Fiori apps.

What Is Demand-Driven Material Requirements Planning (DDMRP)?

In 2011, Carol Ptak and Chad Smith introduced a new concept to the world called *demand-driven material requirements planning*, or DDMRP.

Traditional MRP is fundamentally forecast-driven. However, the supply chain is extremely volatile and uncertain in today's age. The forecasts, which are generated based on historical figures, can't be trusted to be 100 percent accurate. There are a lot of uncertainties that cannot be foreseen and, thus, could result in component shortages. Industry experts calls the supply chain in today's world VUCA—Volatile, Uncertain, Complex, and Ambiguous. DDMRP tries to answer these uncertainties by responding to real-time fluctuations in demand.

Classic MRP operates on the "push" principle and therefore pushes inventory into the system based on forecasts or demands. DDMRP is an innovative multi-echelon pull methodology that is based on three principles—position, protect, and pull.

H. Goel, *Handbook for SAP PP in S/4HANA*, https://doi.org/10.1007/978-1-4842-8566-4_12

Why Is DDMRP Needed?

2021-22 witnessed shortages of semi-conductors like never before. This was because vehicle sales plummeted in early 2020 due to COVID restrictions, which forced automakers to cut short their orders for chips and semi-conductors. The demand for vehicles recovered much faster than predicted, but the semi-conductor manufacturers had already diverted their production toward other applications.

Things change very quickly in today's dynamic supply chain. When demand fluctuates, Classical MRP tries to solve this issue by consuming the buffer stock. While the buffer stock does help in mitigating the shortages, it can only prevent some of the shortages. Also, if you're always keeping buffer stock, it means you're blocking inventory and capital.

The supply chain has tons of variability caused by several factors, such as forecast inaccuracy, logistics delays, and more. While variability cannot be eliminated altogether, inventory costs and component shortages can be mitigated using DDMRP.

DDMRP takes variability out of the equation by using "pull" for materials in a demand-driven approach. Rather than relying on forecast accuracy—and buffering for fluctuations in demand and supply—DDMRP tracks actual usage and manages replenishment through a simple visual system. Buffer inventory is only used to ensure the availability of key items that are deemed to be of strategic importance. With the use of DDMRP, there is less inventory overall and fewer shortages.

DDMRP combines some of the features of Material Requirements Planning (MRP) and Distribution Requirements Planning (DRP) together with the concepts like pull and visibility emphasize lean manufacturing and the theory of constraints and the variability reduction emphasis of Six Sigma.

Components of Demand-Driven Material Requirement Planning

DDMRP methodology is based on three principles—position, protect, and pull. These three principles comprise of five components—Strategic Inventory Positioning, Buffer Profiles and Levels, Dynamic Adjustments, Demand-Driven Planning, and Visible and Collaborative Execution. The first three components fundamentally outline the initial and evolving configuration of the planning model to be used for DDMRP and the last two components define the day-to-day process. Figure 12-1 illustrates this.

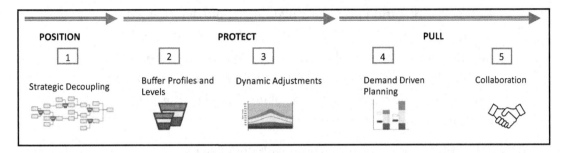

Figure 12-1. *The principles of DDMRP methodology*

Position: The first step is to identify strategic materials that are placed at critical points in the BOM structure. As per the Theory of Constraints method, the critical resources that determine manufacturing limitations are known as *constraints*. These critical materials or constraints must be the prime focus over other components.

Protect: Once the critical components are identified, the next step is to ensure availability of these components by using inventory as a buffer. However, this buffer inventory is not defined as static safety stock. It is rather dynamic.

Pull: The inventory levels of the critical components are continuously monitored and used for managing buffer inventory using an innovative pull technique. Visual cues are used to maintain the buffer inventory within a specified range.

The five components of demand-driven material requirement planning are:

1. **Strategic Inventory Positioning:** These are materials that have significant variability or fluctuations in the demand or supply, materials with very long lead times, or materials with bottleneck in the production capacities. They are the top candidates for DDMRP. The planner should identify these materials and determine the decoupling point.

2. **Buffer Profiles and Levels:** The planner should determine the inventory levels to be stocked (buffer stock) at each decoupling point. Materials with similar variability can be grouped together, relevant buffer profiles can be assigned, and buffer levels can be maintained. The buffer level is calculated based on the average consumption of the materials.

Let's look at some important terms used with buffer sizing:

- **Average daily usage (ADU):** As the name suggests, it refers to average consumption of a material in a period of time.

- **Minimum order quantity (MOQ):** The minimum quantity of an order to be procured from a vendor or to be produced in-house.

- **Decoupled lead time (DLT):** Lead time is usually referred to as the time required to procure a material (i.e., to produce or purchase a material). When none of the components is available, the total time required to procure all the raw materials and produce the semi-finished and finished assemblies, the total time taken is called *cumulative lead time*. However, with the introduction of buffered positions in DDMRP, it can be assumed that stocked positions are available. Therefore, the total time to procure all the components except for the buffered position is referred to as decoupled lead Time (DLT).

Calculation of Buffer Zones

The buffer zone is divided into three zones—Green, Yellow, and Red—as shown in Figure 12-2.

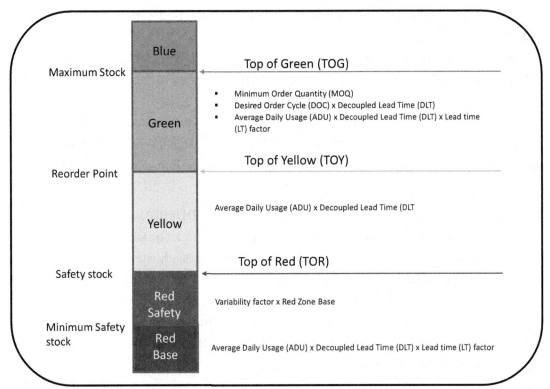

Figure 12-2. Buffer zones

The buffer zones are calculated based on the average consumption over the entire decoupled lead time (i.e., ADU x DLT). Each zone is then calculated as below.

Green zone: Green zone is calculated based on either of the three, whichever is the largest.

- Minimum Order Quantity (MOQ)

- Desired Order Cycle (DOC) x Decoupled Lead Time (DLT)

- Average Daily Usage (ADU) x Decoupled Lead Time (DLT) x Lead Time (LT) factor

The highest point of the green zone is called Top of Green (TOG) and it reflects a comfortable buffer position. When the stock on hand crosses the TOG, it indicates an excessive inventory level and is called Over the Top of Green (OTOG).

Yellow zone: Average Daily Usage (ADU) x Decoupled Lead Time (DLT).

The highest point of the yellow zone is called Top of Yellow (TOY). When the on-hand inventory falls below TOY, then it is considered a warning for the buffer.

Red zone: The red zone is split into two sub-zones—the Red Zone Safety and the Red Zone Base.

Red Zone Base is calculated as Average Daily Usage (ADU) x Decoupled Lead Time (DLT) x Lead time (LT) factor. Red Zone Safety is calculated as variability factor x Red Zone Base.

The Total Red Zone is the sum of the Red Zone Safety and the Red Zone Base.

The highest point of the red zone is called Top of Red (TOR). When the on-hand stock levels falls below the TOR, it calls for urgent and immediate action from the planner.

1. **Dynamic adjustments:** The whole idea behind DDMRP is that the buffer levels should be dynamic and should react quickly to demand/supply situations. The buffer levels are adjusted automatically based on the average daily usage (ADU) of the component. Although the dynamic adjustment is quite robust, it might be necessary to adjust them manually due to several factors like promotions or seasonality, product lifecycle (phase-in or phase-out), and so on.

2. **Demand-driven planning:** The planner can create replenishment orders using the visual planning tools. The orders are created based on the net flow position. The net flow position is calculated based on the following formula:

   Net flow position = Stock on hand + Ordered quantity – Qualified Sales order demand

   In this equation, note the term "qualified" sales order demand. A sales order demand is considered "qualified" if it is past due, due today, or if it is a spike. A day is considered a spike if it is a configurable number of times above ADU (Average Daily Usage). If the net flow position for a component falls below the top of yellow, then a replenishment order is created to reach the inventory up to top of green.

3. **Visible and collaborative execution:** The planners should take action as proposed by the system. The replenishment orders must be converted to production orders or purchase orders. Material lead times or scheduling synchronization alerts can be used to quickly respond to material shortages. Demand-driven replenishment operates on a priority-based pull system and notifies the planner whenever there is a need for urgent action.

SAP adopted the new methodology by the Demand Driven Institute and introduced demand-driven replenishment in SAP S/4HANA Cloud 1708 and SAP S/4HANA 1709. Now that you have read about these DDMRP concepts, it's time to find out how to map these concepts in SAP S/4HANA.

DDMRP in SAP

Setup in the Material Master

Identify the relevant materials for demand-driven MRP and assign the MRP type: D1 (demand-driven MRP, fixing type -1-) in the MRP 1 view of the material master, as shown in Figure 12-3. D1 is a new MRP type for demand-driven replenishment, which has been launched in the S/4HANA release 1709. You must also assign the Lot Sizing Procedure as H1 or HB to replenish up to the maximum stock level. You must also maintain the following fields:

- Minimum Safety Stock: This field acts as Top of Red – Safety

- Safety Stock: This field acts as Top of Red – Base

- Reorder point: This field acts as Top of Yellow

- Maximum stock level: This field acts as Top of Green

These fields are maintained but are eventually overwritten based on the values calculated by DDR and the actual consumption data.

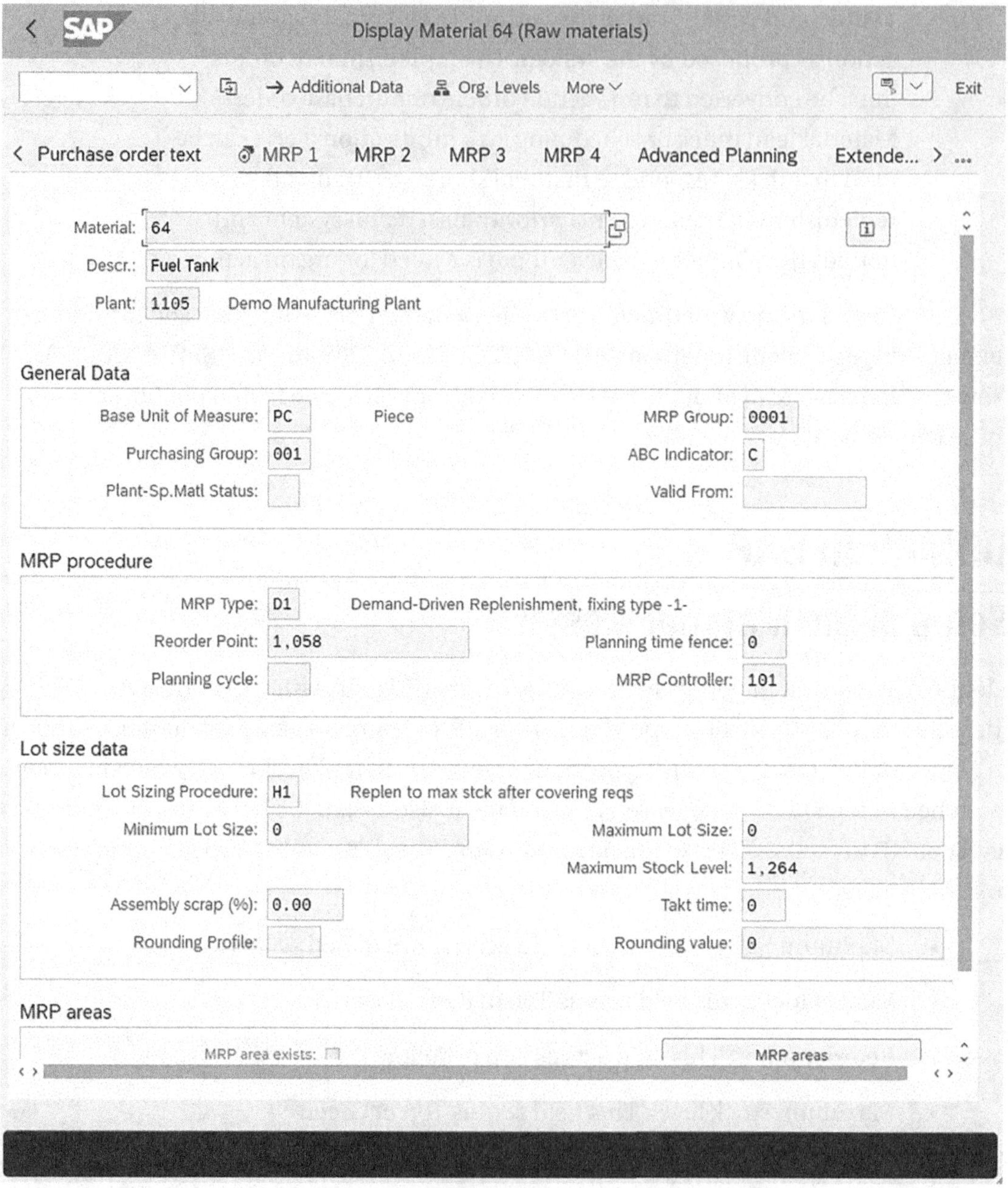

Figure 12-3. *Material master: MRP1 view*

Schedule Product Classification (DD)

You can classify the materials using the Schedule Product Classification app. You can use this app to classify the materials based on several parameters, including Usage Value in % (ABC Classification), BOM Usage (PQR classification), and Coefficient of Variation (XYZ Classification). Based on the classification, the system determines if the product should be replenished using DDMRP and eventually helps assign the buffer profile in the Stock positioning, which is the consequent step of the DDMRP process.

Click the Schedule Product Classification (DD) app in the demand-driven replenishment section of the Fiori apps (see Figure 12-4).

Figure 12-4. *Schedule Product Classification (DD) tile*

Click the New button to schedule a new job to classify the products based on the criteria you would like to specify. In the Product Selection criteria, you must specify the products or product groups that you want to classify—the plant and MRP area. The number of days in the past is used to calculate the material movements during that period.

In the Parameters section, you must specify the values according to how the products should be classified, as shown in Figure 12-5.

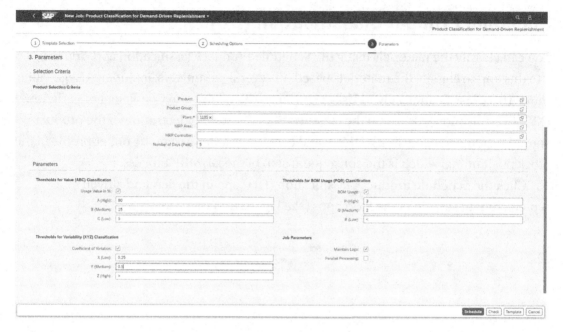

Figure 12-5. *New job: product classification for demand-driven replenishment*

Each product can be classified in three groups according to the defined criteria:

- **ABC Classification:** Materials are classified based on the historical consumption (i.e., it analyzes the material movements in the specified period and determines the proportion of the goods movement). Materials with the highest consumption are classified as A while the materials with the lowest consumption are classified as C. The materials that have a lower proportion of consumption than A materials but higher than C are classified as B.

- **PQR Classification:** Materials are classified based on the usage of a component in the BOMs (i.e., to determine how many BOMs a component is assigned to). The higher number of BOM assignments means the component has a higher relevance for planning.

- **XYZ Classification:** XYZ analysis is used to classify the products based on their variability of demand (i.e., to determine the deviation of demand from the forecast). When the deviation is negligible or lowest, then the products are classified as X, the products with medium to high deviation are classified as Y, and the products with unpredictable demands are classified as Z items.

The Schedule Product Classification app classifies products based on three criteria:

- How frequent and how much is the material used?

- How many finished goods are impacted by the product based on usage in BOM?

- How accurate is the forecast?

These characteristics play a key role in determining the central process of demand-driven replenishment process, since they can help determine how the product should be managed and if there is a need to maintain inventory of the product.

Mass Maintenance of Products (DD)

This app is used to display and change the product details or the master data records for the products that are relevant for DDMRP. The result of classification of the products from the previous step is displayed in this app, as you can see in Figure 12-6. The classification of each product is displayed in the app. You can use the Mass Change function if you want to change the material master data for products. This app can also be used to derive stock positioning of the products based on the classification results.

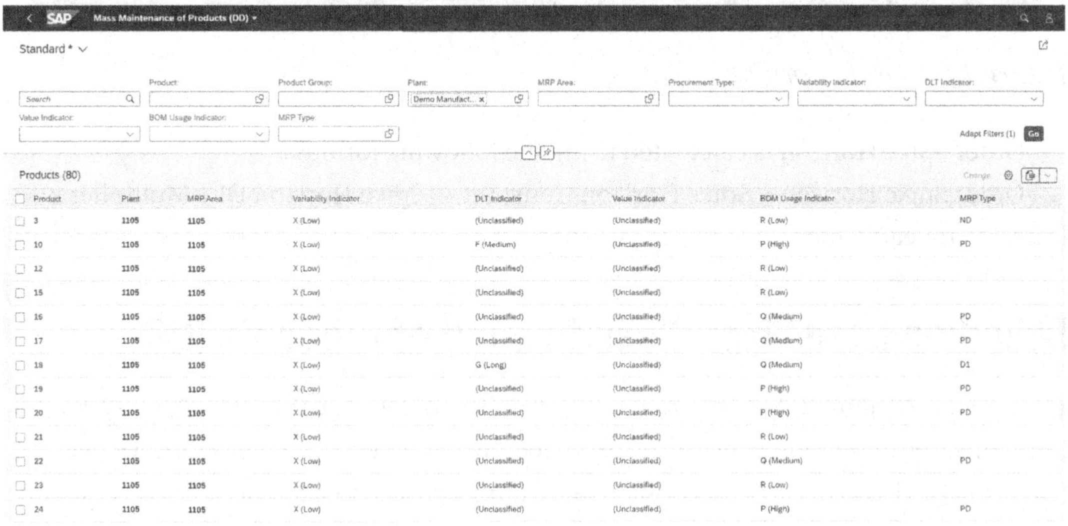

Figure 12-6. *Mass maintenance of products (DD)*

Product classification plays a critical role in determining the variability factor and the lead time factor since these values are calculated based on the classification results, which are later used for buffer proposal calculation.

SAP comes preconfigured with a standard buffer profile, which contains standard values for the variability factor as well as the lead time factor. However, it is not possible to define buffer profile values. It can only be changed using view cluster PPH_DD_PROFILE_ASG_VC with the Transaction Code SM34.

The buffer profile can be defined at the plant level, which contains various fields like spike horizon constant, spike horizon DLT multiplier, spike threshold, and on-hand alert threshold, as shown in Figure 12-7.

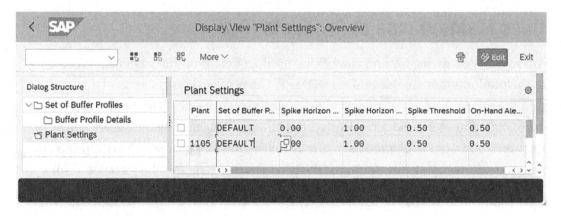

Figure 12-7. Buffer profile: plant

Order Spike Horizon is calculated using the following formula:

Order Spike Horizon = Spike Horizon Constant + (Spike Horizon DLT Multiplier x Decoupled Lead Time)

Schedule Lead Time Classification of Products (DD)

The next step in demand-driven replenishment is to determine the *decoupled lead time*. Lead time determination can only be executed once the decoupling points have been determined. This is because decoupled lead times for the subsequent buffer calculation are determined based on the decoupling points. Decoupled lead times are used to calculate the buffer level.

The Schedule Lead Time Classification of Products (DD) app is used to classify the products based on the decoupled lead time. This is called EFG classification. EFG classification can only be executed once the dispatching characteristics in demand-driven replenishment have been defined. This is because the decoupling points are not known when the DDR process is initiated.

Click the Schedule Lead Time Classification of Products (DD) app in the Demand-Driven Replenishment section of the Fiori apps (see Figure 12-8).

Figure 12-8. *Schedule lead time classification of products (DD) tile*

Now click the New button to schedule a new job to classify the products based on the criteria that you would like to specify. In the product selection criteria, you must specify the products or product groups that you want to classify—the plant and MRP area. The number of days in the past is used to calculate the material movements during that period.

In the Parameters section, you must specify the values according to which products should be classified with EFG classification. The threshold for decoupled lead times can be maintained at three levels—in-house production, external procurement, and stock transfer—as shown in Figure 12-9.

E- products have the shortest lead times according to the specified threshold.

F- products have average lead times according to the specified threshold.

G- products have the longest lead times according to the specified threshold.

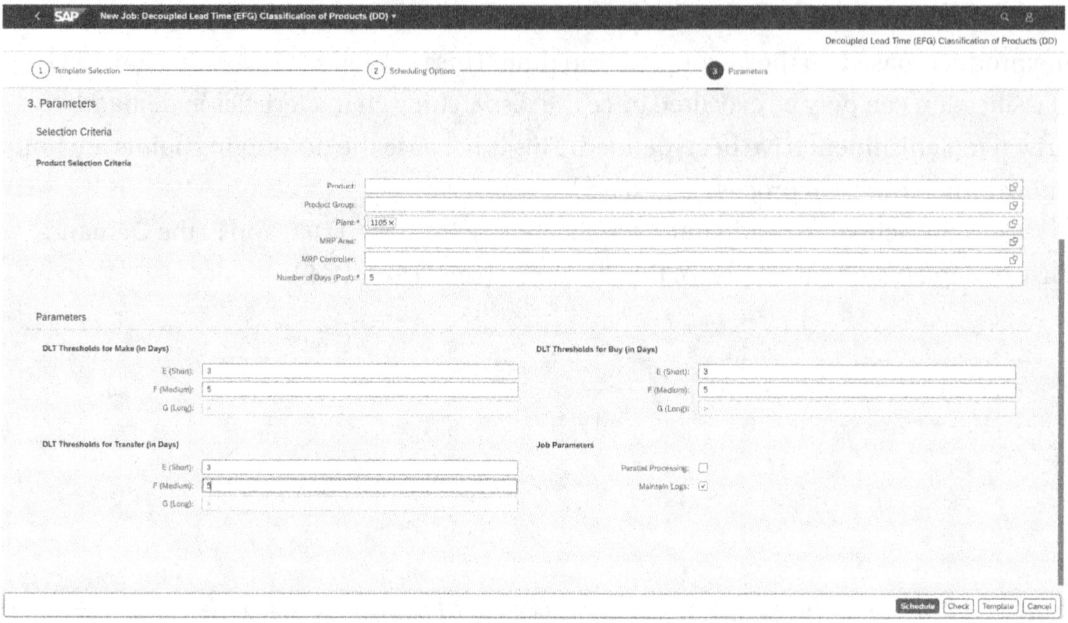

Figure 12-9. *New job: decoupled lead time (EFG) classification of products (DD)*

During EFG classification of the in-house produced materials, all the production/process orders are identified that fall in the analysis horizon. The replenishment lead time (RLT) is calculated based on the time between the order creation date and the final confirmation date. The average RLT is calculated for each material/plant combination. If the RLT cannot be calculated based on this logic, the in-house production time in the material master is considered for the RLT.

Similarly, for externally procured materials, all the purchase orders are identified within the analysis horizon. The replenishment lead time is determined based on the time between the purchase order creation date and the final delivery date. If the RLT cannot be calculated using this logic, the planned delivery time from the purchase info record is used. If the RLT cannot be determined from the info record, the planned delivery time from the material master is used.

Schedule Buffer Proposal Calculation

The next step in demand-driven replenishment is to determine the central buffer zones and buffer levels. It can be calculated based on the average daily usage, decoupled lead time, buffer profiles, and several other factors.

Click the Schedule Buffer Proposal Calculation app in the Demand-Driven
Replenishment section of the Fiori apps, as shown in Figure 12-10.

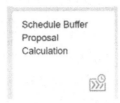

Figure 12-10. *Schedule buffer proposal calculation tile*

In this app, you can schedule a job and specify the scheduling parameters of the
job. For example, as a single job or periodic. In the product selection criteria, you can
specify the Product, Product Group, Plant, or MRP Area, as shown in Figure 12-11. You
can specify if the Average Daily Usage should be calculated. You can specify if you want
to recalculate the decoupled lead time or adopt it from the material master. In addition
to this, you can automatically adopt the buffer level proposal in the Automated Proposal
Processing Options section. If you want to review the buffer level proposals and then
adopt them manually, you must select the Do Not Adopt Proposals option.

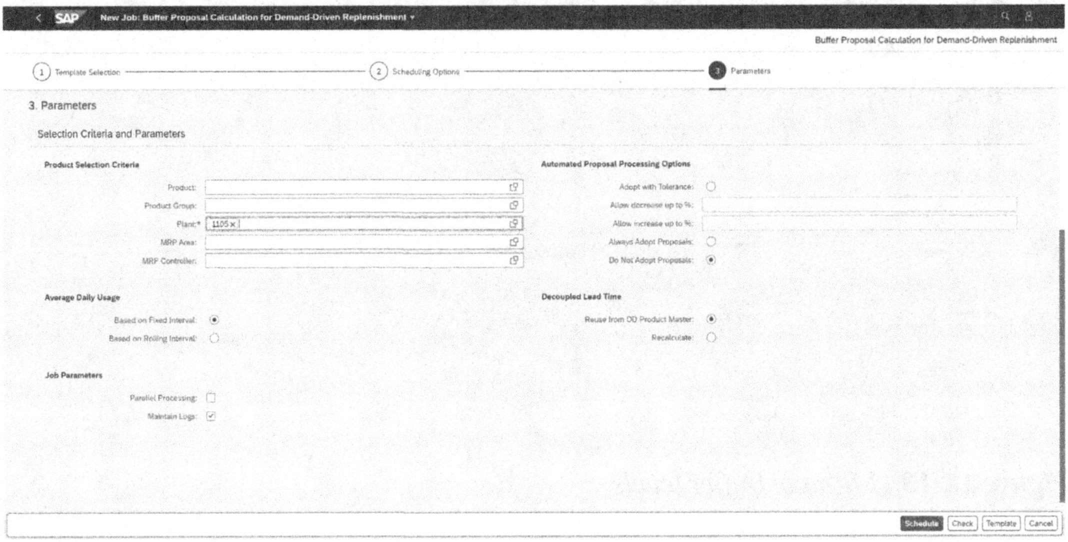

Figure 12-11. *New job: buffer proposal calculation for demand-driven
replenishment*

Manage Buffer Levels

This app is used to ensure that the products are available whenever they're needed since inventory points like the safety stock, reorder point, and maximum stock are calculated.

Click the Manage Buffer Levels app in the Demand-Driven Replenishment section of the Fiori apps, as shown in Figure 12-12.

Figure 12-12. *Manage buffer levels tile*

The Buffer Level field displays the current buffer levels as well as the proposed buffer levels. As you can see in Figure 12-13, the current stock for Product 64 is 1264 pcs, while the proposed stock is 52 pcs.

![Manage buffer levels screen showing a table of products with columns Product, Plant, Max. Stock Today, Buffer Levels (Historical and Proposed), and Average Daily Usage (Historical and Future).]

Product	Plant	Max. Stock Today		
63	1105 Demo Manufacturing Plant	Current: 998.016 M Proposed: 1,301.760 M Change: 30.43% (+303.744 M)		Adopt
64	1105 Demo Manufacturing Plant	Current: 1,264 PC Proposed: 52 PC Change: -95.89% (-1,212 PC)		Adopt
18	1105 Demo Manufacturing Plant	Current: 1,513 PC Proposed: 0 PC Change: -100% (-1,513 PC)		Adopt
65	1105 Demo Manufacturing Plant	Current: 200 PC Proposed: 0 PC Change: -100% (-200 PC)		Adopt

Figure 12-13. *Manage buffer levels*

Figure 12-14 shows the buffer levels. The buffer level so far is quite high as compared to the proposed buffer level today onward. Click the Adopt button if you want to accept the proposed buffer level.

Figure 12-14. *Buffer levels: planning view*

Once the buffer proposal is accepted, you can execute MRP Live using Transaction Code MD01N to generate the replenishment proposals. Now, go to the Stock Requirement list (MD04) to display the demand and supply situation. New replenishment orders are generated and inventory points, like safety stock, reorder point, and maximum stock are updated in the Demand-Driven Replenishment view of the Stock Requirement List, as shown in Figure 12-15. These inventory points have been calculated by the DDR process.

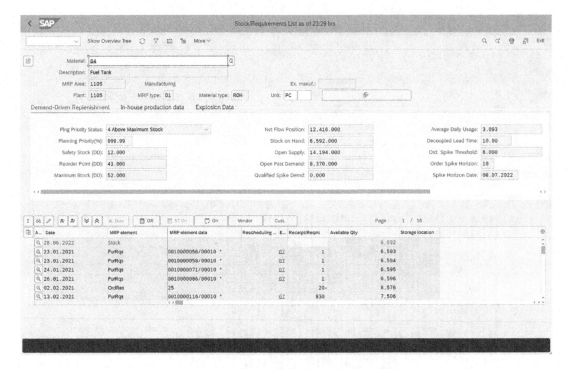

Figure 12-15. *Stock requirement list: demand-driven replenishment*

The replenished can be triggered by MRP, as you saw in the previous example. However, the replenishment can also be triggered by Fiori apps for demand-driven replenishment. The next section looks at how to execute replenishments in DDR using Fiori apps.

Replenishment Execution by On-Hand Status

Click the Replenishment Execution by On-Hand Status app in the Demand-Driven Replenishment section of the Fiori apps (see Figure 12-16).

Figure 12-16. *Replenishment execution by on-hand status tile*

The Fiori app called Replenishment Execution by On-Hand Status displays the existing inventory in the warehouse and determines if the on-hand stock is sufficient for production (see Figure 12-17).

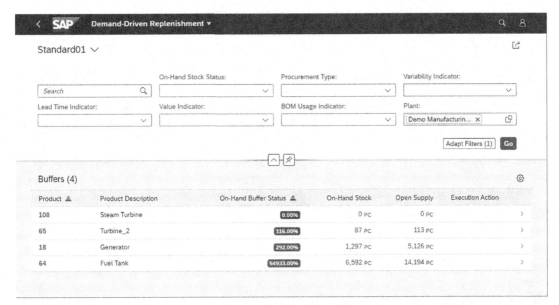

Figure 12-17. *Replenishment execution by on-hand status*

You can click the > button in the Execution Action. The procurement proposals can be modified as needed. For example, planned orders can be edited, deleted, or converted into production/process orders and purchase requisitions can be edited or deleted, as shown in Figure 12-18.

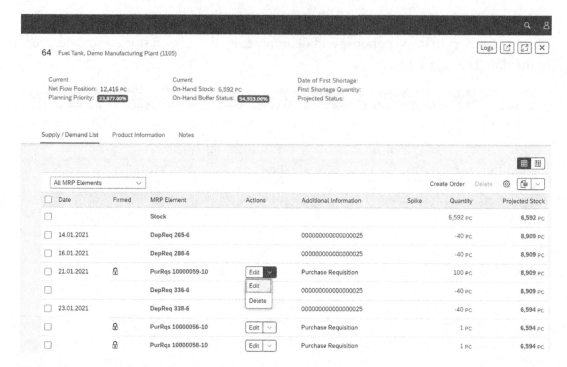

Figure 12-18. *Replenishment details*

Replenishment Planning by Planning Priority

The Fiori app called Replenishment Planning by Planning Priority is used to postprocess the output of the planning run. Click the Replenishment Planning by Planning Priority app in the Demand-Driven Replenishment section of the Fiori apps (see Figure 12-19).

Figure 12-19. *Replenishment planning by planning priority tile*

The output screen displays the buffer level of all the products. The output is sorted based on the planning priority. The app also displays other important fields, like Net Flow Position, Proposed Quantity for Replenishment, Planning Priority Status, and so on. As you can see in Figure 12-20, the stock of material 108 is below demand, so the app has generated a replenishment proposal of 1454 pcs. You can click the Create Supply button to trigger this replenishment.

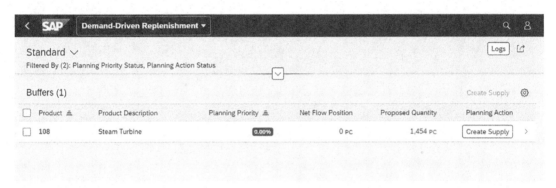

Figure 12-20. *Replenishment planning by planning priority*

Summary

In this chapter, you learned about the latest MRP procedure—demand-driven replenishment. The chapter discussed some of the components of DDMRP, including strategic inventory positioning, buffer profiles, and so on. It also discussed how demand-driven replenishment is performed in SAP and how to execute DDMRP using the Fiori apps.

The next chapter discusses Predictive MRP (pMRP), which is the latest innovation in SAP S/4HANA that can be used to identify potential capacity constraints in a long-term planning horizon.

CHAPTER 13

Predictive MRP

Predictive Material Requirements Planning (pMRP) helps you determine capacity issues for materials planned with demand driven replenishment. In this chapter, you learn about the Fiori apps—Schedule pMRP Simulation Creation and Process pMRP Simulations—which are used for executing pMRP in SAP S/4HANA.

What Is Predictive MRP?

Predictive Material and Resource Planning (pMRP) is a new functionality launched by SAP on the S/4HANA 1909 release. pMRP aims to identify capacity issues that may happen in the long run so that planner can evaluate potential solutions to solve capacity constraints. The production planner can simulate a requirements plan for a long-term planning horizon to analyze demands, resources, and capital expenditures. This helps with informed make-or-buy decisions.

Figure 13-1 shows the process flow of pMRP or predictive material and resource planning.

pMRP starts defining a simulation scenario by determining which data from the MRP should be considered as reference data by the simulation in pMRP.

Planners can copy a simulation to create multiple simulations to compare. Within a simulation, planners can display capacity issues. Then the planner can make changes to the capacity of work centers or to the quantity of top-level demands. Planners can also display the multi-level bill of material, start a preproduction on the component level, or change the source of the supply to solve capacity issues. These changes are only simulations, which the planner can compare to analyze the impact of the changes on the delivery performance or the capacity situation. When planners decide to implement simulation results in the operative MRP, they can then release the simulation.

© Himanshu Goel 2022
H. Goel, *Handbook for SAP PP in S/4HANA*, https://doi.org/10.1007/978-1-4842-8566-4_13

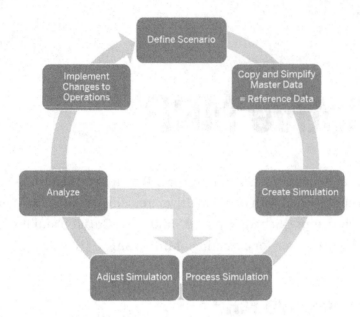

Figure 13-1. The predictive MRP process

Prerequisites for pMRP

You must ensure that all the master data relevant to SAP PP exists.

- Material Master

- Bill of Material

- Work Center/Resources

- Routing/Master Recipe

- Production Version

Note   The Predictive Material and Resource Planning solution has been developed completely to run on the Fiori Launchpad; there are no transactions available for pMRP.

Create the Planned Independent Requirements

The first step is to create forecasts in the form of PIRs. The PIRs are used to produce or procure materials or components in advance so that materials can be shipped when sales orders are received from customers. PIRs play a very important role when the lead time to procure components is quite long and the lead time for supplying finished products to customer is much shorter.

You can create PIRs with Transaction Code MD61 or you can use the Fiori App called Maintain PIRs. Figure 13-2 shows the PIRs that have been created for a monthly bucket.

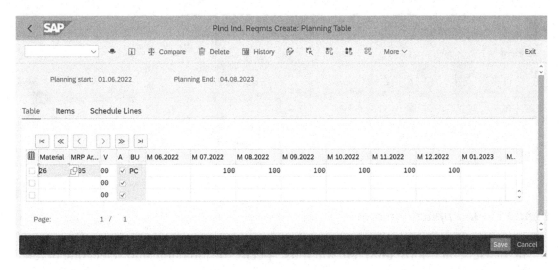

Figure 13-2. *Maintain PIRs*

Schedule pMRP Simulation Creation

The first step in the pMRP simulation process is to define the reference data for the simulation. The same reference data can be used for multiple simulations. The planner can change the reference data and thus simulate several scenarios and then choose the one that works best.

The planner can schedule jobs to create pMRP simulations using the Schedule pMRP Simulation Creation app, as shown in Figure 13-3. The system uses the operative data that's used for material requirement planning and modifies it to be used in a simplified form. This data is called *reference data* in pMRP. Multiple simulations can be created using the same reference data. You can also create several scheduling jobs and create simulations using different reference data.

Figure 13-3. *Schedule pMRP simulation creation tile*

Click the Create button to create a new simulation job, as shown in Figure 13-4.

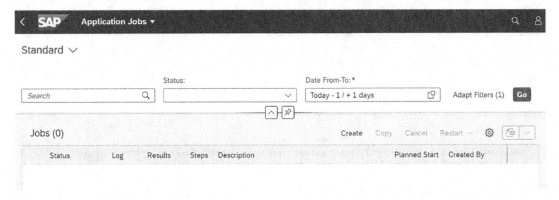

Figure 13-4. *Application jobs*

In the General Information tab, you must specify the job name and select one of the job templates from the following template list:

- Creation of pMRP Simulations via Work Centers

- Creation of pMRP Simulations via Top-Level Materials

- Creation of pMRP Simulations via Components

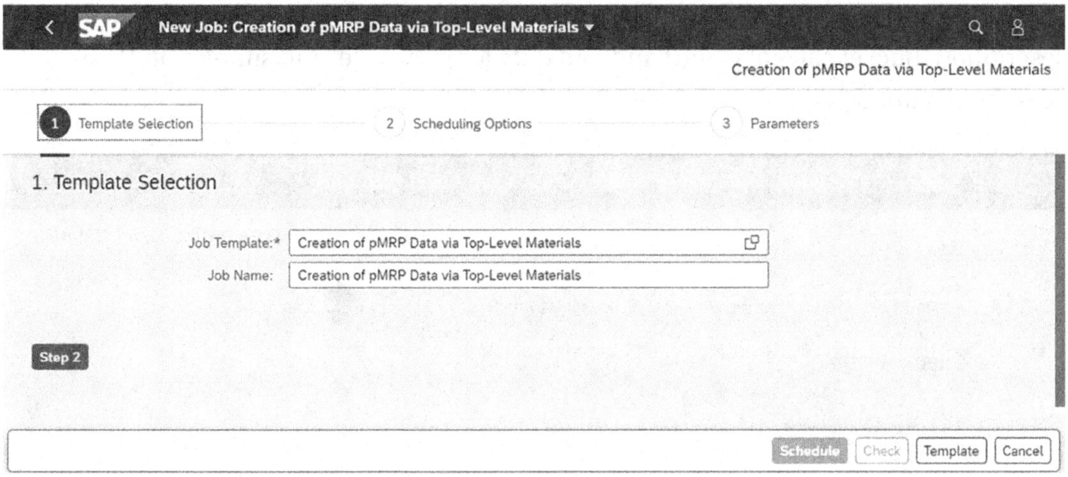

Figure 13-5. *Creating pMRP simulations via top-level materials: template selection*

In the Scheduling Options view, you can define the frequency of the job run. For example, you can pick single job or recurring job. You can also define the data and time of the job run. (See Figure 13-6).

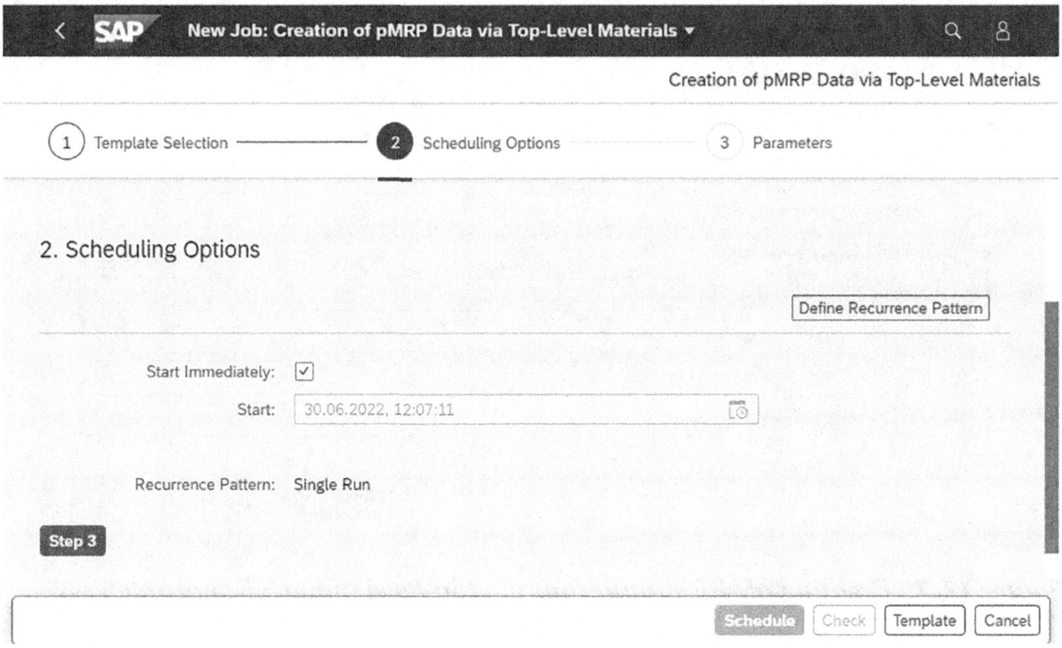

Figure 13-6. *Creating pMRP simulations via top-level materials: scheduling options*

In the Parameter tab, add or edit the values for ID for reference plan, reference description, bucket category, start and end date for reference, and simulation ID, as shown in Figure 13-7.

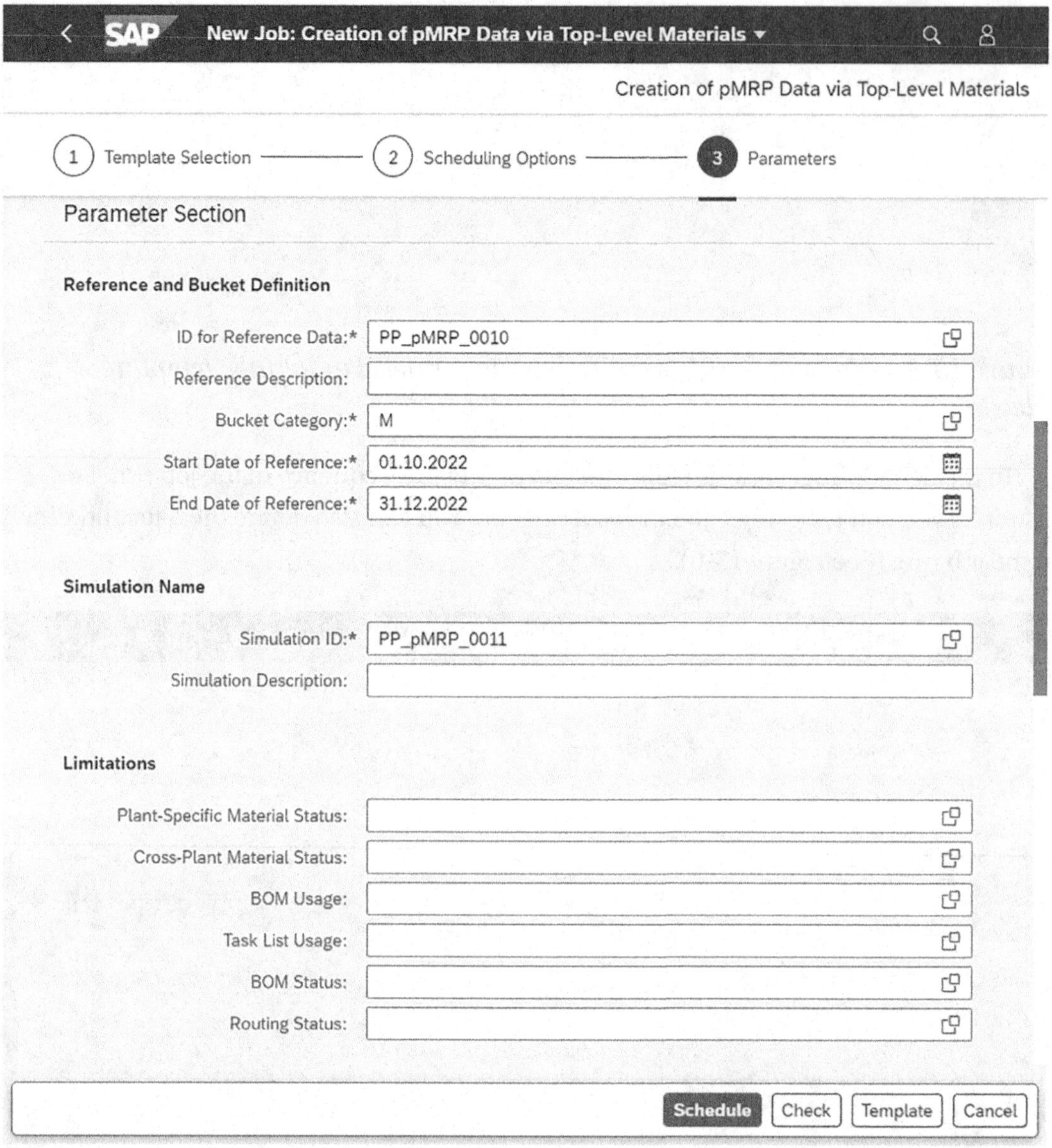

Figure 13-7. *Creating pMRP simulations via top-level materials: parameters*

Also enter the plant and material into the Object Selection section on the same screen, as shown in Figure 13-8. Then click the Schedule button to execute the job.

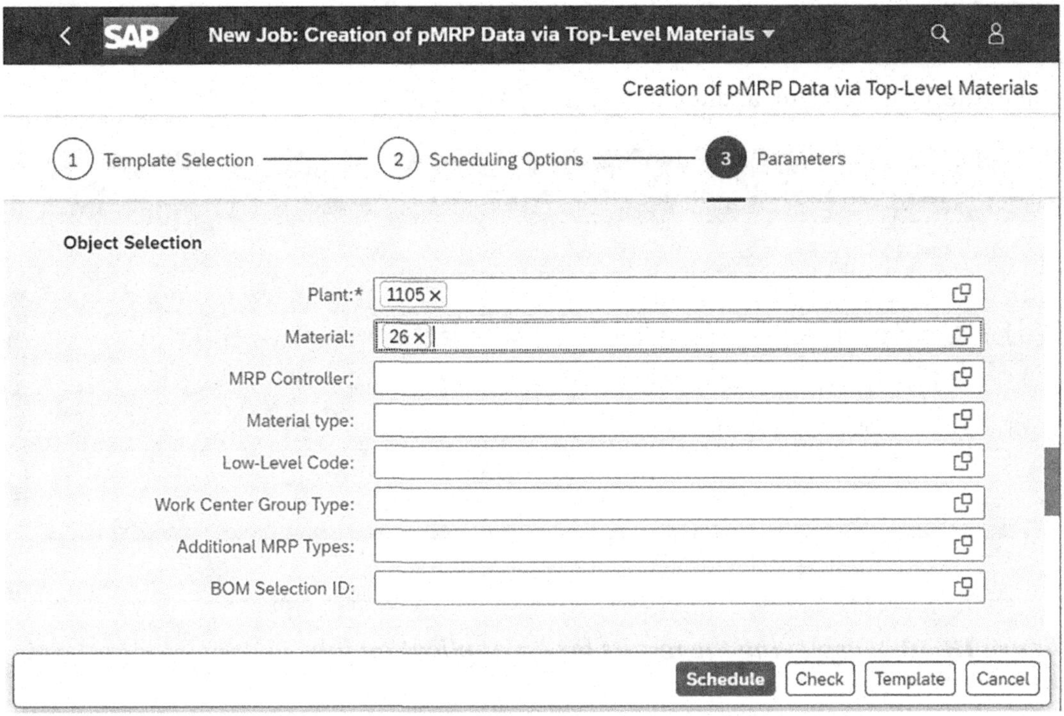

Figure 13-8. *Creating pMRP simulations via top-level materials: parameters: object selection*

Figure 13-9 shows a list of all the jobs that have been executed for pMRP simulations. You can also see if the job was executed successfully or with errors or warnings.

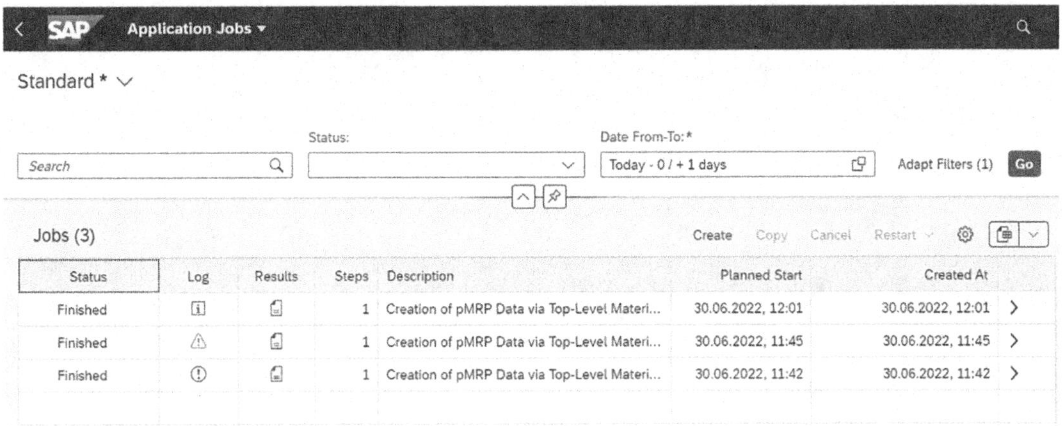

Figure 13-9. *Application job status*

Click the page icon in the Results column to display the results of the pMRP simulation run. A new window opens and displays the results of the job. Click the cube icon in the Type Column, as shown in Figure 13-10.

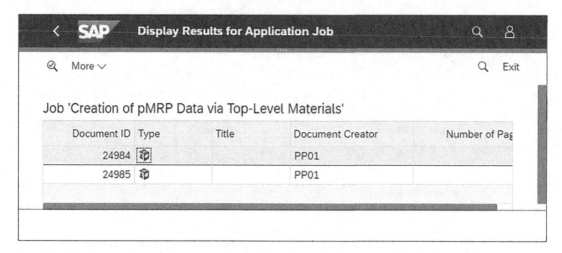

Figure 13-10. *Displaying the results for an application job*

Figure 13-11 displays a list of all the materials that were simulated during the pMRP simulation run. If there are any errors in the simulation run, they are displayed in the comment field against each material.

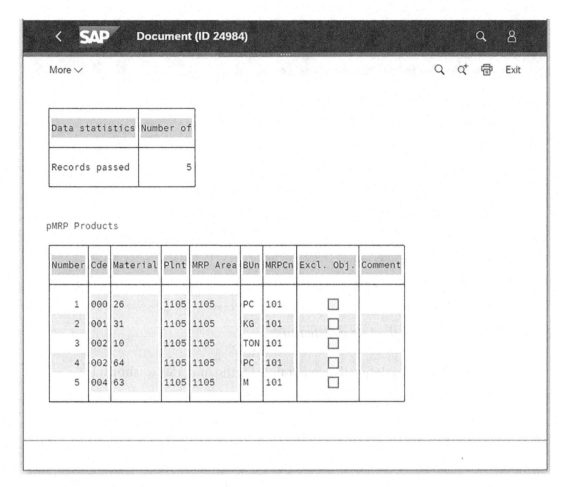

Figure 13-11. *Document: logs of pMRP simulation*

Define Flexible Constraints

You can use this app to define constraints that should be considered during the simulations. The constraints can be defined for a single material or multiple materials that are produced in-house or procured externally from other vendors or from other plants (stock-transfer). These constraints are taken into consideration during pMRP simulation and the system will issue messages when a constraint is violated. For example, you can define a constraint quantity for a material in a time period. If the demand quantity exceeds the constraint quantity, it is displayed as `Violated Constraint` in the simulation.

Enter the plant and material, as shown in Figure 13-12, and then click the > icon.

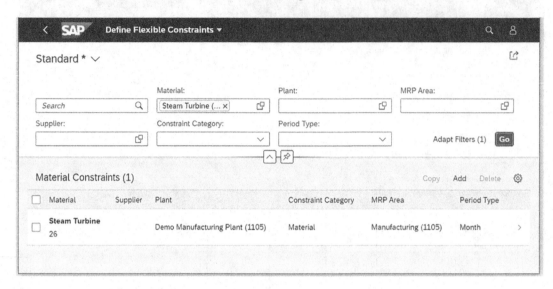

Figure 13-12. *Defining flexible constraints*

Click the Edit button to define the constraints for the material, as shown in Figure 13-13.

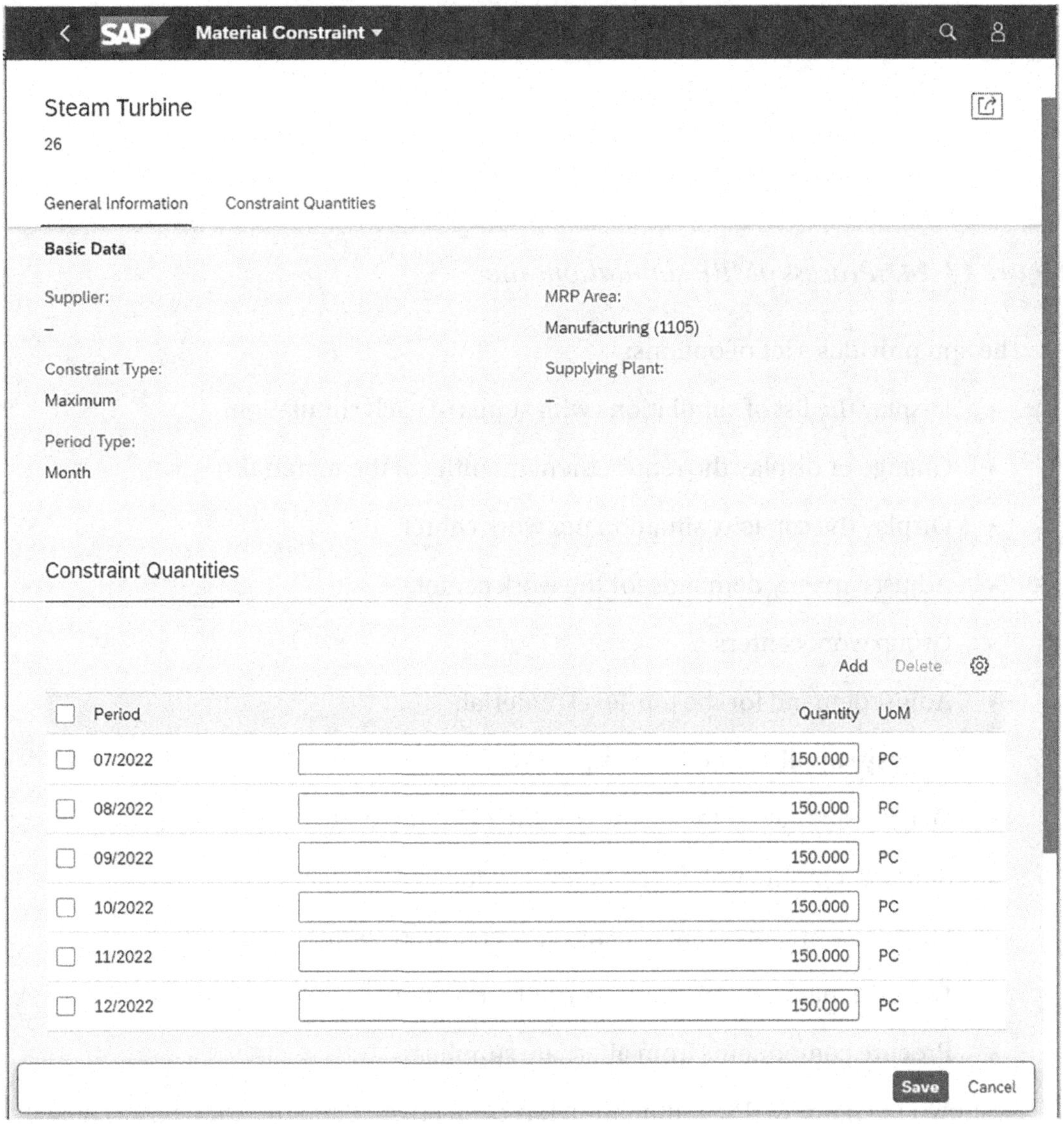

Figure 13-13. *Material constraints*

Process pMRP Simulations

This app is used to create simulations for pMRP (see Figure 13-14). For example, you can change demand quantities and check the impact on the production plan. Likewise, you can adjust the capacities of the work center and make informed decisions for production planning. This could eventually help in reducing inventory costs or delayed delivery to the customer due to capacity constraints.

Figure 13-14. *Process pMRP simulations tile*

The app provides a lot of options:

- Display the list of simulations with status of each simulation.

- Change or display the requirement quantity of the material.

- Display the capacity situation per work center.

- Adjust capacity demands for the work center.

- Group work centers.

- Adjust demand for the top-level material.

- Display supplier for each component.

- Display simulation for all levels of the BOM hierarchy.

- Start a preproduction for in-house produced materials.

- Start early procurement of externally procured components.

- Produce materials on alternate production lines.

- Procure components from alternate suppliers.

As shown in Figure 13-15, a simulation has been created and there are three capacity issues that should be resolved.

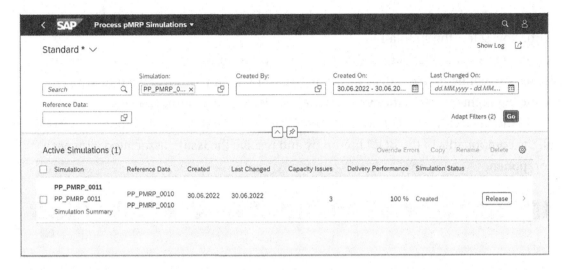

Figure 13-15. *Process pMRP simulations*

Click Simulation Summary and then click the Unresolved Issues view to display all the issues. As shown in Figure 13-16, the issues are caused by capacity overload.

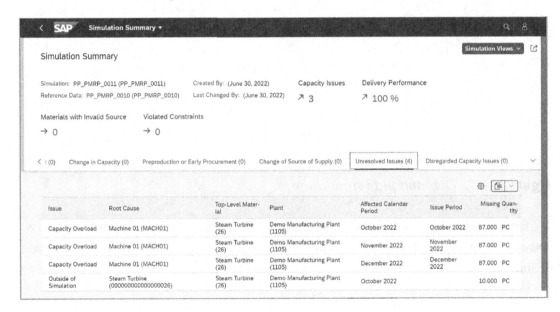

Figure 13-16. *Simulation summary*

To resolve these issues, you must go back to the previous screen by clicking the Back icon. Now select the simulation.

In the Demand Plan Simulation window, the planning periods that have capacity issues are highlighted in red, as shown in Figure 13-17. If you hover the mouse over any of the highlighted weeks, the system will display the issues for that particular week.

In the Inspector panel on the right, click Multi-Level Material Simulation to display all the components in the BOM hierarchy and resolve the issues associated with each component.

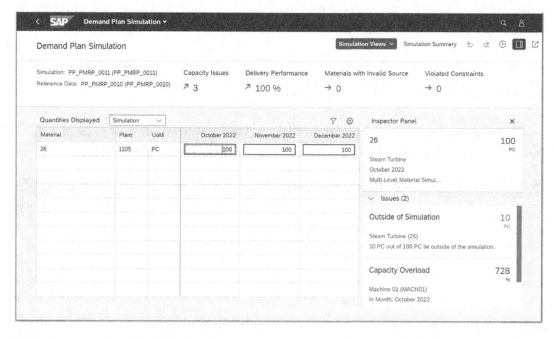

Figure 13-17. *Demand plan simulation*

Figure 13-18 displays the multi-level material simulation for finished material 26. As you can see in the Inspector Panel, there are two issues—Capacity Overload and Outside of Simulation.

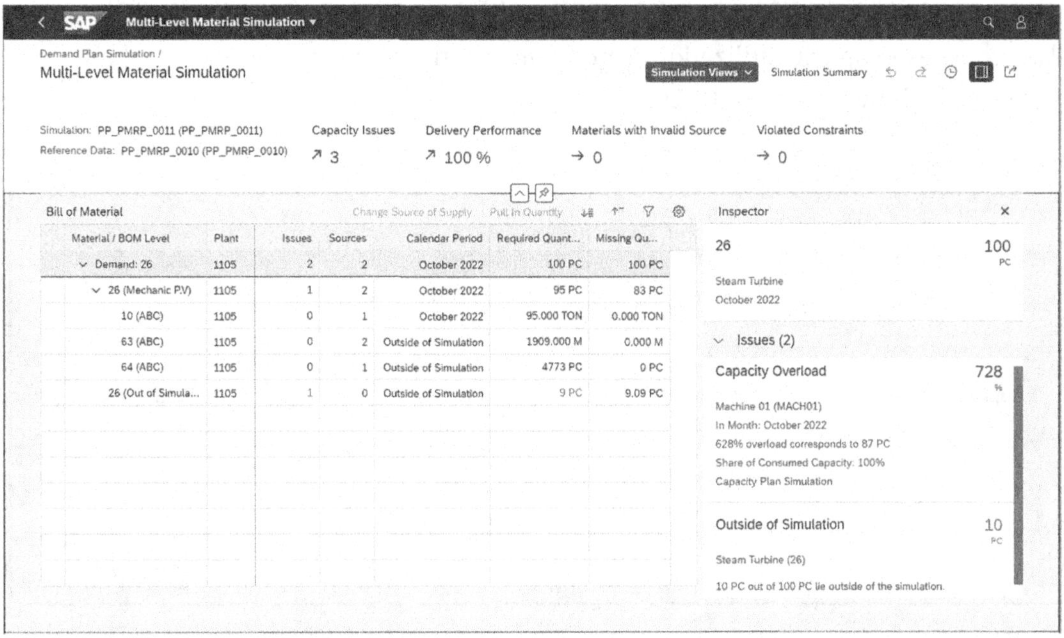

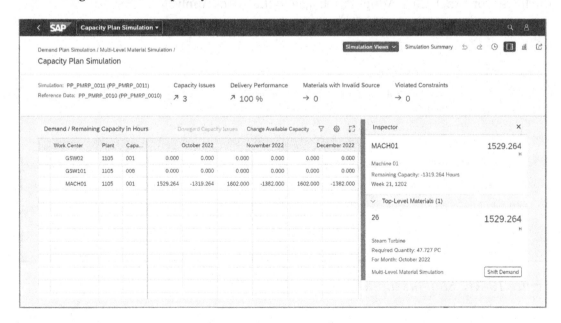

Figure 13-18. *Multi-level material simulation*

Change Available Capacity: Click the Capacity Plan Simulation option to resolve the capacity issue. A new screen is displayed, as shown in Figure 13-19. To resolve the issues, click Change Available Capacity.

Figure 13-19. *Capacity plan simulation*

A popup window appears, and the system displays the capacity situation. The system also proposes a capacity utilization. You can accept the proposal by clicking Adopt Proposal, as shown in Figure 13-20.

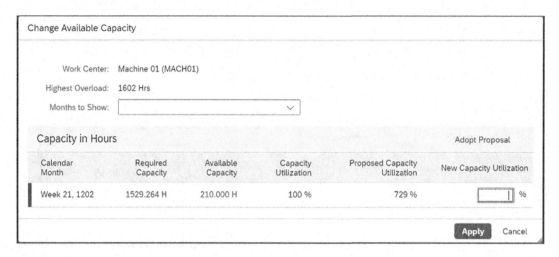

Figure 13-20. *Change available capacity*

Shift Demand: The other way to resolve this issue is to shift demand, as shown in Figure 13-19.

A new window appears, as shown in Figure 13-21. Click the Shift Demand option in the Inspector panel. Click Adopt Proposal and then click Apply.

Shift Top-Level Demand

General Information

Work Center:	Machine 01 (MACH01)
Top-Level Material:	Steam Turbine (26)
Shift Demand From:	October 2022
Shift Demand To:	

Planned Capacity (1)   Adopt Proposal

Production Month	Remaining Capacity	For Month	Available Quantity	Proposed Quantity	Quantity
October 2022	9.456	October 2022	13 PC	13 PC	13 PC

Unassigned: 0 PC

Apply   Cancel

Figure 13-21. *Shift the top-level demand*

If you go back to the Demand Plan Simulation screen (see Figure 13-22), you can see that the quantity for the month of October has been reduced to 13.

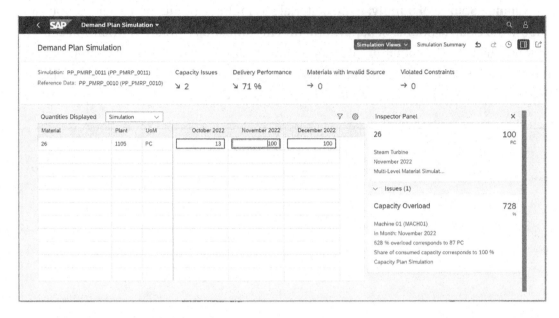

Figure 13-22. *Demand plan simulation*

Now click the quantity in November to display issues in the Inspector Panel and then click Multi-Level Material Simulation. See Figure 13-23.

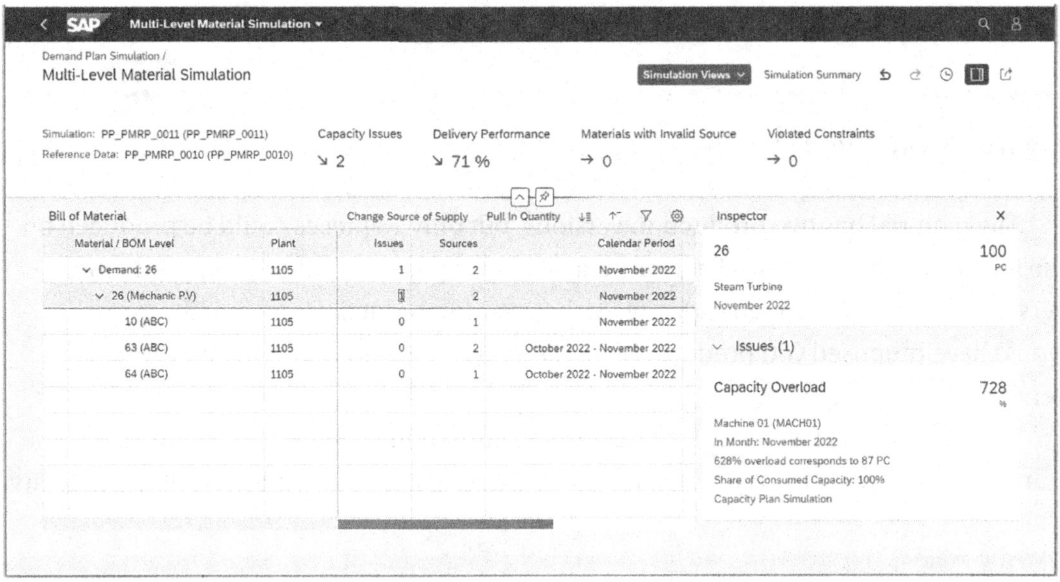

Figure 13-23. *Multi-level material simulation*

As shown in Figure 13-24, there are two ways to solve this issue—Change Source of Supply or Pull In Quantity.

Change Source of Supply: If the material has multiple production versions, you can choose the Change Source of Supply option. This function is preferred when you can produce the material with multiple production versions and do not want to preproduce the material. Select the material and click Change Source of Supply. The system will display the required quantity and the missing quantity.

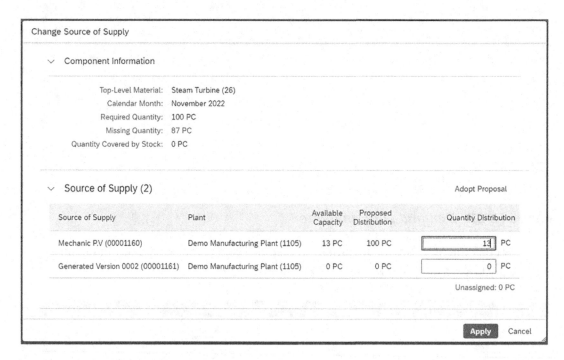

Figure 13-24. *Change source of supply*

The material has two production versions, but only 13 pieces could be produced on the first production version. There is no available capacity on the second production version. If there was enough capacity on the second production version, the system would have proposed you produce the remaining 87 pieces on the second production version.

If you go back to the Multi-Level Material Simulation, as shown in Figure 13-25, you can still see these issues. Try to resolve these issues using other option—Pull In Quantity.

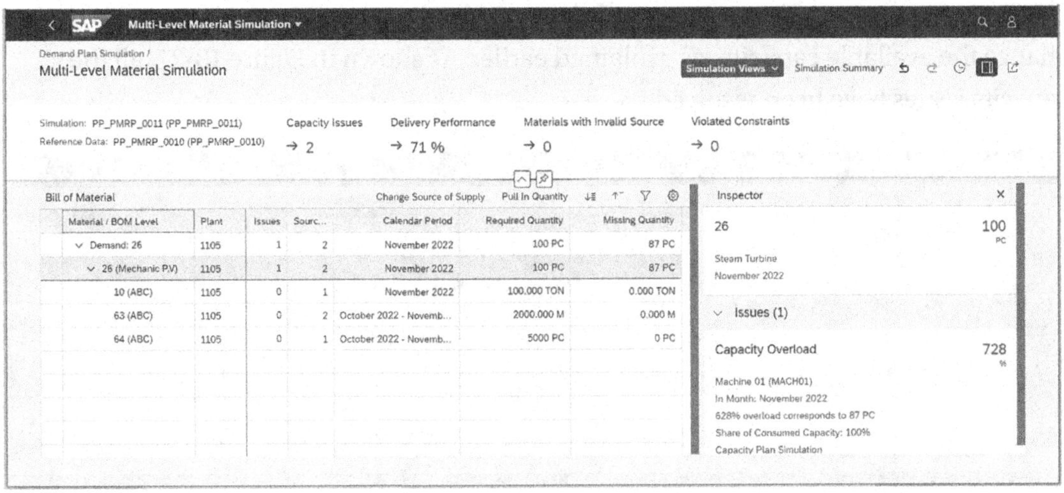

Figure 13-25. *Multi-level material simulation*

A new popup window appears, as shown in Figure 13-26. There is a shortage of one component, so the system is trying preproduction or early procurement. However, there is no available capacity in October, which is why the proposed distribution is 0.

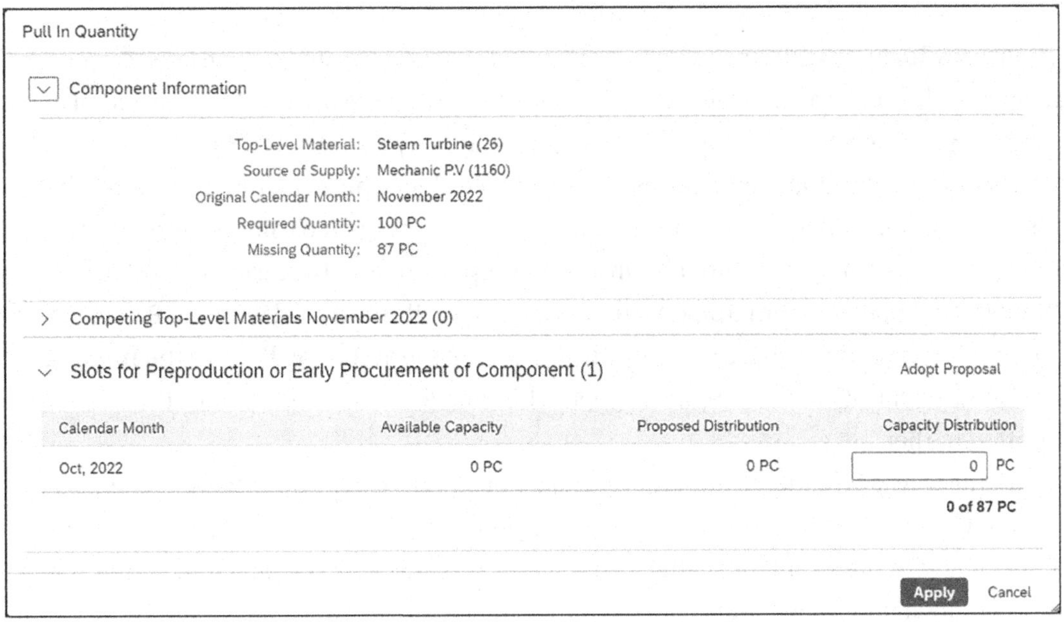

Figure 13-26. *Pull-in quantity*

Since the issues in November couldn't be resolved completely, the best way is to change the available capacity, as explained earlier. As shown in Figure 13-27, all the capacity issues have been resolved.

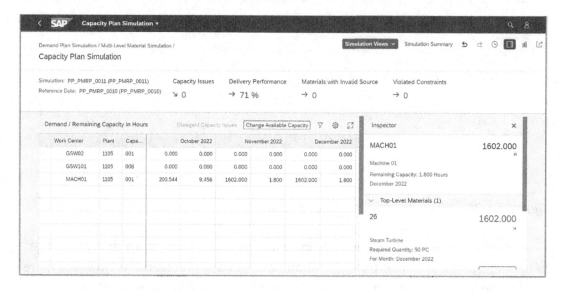

Figure 13-27. *Capacity plan simulation*

Preproduce: As a planner, you have decided that you would like to preproduce the material, which means you'll produce the material in advance before the actual requirement date and keep it in stock to resolve capacity issues. Click Preproduce and the system will automatically propose the available slots where the production can be done. The system will give a proposal to preproduce during an earlier week or month. If the planner is convinced with the proposed preproduction, they can click Adopt Proposal. Then, the system updates the Capacity Distribution field with the Proposed Distribution quantity. Click the Apply button so that the system will move the missing production quantity to the proposed week. This will also resolve the issues that were reported earlier.

In this way, pMRP helps planners simulate capacity issues and resolve issues in several ways, such as by adjusting demand or preproducing materials. Once the planner is satisfied with the simulation, they can release the simulation by clicking the Release icon, as shown in Figure 13-28.

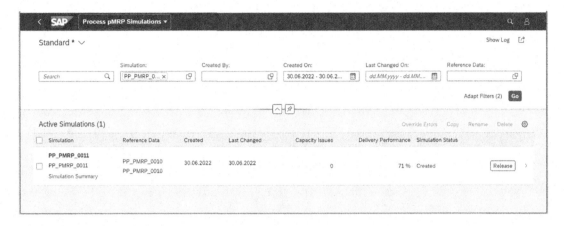

Figure 13-28. *Process pMRP simulations*

Once you release the simulation, the planned independent requirements are generated with active version 00 for materials planned via demand driven replenishment. For the top-level materials, you can select the requirement version manually, as shown in Figure 13-29.

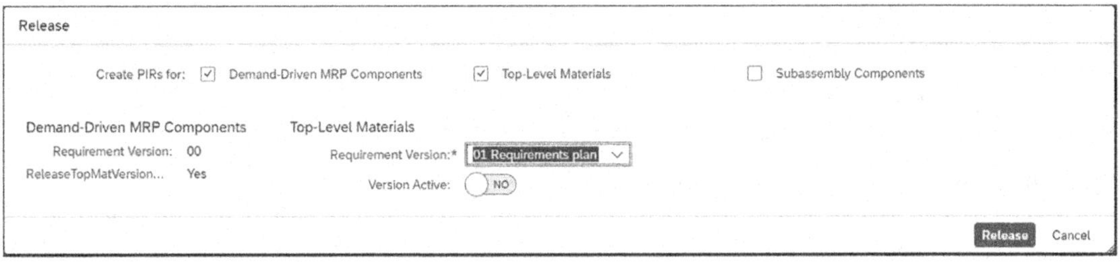

Figure 13-29. *Release*

Summary

In this chapter, you learned about pMRP (predictive material and resource planning), which is the latest innovation in SAP S/4HANA. The chapter also discussed several methods that the system can propose to solve capacity issues.

So far, the book has covered all the processes and functionalities offered in SAP S/4HANA PP. The next chapter discusses reports and other analytical tools that are available from the SAP S/4HANA GUI, as well as Fiori apps.

CHAPTER 14

Reporting and Analytics

This chapter discusses several reports and tools that can be used for reporting and analysis purposes. They can be executed using SAP GUI. It also discusses the latest monitoring tools available in Fiori apps.

A lot of reports and analytic tools are available in SAP that give you strategic insight into your business operations. This chapter discusses reports that can help you make informed decisions. You can use standard reports for analyzing master data, the production planning process, order management, stock analysis, and so on.

Materials List

You can use the materials list to display materials in a plant. Choose Logistics ➤ Production ➤ Master Data ➤ Material Master ➤ Other ➤ Materials List. You can also use Transaction Code MM60 to display the materials list.

Enter the materials or manufacturer part number or simply enter the plant to display all the materials in the plant, as shown in Figure 14-1. You can enter additional selection criteria, such as the material type and material group, or you can display the materials created by a specific user. The Valuated Materials Only indicator displays only the materials for which accounting data has been created.

© Himanshu Goel 2022
H. Goel, *Handbook for SAP PP in S/4HANA*, https://doi.org/10.1007/978-1-4842-8566-4_14

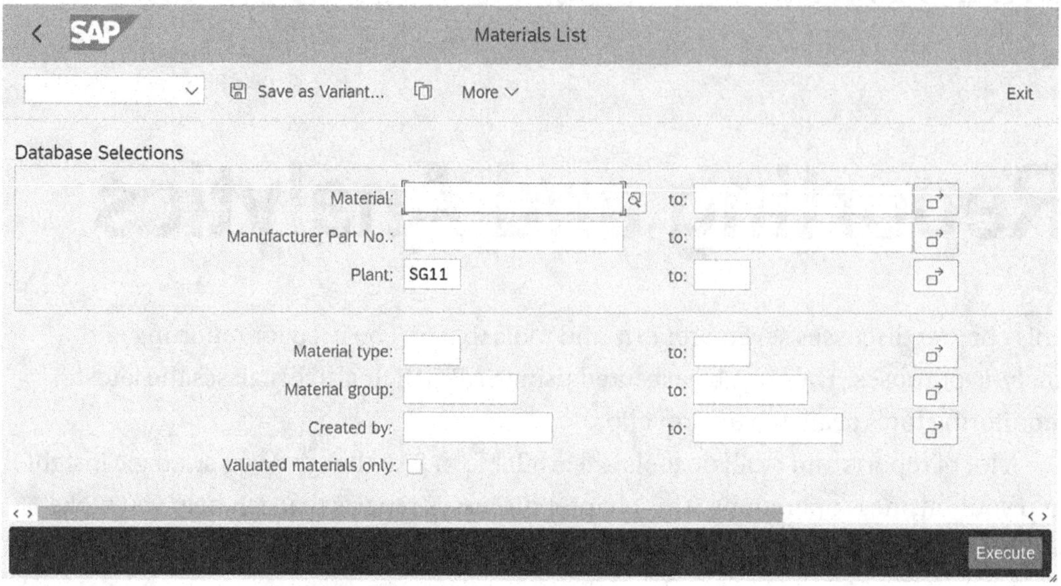

Figure 14-1. *Materials list: selection screen*

Based on the selection criteria, the system displays the materials and other relevant information, like the plant, material description, material type, material group, MRP type, valuation class, price, currency, and so on, as shown in Figure 14-2.

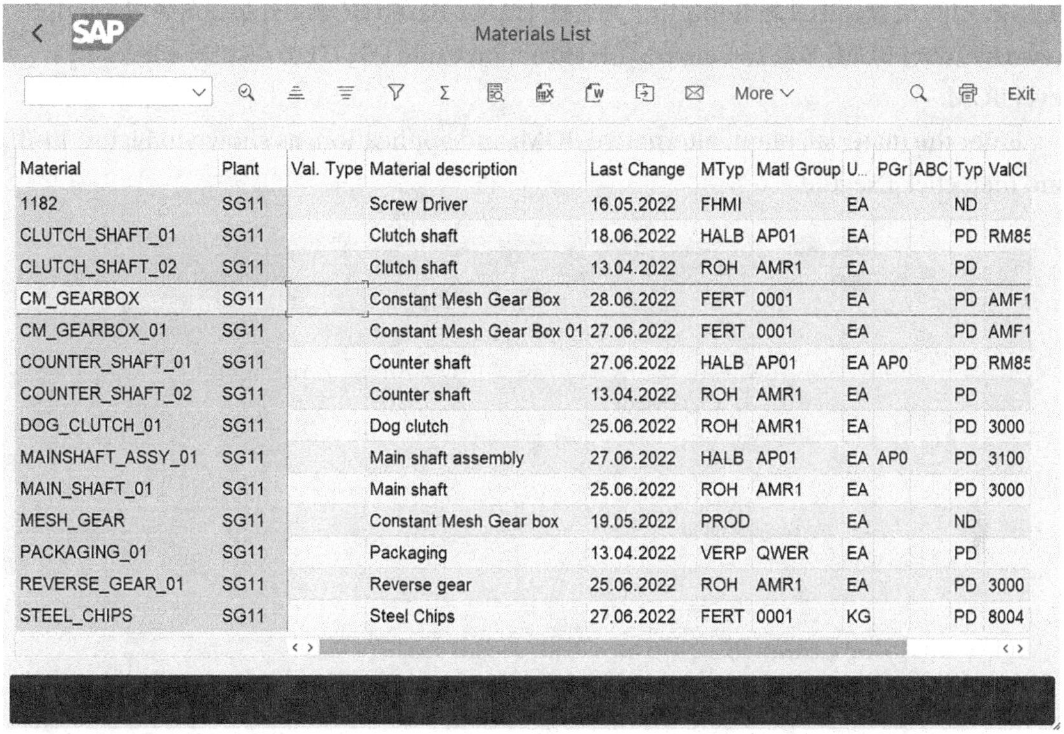

Material	Plant	Val. Type	Material description	Last Change	MTyp	Matl Group	U..	PGr	ABC	Typ	ValCl
1182	SG11		Screw Driver	16.05.2022	FHMI		EA			ND	
CLUTCH_SHAFT_01	SG11		Clutch shaft	18.06.2022	HALB	AP01	EA			PD	RM85
CLUTCH_SHAFT_02	SG11		Clutch shaft	13.04.2022	ROH	AMR1	EA			PD	
CM_GEARBOX	SG11		Constant Mesh Gear Box	28.06.2022	FERT	0001	EA			PD	AMF1
CM_GEARBOX_01	SG11		Constant Mesh Gear Box 01	27.06.2022	FERT	0001	EA			PD	AMF1
COUNTER_SHAFT_01	SG11		Counter shaft	27.06.2022	HALB	AP01	EA	APO		PD	RM85
COUNTER_SHAFT_02	SG11		Counter shaft	13.04.2022	ROH	AMR1	EA			PD	
DOG_CLUTCH_01	SG11		Dog clutch	25.06.2022	ROH	AMR1	EA			PD	3000
MAINSHAFT_ASSY_01	SG11		Main shaft assembly	27.06.2022	HALB	AP01	EA	APO		PD	3100
MAIN_SHAFT_01	SG11		Main shaft	25.06.2022	ROH	AMR1	EA			PD	3000
MESH_GEAR	SG11		Constant Mesh Gear box	19.05.2022	PROD		EA			ND	
PACKAGING_01	SG11		Packaging	13.04.2022	VERP	QWER	EA			PD	
REVERSE_GEAR_01	SG11		Reverse gear	25.06.2022	ROH	AMR1	EA			PD	3000
STEEL_CHIPS	SG11		Steel Chips	27.06.2022	FERT	0001	KG			PD	8004

Figure 14-2. *Materials list*

This report can be quite useful if you want to analyze the materials that are created for your plant or for a material type or material group in a plant. You can also export the list to an Excel file by choosing List ➤ Export ➤ Spreadsheet.

Report for Bill of Materials

Several reports are available for analyzing a bill of materials (BOMs). You can display a multilevel BOM or use the where-used list for components.

Explode: Level-by-Level BOM

If you created a complex bill of material with several levels of semifinished assemblies and you want to display everything in a single screen, you can use the Explode: Level by Level BOM report. Access this report by choosing Logistics ➤ Production ➤ Master

Data ➤ Bills of Material ➤ Reporting ➤ SAP HANA-Based BOM Explosion ➤ Explode: Level by Level BOM. You can also use Transaction Code CS11H to display a level-by-level BOM.

Enter the material, plant, alternative BOM, and application, as shown in Figure 14-3, and then click Execute.

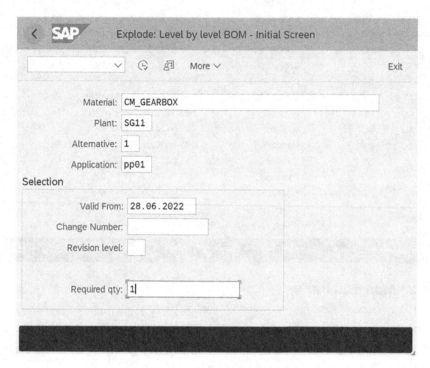

Figure 14-3. *Explode level-by-level BOM: initial screen*

Figure 14-4 displays all the components that are needed to produce the finished assembly in a level-by-level structure.

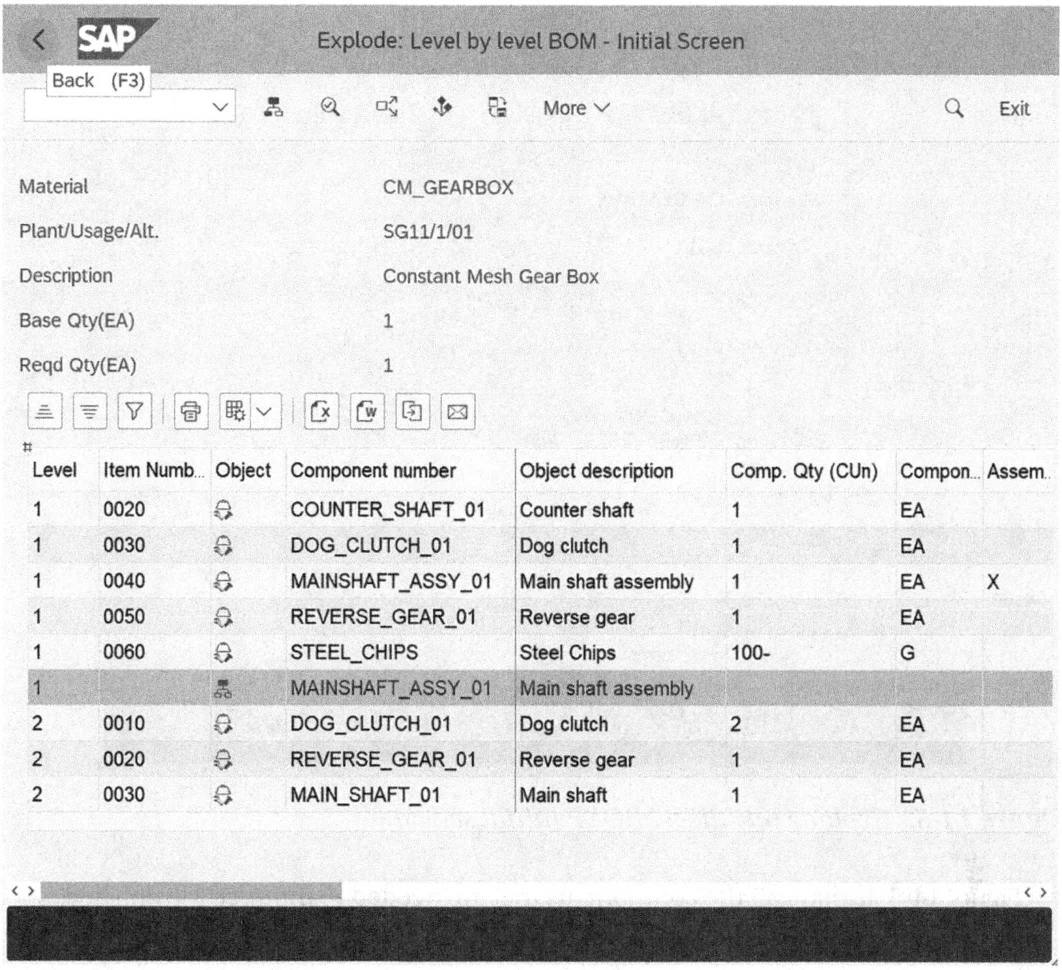

# Level	Item Numb...	Object	Component number	Object description	Comp. Qty (CUn)	Compon...	Assem...
1	0020		COUNTER_SHAFT_01	Counter shaft	1	EA	
1	0030		DOG_CLUTCH_01	Dog clutch	1	EA	
1	0040		MAINSHAFT_ASSY_01	Main shaft assembly	1	EA	X
1	0050		REVERSE_GEAR_01	Reverse gear	1	EA	
1	0060		STEEL_CHIPS	Steel Chips	100-	G	
1			MAINSHAFT_ASSY_01	Main shaft assembly			
2	0010		DOG_CLUTCH_01	Dog clutch	2	EA	
2	0020		REVERSE_GEAR_01	Reverse gear	1	EA	
2	0030		MAIN_SHAFT_01	Main shaft	1	EA	

Screen header fields:

Material: CM_GEARBOX
Plant/Usage/Alt.: SG11/1/01
Description: Constant Mesh Gear Box
Base Qty(EA): 1
Reqd Qty(EA): 1

Explode: Level by level BOM - Initial Screen

Figure 14-4. Explode level-by-level BOM

Explode Multilevel BOM

Similar to the CS11H Explode: Level by Level BOM report, the Explode: Multilevel BOM report can display multilevel BOMs. Choose Logistics ➤ Production ➤ Master Data ➤ Bills of Material ➤ Reporting ➤ SAP HANA-Based BOM Explosion ➤ Explode: Multilevel BOM. You can also use Transaction Code CS12H to display a multilevel BOM.

Enter the material, plant, alternative BOM, and application, as shown in Figure 14-5, and click Execute.

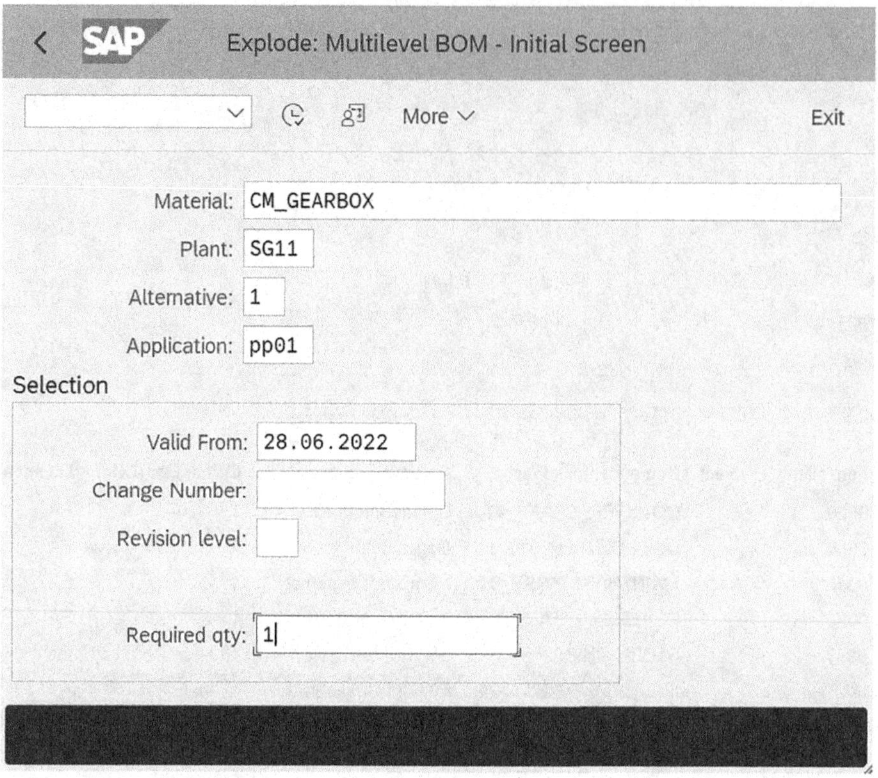

Figure 14-5. *Explode multilevel BOM: initial screen*

Figure 14-6 displays all the components that are needed to produce the finished assembly in a multilevel structure.

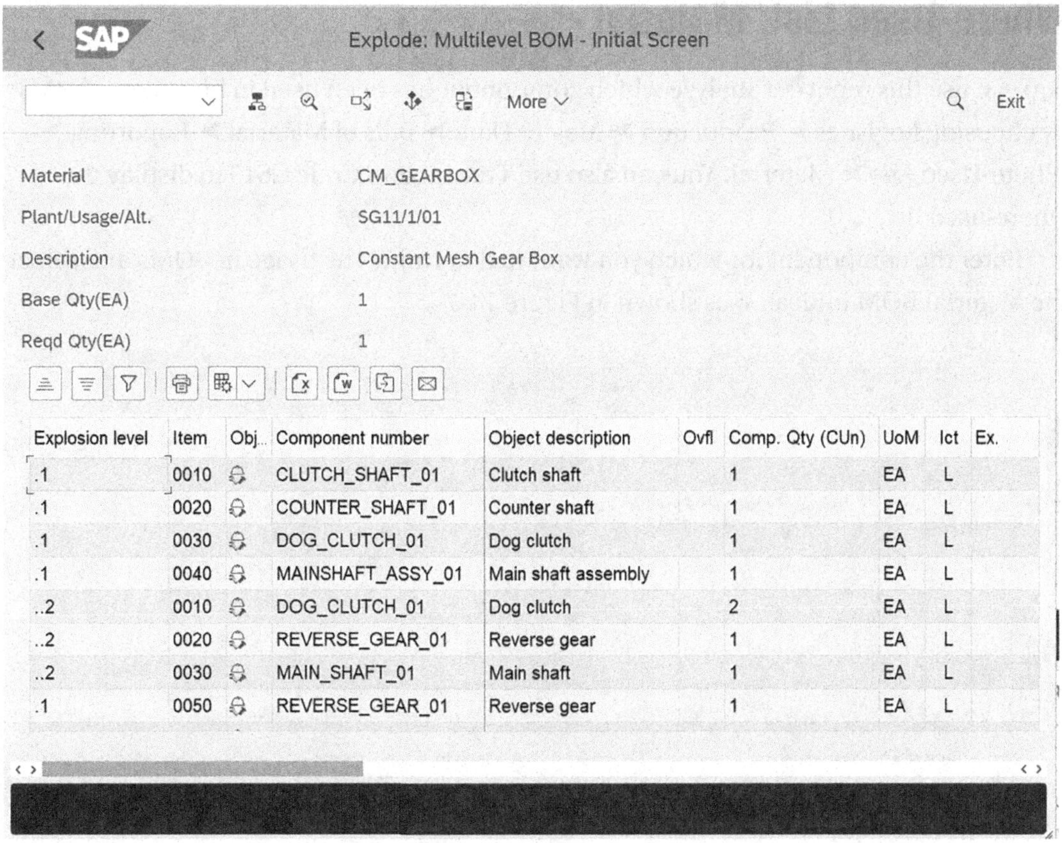

Figure 14-6. *Explode multilevel BOM*

The CS11H and CS12H reports are quite similar except for the fact that the CS11H report displays the components level-by-level (i.e., all the materials at level 1 are displayed first and then all the components at second level, and so on). Once all the components at level 1 are displayed, the components of level 1 are displayed. Whereas in CS12H, the components are displayed in a multilevel hierarchy. The first level of the component is displayed and then all the components required to produce level 1 are displayed in a hierarchical way.

Where-Used List: Material

You can use this report to analyze which component has been used in how many BOMs by choosing Logistics ➤ Production ➤ Master Data ➤ Bills of Material ➤ Reporting ➤ Where-Used List ➤ Material. You can also use Transaction Code CS15 to display the where-used list.

Enter the component for which you want to determine the usage in BOMs and select the Material BOM indicator, as shown in Figure 14-7.

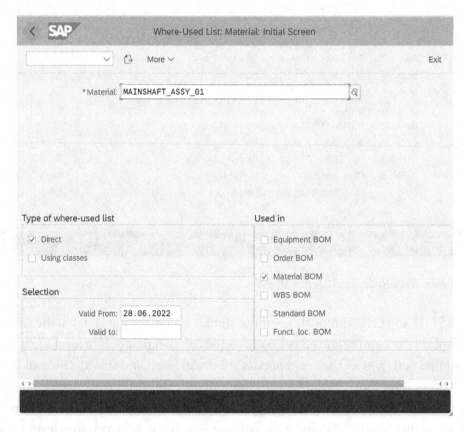

Figure 14-7. *Where-used list: material: initial screen*

A new screen appears where you must enter the required quantity or resulting quantity and then click Execute.

The output displays a list of all the BOMs that use the component entered on the initial screen, as shown in Figure 14-8.

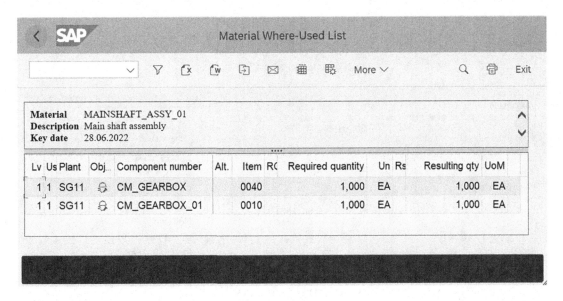

Figure 14-8. *Material where-used list*

Multiple Material Where-Used List

Similar to CS15, the where-used list, you can use report CS15M to display usage of multiple materials in the BOM. Choose Logistics ➤ Production ➤ Master Data ➤ Bills of Material ➤ Reporting ➤ Where-Used List ➤ Multiple Material. You can also use Transaction Code CS15M to display the where-used list for multiple materials.

You can enter multiple materials, as shown in Figure 14-9, or you can enter a range of materials to display the usage of selected materials in the BOM. Click Execute.

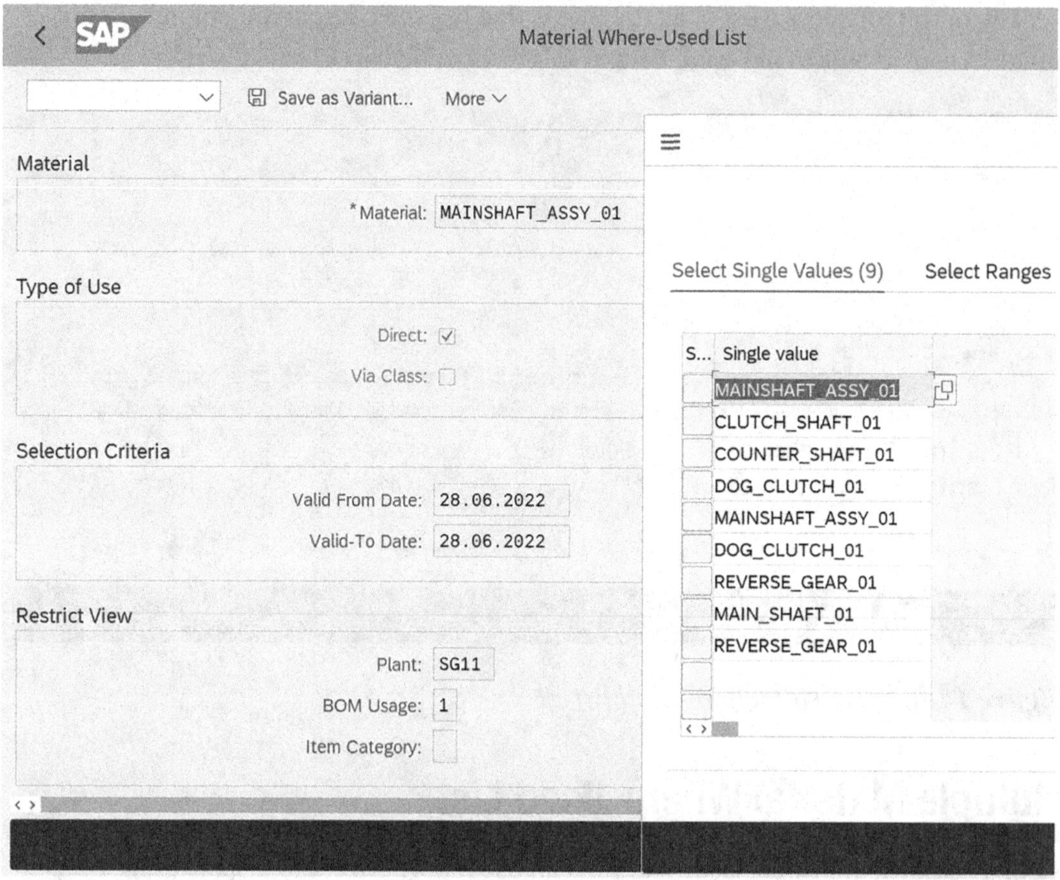

Figure 14-9. *Material where-used list: initial screen*

The output list shows all the materials where the material is assigned as a component in the bill of material, as shown in Figure 14-10.

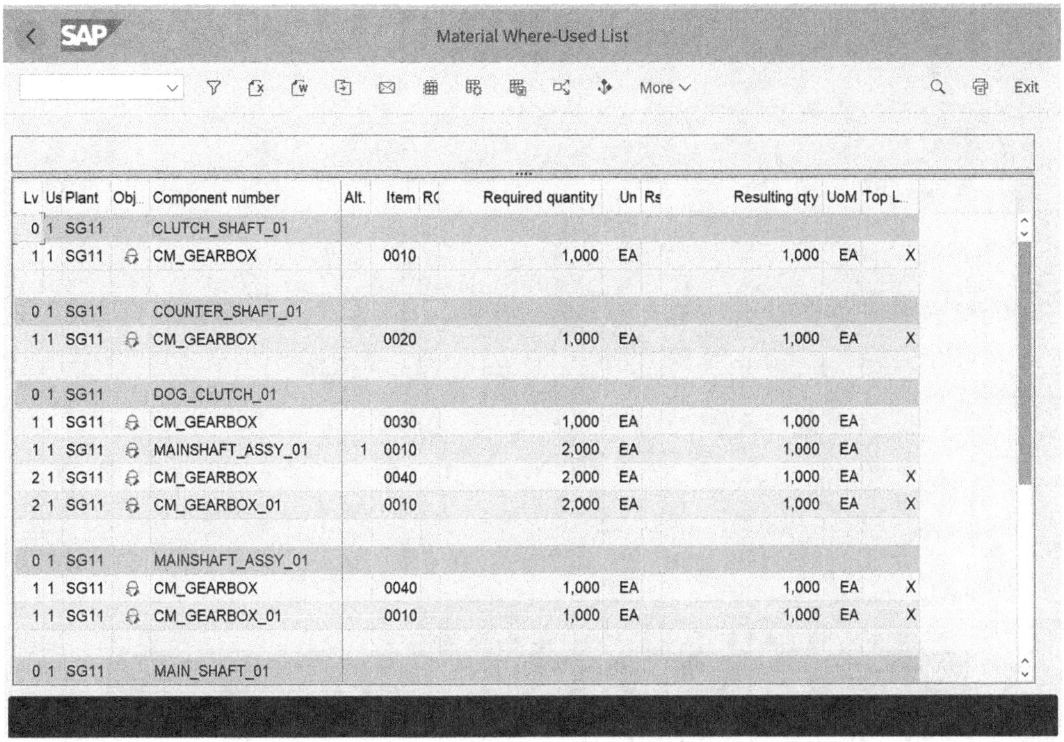

Figure 14-10. *Material where-used list*

Report for Work Center

This section discusses a few reports that can help when reporting and analyzing work centers.

Work Center List

You can use the Work Center List report to display all work centers in a plant. Do so by choosing Logistics ➤ Production ➤ Master Data ➤ Work Centers ➤ Reporting ➤ Work Center List or use Transaction Code CR05. Enter the plant and click Execute, as shown in Figure 14-11.

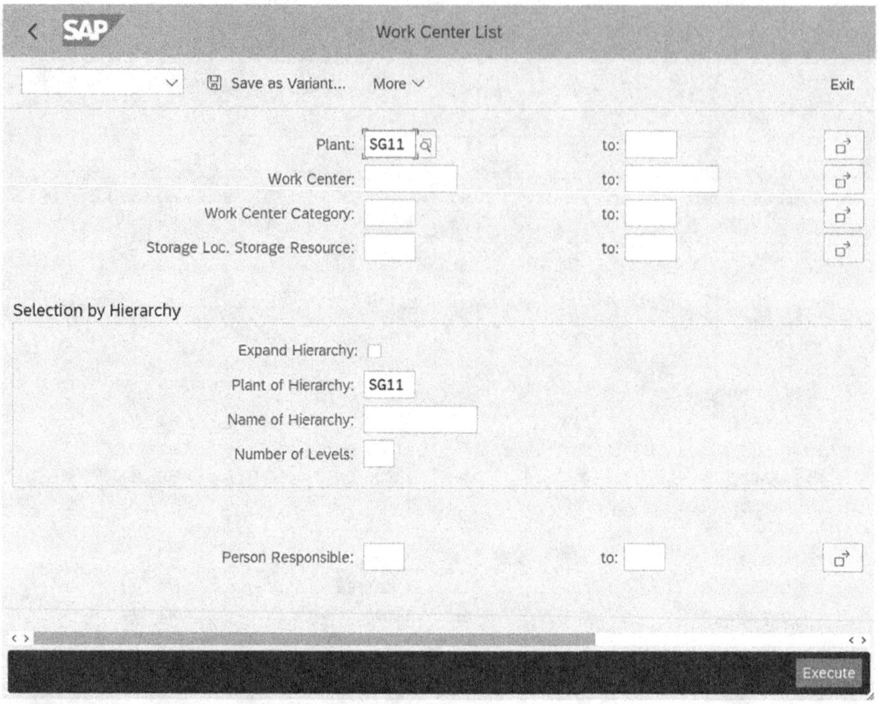

Figure 14-11. *Work center list: selection screen*

The output list displays all the work centers in plant SG11, as shown in Figure 14-12.

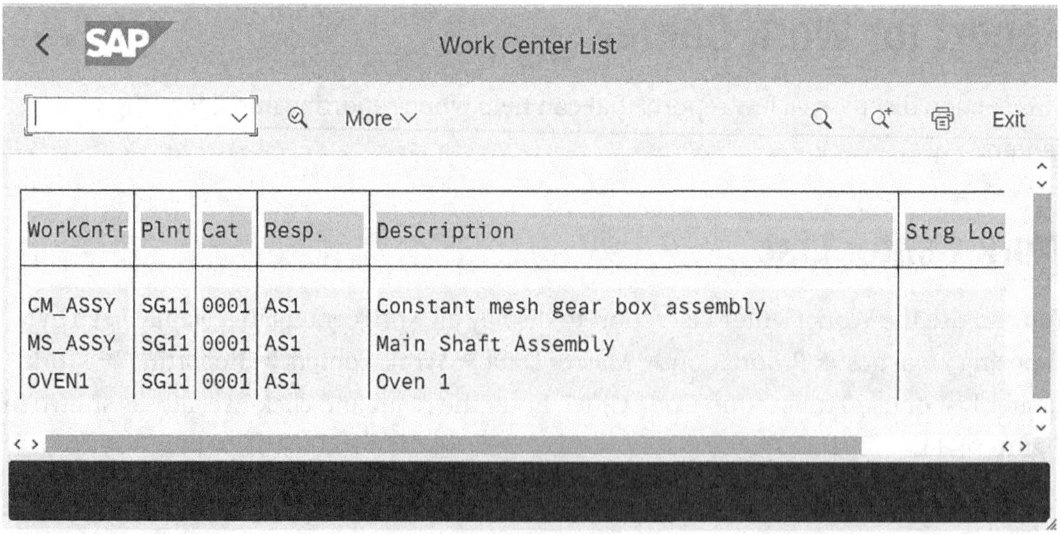

Figure 14-12. *Work center list*

Cost Center Assignment

You can use the Cost Center Assignment report to display an assignment of cost centers to the work centers in a plant by choosing Logistics ➤ Production ➤ Master Data ➤ Work Centers ➤ Reporting ➤ Cost Center Assignment or using Transaction Code CR06. Enter the plant and click Execute, as shown in Figure 14-13.

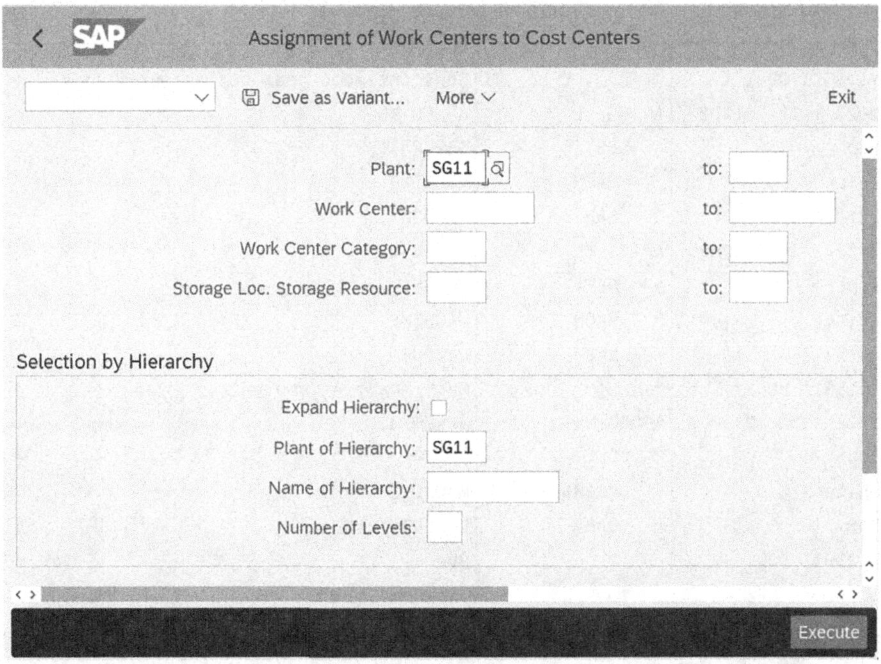

Figure 14-13. *Assignment of work centers to cost centers: initial screen*

The output list displays the cost centers per work centers as well as the activities assigned, as shown in Figure 14-14.

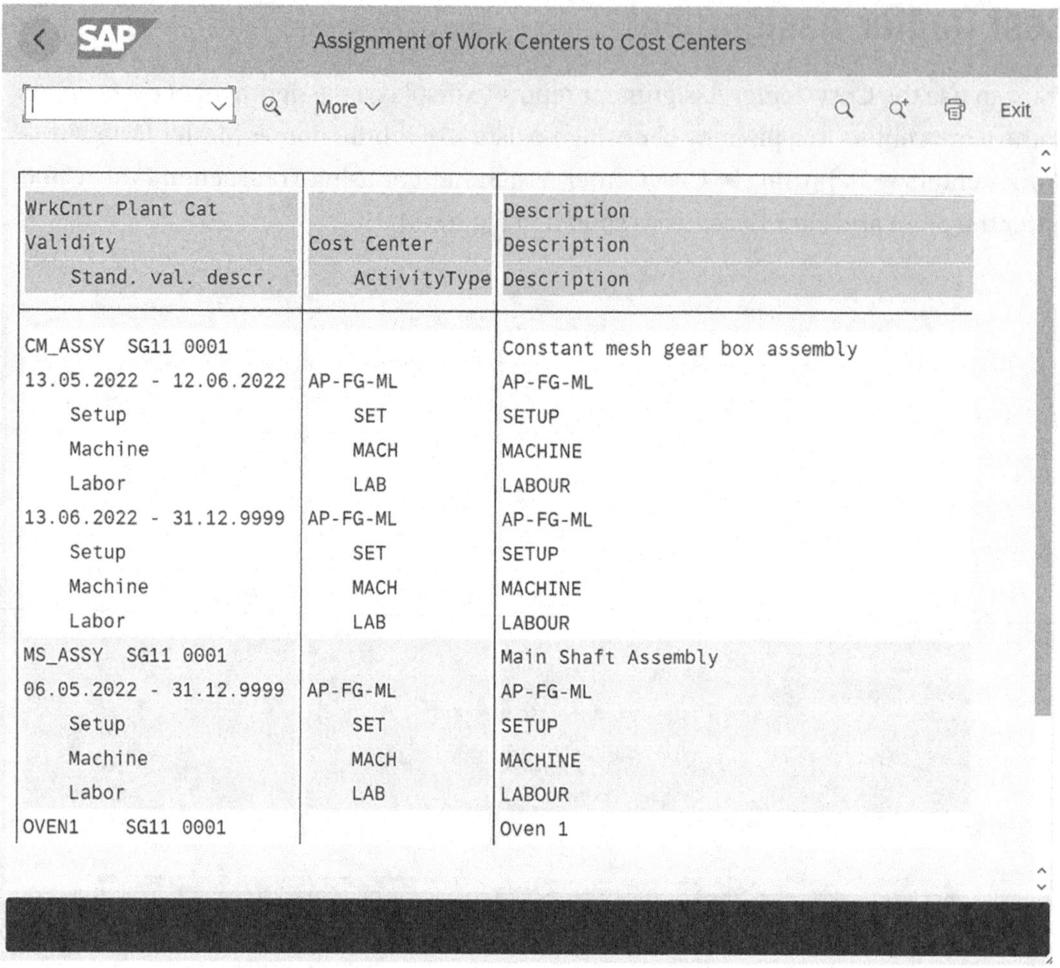

WrkCntr Plant Cat / Validity / Stand. val. descr.	Cost Center / ActivityType	Description
CM_ASSY SG11 0001		Constant mesh gear box assembly
13.05.2022 - 12.06.2022	AP-FG-ML	AP-FG-ML
Setup	SET	SETUP
Machine	MACH	MACHINE
Labor	LAB	LABOUR
13.06.2022 - 31.12.9999	AP-FG-ML	AP-FG-ML
Setup	SET	SETUP
Machine	MACH	MACHINE
Labor	LAB	LABOUR
MS_ASSY SG11 0001		Main Shaft Assembly
06.05.2022 - 31.12.9999	AP-FG-ML	AP-FG-ML
Setup	SET	SETUP
Machine	MACH	MACHINE
Labor	LAB	LABOUR
OVEN1 SG11 0001		Oven 1

Figure 14-14. *Assignment of work centers to cost centers*

Stock/Requirements List

The stock requirement list is used to display the real-time stock situation and all the demand and supply elements. This is (arguably) the most important report for the logistics function in SAP, as it displays anything and everything happening in the logistics area. This is a dynamic list that displays a real-time situation every time the report is executed using Transaction Code MD04.

Demand Elements: These are MRP elements that generate the requirements for the material stock and thus credit (or reduce) the stock in the plant or warehouse. Demand elements are, thus, represented as -ve stock in Stock Requirement list (Transaction Code MD04).

Some of the most common demand elements displayed in MD04 are as follows:

- Concrete demands for finished goods from customers in terms of sales orders or schedule lines

- Planned independent requirements for finished goods coming from S&OP: sales forecast.

- Material reservations

- Dependent requirements for a semifinished or raw material

Supply elements: These are MRP elements that fulfill the requirements and thus debit (or add) the stock in the plant or warehouse. Supply elements are represented with +ve stock in the stock requirement list (Transaction Code MD04).

Some of the most common supply elements in MD04 are as follows:

- Purchase requisitions for externally procured materials which are then converted to purchase orders

- Planned orders for in-house produced materials which are subsequently converted to production orders

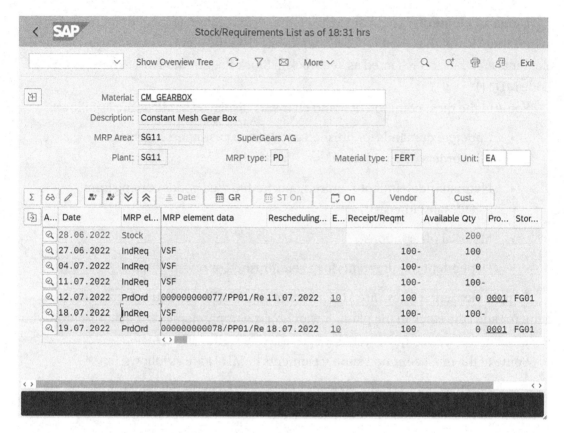

Figure 14-15. *Stock requirement list*

The system generates the exception messages to attract the planner's attention. The planner can double-click the exception message and view the details of the exception message at the bottom of the screen. In Figure 14-15, you can see the exception message 10, which means Reschedule In. This is one of the most common exception messages a planner will observe. Another common exception message is 15, which means Reschedule Out. For rescheduling exception messages, the system proposes a date in the Rescheduling Date column.

Table 14-1 shows a list of exception messages available in the stock requirement list together with the selection groups.

Table 14-1. *Exception Messages*

Selection Group	Exception No.	Exception Message
1	69	Recursive BOM components possible
	2	New and opening date in the past
	5	Opening date in the past
2	3	New and start date in the past
	6	Start date in the past
	63	Production start before order start
3	4	New and finish date in the past
	7	Finish date in the past
	64	Production finish after order finish
4	1	Newly created order proposal
	42	Order proposal has been changed
	44	Order proposal re-exploded
	46	Order proposal has been manually changed
	61	Scheduling: Customizing inconsistent
	62	Scheduling: Master data inconsistent
	80	Reference to retail promotion
	82	Item is blocked
5	50	No BOM exists
	52	No BOM selected
	53	No BOM explosion due to missing config.
	55	Phantom assembly not exploded

(*continued*)

Table 14-1. (*continued*)

Selection Group	Exception No.	Exception Message
6	25	Excess stock
	26	Excess in individual segment
	27	Excess stock applied to superceding mat.
	27	Underdelivery tolerance
	40	Coverage not provided by master plan
	56	Shortage in the planning time fence
	57	Disc. matl partly replaced by follow-up
	58	Uncovered reqmt after effective-out date
	59	Receipt after effective-out date
	60	Disc., rec. applied to superceding mat.
	70	Max. release qty - quota exceeded
	96	Stock fallen below safety stock level
7	10	Reschedule in
	15	Reschedule out
	20	Cancel process
	30	Plan process according to schedule
8	98	Abnormal end of materials planning

You can click the Show Overview Tree button to display the Order Report, as shown in Figure 14-16. You can display all the components required for the order. This is a multilevel report that displays the components and their receipt elements. The order report can help you determine any potential issues in the production of the assemblies or procurement of the components. The order report can also be executed using Transaction Code MD4C.

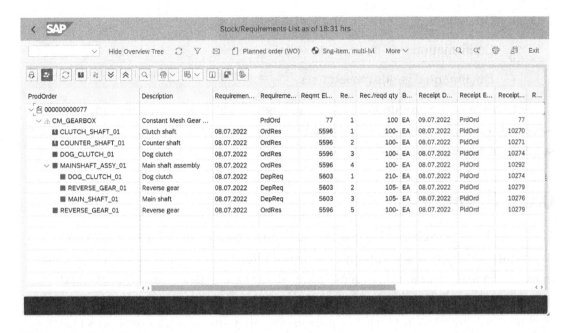

Figure 14-16. Order report

MRP List

The MRP List is almost similar to the MD04: Stock Requirement list except for the fact that the MRP List is static. The MRP List shows the situation that was a result of last MRP run. The MRP List can be executed using Transaction Code MD05, which gives users the flexibility to check the results of last MRP run and, if needed, compare the situation with the current situation.

The Order Information System

The Order Information System is a report to display all the information for production/ planned orders. The report can be executed using Transaction Code COOIS (or COOISPI if you're using PP-PI) and can be executed at several levels to display different sets of data. If you're in PP-PI, you can use the COOISP report. These levels are called lists. Some of the most commonly used lists are:

- Order header
- Components

443

- Operations
- Confirmation
- Documented goods movements

You can filter the production order by a range of selection parameters on the selection screen; for example, by material, plant, order type, MRP controller, production supervisor, system status, and so on.

Order Headers

The Order Header list is used to display the header level information of the planned or production orders. This is probably the most often used list, and it's used to display information like the material, order number, order type, order quantity, confirmed quantity, delivered quantity, start date/time, end date/time, system status, and so on, as shown in Figure 14-17. The list is quite useful for getting a quick sneak peek into the overall production situation.

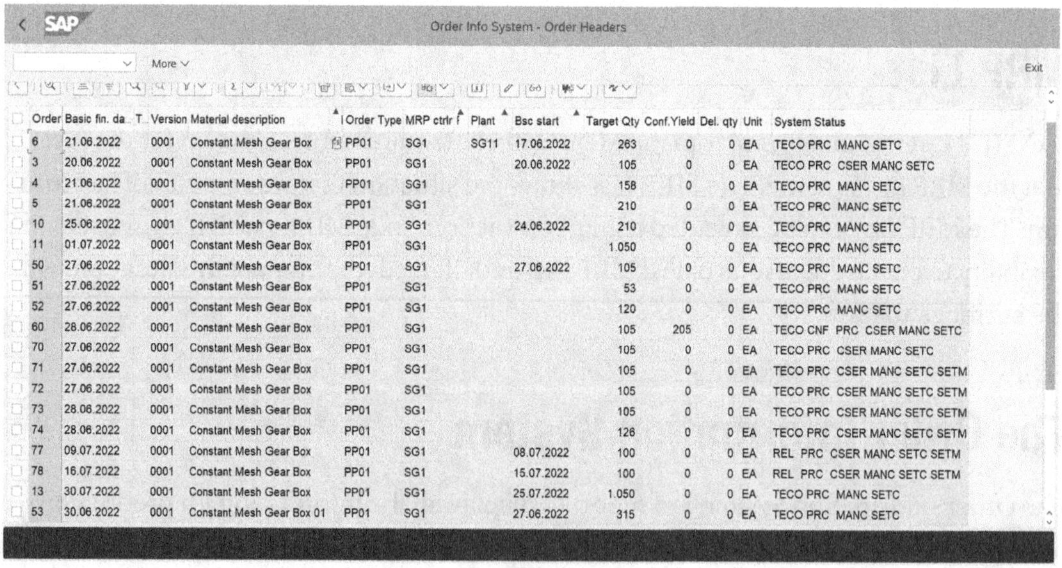

Order	Basic fin. da	T	Version	Material description	Order Type	MRP ctrlr	Plant	Bsc start	Target Qty	Conf.Yield	Del. qty	Unit	System Status
6	21.06.2022		0001	Constant Mesh Gear Box	PP01	SG1	SG11	17.06.2022	263	0	0	EA	TECO PRC MANC SETC
3	20.06.2022		0001	Constant Mesh Gear Box	PP01	SG1		20.06.2022	105	0	0	EA	TECO PRC CSER MANC SETC
4	21.06.2022		0001	Constant Mesh Gear Box	PP01	SG1			158	0	0	EA	TECO PRC MANC SETC
5	21.06.2022		0001	Constant Mesh Gear Box	PP01	SG1			210	0	0	EA	TECO PRC MANC SETC
10	25.06.2022		0001	Constant Mesh Gear Box	PP01	SG1		24.06.2022	210	0	0	EA	TECO PRC MANC SETC
11	01.07.2022		0001	Constant Mesh Gear Box	PP01	SG1			1.050	0	0	EA	TECO PRC MANC SETC
50	27.06.2022		0001	Constant Mesh Gear Box	PP01	SG1		27.06.2022	105	0	0	EA	TECO PRC MANC SETC
51	27.06.2022		0001	Constant Mesh Gear Box	PP01	SG1			53	0	0	EA	TECO PRC MANC SETC
52	27.06.2022		0001	Constant Mesh Gear Box	PP01	SG1			120	0	0	EA	TECO PRC MANC SETC
60	28.06.2022		0001	Constant Mesh Gear Box	PP01	SG1			105	205	0	EA	TECO CNF PRC CSER MANC SETC
70	27.06.2022		0001	Constant Mesh Gear Box	PP01	SG1			105	0	0	EA	TECO PRC CSER MANC SETC
71	27.06.2022		0001	Constant Mesh Gear Box	PP01	SG1			105	0	0	EA	TECO PRC CSER MANC SETC SETM
72	27.06.2022		0001	Constant Mesh Gear Box	PP01	SG1			105	0	0	EA	TECO PRC CSER MANC SETC SETM
73	28.06.2022		0001	Constant Mesh Gear Box	PP01	SG1			105	0	0	EA	TECO PRC CSER MANC SETC SETM
74	28.06.2022		0001	Constant Mesh Gear Box	PP01	SG1			126	0	0	EA	TECO PRC CSER MANC SETC SETM
77	09.07.2022		0001	Constant Mesh Gear Box	PP01	SG1		08.07.2022	100	0	0	EA	REL PRC CSER MANC SETC SETM
78	16.07.2022		0001	Constant Mesh Gear Box	PP01	SG1		15.07.2022	100	0	0	EA	REL PRC CSER MANC SETC SETM
13	30.07.2022		0001	Constant Mesh Gear Box	PP01	SG1		25.07.2022	1.050	0	0	EA	TECO PRC MANC SETC
53	30.06.2022		0001	Constant Mesh Gear Box 01	PP01	SG1		27.06.2022	315	0	0	EA	TECO PRC MANC SETC

Figure 14-17. *Order info system: order headers*

Components

The Components list is used to display the semifinished assemblies or components
required to produce an order. Based on the selection criteria, the report displays
information such as the order number, material (component or semifinished assembly
from the order), requirement quantity, requirement date, quantity withdrawn, BOM
item number, activity (operation number based on component allocation), and so on, as
shown in Figure 14-18.

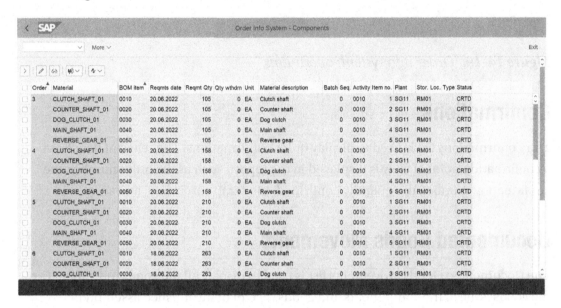

Figure 14-18.   *Order info system: components*

Operations

The Operations list is used to display all the required operations for the order. The
list displays important fields, such as order, activity, work center, operation quantity,
confirmed quantity, start date, end date, system status of the operation, and so on, as
shown in Figure 14-19. This list can be used to determine the daily workload on each
work center.

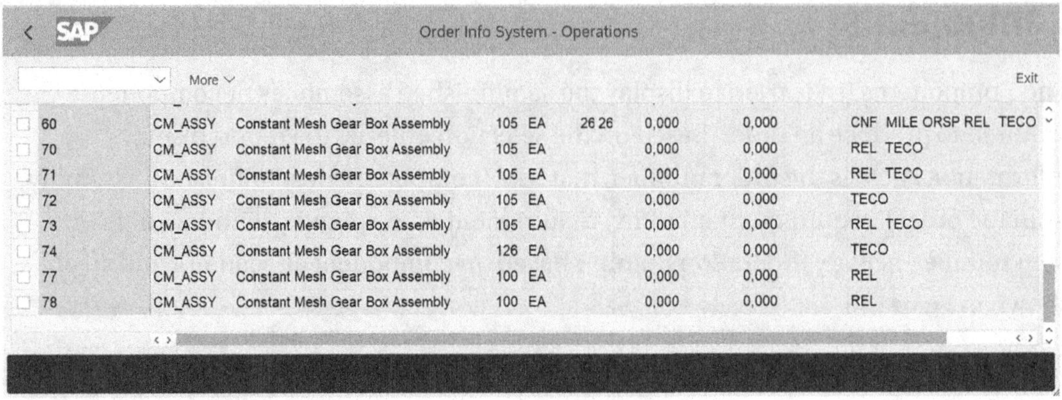

Figure 14-19. *Order info system: operations*

Confirmations

The Confirmations list is used to display order confirmations. The relevant data from a confirmation point of view is displayed in the report, such as the order number, the confirmation number, the quantity confirmed, the scrap confirmed, and so on.

Documented Goods Movements

The Documented Goods Movements list is used to display all the goods movement (i.e., the goods issue of the components and goods receipt of the finished assembly).

Fiori Apps

Several Fiori apps are available in the Production Planning module, which can be used for reporting and analysis. The following list includes are some of the Fiori apps most commonly used in SAP PP:

- Monitor Material Coverage

- Manage Material Coverage

- Monitor External Requirements

- Manage External Requirements

- Monitor Internal Requirements

- Manage Internal Requirements

- Monitor Production Orders or Process Orders

- Manage Production Orders or Process Orders

- Display MRP Master Data Issues

- Capacity Scheduling Table

- Explode Bills of Material

- Monitor Capacity Utilization

Monitor Material Coverage (F0247)

This app is used to monitor the stock situation of all the materials in a selected area of
responsibility. You can define the shortage definition and time horizon for the materials
that you want to monitor. Based on the shortage definition, the system determines which
materials have shortages in the specified time horizon, as shown in Figure 14-20.

Figure 14-20. *Monitor material coverage*

Manage Material Coverage (F0251)

This app is used to solve shortages, as determined in the Monitor Material Coverage app. You can simulate different proposals proposed by the system and choose the one that best suits you, as shown in Figure 14-21.

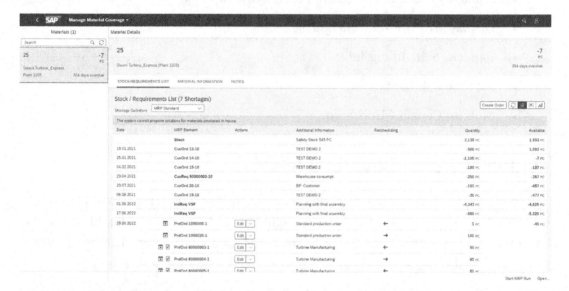

Figure 14-21. *Manage material coverage*

Monitor External Requirements (F0246)

This app is used to monitor the uncovered requirements that are created from sales orders or stock transport orders in a selected area of responsibility. You can define the shortage definition and time horizon for the materials that you want to monitor. Based on the shortage definition, the system determines the uncovered external requirements in the specified time horizon, as shown in Figure 14-22.

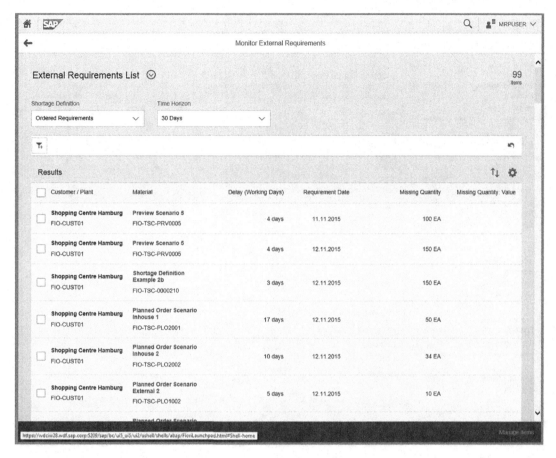

Figure 14-22. *Monitor external requirements*

Manage External Requirements (F0250)

This app is used to solve the shortages determined in the Monitor External Requirements app. You can simulate different proposals proposed by the system and choose the one that's best suited for you, as shown in Figure 14-23.

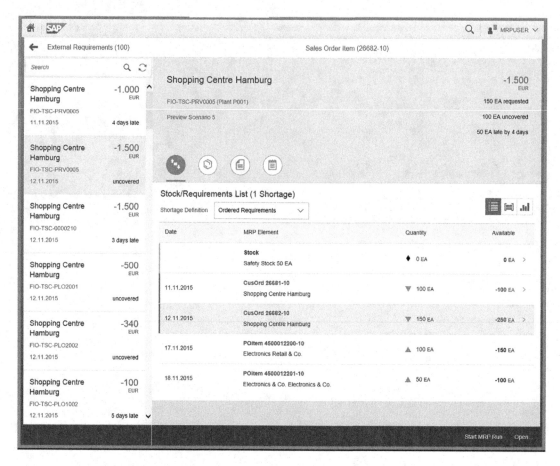

Figure 14-23. *Manage external requirements*

Monitor Internal Requirements (F0263)

This app is used to monitor all the internal requirements generated from orders, such as production order, process orders, maintenance orders, and so on. The app is used to ensure that all the required components are available on time and in the required quantity. You can define the shortage definition and time horizon for the components that you want to monitor. Based on the shortage definition, the system determines the uncovered internal requirements in the specified time horizon, as shown in Figure 14-24.

Figure 14-24. *Monitor internal requirements*

Manage Internal Requirements (F0270)

This app is used to solve the shortages determined in the Monitor Internal Requirements app. You can simulate different proposals proposed by the system and choose the one that is best suited for you, as shown in Figure 14-25.

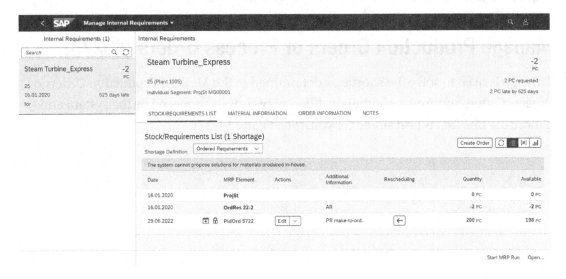

Figure 14-25. *Manage internal requirements*

Monitor Production Orders or Process Orders (F0266A)

This app is used to monitor the production or process order in the specified area of responsibility. You can determine if the materials will be available on-time for pegged requirements. Similarly, you can check the operations status and quantity confirmed per operation, and so on. The system can also determine if the order will be finished on time or will be late based on the shortage definition. (See Figure 14-26).

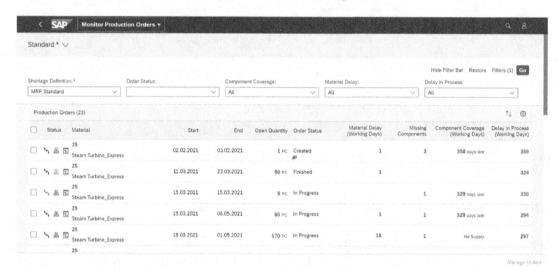

Figure 14-26. *Monitor production or process orders*

Manage Production Orders or Process Orders (F0273)

This app is used to solve the shortages determined in the Monitor Production Orders or Process Orders app. You can simulate different proposals proposed by the system and choose the one that is best suited for you. (See Figure 14-27).

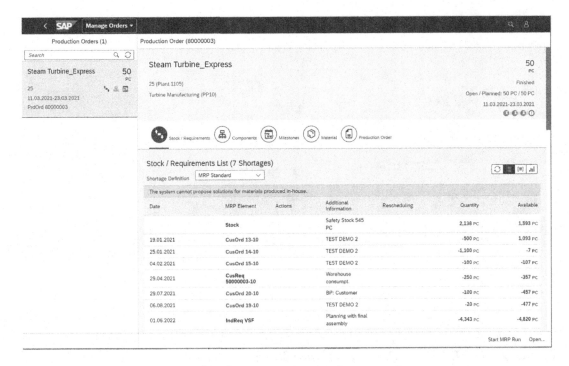

Figure 14-27. *Manage production or process orders*

Display MRP Master Data Issues (S230P)

You can use this app to display all the issues related to the master data that were
identified during the planning run using MRP Live. The app displays all the error
messages as well as success messages for the last MRP Live run. You can accept certain
issues and use filters to restrict the issues. (See Figure 14-28).

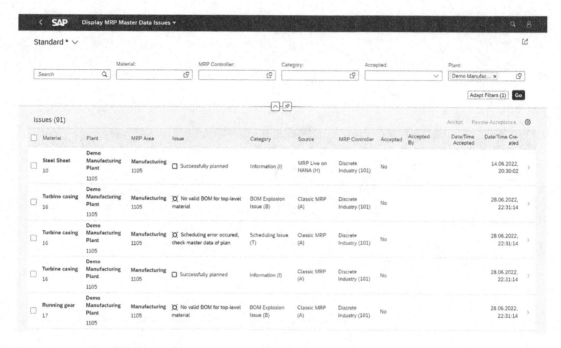

Figure 14-28. *Display MRP master data issues*

Capacity Scheduling Table (S21OP)

This app can be used to prioritize and preschedule orders to be dispatched from a work center. You can select the source of the supply (i.e., production version) and the work centers to dispatch the orders on the selected dates. The app proposes to use the work center that has the available capacity to meet the requirements. You can switch the production version if the capacity is inadequate or you can also reschedule orders. (See Figure 14-29).

Figure 14-29. *Capacity scheduling table*

Explode Bills of Material (S23OP)

You can use this app to display the overall structure of a bill of material for a finished
assembly. The app displays all the semifinished assemblies as well as the components
that are required to produce the finished assembly. (See Figure 14-30).

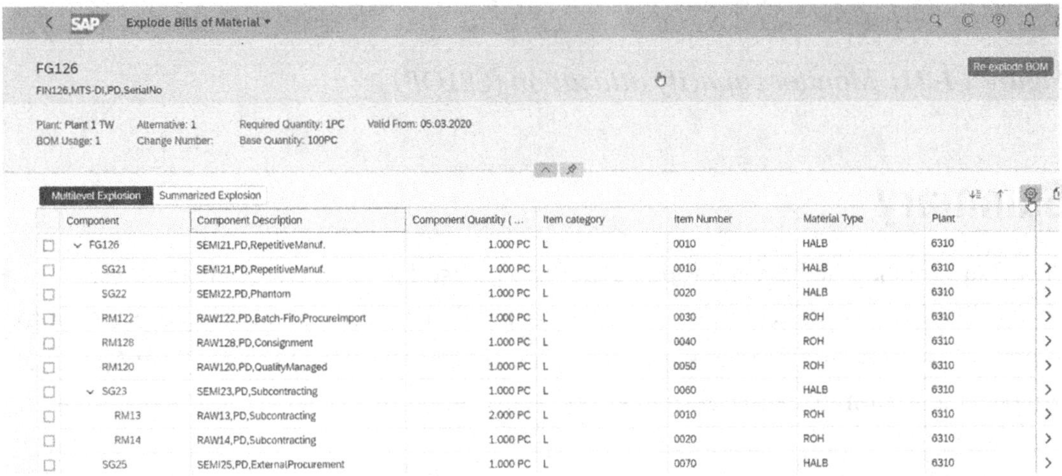

Figure 14-30. *Explode bills of material*

Monitor Capacity Utilization (S210P)

You can use this app to monitor the capacity utilization of the work center or resources. The list displays all the work centers and a quick overview of the load situation so that you can react to overload situations or assign orders to work centers that are underutilized, as shown in Figure 14-31.

You can select the evaluation profile to determine which orders or operations should be taken into account You can also select the evaluation horizon to restrict the time frame of your evaluation.

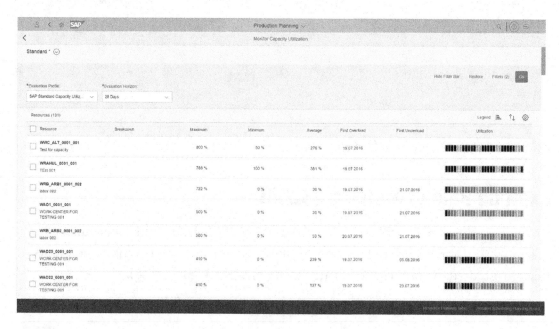

Figure 14-31. *Monitor capacity utilization (S210P)*

Summary

This chapter discussed several reports that can be used to report or analyze master objects like BOM or work center, or to analyze the demand versus supply situation, or to review production order information. The chapter also discussed several Fiori Apps that can be used to monitor and control supply chain elements.

Index

© Himanshu Goel 2022
H. Goel, *Handbook for SAP PP in S/4HANA*, https://doi.org/10.1007/978-1-4842-8566-4

Printed in the United States
by Baker & Taylor Publisher Services